STUDENT TESTED, FACULTY APPROVED

THE PSYCH SOLUTION

D0598672

Every 4LTR Press solution includes:

Visually Engaging Textbook

Online Study Tools

Tear-out Review Cards

Interactive eBook

Heading Numbers Connect Print & eBook

STUDENT RESOURCES:
- Interactive eBook
- Auto-Graded Quizzes
- Flashcards
- Interactive Practice
- Games
- Videos
- Review Cards

INSTRUCTOR RESOURCES:
- All Student Resources
- Engagement Tracker
- First Day of Class Instructions
- LMS Integration
- Instructor's Manual
- Test Bank
- PowerPoint® Slides
- Instructor Prep Cards

Students sign in at **www.cengagebrain.com**

Instructors sign in at **www.cengage.com/login**

"The prose in **PSYCH** is cleverly and enticingly written, which makes a three chapter assignment more enjoyable. Additionally, the tear-out cards at the end of each book are great study guides. " – **Diego**, Student, *Santa Ana College*

JULY 2010
4LTR Press adds eBooks in response to a 10% uptick in digital learning preferences.

Engagement Tracker launches, giving faculty a window into student usage of digital tools.

1 out of every 3 (1,400) schools has adopted a 4LTR Press solution.

750,000 students are IN.

AUGUST 2010

NOVEMBER 2010

Third party research confirms that 4LTR Press digital solutions improve retention and outcomes.

IN 2011

CourseMate
Students access the 4LTR Press website at 4x's the industry average.

IN 2011

60 unique solutions across multiple course areas validates the 4LTR Press concept.

IN 2011

1 out of every 2 (2,000) schools has a 4LTR Press adoption.

APRIL 2011

2,000

Over 1 million students are IN.

We're always evolving. Join the 4LTR Press In-Crowd on Facebook at www.facebook.com/4ltrpress

AUGUST 2011

IN 2011

2012 AND BEYOND

WADSWORTH
CENGAGE Learning·

PSYCH, **Third Edition**
Spencer A. Rathus

Editor in Chief: Linda Ganster

Publisher: Jon-David Hague

Senior Acquisitions Editor: Jaime Perkins

Developmental Editors: Linda Stewart and
Shannon LeMay-Finn

Assistant Editor: Jessica Alderman

Editorial Assistant: T. Christian Holland

Media Editor: Mary Noel

Marketing Manager: Jessica Egbert

Executive Marketing Communications
Manager: Talia Wise

Product Development Manager,
4LTR Press: Steven E. Joos

Senior Content Project Manager: Michelle
Clark

Art Director: Pamela Galbreath

Manufacturing Planner: Karen Hunt

Image and Text Rights Acquisitions Specialist:
Don Schlotman

Production Service/Project Manager: Graphic
World Inc./Cassie Carey

Photo Researcher: Bill Smith Group

Text Researcher: Bill Smith Group

Interior Designer: Trish Knapke

Cover Designer: Trish Knapke

Cover Image: Masterfile Royalty Free

Compositor: Graphic World Inc.

Library of Congress Control Number: 2012942035

Student Edition:

ISBN-13: 978-1-133-96080-5

ISBN-10: 1-133-96080-4

Wadsworth
20 Davis Drive
Belmont, CA 94002-3098
USA

Cengage Learning is a leading provider of customized learning solutions with
office locations around the globe, including Singapore, the United Kingdom,
Australia, Mexico, Brazil, and Japan. Locate your local office at
www.cengage.com/global.

Cengage Learning products are represented in Canada by Nelson Education, Ltd.

To learn more about Wadsworth, visit **www.cengage.com/Wadsworth**

Purchase any of our products at your local college store or at our preferred
online store **www.CengageBrain.com.**

Ad images:
Inside front cover
© iStockphoto.com/sdominick
© iStockphoto.com/A-Digit
© iStockphoto.com/alexsl

Page i
© iStockphoto.com/CostinT
© iStockphoto.com/photovideostock
© iStockphoto.com/Leontura

Inside back cover
© Cengage Learning

Printed in the United States of America
1 2 3 4 5 6 7 16 15 14 13 12

PSYCH

BRIEF CONTENTS

Masterfile (Royalty-Free Div.)

gabczi/Shutterstock.com

© marco betti/Alamy

PSYCH

CONTENTS

Image Source Photography/Veer

© Bruce Coleman Inc./Alamy

Blend Images/Jupiterimages

Rubberball/Mike Kemp/Jupiterimages

© Ocean/Corbis

© Michael Newman/Photo Edit

Susan Kuklin/Photo Researchers, Inc.

©C Squared Studio/Getty Images

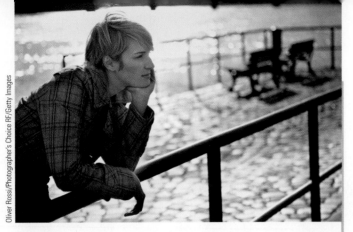

Oliver Rossi/Photographer's Choice RF/Getty Images

Workbook Stock/Jupiterimages/Getty Images

Michael Blann/Stone/Getty Images

David Buffington/Digital Vision/Getty Images

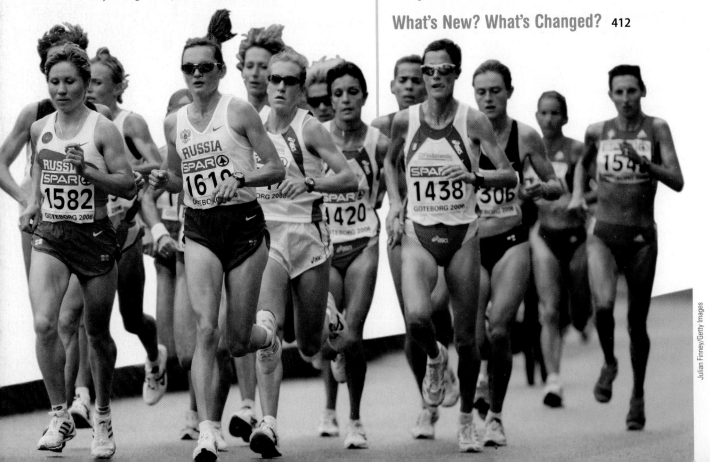

Julian Finney/Getty Images

THE IN-CROWD

Share your 4LTR Press story on Facebook at
www.facebook.com/4ltrpress for a chance to win.

To learn more about the
In-Crowd opportunity 'like'
us on Facebook.

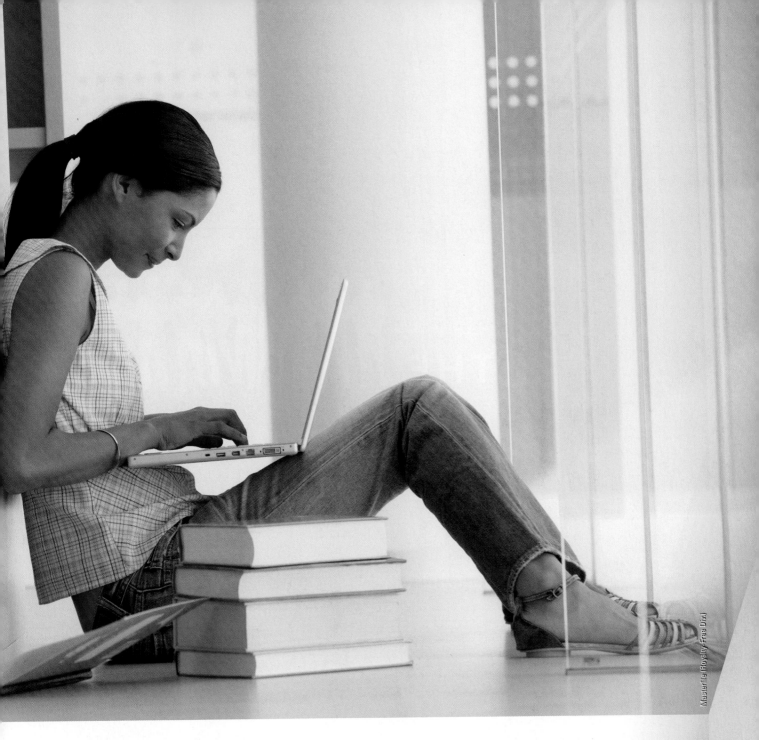

Masterfile (Royalty-Free Div.)

LEARNING OUTCOMES

1-1 Define psychology

1-2 Describe the various fields of psychology

1-3 Describe the origins of psychology and identify people who made significant contributions to the field

1-4 Identify the theoretical perspectives from which today's psychologists view behavior and mental processes

1-5 Explain how psychologists study behavior and mental processes, focusing on critical thinking, research methods, and ethical considerations

 STUDY TOOLS ▶

After you read the chapter, go to the Study Tools at the end of the chapter, page 23.

ARISTOTLE

© The Art Gallery Collection / Alamy

How do we number Aristotle's contributions to psychology?

1. He argued that science could rationally treat only information gathered by the senses.

2. He numbered the so-called five senses of vision, hearing, smell, taste, and touch.

3. He explored the nature of cause and effect.

4. He pointed out that people differ from other living things in their capacity for rational thought.

5. He outlined laws of *associationism* that have lain at the heart of learning theory for more than 2,000 years.

6. He also declared that people are more motivated to seek pleasure and avoid pain—a view that remains as current today as it was in ancient Greece.

1-3 Where Psychology Comes From: A History

Have you heard the expression "Know thyself"? It was proposed by the ancient Greek philosopher Socrates more than 2,000 years ago. Psychology, which is in large part the endeavor to know ourselves, is as old as history and as modern as today. Knowledge of the history of psychology allows us to appreciate its theoretical conflicts, its place among the sciences, the evolution of its methods, and its social and political roles.

Another ancient contributor to psychology was the Greek philosopher Aristotle (384–322 BCE). Aristotle argued that human behavior, like the movements of the stars and the seas, is subject to rules and laws. Then he delved into his subject matter topic by topic:

TRUTH ARISTOTLE WROTE A BOOK ON PSYCHOLOGY WITH CONTENTS SIMILAR TO THE BOOK YOU ARE NOW HOLDING MORE THAN 2,000 YEARS AGO. IN FACT, THE OUTLINE FOR THIS BOOK COULD HAVE BEEN WRITTEN BY ARISTOTLE. HIS *PERI PSYCHES* BEGINS WITH A HISTORY OF PSYCHOLOGICAL THOUGHT AND HISTORICAL PERSPECTIVES ON THE NATURE OF THE MIND AND BEHAVIOR.

personality, sensation and perception, thought, intelligence, needs and motives, feelings and emotion, and memory.

Other ancient Greek philosophers also contributed to psychology. Around 400 BCE, Democritus suggested that we could think of behavior in terms of a body and a mind. (Contemporary psychologists still talk about the interaction of biological and mental processes.) He pointed out that our behavior is influenced by external stimulation. Democritus was one of the first to raise the question of whether there is free will or choice. Putting it another way, where do the influences of others end and our "real selves" begin?

Socrates suggested that we should rely on rational thought and **introspection**—careful examination of one's own thoughts and emotions—to gain self-knowledge. He also pointed out that people are social creatures who influence one another.

Had we room enough and time, we could trace psychology's roots to thinkers farther back in time than the ancient Greeks, and we could trace its development through the great thinkers of the Renaissance. As it is, we must move on to the development of psychology as a laboratory science during the second half of the 19th century. Some historians set the marker date at 1860. It was then that Gustav Theodor Fechner (1801–1887) published his landmark book *Elements of Psychophysics*, which showed how physical events (such as lights and sounds) are related to psychological sensation and perception. Fechner also showed how we can scientifically measure the effect of these events. Most historians set the debut of modern psychology as a laboratory science in the year 1879, when Wilhelm Wundt established the first psychological laboratory in Leipzig, Germany.

 TRUTH SOCRATES SUGGESTED A RESEARCH METHOD THAT IS STILL USED IN PSYCHOLOGY—INTROSPECTION, WHICH IS BASED ON SOCRATES' ADVICE TO "KNOW THYSELF," WHICH HAS REMAINED A MOTTO OF PSYCHOLOGY EVER SINCE.

introspection
deliberate looking into one's own cognitive processes to examine one's thoughts and feelings

1-3a STRUCTURALISM

The German psychologist Wilhelm Wundt (1832–1920) looked as if he were going to be a problem child. He did poorly in elementary school—his mind would wander—and he had to repeat a grade. Eventually he attended medical school because he wanted to earn a good living.

structuralism
the school of psychology that argues that the mind consists of three basic elements—sensations, feelings, and images—that combine to form experience

functionalism
the school of psychology that emphasizes the uses or functions of the mind rather than the elements of experience

But he did not like working with patients and dedicated himself to philosophy and psychology.

Like Aristotle, Wundt saw the mind as a natural event that could be studied scientifically, like light, heat, and the flow of blood. Wundt used introspection to try to discover the basic elements of experience.

Wundt and his students founded the school of psychology called *structuralism*. **Structuralism** attempted to break conscious experience down into *objective* sensations, such as sight or taste, and *subjective* feelings, such as emotional responses, and mental images such as memories or dreams. Structuralists believed that the mind functions by combining objective and subjective elements of experience.

1-3b FUNCTIONALISM

Toward the end of the 19th century, psychologist William James (1842–1910) became a major figure in the development of psychology in the United States. He focused on the relation between conscious experience and behavior. He argued, for example, that the stream of consciousness is fluid and continuous. Introspection convinced him that experience cannot be broken down into objective sensations and subjective feelings as the structuralists maintained.

James was a founder of the school of **functionalism**, which focused on behavior as well as the mind or consciousness. Functionalists looked at how our experience helps us function more adaptively in our environments—for example, how habits help us cope with common situations. (When eating with a spoon, we do not create an individual plan to bring each morsel of food to our mouths.) They also turned to the laboratory for direct observations as a way to supplement introspection. Structuralists tended to ask, "What are the pieces that make up thinking and experi-

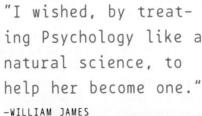

"I wished, by treating Psychology like a natural science, to help her become one."
—WILLIAM JAMES

ence?" In contrast, functionalists tended to ask, "How do behavior and mental processes help people adapt to the requirements of their lives?"

James was also influenced by Charles Darwin's (1809–1882) theory of evolution. Earlier in the 19th century, the British naturalist Darwin had argued that organisms with adaptive features—that is, the "fittest"—survive and reproduce. Functionalists adapted Darwin's theory and proposed that adaptive behavior patterns are learned and maintained. Maladaptive behavior patterns tend to drop out, and only the fittest behavior patterns survive. These adaptive actions tend to be repeated and become habits. James wrote that "habit is the enormous flywheel of society." Habit keeps the engine of civilization running.

1-3c BEHAVIORISM

Imagine you have placed a hungry rat in a maze. It meanders down a pathway that ends in a T. It can then turn left or right. If you consistently reward the rat with food for turning right at this point, it will learn to turn right when it arrives there, at least when it is hungry. But what does the rat *think* when it is learning to turn right?

Does it seem absurd to try to place yourself in the "mind" of a rat? So it seemed to John Broadus Watson (1878–1958), the founder of American behaviorism. Watson was asked to consider the contents of a rat's "mind" as one of the requirements for his doctoral degree, which he received from the University of Chicago in 1903. Functionalism was the dominant view of psychology at the University of Chicago, and functionalists were concerned with the stream of consciousness as well as observable behavior. But Watson (1913) believed that if psychology was to be a natural science, like physics or chemistry, it must limit itself to observable, measurable events—that is, to behavior alone—hence the term *behaviorism*.

FIGURE 1.2 | The Power of Reinforcement

In the photo we see a feathered friend that has learned to drop shapes into their proper places through reinforcement. Behaviorists teach animals complex behaviors such as this by first reinforcing approximations to the goal (or target behavior). As time progresses, closer approximations are demanded before reinforcement is given.

Tom McHugh/Photo Researchers, Inc.

Behaviorism is the school of psychology that focuses on learning observable behavior. The term *observable* refers to behaviors that are observable by means of specialized instruments, such as heart rate, blood pressure, and brain waves. These behaviors are *public*—they can be measured easily and different observers would agree about their existence and features. Given their focus on behavior, behaviorists define psychology as the scientific study of *behavior*, not of *behavior and mental processes*.

B. F. Skinner (1904–1990) also contributed to behaviorism. He believed that organisms learn to behave in certain ways because they have been **reinforced** for doing so—that is, their behavior has a positive outcome. He demonstrated that laboratory animals can be trained to carry out behaviors through strategic use of reinforcers, such as food. He trained rats to turn in circles, climb ladders, and push toys across the floor.

Because Skinner demonstrated that remarkable combinations of behaviors could be taught by means of reinforcement, many psychologists adopted the view that, in principle, one could explain complex human behavior in terms of thousands of instances of learning through reinforcement (see Figure 1.2).

1-3d GESTALT PSYCHOLOGY

In the 1920s, another school of psychology—**Gestalt psychology**—was prominent in Germany. In the 1930s, the three founders of the school—Max Wertheimer (1880–1943), Kurt Koffka (1886–1941), and Wolfgang Köhler (1887–1967)—left Europe to escape the Nazi threat. They carried on their work in the United States, giving further impetus to the growing American ascendance in psychology.

Gestalt psychologists focused on perception and how perception influences thinking and problem solving. The German word *Gestalt* translates roughly to "pattern" or "organized whole." In contrast to behaviorists, Gestalt psychologists argued that we cannot hope to understand human nature by focusing only on overt behavior. In contrast to structuralists, they claimed that we cannot explain human perceptions, emotions, or thought processes in terms of basic units. Perceptions are *more* than the sums of their parts: Gestalt psychologists saw our perceptions as wholes that give meaning to parts, as we see in Figure 1.3.

Gestalt psychologists showed that we tend to perceive separate pieces of information as integrated wholes depending on the contexts in which they occur. In Figure 1.3A, the dots in the centers of the con-

behaviorism
the school of psychology that defines psychology as the study of observable behavior and studies relationships between stimuli and responses

reinforcement
a stimulus that follows a response and increases the frequency of the response

Gestalt psychology
the school of psychology that emphasizes the tendency to organize perceptions into wholes and to integrate separate stimuli into meaningful patterns

FIGURE 1.3 | The Importance of Context

A. Are the dots in the center of the configurations the same size? Why not take a ruler and measure them?

B. Is the second symbol in each line the letter *B* or the number *13*?

C. Which of the gray squares is brighter?

psychoanalysis
the school of psychology that emphasizes the importance of unconscious motives and conflicts as determinants of human behavior

figurations are the same size, yet we may perceive them as being different in size because of their surroundings. The second symbol in each line in part B is identical, but in the top row we may perceive it as a B and in the bottom row as the number 13. The symbol has not changed, but its context has. The inner squares in part C are equally bright, but they do not appear so because of their contrasting backgrounds.

Gestalt psychologists believed that learning could be active and purposeful, not merely responsive and mechanical as in Watson's and Skinner's experiments. They demonstrated that much learning, especially in problem solving, is accomplished by *insight*, not by mechanical repetition.

Consider Köhler's research with chimpanzees, as shown in Figure 1.4. At first, the chimp is unsuccessful in reaching bananas suspended from the ceiling. Then he suddenly stacks the boxes and climbs up to reach the bananas. It seems the chimp has experienced a sudden reorganization of the mental elements of the problem—that is, he has had a "flash of insight." Köhler's findings suggest that we often manipulate the elements of problems until we group them in such a way that we can reach a goal. The manipulations may take quite some time as mental trial and error proceeds. But once the proper grouping has been found, we seem to perceive it all of a sudden.

1-3e PSYCHOANALYSIS

Psychoanalysis is the name of both the theory of personality and the method of psychotherapy developed by Sigmund Freud (1856–1939). As a theory of person-

ality, psychoanalysis proposes that much of our lives is governed by unconscious ideas and impulses that originate in childhood conflicts. As a method of psychotherapy, psychoanalysis aims to help patients gain insight into their conflicts and to find socially acceptable ways of expressing wishes and gratifying needs. We'll discuss psychoanalysis in more depth in Chapter 10.

SIGMUND FREUD

Mansell/Time Life Pictures/Getty Images

1-4 How Today's Psychologists View Behavior and Mental Processes

Today, we no longer find psychologists who describe themselves as structuralists or functionalists. Although the school of Gestalt psychology gave birth to current research approaches in perception and problem solving, few would label themselves Gestalt psychologists. But we do find Gestalt *therapists* who focus on helping clients integrate conflicting parts of their personality (making themselves "whole"). The numbers of orthodox behaviorists and psychoanalysts have been declining (Robins et al., 1999). Many con-

FIGURE 1.4 | Some Insight into Insight

At first, the chimpanzee cannot reach the bananas hanging from the ceiling. After some time has passed, the chimp has an apparent "flash of insight" and piles the boxes on top of one another to reach the fruit.

© Cengage Learning 2012

temporary psychologists in the behaviorist tradition look on themselves as social-cognitive theorists.

The history of psychological thought has taken many turns, and contemporary psychologists differ in their approaches. Today, there are several broad, influential perspectives in psychology: biological, cognitive, humanistic–existential, psychodynamic, learning, and sociocultural. Each approaches its topics in its own way.

1-4a THE BIOLOGICAL PERSPECTIVE

Psychologists with a **biological perspective** seek the relationships between the brain, hormones, heredity, and evolution, on the one hand, and behavior and mental processes on the other. Psychologists assume that thoughts, fantasies, and dreams—and the inborn or instinctive behavior patterns of various species—are made possible by the nervous system and especially by the brain.

Biologically oriented psychologists also study the role of heredity in behavior and mental processes such as psychological disorders, criminal behavior, and thinking. Generally speaking, our heredity provides a broad range of behavioral and mental possibilities. Environmental factors interact with inherited factors to determine specific behavior and mental processes.

Biologically oriented psychologists focus on the evolution of behavior and mental processes as well. Charles Darwin argued that in the age-old struggle for existence, only the fittest (most adaptive) organisms manage to reach maturity and reproduce. For example, fish that swim faster or people who are naturally immune to certain diseases are more likely to survive and transmit their genes to future generations. Therefore, species tend to evolve in adaptive directions. Evolutionary psychologists suggest that much human social behavior, such as aggressive behavior and mate selection, has a hereditary basis. People may be influenced by social rules, cultural factors, and personal choice, but evolutionary psychologists believe that inherited tendencies sort of whisper in people's ears and tend to move them in certain directions.

Mary Evans/Photo Researchers, Inc.

CHARLES DARWIN

1-4b THE COGNITIVE PERSPECTIVE

Psychologists with a **cognitive** perspective venture into the realm of mental processes to understand human nature. They investigate the ways we perceive and mentally represent the world, how we learn, remember the past, plan for the future, solve problems, form judgments, make decisions, and use language. Cognitive psychologists, in short, study those things we refer to as the *mind*.

The cognitive tradition has roots in Socrates' advice to "Know thyself" and in his suggested method of introspection. We also find cognitive psychology's roots in structuralism, functionalism, and Gestalt psychology, each of which, in its own way, addressed issues that are of interest to cognitive psychologists.

1-4c THE HUMANISTIC–EXISTENTIAL PERSPECTIVE

The humanistic–existential perspective is cognitive in flavor, yet it emphasizes the role of subjective (personal) experience. Let's consider each of the parts of this perspective: *humanism* and *existentialism*.

Humanism stresses the human capacity for self-fulfillment and the central roles of consciousness, self-awareness, and decision making. Humanists believe that self-awareness, experience, and choice permit us, to a large extent, to "invent ourselves" and our ways of relating to the world as we progress through life. Consciousness—our sense of being in the world—is seen as the force that unifies our personalities. *Existentialism* views people as free to choose and as being responsible for choosing ethical conduct. Grounded in the work of Carl Rogers (1951) and Abraham Maslow (1970), the humanistic–existential perspective has many contemporary adherents (Elkins, 2009).

1-4d THE PSYCHODYNAMIC PERSPECTIVE

In the 1940s and 1950s, psychodynamic theory dominated the practice of psychotherapy and was influential in scientific psychology and the arts. Most psychotherapists were psychodynamically oriented. Many renowned artists and writers consulted psycho-

biological perspective the approach to psychology that seeks to understand the nature of the links between biological processes and structures such as the functioning of the brain, the endocrine system, and heredity, on the one hand, and behavior and mental processes, on the other

cognitive having to do with mental processes such as sensation and perception, memory, intelligence, language, thought, and problem solving

social-cognitive theory

a school of psychology in the behaviorist tradition that includes cognitive factors in the explanation and prediction of behavior; formerly termed *social learning theory*

sociocultural perspective

the view that focuses on the roles of ethnicity, gender, culture, and socioeconomic status in behavior and mental processes

dynamic therapists as a way to liberate the expression of their unconscious ideas. Today, Freud's influence continues to be felt, although it no longer dominates psychotherapy. Contemporary psychologists who follow theories derived from Freud are likely to call themselves *neoanalysts*. Famous neoanalysts such as Karen Horney (1885–1952) and Erik Erikson (1902–1994) focused less on unconscious processes and more on conscious choice and self-direction.

1-4e PERSPECTIVES ON LEARNING

Many contemporary psychologists study the effects of experience on behavior. Learning, to them, is the essential factor in describing, explaining, predicting, and controlling behavior. The term *learning* has different meanings to psychologists of different persuasions, however. Some students of learning find roles for consciousness and insight. Others do not. This distinction is found today among those who adhere to the behavioral and social-cognitive perspectives.

Early proponents of behaviorism, like John B. Watson, viewed people as doing things because of their learning histories, their situations, and rewards, not because of conscious choice. Like Watson, contemporary behaviorists emphasize environmental influences and the learning of habits through repetition and reinforcement. **Social-cognitive theorists**, in contrast, suggest that people can modify and create their environments. They also grant *cognition* a key role. They note that people engage in intentional learning by observing others. Since the 1960s, social-cognitive theorists have gained influence in the areas of personality development, psychological disorders, and psychotherapy.

1-4f THE SOCIOCULTURAL PERSPECTIVE

The profession of psychology focuses mainly on the individual and is committed to the dignity of the individual. However, many psychologists believe we cannot understand people's behavior and mental processes without reference to their diversity (Alarcón et al., 2009).

The **sociocultural perspective** addresses many of the ways that people differ from one another. It studies the influences of ethnicity, gender, culture, and socioeconomic status on behavior and mental processes (Sanchez et al., 2009; Vodosek, 2009). For example,

David Buffington/PhotoDisc/Jupiterimages

what is often seen as healthful, self-assertive, outspoken behavior by most U.S. women may be interpreted as brazen behavior in Latin American or Asian American communities.

Ethnicity

One kind of diversity involves ethnicity. Members of an *ethnic group* share their cultural heritage, race, language, or history. The experiences of various ethnic groups in the United States highlight the impact of social, political, and economic factors on human behavior and development (Phinney & Ong, 2007).

In the 1940s, Kenneth Bancroft Clark (1914–2005) and Mamie Phipps Clark (1917–1983) conducted research that showed the negative effects of school segregation on African American children. In one such study, African American children were shown white and brown dolls and asked to "Give me the pretty doll," or "Give me the doll that looks bad." Most children's choices showed that they preferred the white dolls over the brown ones. The Clarks concluded that the children had swallowed the larger society's prejudiced views that favored European Americans. The Clark's research was cited by the Supreme Court in 1954 when it overturned the "separate but equal" schools doctrine that had allowed inequalities in school services for various ethnic groups.

How did research by Kenneth Clark and Mamie Phipps Clark influence a Supreme Court decision?

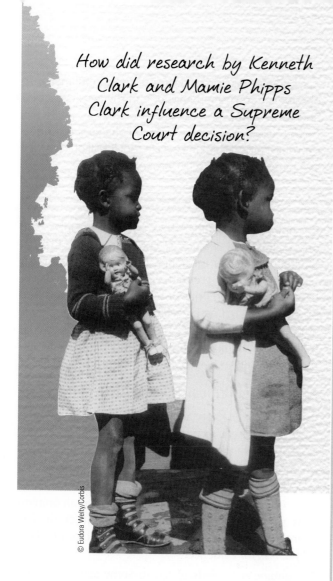

© Eudora Welty/Corbis

Latin American and Asian American psychologists have also made their mark. Jorge Sanchez was among the first to show how intelligence tests are culturally biased—to the disadvantage of Mexican American children. Latina American psychologist Lillian Comas-Diaz (e.g., 2008) has edited a journal on multicultural mental health. Asian American psychologist Richard M. Suinn (e.g., 2001) studies mental health and the development of identity among Asians and Asian Americans.

Gender

Gender refers to the culturally defined concepts of *masculinity* and *femininity*. Gender is not fully defined by anatomic sex. It involves a complex web of cultural expectations and social roles that affect people's self-concepts and hopes and dreams as well as their behavior.

iStockphoto.com/desuza.communications

FICTION IT IS NOT TRUE THAT MEN RECEIVE THE MAJORITY OF DOCTORAL DEGREES IN PSYCHOLOGY. WOMEN DO.

Just as members of ethnic minority groups have experienced prejudice, so too have women.

Although American women have attended college only since 1833, when Oberlin College opened its doors to women, most American college students today are in fact women. Women now receive the majority of undergraduate degrees in psychology and, as shown in Figure 1.1 (refer back to page 4), some 78% of the doctoral degrees (American Psychological Association, 2009).

TRUTH THE FIRST FEMALE PRESIDENT OF THE AMERICAN PSYCHOLOGICAL ASSOCIATION, MARY WHITON CALKINS, DID TURN DOWN THE DOCTORAL DEGREE THAT WAS OFFERED TO HER FROM RADCLIFFE.

Women have made indispensable contributions to psychology. Mary Whiton Calkins (1863–1930) introduced the method of paired associates to study memory (see Chapter 7), discovered the primacy and recency effects, and engaged in research into the role of the frequency of repetition in the vividness of memories. Calkins had studied psychology at Harvard University, which she had to attend as a "guest student," because

At a time when men dominated the discipline of psychology, Mary Whiton Calkins was one of the pioneers who fought the male-centered bias and encouraged psychology to incorporate the values of the "new woman" (D. Rogers, 2009). She pioneered research in memory at Wellesley College, where she founded a psychology laboratory in 1891. She introduced the method of paired associates, discovered the primacy and recency effects, and engaged in research into the role of the frequency of repetition in the vividness of memories.

© Archives of the History of American Psychology. The Center for the History of Psychology—The University of Akron

Harvard was not yet admitting women. When she completed her Ph.D. requirements, Harvard would not award her the degree because of her sex. Instead, Harvard offered to grant her a doctorate from its sister school, Radcliffe. As a form of protest, Calkins declined the offer. Even without the Ph.D., Calkins went on to become president of the American Psychological Association.

In more recent years, Mary Salter Ainsworth (1913–1999) revolutionized our understanding of attachment between parents and children by means of her cross-cultural studies. Elizabeth Loftus (e.g., Laney & Loftus, 2009) has shown that our memories are not snapshots of the past. Instead, they often consist of something old (what actually happened), something new (that is, influenced by more recent events), something borrowed (for example, further shaped by our biases and prejudices), and something blue (altered by tinges of color or emotion).

The contributions of members of diverse ethnic groups and women have broadened our understanding of the influences of ethnicity and gender on behavior and mental processes. They have also increased our knowledge of differences among Europeans. For example, Southern European singles (from Italy, Greece, and Portugal, for example) are more likely than Northern European singles (from the United Kingdom, France, Germany, and Scandinavia) to live with their parents until they get married (Giuliano, 2007). The researcher suggests that the family ties of Southern Europeans seem to be relatively stronger.

1-5 How Psychologists Study Behavior and Mental Processes

Does alcohol cause aggression? Does watching violence on TV cause children to be violent? Why do some people hardly ever think of food, whereas others are obsessed with it and snack all day? Why do some unhappy people attempt suicide, whereas others don't? How does having people of different ethnic backgrounds collaborate in their work affect feelings of prejudice?

Many of us have expressed opinions—maybe strong opinions—on questions like these. But as we saw in our discussion of people who claim to be abducted by aliens from outer space, scientists insist on evidence.

Psychologists, like other scientists, use careful means to observe and measure behavior and the factors that influence behavior.

The need for evidence is one of the keys to critical thinking. Critical thinking is a life tool for all of us as well as a pathway toward scientific knowledge.

1-5a CRITICAL THINKING

Psychologists are guided by scientific principles, and one hallmark of science is critical thinking. **Critical thinking** has many meanings. On one level, it means taking nothing for granted—not believing things just because they are in print or because they were uttered by authority figures or celebrities. On another level, critical thinking refers to a process of thoughtfully analyzing and probing the questions, statements, and arguments of others.

Principles of Critical Thinking

1. *Be skeptical:* Keep an open mind. Politicians and advertisers try to persuade you. Are some of your attitudes and beliefs superficial or unfounded? Accept nothing as the truth until you have examined the evidence.

2. *Insist on evidence:* It is not sufficient that an opinion is traditional, that it appears in print or on the Internet, or that it is expressed by a doctor or a lawyer. Ask for evidence.

3. *Examine definitions of terms:* Some statements are true when a term is defined in one way but not when it is defined in another way. Consider the statement, "Head Start programs have raised children's IQs." The correctness of the statement depends on the definition of IQ. (You will see later in the text that *IQ* is not the same thing as *intelligence*.)

4. *Examine the assumptions or premises of arguments:* Consider the statement that one cannot learn about human beings by engaging in research with animals. One premise in the statement seems to be that human beings are not animals. We are, of course.

5. *Be cautious in drawing conclusions from evidence:* For many years, studies had shown that most clients who receive psychotherapy improve. It was therefore generally assumed that psychotherapy worked. Some 40 years ago, however, psychologist Hans Eysenck pointed out that most psychologically troubled people who did *not* receive psychotherapy also improved. The question thus becomes whether people receiving psychotherapy are *more* likely to improve than those who do not. Current research on the effectiveness of psychotherapy therefore compares the bene-

fits of therapy techniques to the benefits of other techniques or no treatment at all. Be especially skeptical of anecdotes. When you hear "I know someone who . . . ," ask yourself whether this person's reported experience is satisfactory as evidence.

6. *Consider alternative interpretations of research evidence:* Does alcohol cause aggression? Later in the chapter we report evidence that there is a *connection*, or *correlation*, between alcohol and aggression. But does the evidence show that drinking *causes* aggression? Might other factors, such as gender, age, or willingness to take risks, account for both drinking and aggressive behavior?

7. *Do not oversimplify:* Most human behavior involves complex interactions of genetic and environmental influences. For example, consider the issue of whether psychotherapy helps people with psychological problems. A broad answer to this question—a simple yes or no—might be oversimplifying. It is more worthwhile to ask: What *type* of psychotherapy, practiced by *whom*, is most helpful for *what kind of problem*?

8. *Do not overgeneralize:* Again, consider the statement that one cannot learn about humans by engaging in research with animals. Is the truth of the matter an all-or-nothing issue? Are there certain kinds of information we can obtain about people from research with animals? What kinds of things are you likely to learn only through research with people?

9. *Apply critical thinking to all areas of life.*

1-5b THE SCIENTIFIC METHOD

The **scientific method** is an organized way of using experience and testing ideas to expand and refine knowledge. Psychologists do not necessarily follow the steps of the scientific method as we might follow a recipe in a cookbook, but research is guided by certain principles.

Psychologists usually begin by *formulating a research question*. Research questions can have many sources. Our daily experiences, psychological theory, and even folklore all help generate questions for research. Daily experience in using day-care centers may motivate us to conduct research on whether day care affects the development of social skills or the bonds of attachment between children and their parents. Social-cognitive principles of observational learning may prompt research on the effects of TV violence. Research questions may also arise from common knowledge. Consider familiar adages such as "misery loves company" and "opposites attract." Psychologists

may ask: *Does* misery love company? *Do* opposites attract?

A research question may be studied as a question or reworded as a *hypothesis* (see Figure 1.5). A **hypothesis** is a statement about behavior or mental processes that is testable through research. A hypothesis about day care might be that preschoolers who are placed in day care will acquire greater social skills in relating to peers than preschoolers who are cared for in the home.

Psychologists next examine the research question or *test the hypothesis* through controlled methods such as the experiment. For example, we could take a group of preschoolers who attend day care and another group who do not and introduce each to a new child in a con-

scientific method
an organized way of using experience and testing ideas to expand and refine knowledge

hypothesis
in psychology, a specific statement about behavior or mental processes that is tested through research

FIGURE 1.5 | The Scientific Method

The scientific method is a systematic way of organizing and expanding scientific knowledge.

© Cengage Learning 2012

correlation

an association or relationship among variables, as we might find between height and weight or between study habits and school grades

selection factor

a source of bias that may occur in research findings when participants are allowed to choose for themselves a certain treatment in a scientific study

sample

part of a population

population

a complete group of interest to researchers, from which a sample is drawn

trolled setting such as a child-research center. We could then observe how children in each group interact with the new acquaintance.

Psychologists draw conclusions about their research questions or the accuracy of their hypotheses on the basis of their observations or findings. When their observations do not bear out their hypotheses, they may modify the theories from which the hypotheses were derived. Research findings often suggest refinements to psychological theories and new avenues of research. In our research on day care, we might find that children in day care show greater social skills than children who are cared for in the home (Belsky et al., 2001).

As psychologists draw conclusions from research evidence, they are guided by principles of critical thinking. For example, they try not to confuse **correlations**—or associations—between findings with cause and effect. Although more aggressive children apparently spend more time watching violent TV shows, it may be erroneous to conclude from this kind of evidence that TV violence *causes* aggressive behavior. A **selection factor** may be at work because the children being studied choose (select) for themselves what they will watch. Perhaps more aggressive children are more likely than less aggressive children to tune in to violent TV shows.

TRUTH IT IS TRUE THAT YOU COULD SURVEY MILLIONS OF VOTERS AND STILL NOT PREDICT THE OUTCOME OF A PRESIDENTIAL ELECTION.

1-5c SAMPLES AND POPULATIONS

Consider a piece of history that never quite happened: The Republican candidate Alf Landon defeated the incumbent president, Franklin D. Roosevelt, in 1936. Or at least Landon did so in a poll conducted by a popular magazine of the day, the *Literary Digest*. In the actual election, however, Roosevelt routed Landon by a landslide. In effect, the *Digest* accomplished something like this when they predicted a Landon victory. How was so great a discrepancy possible?

The *Digest*, you see, had surveyed voters by phone. Today, telephone sampling is still widely practiced, but the *Digest* poll was taken during the Great Depression, when people who had telephones were much wealthier than those who did not. People at higher income levels are also more likely to vote Republican, in this case, for Landon. Question: Is telephone sampling valid if it omits people—like many college students!—whose only telephone is a cellphone?

The *Digest* poll failed because of its method of sampling. A **sample** is a segment of a **population** that must be drawn so that it accurately *represents* that population. Only representative samples allow us to *generalize*—or *extend*—our findings from research samples to target populations, such as U.S. voters, and not subgroups such as southern Californians or European American members of the middle class.

1-5d PROBLEMS IN GENERALIZING FROM PSYCHOLOGICAL RESEARCH

Many factors must be considered when interpreting the accuracy of the results of scientific research. One is the nature of the research sample. Later in the chapter, we consider research in which the participants were drawn from a population of college men who were social drinkers. That is, they tended to drink at social gatherings but not when alone. Whom do college men represent other than themselves? To whom can we extend, or generalize, the results? For one thing, they do not extend to college women, who, as we see in Chapter 4, are affected more quickly than men are by alcohol.

Also, compared to the general adult male population, college men are younger and score higher on intelligence tests. Social drinkers may also differ biologically and psychologically from alcoholics, who have difficulty controlling their drinking.

By and large, we must also question whether findings of research with men can be generalized to women, and

Does this telephone make me look rich?

whether research with European American men can be extended to members of ethnic minority groups.

Random and Stratified Sampling

One way to achieve a representative sample is by means of random sampling. In a **random sample**, each member of a population has an equal chance of being selected to participate. Researchers can also use a **stratified sample**, which is selected so that identified subgroups in the population are represented proportionately in the sample. For instance, 13% of the American population is African American. A stratified sample would thus be 13% African American. As a practical matter, a large randomly selected sample will show reasonably accurate stratification. A random sample of 1,500 people will represent the broad American population reasonably well. However, a sample of 20,000 European Americans or men will not.

Large-scale magazine surveys of sexual behavior ask readers to fill out and return questionnaires. Although many thousands of readers complete the questionnaires and send them in, do the survey respondents represent the American population? Probably not. These and similar studies may be influenced by **volunteer bias**. People who offer or volunteer to participate in research studies differ systematically from people who do not. In the case of research on sexual behavior, volunteers may represent subgroups of the population—or of readers of the magazines in question—who are willing to disclose intimate information and therefore may also be likely to be more liberal in their sexual behavior (Rathus et al., 2011). Volunteers may also be more interested in research than other people, as well as have more spare time. How might such volunteers differ from the population at large? How might such differences slant or bias the research outcomes?

1-5e METHODS OF OBSERVATION

Many people consider themselves experts on behavior and mental processes. How many times, for example, have you or someone else been eager to share a life experience that proves some point about human nature?

We see much during our lifetimes, but our personal observations tend to be fleeting and unsystematic. We sift through experience for the things that interest us. We often ignore the obvious because it does not fit our assumptions about the way things ought to be. Scientists, however, have devised more controlled ways of observing others. Let's consider three of them: the case study, the survey, and naturalistic observation.

The Case Study

Case studies collect information about individuals and small groups. Many case studies are clinical; that is, they are descriptions of a person's psychological problems and how a psychologist treated them. Case studies are sometimes used to investigate rare occurrences, as in the case of Chris Sizemore, who was diagnosed with dissociative identity disorder ("multiple personalities"). A psychiatrist identified three distinct personalities in Chris. Her story was made into a movie called *The Three Faces of Eve* (a fictitious name). One personality, "Eve White," was a mousy, well-meaning woman. "Eve Black," a flirtatious and promiscuous personality sometimes emerged and took control of Eve. A third personality, "Jane," was well-adjusted and integrated parts of the personalities of the Eves.

Case studies are subject to inaccuracies. We find gaps and factual errors in people's memories (Bernstein & Loftus, 2009). People may also distort their pasts to please or to antagonize the interviewer. Interviewers may also have certain expectations and may subtly encourage participants to fill in gaps in ways that are consistent with these expectations. Psychoanalysts, for example, have been criticized for guiding people who seek their help into viewing their own lives from the psychodynamic perspective (Hergenhahn, 2009). No wonder, then, that many people provide "evidence" that is consistent with psychodynamic theory—such as, "My parents' inept handling of my toilet training is the source of my compulsive neatness." However, interviewers of *any* theoretical viewpoint may indirectly prod people into saying what they want to hear.

"All generalizations are dangerous, even this one."
—ALEXANDRE DUMAS

iStockphoto.com/Chris Pecorano

random sample
a sample drawn so that each member of a population has an equal chance of being selected to participate

stratified sample
a sample drawn so that identified subgroups in the population are represented proportionately in the sample

volunteer bias
a source of bias or error in research reflecting the prospect that people who offer to participate in research studies differ systematically from people who do not

case study
a carefully drawn biography that may be obtained through interviews, questionnaires, and psychological tests

The Survey

Just as computers and pollsters predict election results and report national opinion on the basis of scientifically selected samples, psychologists conduct **surveys** to learn about behavior and mental processes that cannot be observed in the natural setting or studied experimentally. Psychologists conducting surveys may employ questionnaires and interviews or examine public records. One of the advantages of the survey is that by distributing questionnaires and analyzing answers with a computer, psychologists can study many thousands of people at a time (Schwartz, 2007).

One of the best-known surveys, the so-called Kinsey reports, provided surprising information about people's sexual behavior during the middle of the 20th century, a time of widespread sexual repression in the United States. Alfred Kinsey and his colleagues published two surveys of sexual behavior, based on interviews: *Sexual Behavior in the Human Male* (1948) and *Sexual Behavior in the Human Female* (1953). The nation was shocked to hear that masturbation was virtually universal in his sample of men in a day when masturbation was still widely thought to impair health. At the time, it was also widely believed that nearly all single women were virgins. Yet Kinsey found that about 1 woman in 3 who remained single at age 25 reported having engaged in sexual intercourse.

In the film biography *Kinsey*, Liam Neeson played Alfred Kinsey, the scientist who investigated human sexuality during a time when even talking about sex was considered indecent.

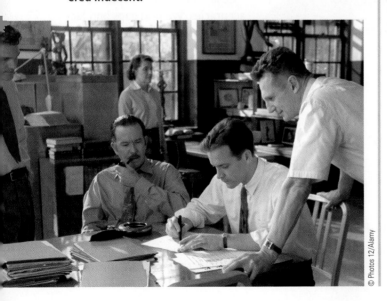

Jane Goodall's naturalistic observations revealed that chimpanzees— like humans—use tools and greet one another with a kiss.

Surveys, like case studies, also have sources of inaccuracy (Schwartz, 2007). People may recall their behavior inaccurately or deny or lie about it. Some people try to ingratiate themselves with their interviewers by answering in a socially desirable direction. The Kinsey studies all relied on male interviewers, but it has been speculated that female interviewees might have been more open with female interviewers. Similar problems may occur when interviewers and the people surveyed are from different ethnic or socioeconomic backgrounds. Other people may falsify attitudes and exaggerate problems to draw attention to themselves or to intentionally foul up the results.

Consider some survey errors caused by inaccurate self-reports of behavior. If people brushed their teeth as often as they claimed and used the amount of toothpaste they indicated, three times as much toothpaste would be sold in the United States as is actually sold (Koerber et al., 2006). People also overreport the extent to which they follow doctors' orders (Wilson et al., 2009) and underreport how much they smoke (Swan et al., 2007). Why do you think this is so?

Naturalistic Observation

You use **naturalistic observation**—that is, you observe people in their natural habitats—every day. Naturalistic observation allows psychologists and other scientists to observe behavior where it happens, or "in the field."

Observers use unobtrusive measures to avoid interfering with the behaviors they are observing. For example, Jane Goodall has observed the behavior of chimpanzees in their natural environment to learn about their social behavior, sexual behavior, use of tools, and other facts of chimp life (Peterson, 2006; Pusey et al., 2008). Her observations have shown us that (a) we were incorrect to think that only humans use tools and (b) kissing on the lips, as a greeting, is used by chimps as well as humans.

1-5f CORRELATION

Are people with higher intelligence more likely to do well in school? Are people with a stronger need for achievement likely to climb higher up the corporate ladder? What is the relationship between stress and health?

Such questions are often answered by means of the **correlational method**. Correlation follows observation. By using the correlational method, psychologists investigate whether observed behavior or a measured trait is related to, or correlated with, another. Consider the variables of intelligence and academic performance. These variables are assigned numbers such as intelligence test scores and academic averages. Then the numbers are mathematically related and expressed as a **correlation coefficient** (*r*). A correlation coefficient is a number that varies from *r* = +1.00 to *r* = −1.00.

Studies report *positive correlations* between intelligence test scores and academic achievement, as measured, for example, by grade point averages. That is, the higher people score on intelligence tests, the better their academic performance is likely to be. Intelligence test scores tend to be positively correlated (about *r* = +0.30 to *r* = +0.60) with academic achievement (see Figure 1.6). But factors *other* than performance on intelligence tests also contribute to academic success. These include desire to get ahead, self-discipline, ability to manage stress, and belief in one's ability to succeed (Duckworth & Seligman, 2005; Jennings et al., 2009; Thomas, 2008).

Many correlations are *negative correlations*; that is, as one variable increases, the other variable decreases. For example, there is a negative correlation between

correlational method a mathematical method of determining whether one variable increases or decreases as another variable increases or decreases

correlation coefficient a number between +1.00 and −1.00 that expresses the strength and direction (positive or negative) of the relationship between two variables

---

FIGURE 1.6 | Positive and Negative Correlations

When there is a positive correlation between variables, as there is between intelligence and achievement, one increases as the other increases. By and large, the higher people score on intelligence tests, the better their academic performance is likely to be, as in the diagram on the left. (Each dot represents an individual's intelligence test score and grade point average.) But there is a negative correlation between stress and health. As the amount of stress we experience increases, the functioning of our immune system tends to decrease.

Positive correlation, as found between intelligence and academic achievement

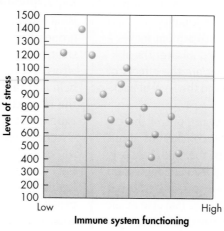

Negative correlation, as found between stress and functioning of the immune system

© Cengage Learning 2012

What kind of correlation would you expect between teenagers' grades in school and their numbers of delinquent acts? Why?

liquidlibrary/Jupiterimages

experiment
a scientific method that seeks to confirm cause-and-effect relationships by introducing independent variables and observing their effects on dependent variables

independent variable
a condition in a scientific study that is manipulated so that its effects may be observed

dependent variable
a measure of an assumed effect of an independent variable

experimental groups
in experiments, groups whose members obtain the treatment

control groups
in experiments, groups whose members do not obtain the treatment, while other conditions are held constant

stress and health. As the amount of stress affecting us increases, the functioning of our immune system decreases. Under high levels of stress, many people show poorer health.

What kinds of correlations (positive or negative) would you expect to find among behavior patterns such as the following: Churchgoing and crime? Language ability and musical ability? Grades in school and delinquency? Why?

Correlational research may suggest, but does not prove, cause and effect. For example, it may seem logical to assume that high intelligence makes it possible for children to profit from education. However, research has also shown that education contributes to higher scores on intelligence tests (Nisbett, 2009). Preschoolers who are placed in stimulating Head Start programs later attain higher scores on intelligence tests than age-mates who did not have this experience. What of the link between stress and health? Does stress impair health, or is it possible that people in poorer health encounter more stress?

1-5g THE EXPERIMENTAL METHOD

The preferred method for answering questions about cause and effect is the experiment. In an **experiment**, a group of participants obtains a treatment, such as a dose of alcohol, a change in room temperature, or perhaps an injection of a drug. The participants are then observed to determine whether the treatment makes a difference in their behavior. Does alcohol alter the ability to take tests, for example? What are the effects of differences in room temperatures and the level of background noise?

Experiments allow psychologists to control the experiences of participants and draw conclusions about cause and effect (Roediger & McCabe, 2007). A psychologist may theorize that alcohol leads to aggression because it reduces fear of consequences or because it energizes the activity levels of drinkers (Sayette et al., 2009). She or he may then hypothesize that a treatment in which participants receive a specified dosage of alco-

hol will lead to increases in aggression. Let's follow the example of the effects of alcohol on aggression to further our understanding of the experimental method.

Independent and Dependent Variables

In an experiment to determine whether alcohol causes aggression, participants are given an amount of alcohol and its effects are measured. In this case, alcohol is an **independent variable**. The presence of an independent variable is manipulated by the experimenters so that its effects may be determined. The independent variable of alcohol may be administered at different levels, or doses, from none or very little to enough to cause intoxication or drunkenness.

The measured results, or outcomes, in an experiment are called **dependent variables**. The presence of dependent variables presumably depends on the independent variables. In an experiment to determine whether alcohol influences aggression, aggressive behavior would be a dependent variable. Other dependent variables of interest might include sexual arousal, visual-motor coordination, and performance on cognitive tasks such as math problems.

In an experiment on the relationships between temperature and aggression, temperature would be an independent variable and aggressive behavior would be a dependent variable. We could set temperatures from below freezing to blistering hot and study its effects on aggression. We could also use a second independent variable such as social provocation; we could insult some participants but not others and see whether insults affect their level of aggression. This method would allow us to study how two independent variables—temperature and social provocation—affect aggression, by themselves and together.

Experimental and Control Groups

Ideal experiments use experimental groups and control groups. Participants in **experimental groups** obtain the treatment. Members of **control groups** do not. Every effort is made to ensure that all other conditions are held constant for both groups. This method enhances the researchers' confidence that the outcomes of the experiment are caused by the treatments and not by chance factors or chance fluctuations in behavior.

For example, in an experiment on the effects of alcohol on aggression, members of the experimental group would ingest alcohol, and members of the control group would not (Eriksson, 2008). The researcher would then measure how much aggression was shown by each group.

18   What Is Psychology?

Blinds and Double Blinds

One experiment on the effects of alcohol on aggression (Boyatzis, 1974) reported that men at parties where beer and liquor were served acted more aggressively than men at parties where only soft drinks were served. But participants in the experimental group knew they had drunk alcohol, and those in the control group knew they had not. Aggression that appeared to result from alcohol might not have reflected drinking per se. Instead, it might have reflected the participants' expectations about the effects of alcohol. People tend to act in stereotypical ways when they believe they have been drinking alcohol (Eriksson, 2008). For instance, men tend to become less anxious in social situations, more aggressive, and more sexually aroused. To what extent do these behavior patterns reflect the direct effects of alcohol on the body, and to what extent do they affect people's *beliefs* about the effects of alcohol?

In medicine, physicians sometimes give patients **placebos** (a fake treatment, such as sugar pills, that appears to be genuine) when the patient insists on having a medical cure but the physician does not believe that medicine is necessary. When patients report that placebos have helped them, it is because they expected the pills to be of help and not because of the biochemical effects of the pills. Placebos are not limited to sugar pills. Interestingly, the taste of vodka and tonic water is almost impossible to distinguish from tonic water alone. Therefore, tonic water can be used as a placebo in experiments on the effects of alcohol. Moreover, if participants believe they have drunk alcohol but have actually been given tonic water only, we may conclude that changes in their behavior result from their beliefs about the effects of alcohol and not from alcohol itself.

Well-designed experiments control for the effects of expectations by creating conditions under which participants are unaware of, or **blind** to, the treatment. Placebos are one way of keeping participants blind as to whether they have received a particular treatment. Yet researchers may also have expectations. They may be "rooting for" a certain treatment outcome, a phenomenon known as *experimenter bias*. For instance, tobacco company executives may wish to show that cigarette smoking is harmless. In such cases, it is useful if the people measuring the experimental outcomes are unaware of which participants have received the treatment. Studies in which neither the participants nor the experimenters know who has obtained the treatment are called **double-blind studies**.

Neither the participants nor the researchers know who is receiving the real treatment in many experiments. For example, the Food and Drug Administration requires double-blind studies before it allows the marketing of new drugs. The drug and the placebo look and taste alike. Experimenters assign the drug or placebo to participants at random. Neither the participants nor the observers know who is taking the drug and who is taking the placebo. After the final measurements have been made, a neutral panel (a group of people who have no personal stake in the outcome of the study) judges whether the effects of the drug differed from those of the placebo.

TRUTH IT IS TRUE THAT NEITHER THE PARTICIPANTS NOR THE RESEARCHERS KNOW WHO IS RECEIVING THE REAL TREATMENT IN MANY EXPERIMENTS.

In one double-blind study on the effects of alcohol on aggression, Alan Lang and his colleagues (1975) pretested a highball of vodka and tonic water to determine that it could not be discriminated by taste from tonic water alone. They then recruited college men who described themselves as "social drinkers" to participate in the study. Some of the men drank vodka and tonic water. Others drank tonic water only. Of the men who drank vodka, half were misled into believing they had drunk tonic water only (see Figure 1.7). Of those who drank tonic water only, half were misled into believing their drink contained vodka. Thus, half the participants were blind to their treatment. Experimenters defined aggression as pressing a lever that participants believed would deliver an electric shock to another person. The researchers who measured the men's aggressive responses were also blind concerning which participants had drunk vodka.

The research team found that men who believed that they had drunk vodka responded more aggressively (selected a higher level of shock) in response to a provocation than men who believed that they had drunk tonic water only. The actual content of the drink was immaterial. That is, the men's *belief* about what

placebo
a bogus treatment that has the appearance of being genuine

blind
in experimental terminology, unaware of whether or not one has received a treatment

double-blind study
a study in which neither the subjects nor the observers know who has received the treatment

they drank affected their behavior more than what they actually consumed. The results of the Lang study differ dramatically from those reported by Boyatzis, perhaps because the Boyatzis study did not control for the effects of expectations or beliefs about alcohol.

1-5h ETHICS OF RESEARCH WITH HUMANS

If the Lang group were running their experiment today rather than in the 1970s, they would probably have been denied permission to do so by a university ethics review committee. Why? Because the researchers gave some participants alcohol to drink—a potentially harmful treatment, especially to participants who might have drinking problems—and deceived the entire group about the purposes and methods of the study. Was their method ethical?

Psychologists adhere to a number of ethical standards that are intended to promote individual dignity, human welfare, and scientific integrity. The standards are also intended to ensure that psychologists do not undertake research methods or treatments that are harmful. In virtually all institutional settings, including colleges, hospitals, and research foundations, ethics review committees help researchers consider the potential harm of their methods and review proposed studies according to ethical guidelines. When such committees find that proposed research might be unacceptably harmful to participants, they may withhold approval until the proposal has been modified. Ethics review committees also weigh the potential benefits of research against the potential harm.

Today, individuals must provide **informed consent** before they participate in research (Knaus et al., 2012). Having a general overview of the research and the opportunity to choose not to participate apparently give them a sense of control and decrease the stress of participating (Fisher, 2009). Is there a way in which participants in the Lang study could have provided informed consent? What do you think?

Psychologists keep the records of research participants and clients confidential because they respect people's privacy and because people are more likely to express their true thoughts and feelings when researchers or therapists keep their disclosures confidential (Fisher, 2009). Sometimes, conflicts of interest arise, as

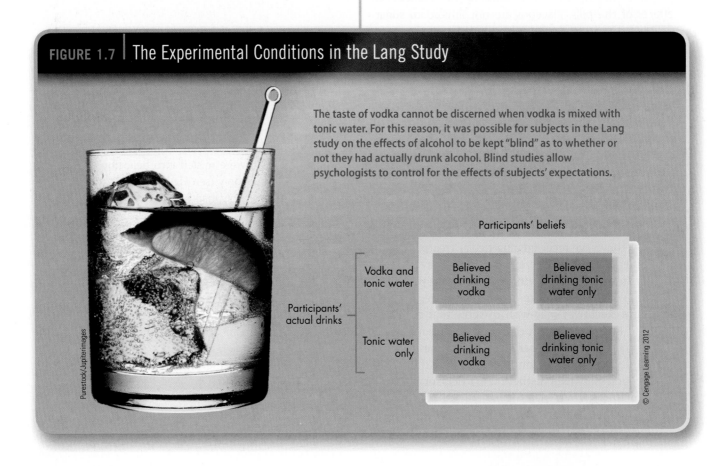

FIGURE 1.7 | The Experimental Conditions in the Lang Study

The taste of vodka cannot be discerned when vodka is mixed with tonic water. For this reason, it was possible for subjects in the Lang study on the effects of alcohol to be kept "blind" as to whether or not they had actually drunk alcohol. Blind studies allow psychologists to control for the effects of subjects' expectations.

Participants' beliefs

Participants' actual drinks

Vodka and tonic water — Believed drinking vodka | Believed drinking tonic water only

Tonic water only — Believed drinking vodka | Believed drinking tonic water only

Purestock/Jupiterimages

© Cengage Learning 2012

when a client threatens to harm someone, and the psychologist feels an obligation to warn the victim (Knaus et al., 2012).

Some studies could not be conducted if participants know what the researchers were trying to learn or which treatment they had received (for example, a new drug or a sugar pill). According to the American Psychological Association's *Handbooks of Ethics in Psychology* (Knaus et al., 2012), psychologists may use deception only when they believe the benefits of the research outweigh its potential harm, when they believe the individuals might have been willing to participate if they had understood the benefits of the research, and when participants are **debriefed** afterward—that is, the purposes and methods of the research are explained.

Participants in the Lang study on alcohol and aggression were deceived in two ways. The researchers (a) misinformed them about what they were drinking and (b) told them they were shocking other participants when they were actually only pressing switches on an unconnected control board. (*Aggression* was defined for purposes of the study as pressing these switches.) The study could not have been run without deception, but the ethics of deceiving research participants remains debated.

> "An act has no ethical quality whatever unless it be chosen out of several all equally possible."
> —WILLIAM JAMES

debrief
to explain the purposes and methods of a completed procedure to a participant

havior. For instance, a lesion in one part of a brain structure causes a rat to overeat. A lesion elsewhere causes the rat to go on a crash diet. Psychologists generalize to humans from experiments such as these in the hope of finding solutions to problems such as eating disorders (Mehta & Gosling, 2008). Proponents of the use of animals in research argue that major advances in medicine and psychology could not have taken place without them (Ringach & Jentsch, 2009). For example, we would know much less about how experimental drugs affect cancerous growths and the brain.

According to the ethical guidelines of the American Psychological Association, animals may be harmed only when there is no alternative and when researchers believe that the benefits of the research justify the harm (American Psychological Association, 2002; Fisher, 2009).

Now that we have an overview of psychology as a science, we will move on to the connections between psychology and biology in Chapter 2. Psychologists assume that our behaviors and our mental processes are related to biological events. In Chapter 2 we consider the evidence for this assumption.

1-5i ETHICS OF RESEARCH WITH ANIMALS

Psychologists and other scientists frequently use animals to conduct research that cannot be carried out with humans. For example, experiments on the effects of early separation from the mother have been done with monkeys and other animals. Such research has helped psychologists investigate the formation of parent–child bonds of attachment.

Experiments with infant monkeys highlight some of the ethical issues faced by psychologists and other scientists who contemplate potentially harmful research. Psychologists and biologists who study the workings of the brain destroy sections of the brains of laboratory animals to learn how they influence be-

Percent of new doctoral degrees in psychology earned by women

78

1879

Year that Wilhelm Wundt established the first psych lab

+1.00 to -1.00

Range of possible correlation coefficients

0

As a correlation coefficient, means that there is no linear relationship between the variables

STUDY TOOLS ▶ 1

Ready to study? In the book, you can:

- ↻ Review what you've read with Fill-Ins and Multiple Choice quizzes (below).
- ↻ Rip out Chapter Review card (in the back).

Or you can go online to CourseMate at www.cengagebrain.com for these resources:

- ↻ Complete Practices Quizzes to prepare for tests.
- ↻ Review Key Terms Flash Cards (online or print).
- ↻ Play games to master concepts.

FILL-INS

Answers can be found in the back of the book, starting on page 368.

1. Psychology is defined as the study of _____ and mental processes.

2. _____ psychologists evaluate problems such as anxiety and depression through interviews and psychological tests.

3. _____ founded the school of structuralism.

4. _____ psychologists saw our perceptions as wholes that give meaning to parts.

5. _____ psychologists note that only the fittest organisms reach maturity and reproduce, thereby transmitting their genes to future generations and causing species to evolve in adaptive directions.

6. Kenneth and Mamie Phipps _____ conducted research that influenced a Supreme Court decision on segregated schools.

7. Samples must accurately represent the target _____.

8. In the _____, a large sample of people answer questions about their attitudes or behavior.

9. Ideal experiments use experimental and _____ groups.

10. Psychologists adhere to _____ standards that help promote the dignity of the individual, maintain scientific integrity, and protect research participants and clinical clients from harm.

1. Psychology is defined as the scientific study of
   a. **behavior and mental processes.**
   b. **diagnosis and treatment of behavioral disorders.**
   c. **conscious and unconscious mental processes.**
   d. **the mind.**

2. School psychologists are employed by school districts to
   a. **develop achievement and aptitude tests.**
   b. **identify and assist students who have problems that interfere with their learning.**
   c. **assess the development of children in the school system.**
   d. **develop curriculum for teachers to deliver.**

3. What distinguished Wilhelm Wundt's contribution from other contributions to psychology?
   a. **He wrote the first textbook of psychology.**
   b. **He defined psychology as the science of behavior.**
   c. **He established psychology as a laboratory science.**
   d. **He studied insight in lower animals.**

4. The school of psychology that places unconscious impulses and desires at the center of human behavior is
   a. **psychoanalysis.**
   b. **humanism-existentialism.**
   c. **functionalism.**
   d. **Gestalt psychology.**

5. The first female president of the American Psychological Association was
   a. **Mary Ainsworth.**   c. **Karen Horney.**
   b. **Elizabeth Loftus.**   d. **Mary Whiton Calkins.**

6. A(n) _____ is a specific statement about behavior or mental processes that is tested through research.
   a. **observation**   c. **theory**
   b. **scientific method**   d. **hypothesis**

7. In a _____, each member of a population has an equal chance of being selected to participate.
   a. **random sample**
   b. **selection sample**
   c. **stratified sample**
   d. **free sample**

8. A disadvantage of survey research is _____. For example, people tend to overrate behaviors like church attendance and proper hygiene.
   a. **inaccurate self-report**
   b. **too much detail**
   c. **that people are too honest**
   d. **too few survey companies**

9. You design a test of intelligence. On the theory that intelligence is related to academic performance, you use _____ to test the relationship between performance on your new test and grades in school.
   a. **an experimental method**
   b. **a test-retest method**
   c. **the correlational method**
   d. **naturalistic observation**

10. Dr. Liu was interested in testing the effects of violent television on six-year-old children. She showed one group a particularly violent episode of *Power Rangers* and another group watched a short nonviolent episode of an old Bill Cosby show. She then observed the groups in the playground and measured their behaviors. What is the dependent variable in this study?
    a. **Bill Cosby and his family**
    b. **Violent or nonviolent TV show**
    c. **The behavior on the playground**
    d. **The amount of time watching TV**

USE THE TOOLS.

- Rip out the Review Cards in the back of your book to study.

Or Visit CourseMate to:

- Read, search, highlight, and take notes in the Interactive eBook
- Review Flashcards (Print or Online) to master key terms
- Test yourself with Auto-Graded Quizzes
- Bring concepts to life with Games, Videos, and Animations!

Go to CourseMate for PSYCH3 to begin using these tools. Access at **www.cengagebrain.com**

Complete the Speak Up survey in CourseMate at www.cengagebrain.com

f Follow us at www.facebook.com/4ltrpress

LEARNING OUTCOMES

2-1 Describe the nervous system, including neurons, neural impulses, and neurotransmitters

2-2 List the structures of the brain and their functions

2-3 Explain the role of the endocrine system and list the endocrine glands

2-4 Describe evolutionary psychology and the connections between heredity, behavior, and mental processes

 STUDY TOOLS ▶ After you read the chapter, go to the Study Tools at the end of the chapter, page 54.

CHAPTER 2

Biology and
PSYCHOLOGY

"Gage is no longer Gage," said those who had known him before the accident.

There are many key characters in the history of psychology, and some of them did not arrive there intentionally. One of these was a promising railroad worker who was helping our young nation stretch from coast to coast. His name was Phineas Gage. Gage was highly admired by his friends and coworkers. But all that changed one day in 1848. While he was tamping down the blasting powder for a dynamite charge, Gage accidentally set the powder off. The inch-thick metal tamping rod shot upward through his cheek and brain and out the top of his head.

If the trajectory of the rod had been slightly different, Gage would have died. Although Gage fell back in a heap, he was miraculously alive. His coworkers watched in shock as he stood up a few moments later and spoke. While the local doctor marveled at the hole through Gage's head, Gage asked when he'd be able to return to work. Two months later, Gage's external wounds had healed, but the psychological aspects of the wound were now obvious. His former employer, who had regarded him as "the most efficient and capable foreman in their employ previous to his injury" (Harlow, 1868), refused to rehire him because he had changed so much:

The equilibrium or balance, so to speak, between his intellectual faculties and animal propensities, seems to have been destroyed. He is ... irreverent, indulging at times in the grossest profanity (which was not previously his custom). [He showed little consideration for other people, was] impatient of restraint or advice when it conflicts with his desires ... obstinate, yet capricious and vacillating, devising many plans of future operation, which are no sooner arranged than they are abandoned in turn for others ... But all had not been lost in Gage's brain. In fact, many of his intellectual skills were just fine, apparently untouched.

Generations of researchers—psychologists, physicians, biologists, neuroscientists—have wondered how the changes in Gage's personality might have been caused by the damage to his brain. Perhaps the trajec-

---

"Gage is no longer Gage."

TRUTH OR *FICTION*

WHAT DO YOU THINK? FOLKLORE, COMMON SENSE, OR NONSENSE? CIRCLE THE T FOR "TRUTH" OR THE F FOR "FICTION," AND CHECK THE ACCURACY OF YOUR ANSWERS AS YOU READ THROUGH THE CHAPTER.

T	F	A SINGLE CELL CAN STRETCH ALL THE WAY FROM YOUR SPINE TO YOUR TOE.
T	F	MESSAGES TRAVEL IN THE BRAIN BY MEANS OF ELECTRICITY.
T	F	A BRAIN CELL CAN SEND OUT HUNDREDS OF MESSAGES EACH SECOND—AND MANAGE TO CATCH SOME REST IN BETWEEN.
T	F	FEAR CAN GIVE YOU INDIGESTION.
T	F	THE HUMAN BRAIN IS LARGER THAN THAT OF ANY OTHER ANIMAL.
T	F	IF A SURGEON WERE TO STIMULATE A CERTAIN PART OF YOUR BRAIN ELECTRICALLY, YOU MIGHT SWEAR THAT SOMEONE HAD STROKED YOUR LEG.
T	F	CHARLES DARWIN WAS NEARLY EXCLUDED FROM THE VOYAGE THAT LED TO THE DEVELOPMENT OF HIS THEORY OF EVOLUTION BECAUSE THE CAPTAIN OF THE SHIP DID NOT LIKE THE SHAPE OF HIS NOSE.

neuron

a specialized cell of the nervous system that receives and transmits messages

glial cells

cells that remove dead neurons and waste products from the nervous system, nourish and insulate neurons, form myelin, and play a role in neural transmission of messages

tory of the rod spared parts of the frontal lobes that are involved in language and movement but damaged areas connected with personality and emotional response (Damasio, 2000; Wagar & Thagard, 2004). In this chapter, we will learn about the frontal lobes of the brain and much more. We will travel from the small to the large—from the microscopic brain cells that hold and transmit information, to the visible structures that provide the basis for functions such as memory, speech, sensation, thought, planning, and voluntary movement.

2-1 The Nervous System: On Being Wired

The nervous system is a system of nerves involved in thought processes, heartbeat, visual–motor coordination, and so on. The nervous system contains the brain, the spinal cord, and other parts that make it possible for us to receive information from the world outside and to act on that world.

The nervous system is composed of cells, most of which are *neurons*, which is where we will begin our study of the nervous system.

2-1a NEURONS: INTO THE FABULOUS FOREST

Within our brains lies a fabulous forest of nerve cells, or neurons. **Neurons** are specialized cells of the nervous system that conduct impulses. Neurons can be visualized as having branches, trunks, and roots—something like trees. As we voyage through this forest, we see that many nerve cells lie alongside one another like a thicket of trees. But neurons can also lie end to end, with their "roots" intertwined with the "branches" of the neurons that lie below. Neurons receive "messages" from a number of sources such as light, other neurons, and pressure on the skin, and they can pass these messages along in a complex biological dance. We are born with more than 100 billion neurons. Most of them are found in the brain.

The nervous system also contains **glial cells**. Glial cells remove dead neurons and waste products from the nervous system; nourish and insulate neurons; form a fatty, insulating substance called *myelin*; and play a role in neural transmission of messages. But neurons occupy center stage in the nervous system. The messages transmitted by neurons somehow account for phenomena ranging from the perception of an itch from a mosquito bite to the coordination of a

---

FIGURE 2.1 | The Anatomy of a Neuron

SENDING NEURON   RECEIVING NEURON

Neural impulse

Axon

Axon terminals

Dendrites

Nucleus

Cell body (soma)

Myelin sheath

Closeup of axon terminal button and synapse

Neurotransmitters

Synaptic cleft   Receptor sites

"Messages" enter neurons through dendrites, are transmitted along the trunk-like axon, and then are sent from axon terminal buttons to muscles, glands, and other neurons. Axon terminal buttons contain sacs of chemicals called *neurotransmitters*. Neurotransmitters are released into the *synaptic cleft*, where many of them bind to *receptor sites* on the dendrites of the receiving neuron.

skier's vision and muscles to the composition of a concerto to the solution of an algebraic equation.

Neurons vary according to their functions and their location. Neurons in the brain may be only a fraction of an inch in length, whereas others in the legs are several feet long. Most neurons include a cell body, dendrites, and an axon (see Figure 2.1). The cell body contains the core or *nucleus* of the cell. The nucleus uses oxygen and nutrients to generate the energy needed to carry out the work of the cell. Anywhere from a few to several hundred short fibers, or **dendrites**, extend like roots from the cell body to receive incoming messages from thousands of adjoining neurons.

Each neuron has an **axon** that extends like a trunk from the cell body. Axons are very thin, but those that carry messages from the toes to the spinal cord extend several feet. Like tree trunks, axons can branch off in different directions. Axons end in small, bulb-shaped structures called *axon terminals* or *terminal buttons*. Neurons carry messages in one direction only: from the dendrites or cell body through the axon to the axon terminals. The messages are then transmitted from the terminal buttons to other neurons, muscles, or glands.

As a child matures, the axons of neurons become longer and the dendrites and terminals proliferate, creating vast interconnected networks for the transmission of complex messages. The number of glial cells also increases as the nervous system develops, contributing to its dense appearance.

Myelin

The axons of many neurons are wrapped tightly with white, fatty **myelin** that makes them look like strings of sausages under the microscope (Figure 2.1). The fat insulates the axon from electrically charged atoms, or *ions*, found in the fluids that surround the nervous system. The myelin sheath minimizes leakage of the electrical current being carried along the axon, thereby allowing messages to be conducted more efficiently.

Myelination is part of the maturation process that leads to a child's ability to crawl and walk during the first year. Infants are not physiologically "ready" to engage in visual–motor coordination and other activities until the coating process reaches certain levels. In people with the disease multiple sclerosis, myelin is replaced with a hard fibrous tissue that throws off the timing of nerve impulses and disrupts muscular control.

Afferent and Efferent Neurons

If someone steps on your toes, the sensation is registered by receptors or sensory neurons near the surface of your skin. Then it is transmitted to the spinal cord and brain through *sensory neurons*, or **afferent neurons**, which can be as long as 2 to 3 feet in length. In the brain, subsequent messages might be conveyed by associative neurons that are only a few thousandths of an inch long. You experience the pain through this process and perhaps entertain some rather nasty thoughts about the perpetrator, who is now apologizing and begging for understanding.

Long before you arrive at any logical conclusions, however, *motor neurons*, or **efferent neurons**, send messages to your foot so that you withdraw it and begin an impressive hopping routine. Efferent neurons transmit messages from the brain or spinal cord to muscles and glands. Other efferent neurons stimulate glands so that your heart is beating more rapidly, you are sweating, and the hair on the back of your arms has become erect! Being a good sport, you say, "Oh, it's nothing." But considering all the neurons involved, it really is something, isn't it?

TRUTH IT IS TRUE THAT A SINGLE CELL CAN STRETCH ALL THE WAY FROM YOUR SPINE TO YOUR TOE.

In case you think that afferent and efferent neurons will be hard to distinguish because they sound pretty much the SAME to you, remember that they *are* the "SAME." That is, Sensory Afferent, and Motor Efferent.

2-1b THE NEURAL IMPULSE: "THE BODY ELECTRIC"[1]

In the 18th century, the Italian physiologist Luigi Galvani (1737–1798) conducted a shocking experiment in a rainstorm. While his neighbors had the sense to remain indoors, Galvani and his wife were out on the porch connecting lightning rods to the heads of dissected frogs whose legs were connected by wires to a well of water. When lightning blazed above, the frogs' muscles

---

[1] From Walt Whitman's *Leaves of Grass*.

dendrites
rootlike structures, attached to the cell body of a neuron, that receive impulses, or incoming messages, from other neurons

axon
a long, thin part of a neuron that transmits impulses to other neurons from bulb-shaped structures called *axon terminals or terminal buttons*

myelin
a fatty substance that encases and insulates axons, facilitating transmission of neural impulses

afferent neurons
neurons that transmit messages from sensory receptors to the spinal cord and brain; also called *sensory neurons*

efferent neurons
neurons that transmit messages from the brain or spinal cord to muscles and glands; also called *motor neurons*

neural impulse
the electrochemical discharge of a nerve cell, or neuron

polarize
to ready a neuron for firing by creating an internal negative charge in relation to the body fluid outside the cell membrane

resting potential
the electrical potential across the neural membrane when it is not responding to other neurons

depolarize
to reduce the resting potential of a cell membrane from about 70 millivolts toward zero

action potential
the electrical impulse that provides the basis for the conduction of a neural impulse along an axon of a neuron

contracted. Galvani was demonstrating that the messages—or **neural impulses**—that travel along neurons are electrochemical in nature.

Neural impulses are messages that travel within neurons at somewhere between two (in nonmyelinated neurons) and 225 miles an hour (in myelinated neurons). This speed is not impressive when compared with that of an electrical current in a toaster oven or a lamp, which can travel at close to the speed of light—over 186,000 miles per second. Distances in the body are short, however, and a message will travel from a toe to the brain in perhaps 1/50th of a second.

An Electrochemical Voyage

The process by which neural impulses travel is electrochemical. Chemical changes take place within neurons that cause an electrical charge to be transmitted along their lengths. Neurons and body fluids contain *ions*—positively or negatively charged atoms. In a resting state—that is, when a neuron is not being stimulated by its neighbors—negatively charged chloride (Cl⁻)

ions are plentiful within the neuron, contributing to an overall negative charge in relation to the outside. The difference in electrical charge readies, or **polarizes**, a neuron for firing by creating an internal negative charge in relation to the body fluid outside the cell membrane. The electrical potential across the neural membrane when it is not responding to other neurons—its **resting potential**—is about −70 millivolts in relation to the body fluid outside the cell membrane.

When an area on the surface of the resting neuron is adequately stimulated by other neurons, the cell membrane in the area changes its permeability to allow positively charged sodium ions to enter. Thus the area of entry becomes positively charged, or **depolarized**, with respect to the outside (see Figure 2.2A). The permeability of the cell membrane then changes again, allowing no more sodium ions to enter (see Figure 2.2B).

The electrical impulse that provides the basis for the conduction of a neural impulse along an axon of a neuron is termed its **action potential**. The inside of the cell axon at the disturbed area has an action potential of 110 millivolts. This action potential, added to the −70 millivolts that characterizes the resting potential, brings the membrane voltage to a positive charge of about +30 to +40 millivolts (see Figure 2.3). This inner change causes the next section of the cell to become

©American Images Inc./Getty Images

FIGURE 2.2 | Changes in Electrical Charges as a Neural Impulse Is Transmitted Along the Length of an Axon

Electrical charges inside and outside axons are measured by microscopic glass tubes placed inside and outside the cell membranes of axons. As shown in part A, when an axon is at rest, it has a negative charge of about −70 millivolts. But when sodium ions enter and the area of entry is depolarized, as shown in part B, the charge in that part of the axon rises to +30 to +40 millivolts. The change causes the next part of the cell membrane to become permeable to sodium ions, continuing the transmission of the neural impulse along the axon.

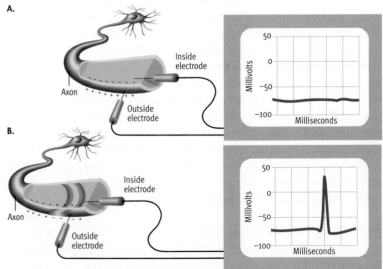

permeable to sodium ions. At the same time, other positively charged (potassium) ions are being pumped out of the area of the cell that was previously affected, which returns the area to its resting potential. In this way, the neural impulse is transmitted continuously along an axon. Because the impulse is created anew as it progresses, its strength does not change.

Firing: How Messages Voyage from Neuron to Neuron

The conduction of the neural impulse along the length of a neuron is what is meant by *firing*. When a rifle fires, it sends a bullet speeding through its barrel and discharges it at more than 1,000 feet per second. Neurons also fire, but instead of a barrel, a neuron has an axon. Instead of discharging a bullet, it releases *neurotransmitters*.

Some neurons fire in less than 1/1,000th of a second. When they fire, neurons transmit messages to other neurons, muscles, or glands. However, neurons will not fire unless the incoming messages combine to reach a certain strength, which is defined as the *threshold* at which a neuron will fire. A weak message may cause a temporary shift in electrical charge at some point along the cell membrane, but this charge will dissipate if the neuron is not stimulated to its threshold.

Every time a neuron fires, it transmits an impulse of the same strength. This occurrence is known as the **all-or-none principle.** That is, either a neuron fires or it doesn't. Neurons fire more often when they have been stimulated by larger numbers of other neurons. Stronger stimuli cause more frequent firing, but again, the strength of each firing remains the same.

MESSAGES WITHIN NEURONS *DO* TRAVEL BY MEANS OF ELECTRICITY. HOWEVER, COMMUNICATION *BETWEEN* NEURONS IS CARRIED OUT DIFFERENTLY.

For a few thousandths of a second after firing, a neuron is in a **refractory period**; that is, it is insensitive to messages from other neurons and will not fire. This period is a time of recovery during which sodium is prevented from passing through the neuronal membrane. Because such periods of "recovery" might occur hundreds of times per second, it seems a rapid recovery and a short rest indeed.

The Synapse: On Being Well-Connected

A neuron relays its message to another neuron across a junction called a **synapse**. A synapse consists of an axon terminal from the transmitting neuron, a dendrite, or the body of a receiving neuron, and a fluid-filled gap

IT IS TRUE THAT NEURONS IN THE BRAIN CAN SEND OUT HUNDREDS OF MESSAGES EACH SECOND—AND MANAGE TO CATCH SOME REST IN BETWEEN. THAT "REST" IS TERMED THE *REFRACTORY PERIOD*.

all-or-none principle
the fact that a neuron fires an impulse of the same strength whenever its action potential is triggered

refractory period
a phase following firing during which a neuron is less sensitive to messages from other neurons and will not fire

synapse
a junction between the axon terminals of one neuron and the dendrites or cell body of another neuron

FIGURE 2.3 | Changes in Electrical Charges as a Neural Impulse Is Transmitted Across an Axon

The resting potential of a segment of a cell axon is about −70 millivolts. But the inside of the cell axon at the disturbed area has an action potential of about 110 millivolts. When we add this figure to the −70 millivolts that characterize the resting potential, we bring the membrane voltage to a positive charge of about +30 to +40 millivolts. The inner change causes the next section of the cell to become permeable to sodium ions. In this way, the neural impulse is transmitted continuously along an axon.

© Cengage Learning 2012

neurotransmitters
chemical substances involved in the transmission of neural impulses from one neuron to another

receptor site
a location on a dendrite of a receiving neuron tailored to receive a neurotransmitter

acetylcholine (ACh)
a neurotransmitter that controls muscle contractions

hippocampus
a structure of the brain that is involved in memory formation

dopamine
a neurotransmitter that affects the ability to perceive pleasure, voluntary movement, and learning and memory; it is involved in Parkinson's disease and appears to play a role in schizophrenia

between the two that is called the *synaptic cleft* (see Figure 2.1). Although the neural impulse is electrical, it does not jump across the synaptic cleft like a spark. Instead, when a nerve impulse reaches a synapse, axon terminals release chemicals into the synaptic cleft like myriad ships being cast into the sea. Scientists have identified a few dozen of these chemicals to date. Let's consider a few that are usually of the greatest interest to psychologists.

2-1c
NEUROTRANSMITTERS: THE CHEMICAL KEYS TO COMMUNICATION

Sacs called *synaptic vesicles* in the axon terminals contain **neurotransmitters**—the chemical keys to communication (see Figure 2.1). When a neural impulse (action potential) reaches the axon terminal, the vesicles release varying amounts of neurotransmitters into the synaptic cleft. From there, they influence the receiving neuron.

Each kind of neurotransmitter has a unique chemical structure, and each can fit into a specifically tailored harbor, or **receptor site**, on the receiving cell (see Figure 2.1). The analogy of a key fitting into a lock is often used to describe this process. Once released, not all molecules of a neurotransmitter find their way into receptor sites of other neurons. "Loose" neurotransmitters are usually either broken down or reabsorbed by the axon terminal (a process called *reuptake*).

Some neurotransmitters act to *excite* other neurons—that is, to cause other neurons to fire. Other neurotransmitters *inhibit* receiving neurons. That is, they prevent the neurons from firing. The sum of the stimulation—excitatory and inhibitory—determines whether a neuron will fire.

Neurotransmitters are involved in physical processes such as muscle contraction and psychological processes such as thoughts and emotions. Excesses or deficiencies of neurotransmitters have been linked to psychological disorders such as depression and schizophrenia. Let's consider the effects of some neurotransmitters that are of interest to psychologists: acetylcholine (ACh), dopamine, norepinephrine, serotonin, GABA, and endorphins.

Acetylcholine (ACh) is a neurotransmitter that controls muscle contractions. It is excitatory at synapses between nerves and muscles that involve voluntary movement but inhibitory at the heart and some other locations. The effects of *curare* highlight the functioning of ACh. The poison curare is extracted from plants by South American indigenous people and used in hunting. If an arrow tipped with curare pierces the skin and the poison enters the body, it prevents ACh from binding to the receptor sites on neurons. Because ACh helps muscles move, curare causes paralysis. The victim is prevented from contracting the muscles used in breathing and dies from suffocation. Botulism, a disease that stems from food poisoning, prevents the release of ACh and has the same effect as curare.

ACh is normally prevalent in a part of the brain called the **hippocampus**, a structure involved in the formation of memories (Louie & Wilson, 2001). When the amount of ACh available to the brain decreases, as in Alzheimer's disease, memory formation is impaired (Packard, 2009). In one experiment, researchers decreased the ACh available to the hippocampus of laboratory rats. As a result, the rats were incapable of learning their way through a maze, apparently because they could not remember which way to turn at various choice points (Egawa et al., 2002).

Dopamine is a neurotransmitter that acts in the brain and affects the ability to perceive pleasure, voluntary movement, and learning and memory. Nicotine, alcohol, and many other drugs are pleasurable because they heighten levels of dopamine. Deficiencies of dopamine are linked to Parkinson's disease, in which people progressively lose control over their muscles (Fuentes et al., 2009). They develop muscle tremors and jerky, uncoordinated movements.

The psychological disorder *schizophrenia* is characterized by confusion and false perceptions, and it has been linked to dopamine. People with schizophrenia may have more receptor sites for dopamine in an area of the brain that is involved in emotional responding. For this reason, they may "overutilize" the dopamine available in the brain (Neve, 2009; Roth et al., 2009). Overutilization is connected with hallucinations and disturbances of thought and emotion. The phenothiazines, a group of drugs used in the treatment of schizophrenia, inhibit the action of dopamine by blocking some dopamine receptors (Neve, 2009). Because of their action, phenothiazines may have Parkinson's-like side effects, which are usually treated by lowering the dosage or prescribing other drugs that lessen the Parkinson-like effects.

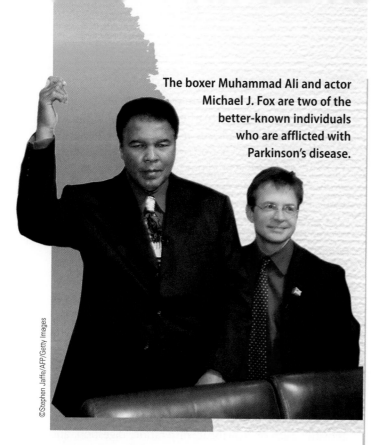

The boxer Muhammad Ali and actor Michael J. Fox are two of the better-known individuals who are afflicted with Parkinson's disease.

©Stephen Jaffe/AFP/Getty Images

Norepinephrine is produced largely by neurons in the brain stem and acts both as a neurotransmitter and as a hormone. It is an excitatory neurotransmitter that speeds up the heartbeat and other body processes and is involved in general arousal, learning and memory, and eating. Excesses and deficiencies of norepinephrine have been linked to mood disorders. Deficiencies of both ACh and norepinephrine particularly impair memory formation (Qi & Gold, 2009).

The stimulants cocaine and amphetamine ("speed") boost norepinephrine (as well as dopamine) production, increasing the firing of neurons and leading to persistent arousal. Amphetamines both facilitate the release of these neurotransmitters and prevent their reuptake. Cocaine also blocks reuptake.

Serotonin is a neurotransmitter that is involved in emotional arousal and sleep. Deficiencies of serotonin have been linked to eating disorders, alcoholism, depression, aggression, and insomnia (Polina et al., 2009; Risch et al., 2009). The drug LSD decreases the action of serotonin and is also believed to increase the utilization of dopamine, which may be the mechanism by which it produces hallucinations.

Gamma-aminobutyric acid (GABA) is another neurotransmitter of great interest to psychologists. One reason is that GABA is an inhibitory neurotransmitter that may help calm anxiety reactions (Cunningham et al., 2009). Tranquilizers and alcohol may quell anxiety by binding with GABA receptors and amplifying its effects. One class of antianxiety drug may also increase the sensitivity of receptor sites to GABA. Other studies link deficiencies of GABA to depression (Karolewicz et al., 2009).

Endorphins are inhibitory neurotransmitters. The word *endorphin* is the contraction of *endogenous morphine. Endogenous* means "developing from within." Endorphins occur naturally in the brain and in the bloodstream and are similar to the narcotic morphine in their functions and effects. They lock into receptor sites for chemicals that transmit pain messages to the brain. Once the endorphin "key" is in the "lock," the pain-causing chemicals are locked out. Endorphins may also increase our sense of competence, enhance the functioning of the immune system, and be connected with the pleasurable "runner's high" reported by many long-distance runners (Shah et al., 2009).

There you have it—a fabulous forest of neurons in which billions upon billions of axon terminals are pouring armadas of neurotransmitters into synaptic clefts at any given time. The combined activity of all these neurotransmitters determines which messages will be transmitted and which ones will not. You experience your sensations, your thoughts, and your control over your body as psychological events, but the psychological events come from billions upon billions of electrochemical events.

We can think of neurons as the microscopic building blocks of the nervous system. Millions upon millions of these neurons gather together to form larger, visible structures that we think of as the parts of the nervous system. We discuss those parts next.

2-1d THE PARTS OF THE NERVOUS SYSTEM

The nervous system consists of the brain, the spinal cord, and the **nerves** linking them to the sensory organs, muscles, and glands. As shown in Figure 2.4, the

norepinephrine
a neurotransmitter whose action is similar to that of the hormone epinephrine and that may play a role in depression

serotonin
a neurotransmitter involved in emotional arousal and sleep; deficiencies of serotonin have been linked to eating disorders, alcoholism, depression, aggression, and insomnia

gamma-aminobutyric acid (GABA)
an inhibitory neurotransmitter that apparently helps calm anxiety

endorphins
inhibitory neurotransmitters that occur naturally in the brain and in the bloodstream and are similar to the narcotic morphine in their functions and effects

nerve
a bundle of axons from many neurons

central nervous system
the brain and spinal cord

peripheral nervous system
the part of the nervous system consisting of the somatic nervous system and the autonomic nervous system

somatic nervous system
the division of the peripheral nervous system that connects the central nervous system with sensory receptors, skeletal muscles, and the surface of the body

autonomic nervous system (ANS)
the division of the peripheral nervous system that regulates glands and activities such as heartbeat, respiration, digestion, and dilation of the pupils

brain and the spinal cord make up the **central nervous system**. If you compare your nervous system to a computer, your central nervous system would be your central processing unit (CPU).

The sensory (afferent) neurons, which receive and transmit messages to the brain and spinal cord, and the motor (efferent) neurons, which transmit messages from the brain or spinal cord to the muscles and glands, make up the peripheral nervous system. In the comparison of the nervous system to a computer, the **peripheral nervous system** makes up the nervous system's peripheral devices—keyboard, mouse, DVD drive, and so on. You would not be able to feed information to your computer's central processing unit without these *peripheral* devices. Other peripheral devices, such as your monitor and printer, allow you to follow what is happening inside your CPU and see what it has done.

The Peripheral Nervous System: The Body's Peripheral Devices

The peripheral nervous system consists of sensory and motor neurons that transmit messages to and from the central nervous system. Without the peripheral nervous system, our brains would be like isolated CPUs. There would be no keyboards, mouses, DVDs, or other ways of inputting information. There would be no monitors, printers, modems, or other ways of displaying or transmitting information. We would be detached from the world. We would not be able to perceive it; we would not be able to act on it. The two main divisions of the peripheral nervous system are the *somatic nervous system* and the *autonomic nervous system.*

The **somatic nervous system** contains sensory (afferent) and motor (efferent) neurons. It transmits messages about sights, sounds, smells, temperature, body positions, and so on, to the central nervous system. Messages transmitted from the brain and spinal cord to the somatic nervous system control purposeful body movements such as raising a hand, winking, or running, as well as the tiny, almost imperceptible movements that maintain our balance and posture.

The **autonomic nervous system (ANS)** also has afferent and efferent neurons and regulates the glands and the muscles of internal organs. Thus, the ANS controls activities such as heartbeat, respiration, digestion, and dilation of the pupils. These activities can occur automatically, while we are asleep. But some of them can be overridden by conscious control. You can breathe at a purposeful pace, for example. Methods like biofeedback and yoga also help people gain voluntary control of functions such as heart rate and blood pressure.

The ANS also has two branches, or divisions: *sympathetic* and *parasympathetic*. These branches have largely opposing effects. Many organs and glands are stimu-

---

FIGURE 2.4 | The Divisions of the Nervous System

The nervous system contains two main divisions: the central nervous system and the peripheral nervous system. The central nervous system consists of the brain and spinal cord. The peripheral nervous system contains the somatic and autonomic systems. In turn, the autonomic nervous system has sympathetic and parasympathetic divisions.

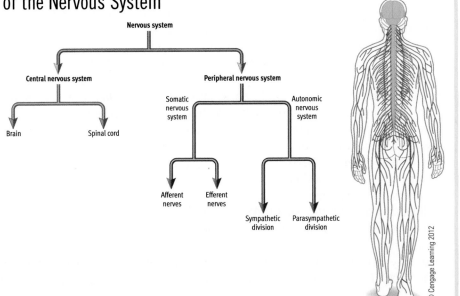

© Cengage Learning 2012

FIGURE 2.5 | The Branches of the Autonomic Nervous System (ANS)

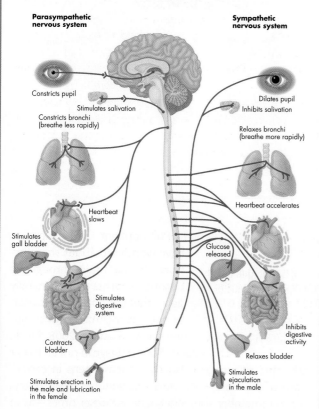

Parasympathetic nervous system

Constricts pupil
Stimulates salivation
Constricts bronchi (breathe less rapidly)
Heartbeat slows
Stimulates gall bladder
Stimulates digestive system
Contracts bladder
Stimulates erection in the male and lubrication in the female

Sympathetic nervous system

Dilates pupil
Inhibits salivation
Relaxes bronchi (breathe more rapidly)
Heartbeat accelerates
Glucose released
Inhibits digestive activity
Relaxes bladder
Stimulates ejaculation in the male

The parasympathetic branch of the AMS generally acts to replenish stores of energy in the body. The sympathetic branch is most active during activities that expend energy. The two branches of the ANS frequently have antagonistic effects on the organs they service.

Weiten W. *Psychology*, 8e. Copyright © 2010. Cengage Learning.

---

lated by both branches of the ANS (see Figure 2.5). When organs and glands are simultaneously stimulated by both divisions, their effects can average out to some degree. In general, the **sympathetic division** is most active during processes that involve spending body energy from stored reserves, such as a fight-or-flight response to a predator or when you find out that your rent is going to be raised. The **parasympathetic division** is most active during processes that replenish reserves of energy, such as eating. When we are afraid, the sympathetic division of the ANS accelerates the heart rate. When we relax, the parasympathetic division decelerates the heart rate. The parasympathetic division stimulates digestive processes, but the sympathetic branch, which can be activated by fear, inhibits diges-

TRUTH FEAR CAN INDEED GIVE YOU INDIGESTION.

tion. Thus fear can give you indigestion. The ANS is of particular interest to psychologists because its activities are linked to various emotions such as anxiety and love.

The Central Nervous System: The Body's Central Processing Unit

The central nervous system consists of the spinal cord and the brain. The **spinal cord** is a true "information superhighway"—a column of nerves as thick as a thumb. It transmits messages from sensory receptors to the brain and from the brain to muscles and glands throughout the body. The spinal cord also carries out some "local government." That is, it responds to some sources of external stimulation through spinal reflexes. A **spinal reflex** is an unlearned response to a stimulus that may require only two neurons—a sensory neuron and a motor neuron (see Figure 2.6). In some reflexes, a third neuron, called an *interneuron*, transmits the neural impulse from the sensory neuron through the spinal cord to the motor neuron.

The spinal cord and brain contain gray matter and white matter. **Gray matter** consists of nonmyelinated neurons. Some of these are involved in spinal reflexes. Others send their axons to the brain. **White matter** is composed of bundles of longer, myelinated (and thus whitish) axons that carry messages to and from the brain. A cross-section of the spinal cord shows that the gray matter, which includes cell bodies, is distributed in a butterfly pattern (see Figure 2.6).

The spinal cord is also involved in reflexes. We blink in response to a puff of air in our faces. We swallow when food accumulates in the mouth. A physician may tap below the knee to elicit the knee-jerk reflex, a sign that the nervous system is operating adequately. Sexual response involves many reflexes. Urinating and defecating are reflexes that occur in response to pressure in the bladder and the rectum. It is your central nervous system that makes you so special. Other

sympathetic division the branch of the ANS that is most active during emotional responses, such as fear and anxiety, that spend the body's reserves of energy

parasympathetic division the branch of the ANS that is most active during processes (such as digestion) that restore the body's reserves of energy

spinal cord a column of nerves within the spine that transmits messages from sensory receptors to the brain and from the brain to muscles and glands throughout the body

spinal reflex a simple, unlearned response to a stimulus that may involve only two neurons

gray matter the grayish neurons and neural segments that are involved in spinal reflexes

white matter axon bundles that carry messages to and from the brain

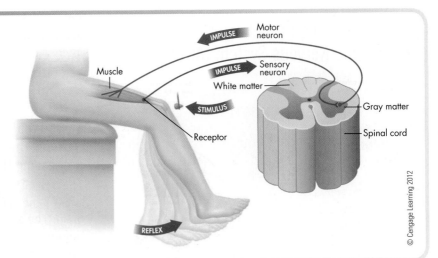

FIGURE 2.6 | The Reflex Arc

Reflexes are inborn, stereotyped behavior patterns that have apparently evolved because they help individuals adapt to the environment even before they can understand and purposefully manipulate the environment. Here we see a cross-section of the spinal cord, highlighting a sensory neuron and a motor neuron, which are involved in the knee-jerk reflex. In some reflexes, interneurons link sensory and motor neurons.

© Cengage Learning 2012

species see more sharply, smell more keenly, and hear more acutely. Other species run faster, or fly through the air, or swim underwater, without the benefit of artificial devices such as airplanes and submarines. But it is your central nervous system that enables you to use symbols and language, the abilities that allow people not only to adapt to their environment but also to create new environments and give them names (Bandura, 1999).

FICTION IT IS NOT TRUE THAT THE HUMAN BRAIN IS LARGER THAN THAT OF ANY OTHER ANIMAL. HOWEVER, OUR BRAINS ACCOUNT FOR A LARGER PERCENTAGE OF OUR BODY WEIGHT THAN DO THE BRAINS OF ELEPHANTS OR WHALES.

2-2 The Brain: Wider Than the Sky

When I was a child, I was told that the human nervous system is more complex than that of any other animal and that our brains are larger than those of any other animal. Now, this last piece of business is not quite true. A human brain weighs about 3 pounds, but the brains of elephants and whales may be four times as heavy. Still, our brains account for a greater part of our body weight than do those of elephants or whales. Our brains weigh about 1/60th of our body weight. Elephant brains weigh about 1/1,000th of their total weight, and whale brains are a paltry 1/10,000th of their weight.

"The Brain—is wider than the Sky—
For—put them side by side—
The one the other will contain
With ease—and you—beside—"
—EMILY DICKINSON

© iStockphoto/stockcam

Philosophers and scientists have wondered about the functions of the brain throughout history. Scientists today generally agree that the mind is a function of the brain (American Psychological Association, 2008; Block, 2009). Some engage in research that attempts to pinpoint exactly what happens in certain parts of the brain when we are listening to music or trying to remember someone's face. At other times—as in the case of Phineas Gage—knowledge has almost literally fallen into their laps. From injuries to the head—some of them minimal, some horrendous—we have learned that brain damage can impair consciousness, perception, memory, and abilities to make plans and decisions. In some cases, the loss of large portions of the brain may result in little loss of function. But the loss of smaller portions in certain locations can cause language problems, memory loss, or death. It has been known for about two centuries that damage to the left side of the brain is connected with loss of sensation or movement on the right side of the body, and vice versa. Thus it has been assumed that the brain's control mechanisms cross over from right to left, and vice versa, as they descend into the body.

Accidents provide unplanned—and uncontrolled—opportunities of studying the brain. Still, scientists learn more about the brain through methods like experimentation, electroencephalography, and brain scans.

2-2a EXPERIMENTING WITH THE BRAIN

The results of disease and accidents (as in the case of Phineas Gage) have shown us that brain injuries can be connected with changes in behavior and mental processes. Scientists have also purposefully damaged part of the brain in laboratory animals to observe the results. For example, damaging one part of the brain region called the *hypothalamus* causes rats to overeat. Damaging another part of the hypothalamus causes them to stop eating. It is as if parts of the brain contain on–off switches for certain kinds of behavior, at least in lower animals.

Because the brain has no receptors for pain, surgeon Wilder Penfield (1969) was able to stimulate parts of human brains with electrical probes. As a result, his patients reported perceiving certain memories. Electrical stimulation of the brain has also shown that parts of the brain are connected with specific kinds of sensations (as of light or sound) or motor activities (such as movement of an arm or leg).

The Electroencephalograph

Penfield stimulated parts of the brain with an electrical current and asked people to report what they experienced. Researchers have also used the **electroencephalograph (EEG)** to record the natural electrical activity of the brain. The EEG (see Figure 2.7) detects minute amounts of electrical activity—called *brain waves*—that pass between the electrodes. Certain brain waves are associated with feelings of relaxation, with various stages of sleep, and with neurological problems such as epilepsy.

Brain-Imaging Techniques

When Phineas Gage had his fabled accident, the only ways to look into the brain were to drill holes or crack it open, neither of which would have contributed to the well-being of the subject. But in the latter years of the 20th century, researchers developed imaging techniques that use the computer's ability to generate images of the parts of the brain from sources of radiation.

Computerized axial tomography (CAT or CT scan), shown in Figure 2.8A, passes X-rays through the head and measures the structures that reflect the beams from various angles, generating a three-dimensional image. The CAT scan reveals deformities in shape and structure that are connected with blood clots, tumors, and other health problems.

A second method, **positron emission tomography (PET scan)**, shown in Figure 2.8B, forms a computer-generated image of the activity of parts of the brain by tracing the amount of glucose used (or metabolized) by these parts. More glucose is metabolized in more active parts of the brain. To trace the metabolism of glucose, a harmless amount of a radioactive compound, called a *tracer*, is mixed with glucose and injected into the bloodstream. When the glucose reaches the brain, the patterns of activity are revealed by measurement of the positrons—positively charged particles—that are given off by the tracer.

electroencephalograph (EEG) a method of detecting brain waves by means of measuring the current between electrodes placed on the scalp

computerized axial tomography (CAT or CT scan) a method of brain imaging that passes a narrow X-ray beam through the head and measures the structures that reflect the beams from various angles, enabling a computer to generate a three-dimensional image

positron emission tomography (PET scan) a method of brain imaging that injects a radioactive tracer into the bloodstream and assesses activity of parts of the brain according to the amount of glucose they metabolize

---

FIGURE 2.7 | The Electroencephalograph (EEG)

The EEG detects brain waves that pass between electrodes that are attached to the scalp. It has been used to reveal electrical activity associated with relaxation and the stages of sleep.

© Richard T. Nowitz/Corbis

magnetic resonance imaging (MRI)

an imaging method that places a person in a magnetic field and uses radio waves to cause the brain to emit signals that reveal shifts in the flow of blood, which, when the brain is being scanned, indicate brain activity

functional MRI (fMRI)

a form of MRI that enables researchers to observe the brain "while it works" by taking repeated scans

medulla

an oblong area of the hindbrain involved in regulation of heartbeat, blood pressure, movement, and respiration

A third imaging technique is **magnetic resonance imaging (MRI)**, which is shown in Figure 2.8C. In MRI, the person lies in a powerful magnetic field and is exposed to radio waves that cause parts of the brain to emit signals, which are measured from multiple angles. MRI relies on subtle shifts in blood flow. (More blood flows to more active parts of the brain, supplying them with oxygen.) **Functional MRI (fMRI)** provides a more rapid picture and therefore enables researchers to observe the brain "while it works" by taking repeated scans while subjects engage in activities such as mental processes and voluntary movements. fMRI can be used to show which parts of the brain are active when we are, say, listening to music, using language, or

playing chess (Krueger et al., 2008; Newman et al., 2009; Stocco & Anderson, 2008).

Some researchers consider the prefrontal cortex to be the "executive center" of the brain, where decisions are made to keep information in working memory and to solve problems. The prefrontal cortex is the part of the frontal lobe (see Figure 2.11 on page 41) that is closest to the front of the brain. Research with the PET scan and MRI supports the view that the prefrontal cortex is where we process much of the information involved in making plans and solving problems (Gilbert et al., 2008; Wang et al., 2008).

2-2b A VOYAGE THROUGH THE BRAIN

Let's begin our tour of the brain with the *hindbrain*, where the spinal cord rises to meet the brain (see Figure 2.9). Here we find three major structures: the *medulla*, the *pons*, and the *cerebellum*. Many pathways pass through the **medulla** to connect the spinal cord to higher levels of the brain. The medulla regulates basic

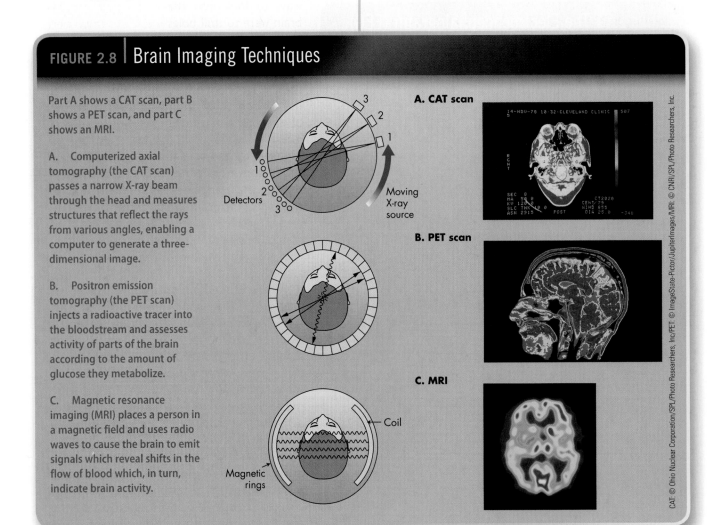

FIGURE 2.8 | Brain Imaging Techniques

Part A shows a CAT scan, part B shows a PET scan, and part C shows an MRI.

A. Computerized axial tomography (the CAT scan) passes a narrow X-ray beam through the head and measures structures that reflect the rays from various angles, enabling a computer to generate a three-dimensional image.

B. Positron emission tomography (the PET scan) injects a radioactive tracer into the bloodstream and assesses activity of parts of the brain according to the amount of glucose they metabolize.

C. Magnetic resonance imaging (MRI) places a person in a magnetic field and uses radio waves to cause the brain to emit signals which reveal shifts in the flow of blood which, in turn, indicate brain activity.

the hairstyles of the day. Your **phenotype** is the manner in which your genetic code manifests itself because of your experiences and environmental circumstances. Your genotype enables you to acquire language. Your phenotype reveals that you are likely to be speaking English if you were reared in the United States or Spanish if you were reared in Mexico (or both, if you are Mexican American).

Your genotype provides what psychologists refer to as your **nature**. Your phenotype represents the interaction of your nature (heredity) and your **nurture** (environmental influences) in the origins of your behavior and mental processes. Psychologists are especially interested in the roles of nature and nurture in intelligence and psychological disorders. Our genotypes provide us with physical traits that set the stage for certain behaviors. But none of us is the result of heredity alone. Environmental factors such as nutrition, learning opportunities, cultural influences, exercise, and (unfortunately) accident and illness also determine our phenotypes and

whether genetically possible behaviors will be displayed. Behavior and mental processes represent the interaction of nature and nurture. A potential Shakespeare who is reared in poverty and never taught to read or write will not create a *Hamlet*.

We normally receive 23 chromosomes from our father's sperm cell and 23 chromosomes from our mother's egg cell (ovum). When a sperm cell fertilizes an ovum, the chromosomes form 23 pairs. The 23rd pair consists of **sex chromosomes**, which determine whether we are female or male. We all receive an X sex chromosome (so called because of the X shape) from our mother. If we also receive an X sex chromosome from our father, we develop into a female. If we receive a Y sex chromosome (named after the Y shape) from our father, we develop into a male.

When people do not have the normal number of 46 chromosomes (23 pairs), physical and behavioral abnormalities may result. Most persons with **Down syndrome**, for example, have an extra, or third, chromosome on the 21st pair. Persons with Down syndrome have a downward-sloping fold of skin at the inner corners of the eyes, a round face, a protruding tongue, and a broad, flat nose. They are cognitively impaired and usually have physical problems that cause death by middle age.

2-4d KINSHIP STUDIES

Kinship studies are ways in which psychologists compare the presence of traits and behavior patterns in people who are biologically related or unrelated to help determine the role of genetic factors in their occurrence. The more *closely* people are related, the more *genes* they have in common. Identical twins share 100% of their genes. Parents and children have 50% of their genes in common, as do siblings (brothers and sisters). Aunts and uncles related by blood have a 25% overlap with nieces and nephews. First cousins share 12.5% of their genes. If genes are involved in a trait or behavior pattern, people who are more closely related should be more likely to show similar traits or behavior. Psychologists and behavioral geneticists are especially interested

phenotype
one's actual development and appearance, as based on one's genotype and environmental influences

nature
the inborn, innate character of an organism

nurture
the sum total of the environmental factors that affect an organism from conception onward

sex chromosomes
the 23rd pair of chromosomes, whose genetic material determines the sex of the individual

Down syndrome
a condition caused by an extra chromosome on the 21st pair and characterized by mental deficiency, a broad face, and slanting eyes

Down syndrome is caused by an extra chromosome on the 21st pair and becomes more likely to occur as the mother's age at the time of pregnancy increases. Persons with Down syndrome have characteristic facial features including downward-sloping folds of skin at the inner corners of the eyes, are intellectually deficient, and usually have health problems that lead to death by middle age.

in running kinship studies with twins and adopted individuals (Plomin & Haworth, 2009).

Twin Studies

The fertilized egg cell (ovum) that carries genetic messages from both parents is called a *zygote*. Now and then, a zygote divides into two cells that separate, so that instead of developing into a single person, it develops into two people with the same genetic makeup. Such people are identical, or **monozygotic (MZ), twins**. If the woman releases two ova in the same month and they are both fertilized, they develop into fraternal, or **dizygotic (DZ), twins**. DZ twins, like other siblings, share 50% of their genes. MZ twins are important in the study of the relative influences of nature (heredity) and nurture (the environment) because differences between MZ twins are the result of nurture. (They do not differ in their heredity—that is, their nature—because their genetic makeup is the same.)

Twin studies compare the presence of traits and behavior patterns in MZ twins, DZ twins, and other people to help determine the role of genetic factors in their occurrence. If MZ twins show greater similarity on a trait or behavior pattern than DZ twins, a genetic basis for the trait or behavior is suggested.

Twin studies show how strongly genetic factors influence physical features. MZ twins are more likely to look alike and to be similar in height, even to have more similar cholesterol levels than DZ twins (Souren et al., 2007). MZ twins also resemble one another more strongly than DZ twins in intelligence and personality traits like sociability, anxiety, friendliness, and conformity, even happiness (Lykken, 2007; McCrae et al., 2000; Veselka et al., 2009). Monozygotic twins are more likely than dizygotic twins to share psychological disorders such as autism, depression, schizophrenia, and vulnerability to alcoholism (Dworzynski et al., 2009; Plomin, 2000; Veenstra-Vanderweele & Cook, 2003). Research also shows that MZ twins are more alike than DZ twins in their blood pressure, brain wave patterns, even in their speech patterns, gestures, and mannerisms (Ambrosius et al., 2008; Lykken, 2007; Wessel et al., 2007).

Of course, twin studies are not perfect. MZ twins may resemble each other more closely than DZ twins partly because they are treated more similarly. MZ twins frequently are dressed identically, and parents sometimes have difficulty telling them apart. One way

Monozygotic twins share 100% of their genes, whereas dizygotic share 50% of their genes.

TWINS

Image Source Photography/Veer

to get around this difficulty is to find and compare MZ twins who were reared in different homes. Then, any similarities between MZ twins reared apart could not be explained by a shared home environment and would appear to be largely a result of heredity. In the fascinating Minnesota Study of Twins Reared Apart (Lykken, 2007), researchers have been measuring the physiological and psychological characteristics of 56 sets of MZ adult twins who were separated in infancy and reared in different homes.

In sum, MZ twins reared apart are about as similar as MZ twins reared together on a variety of measures of intelligence, personality, temperament, occupational and leisure-time interests, and social attitudes. These traits thus would appear to have a genetic underpinning.

Adoption Studies

The results of kinship studies can be confused when relatives share similar environments as well as genes. *Adoption studies* overcome some of this problem by comparing children who have been separated from their parents at an early age (or in which identical twins are separated at an early age) and reared in different environments. Psychologists look for similarities between children and their adoptive and natural parents. When children reared by adoptive parents are more similar to their natural parents in a particular trait, strong evidence exists for a genetic role in the development of that trait.

In later chapters we will see that psychologists have been particularly interested in the use of adoption studies to sort out the effects of nature and nurture in the development of personality traits, intelligence, and various psychological disorders. Such traits and disorders apparently represent the interaction of complex groupings of genes as well as environmental influences.

By the Numbers

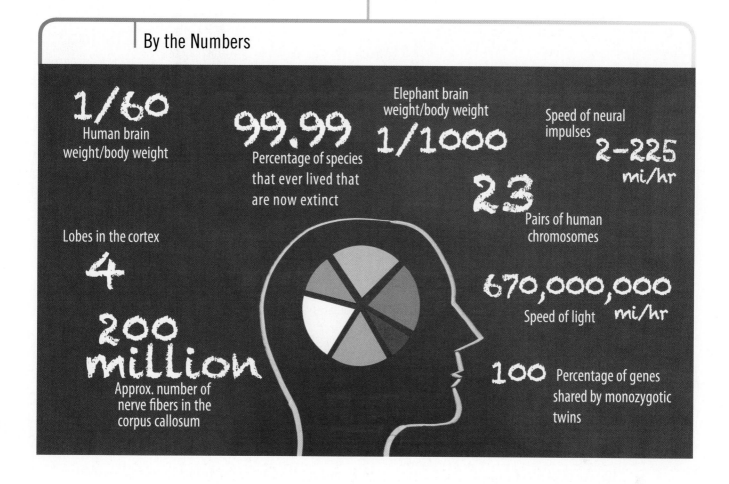

1/60
Human brain weight/body weight

99.99
Percentage of species that ever lived that are now extinct

Elephant brain weight/body weight
1/1000

Speed of neural impulses
2-225 mi/hr

23
Pairs of human chromosomes

Lobes in the cortex
4

200 million
Approx. number of nerve fibers in the corpus callosum

670,000,000 mi/hr
Speed of light

100
Percentage of genes shared by monozygotic twins

STUDY TOOLS ▶ 2

Ready to study? In the book, you can:

⊃ Review what you've read with Fill-Ins and Multiple Choice quizzes (below).

⊃ Rip out Chapter Review card (in the back).

Or you can go online to CourseMate at www.cengagebrain.com for these resources:

⊃ Complete Practices Quizzes to prepare for tests.

⊃ Review Key Terms Flash Cards (online or print).

⊃ Play games to master concepts.

FILL-INS

Answers can be found in the back of the book, starting on page 368.

1. Neurons transmit messages to other neurons by means of chemical substances called _____.

2. Neurons have a cell body, or soma; dendrites, which receive "messages"; and a(n) _____, which extends from the cell body and transmits messages.

3. The axons of many neurons have a fatty insulating sheath called _____.

4. It is theorized that people with the psychological disorder called _____ apparently overutilize the neurotransmitter dopamine.

5. The _____ nervous system regulates the glands and involuntary activities such as heartbeat and digestion.

6. The brain structure called the _____ is involved in balance and coordination.

7. The concept of a struggle for _____ lies at the core of the theory of evolution.

8. Stereotypical behavior patterns that have evolved within a species are called _____.

9. People with _____ syndrome have an extra chromosome on the 21st pair.

10. The behavior of _____ twins is of special interest to psychologists because their genetic endowment is the same.

1. An axon's length can range from a few millimeters to
   a. 1 inch.
   b. 12 inches.
   c. several feet.
   d. up to a mile.

2. A neuron can fire up to a limit of about _____ times per second.
   a. 40
   b. 400
   c. 4,000
   d. 40,000

3. If someone steps on your toes, resulting in pain and the movement of your foot, which of the following describes this process?
   a. Afferent neurons transmit the sensation of pain to the spinal cord and to the brain followed by efferent neurons sending the message to your foot to move.
   b. Efferent neurons transmit the sensation of pain to the spinal cord and to the brain followed by afferent neurons sending the message to your foot to move.
   c. Efferent neurons transmit the sensation of pain to the spinal cord and to the brain followed by efferent neurons sending the message to your foot to move.
   d. Afferent neurons transmit the sensation of pain to the spinal cord and to the brain followed by afferent neurons sending the message to your foot to move.

4. When Charlotte hears something embarrassing, she blushes. Being a student of psychology, she knows that this condition is controlled by the
   a. motor cortex.
   b. autonomic nervous system.
   c. somatosensory cortex.
   d. motor nervous system.

5. Wernicke's aphasia causes
   a. impairment of one's ability to comprehend speech and to think of the proper words to express his or her own thoughts.
   b. one to speak slowly and laboriously in simple sentences.
   c. serious impairment in reading.
   d. an inability to segment words in sounds while reading.

6. An editor gets so upset that she is late in working on a manuscript that she throws up her lunch. This probably occurred because of activity of the
   a. longest neurons in her body.
   b. corpus callosum.
   c. parasympathetic division of her autonomic nervous system.
   d. sympathetic division of her autonomic nervous system.

7. Ellen loses weight and becomes somewhat agitated. Her doctor is most likely to theorize that she is suffering from a deficiency of
   a. epinephrine.
   b. dopamine.
   c. cortisol.
   d. thyroxin.

8. _____ are the most basic building blocks of heredity.
   a. Genes
   b. Hormones
   c. Neurons
   d. Neurotransmitters

9. Dizygotic twins
   a. develop when two ova are fertilized.
   b. share 100% of their genes.
   c. are referred to as identical twins.
   d. demonstrate differences that are the result of nurture.

10. "Messages" travel within neurons by means of _____ and from neuron to neuron by means of _____.
    a. electricity, electricity
    b. neurotransmitters, neurotransmitters
    c. neurotransmitters, electricity
    d. electricity, neurotransmitters

Chung Sung-Jun/Getty Images

LEARNING OUTCOMES

3-1 Define and differentiate between sensation and perception

3-2 Identify the parts of the eye; explain the properties of light and the theories of color vision

3-3 Describe the organization of visual perceptions

3-4 Identify the parts of the ear; describe the sense of hearing

3-5 Describe the chemical senses

3-6 Explain the properties of the skin senses and theoretical explanations for pain

3-7 Describe the kinesthetic and vestibular senses

3-8 Explain why psychologists are skeptical about extrasensory perception

 STUDY TOOLS ▶ After you read the chapter, go to the Study Tools at the end of the chapter, page 82.

CHAPTER 3

Sensation and PERCEPTION

The tsunami that hit the coast of southern Asia in 2004 killed as many as a quarter of a million people. The people were caught off guard, but not the animals.

Along the western coast of Thailand, elephants giving rides to tourists began to trumpet agitatedly hours before the tsunami, just about when the earthquake that fractured the ocean floor sent the big waves rushing toward the shore. An hour before the waves slammed into the area, the elephants began wailing. Before the waves struck, they trooped off to higher ground. Elephants, tigers, leopards, deer, wild boar, water buffalo, monkeys, and reptiles in Sri Lanka's Yala National Park escaped the tsunami unharmed.

People have noticed that animals appear to detect earthquakes, hurricanes, volcanic eruptions, and tsunamis before the earth starts shaking. Some animals are apparently supersensitive to sound, others to temperature, touch, or vibration, which gives them advance warning.

Elephants are particularly sensitive to ground vibrations and probably sensed the earthquake that caused the tsunami in their feet and trunks. Some birds, dogs, tigers, and elephants can sense sound waves whose frequencies are too low for humans to hear. Dogs' superior sense of smell might detect subtle chemical changes in the air that warn them of calamities.

Different animals, then, have different sensory apparatuses, and many of them sense things that people cannot sense. Just how do humans sense the world around them?

Ben Cranke/The Image Bank/Getty Images

Elephants detected the tsunami before the earth started shaking.

TRUTH OR FICTION

WHAT DO YOU THINK? FOLKLORE, COMMON SENSE, OR NONSENSE? CIRCLE THE T FOR "TRUTH" OR THE F FOR "FICTION," AND CHECK THE ACCURACY OF YOUR ANSWERS AS YOU READ THROUGH THE CHAPTER.

T	F	PEOPLE HAVE ONLY FIVE SENSES.
T	F	IF WE COULD SEE WAVES OF LIGHT WITH SLIGHTLY LONGER WAVELENGTHS, WARM-BLOODED ANIMALS WOULD GLOW IN THE DARK.
T	F	PEOPLE SOMETIMES HEAR WHAT THEY WANT TO HEAR.
T	F	WHEN WE MIX BLUE LIGHT AND YELLOW LIGHT, WE OBTAIN GREEN LIGHT.
T	F	MANY PEOPLE EXPERIENCE PAIN "IN" LIMBS THAT HAVE BEEN AMPUTATED.
T	F	SOME PEOPLE CAN READ OTHER PEOPLE'S MINDS.

3-1 Sensation and Perception

Sensation is the stimulation of sensory receptors and the transmission of sensory information to the central nervous system (the spinal cord or brain). Sensory receptors are located in sensory organs such as the eyes and ears, the skin, and elsewhere in the body. Stimulation of the senses is an automatic process. It results from sources of energy, like

sensation
the stimulation of sensory receptors and the transmission of sensory information to the central nervous system

perception
the process by which sensations are organized into an inner representation of the world

absolute threshold
the minimal amount of energy that can produce a sensation

pitch
the highness or lowness of a sound, as determined by the frequency of the sound waves

light and sound, or from the presence of chemicals, as in smell and taste.

Perception is not mechanical. Perception is an *active* process in which sensations are organized and interpreted to form an inner representation of the world (Hafemeister et al., 2010; Rouder & Morey, 2009). Perception may begin with sensation, but it also reflects our experiences and expectations as it makes sense of sensory stimuli. A person standing 15 feet away and a 12-inch-tall doll right next to you may cast similar-sized images on the back of your eye, but whether you interpret the size to be a foot-long doll or a full-grown person 15 feet away is a matter of perception that depends on your experience with dolls, people, and distance.

In this chapter you will see that your perception of the world of changing sights, sounds, and other sources of sensory input depends largely on the so-called five senses: vision, hearing, smell, taste, and touch. But touch is just one of several "skin senses," which also include pressure, warmth, cold, and pain. There are also senses that alert you to your own body position without your having to watch every step you take. As we explore each of these senses, we will find that similar sensations may lead to different perceptions in different people—or to different situations in the same person.

Before we begin our voyage through the senses, let's consider a number of concepts that we use to talk about the relationships between sensations and perceptions: *absolute threshold, subliminal stimulation, difference threshold, signal-detection theory, feature detectors,* and *sensory adaptation.* In doing so, we will learn why we can dim the lights gradually to near darkness without anyone noticing. We will also learn why

"The great art of life is sensation, to feel that we exist, even in pain."

—LORD BYRON

we might become indifferent to the savory aromas of delightful dinners.

3-1a ABSOLUTE THRESHOLD

Nineteenth-century German psychologist Gustav Fechner used the term **absolute threshold** to refer to the weakest level of a stimulus that is necessary to produce a sensation. For example, the absolute threshold for light would be the minimum brightness (physical energy) required to activate the visual sensory system.

Psychophysicists look for the absolute thresholds of the senses by exposing individuals to progressively stronger stimuli until they find the minimum stimuli that the person can detect 50% of the time. These absolute thresholds are not all that absolute, however. Some people are more sensitive than others, and even the same person might have a slightly different response at different times (Rouder & Morey, 2009). Nevertheless, under ideal conditions, our ability to detect stimuli is quite sensitive. (See the box feature, this page.)

How different our lives would be if the absolute thresholds for the human senses differed! If your ears were sensitive to sounds that are lower in **pitch**, you might hear the collisions among molecules of air. If you

FICTION IT IS NOT TRUE THAT PEOPLE HAVE ONLY FIVE SENSES. PEOPLE ACTUALLY HAVE MANY MORE THAN FIVE SENSES.

✱ Absolute Thresholds of the Senses

The following are measures of the absolute thresholds for the human senses of vision, hearing, taste, smell, and touch:

- *Vision:* a candle flame viewed from about 30 miles on a clear, dark night.
- *Hearing:* a watch ticking from about 20 feet away in a quiet room.
- *Taste:* 1 teaspoon of sugar dissolved in 2 gallons of water.
- *Smell:* about one drop of perfume diffused throughout a small house (1 part in 500 million).
- *Touch:* the pressure of the wing of a fly falling on a cheek from a distance of about 0.4 inch

Thinkstock/Jupiterimages

could see light with slightly longer wavelengths, you would see infrared light waves and people and other animals would glow in the dark. Your world would be transformed because heat generates infrared light.

3-1b SUBLIMINAL STIMULATION

Do TV commercials contain words or sexual images that are flashed so briefly on the screen that we do not become conscious of them, but they still influence us? Behaviorist John B. Watson was a pioneer in associating appealing stimuli with products, as auto ads frequently associate attractive women with cars. But most ads make the associations openly.

Sensory stimulation that is below a person's absolute threshold for conscious perception is termed **subliminal stimulation**—and its perception is called *subliminal perception*. Visual stimuli can be flashed too briefly to enable us to process them. Auditory stimuli can be played at a volume too low to consciously hear or can be played backward.

In one experiment, Johan Karremans and his colleagues (2006) repeatedly flashed "Lipton Ice" for about 1/50th of a second—too briefly to be consciously recognized—on a computer screen that was viewed by a group of participants. They flashed a message without a brand name to a control group. Afterward, thirsty participants in the first group showed a preference for Lipton Ice.

3-1c DIFFERENCE THRESHOLD

How much of a difference in intensity between two lights is required before you will detect one as being brighter than the other? The minimum difference in *magnitude* of two stimuli required to tell them apart is their **difference threshold**. As with the absolute threshold, psychologists agree to the standard of a difference in strength that can be detected 50% of the time.

Psychophysicist Ernst Weber discovered through laboratory research that the threshold for perceiving differences in the intensity of light is about 2% (actually closer to 1/60th) of their intensity. This fraction, 1/60th, is known as **Weber's constant** for light. A related concept is the **just noticeable difference (jnd)**—the minimum difference in stimuli that a person can detect. For example, at least 50% of the time, most people can tell if a light becomes just 1/60th brighter or dimmer. Weber's constant for light holds whether we are comparing moderately bright lights or moderately dull lights. But it becomes inaccurate when we compare extremely bright or extremely dull lights.

Weber's constant for noticing differences in lifted weight is 1/53rd. (Round it off to 1/50th, or 2%.) That means if you are strong enough to heft a 100-pound barbell, you would not notice that it was heavier until about 2 pounds were added. Yet if you are a runner who carries 1-pound dumbbells, you would definitely notice if someone slipped you dumbbells even a pound heavier because the increase would be 100%.

What about sound? People are most sensitive to changes in the pitch (frequency) of sounds. The Weber constant for pitch is 1/333, meaning that on average, people can tell when a tone rises or falls in pitch by an extremely small one-third of 1%. (Even a small error in pitch makes singers sound sharp or flat.) Remember this when friends criticize your singing.

The sense of taste is much less sensitive. On average, people cannot detect differences in saltiness of less than 20%. That is why "low-salt" chips that have 15% less salt than your favorite chips do not taste so bad.

3-1d SIGNAL-DETECTION THEORY

From the discussion so far, it might seem that people are simply switched on by certain amounts of stimulation. This is not quite so. People are also influenced by psychological factors. **Signal-detection theory** considers these factors.

According to signal-detection theory, the relationship between a physical stimulus and a sensory response is not fully mechanical (Gigerenzer, 2010). People's ability to detect stimuli such as blips on a radar screen depends not only on the intensity of the blips but also on their training (learning), motivation (desire to perceive blips), and psychological states such as fatigue or alertness (Rouder & Morey, 2009).

The intensity of the signal is one factor that determines whether people will perceive sensory stimuli (signals) or a difference between signals. Another is the

subliminal stimulation
sensory stimulation below a person's absolute threshold for conscious perception

difference threshold
the minimal difference in intensity required between two sources of energy so that they will be perceived as being different

Weber's constant
the fraction of the intensity by which a source of physical energy must be increased or decreased so that a difference in intensity will be perceived

just noticeable difference (jnd)
the minimal amount by which a source of energy must be increased or decreased so that a difference in intensity will be perceived

signal-detection theory
the view that the perception of sensory stimuli involves the interaction of physical, biological, and psychological factors

feature detectors

neurons in the sensory cortex that fire in response to specific features of sensory information such as lines or edges of objects

sensory adaptation

the processes by which organisms become more sensitive to stimuli that are low in magnitude and less sensitive to stimuli that are constant or ongoing in magnitude

sensitization

the type of sensory adaptation in which we become more sensitive to stimuli that are low in magnitude. Also called *positive adaptation*

desensitization

the type of sensory adaptation in which we become less sensitive to constant stimuli. Also called *negative adaptation*

degree to which the signal can be distinguished from background noise. It is easier to hear a friend speaking in a quiet room than in a room in which people are singing and clinking glasses. The sharpness of a person's biological sensory system is still another factor. Is sensory capacity fully developed? Is it diminished by age?

TRUTH PEOPLE DO SOMETIMES HEAR WHAT THEY WANT TO HEAR BECAUSE THAT IS WHAT THEY PAY ATTENTION TO.

We also tend to detect stimuli we are searching for. People sometimes hear what they want to hear. The place in which you are reading this book may be abuzz with signals. If you are focusing your attention on this page, the other signals recede into the background. One psychological factor in signal detection is focusing on signals one considers important.

3-1e FEATURE DETECTORS IN THE BRAIN

Imagine you are standing by the curb of a busy street as a bus approaches. When neurons in your sensory organs—in this case, your eyes—are stimulated by the approach of the bus, they relay information to the sensory cortex in the brain. Nobel Prize winners David Hubel and Torsten Wiesel (1979) discovered that various neurons in the visual cortex of the brain fire in response to particular features of the visual input. Many cells in the brain detect (i.e., fire in response to) lines

I think I can hear a watch ticking on an earlier page.

© Michael Haegele/Corbis

presented at various angles—vertical, horizontal, and in between. Other cells fire in response to specific colors. Because they respond to different aspects or features of a scene, these brain cells are termed **feature detectors**. In the example of the bus, visual feature detectors respond to the bus's edges, depth, contours, textures, shadows, speed, and kinds of motion (up, down, forward, and back). There are also feature detectors for other senses. Auditory feature detectors, for example, respond to the pitch, loudness, and other aspects of the sounds of the bus.

3-1f SENSORY ADAPTATION

Our sensory systems are admirably suited to a changing environment. **Sensory adaptation** refers to the processes by which we become more sensitive to stimuli of low magnitude and less sensitive to stimuli that remain the same, such as the background noises outside the window (Lawless & Heymann, 2010).

Consider how the visual sense adapts to lower intensities of light. When we first walk into a darkened movie theater, we see little but the images on the screen. As we search for our seats, however, we become increasingly sensitive to the faces around us and to the features of the theater. The process of becoming more sensitive to stimulation is referred to as **sensitization**, or *positive adaptation*.

But we become less sensitive to constant stimulation. When we live in a city, for example, we become desensitized to sounds of traffic except, perhaps, for the occasional backfire or siren. The process of becoming less sensitive to stimulation is referred to as **desensitization**, or *negative adaptation*.

Our sensitivities to stimulation provide our brains with information that we use to understand and influence the world outside. Therefore, it is not surprising that psychologists study the ways in which we sense and perceive this information—through vision, hearing, the chemical senses, and still other senses, as we see throughout the remainder of the chapter.

3-2 Vision

Our eyes are literally our "windows on the world." Because vision is our dominant sense, blindness is considered by many to be the most debilitating sensory loss. To understand vision, let's first "look" at light.

3-2a LIGHT

Light is fascinating stuff. It radiates. It illuminates. It dazzles. In almost all cultures, light is a symbol of goodness and knowledge. We speak of genius as "brilliance." People who aren't in the know are said to be "in the dark."

It is **visible light** that triggers visual sensations. Yet visible light is just one small part of a spectrum of electromagnetic energy that surrounds us (see Figure 3.1). All forms of electromagnetic energy move in waves, and different kinds of electromagnetic energy have signature wavelengths:

- *Cosmic rays:* The wavelengths of these rays from outer space are only a few *trillionths* of an inch long.

- *Radio waves:* Some radio signals extend for miles.

- *Visible light:* Roses are red, and violets are blue. Why? Different colors have different wavelengths, with violet the shortest at about 400 *billionths* of a meter in length and red the longest at 700 billionths of a meter.

"IT IS A TERRIBLE THING TO SEE AND HAVE NO VISION."
–HELEN KELLER

Sir Isaac Newton, the British scientist, discovered that sunlight could be broken down into different colors by means of a triangular solid of glass called a *prism* (see Figure 3.1). You can remember the colors of the spectrum, from longest to shortest wavelengths, by using the mnemonic device *Roy G. Biv* (red, orange, yellow, green, blue, indigo, violet). The wavelength of visible light determines its color, or **hue**. The wavelength for red is longer than the wavelength for orange, and so on through the spectrum.

3-2b THE EYE

Consider the major parts of the eye, as shown in Figure 3.2. As with a camera, light enters through a narrow opening and is projected onto a sensitive surface. Light

visible light
the part of the electromagnetic spectrum that stimulates the eye and produces visual sensations

hue
the color of light, as determined by its wavelength

FIGURE 3.1 | The Visible Spectrum

By passing a source of white light, such as sunlight, through a prism, we break it down into the colors of the visible spectrum. The visible spectrum is just a narrow segment of the electromagnetic spectrum. The electromagnetic spectrum also includes radio waves, microwaves, X-rays, cosmic rays, and many others. Different forms of electromagnetic energy have wavelengths that vary from a few trillionths of a meter to thousands of miles. Visible light varies in wavelength from about 400 to 700 *billionths* of a meter. (One meter = 39.37 inches.)

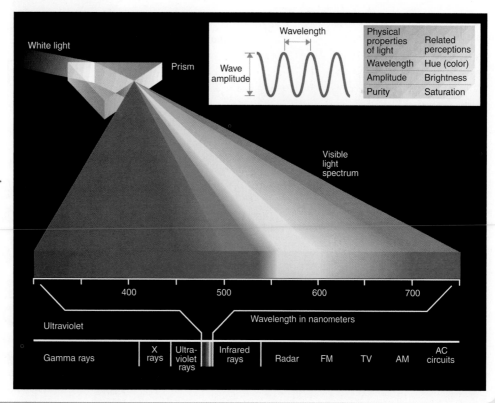

cornea

transparent tissue forming the outer surface of the eyeball

iris

a muscular membrane whose dilation regulates the amount of light that enters the eye

pupil

the black-looking opening in the center of the iris, through which light enters the eye

lens

a transparent body behind the iris that focuses an image on the retina

first passes through the transparent **cornea**, which covers the front of the eye's surface. (The "white" of the eye, or *sclera*, is composed of hard protective tissue.) The amount of light that passes through the cornea is determined by the size of the opening of the muscle called the **iris**, which is the colored part of the eye. The opening in the iris is the **pupil**. The size of the pupil adjusts automatically to the amount of light present. Therefore, you do not have to purposely open your

eyes wider to see better in low lighting—the more intense the light, the smaller the opening. Pupil size is also sensitive to your emotions: We can be truly "wide-eyed with fear."

Once light passes through the iris, it encounters the **lens**. The lens adjusts or accommodates to the image by changing its thickness. Changes in thickness permit a clear image of the object to be projected onto the retina. These changes focus the light according to the distance of the object from the viewer. If you hold a finger at arm's length and slowly bring it toward your nose, you will feel tension in the eye as the thickness of the lens accommodates to keep the retinal image in focus. When people squint to bring an object into focus, they are adjusting the thickness of the lens.

FIGURE 3.2 | The Human Eye

In both the eye and a camera, light enters through a narrow opening and is projected onto a sensitive surface. In the eye, the photosensitive surface is called the retina, and information concerning the changing images on the retina is transmitted to the brain. The retina contains photoreceptors called rods and cones. Rods and cones transmit sensory input back through the bipolar neurons to the ganglion neurons. The axons of the ganglion neurons form the optic nerve, which transmits sensory stimulation through the brain to the visual cortex of the occipital lobe.

© Cengage Learning 2013

The **retina** consists of cells called **photoreceptors** that are sensitive to light (photosensitive). There are two types of photoreceptors: *rods* and *cones*. The retina (see Figure 3.2) contains several layers of cells: the rods and cones, **bipolar cells**, and **ganglion cells**. All of these cells are neurons. The rods and cones respond to light with chemical changes that create neural impulses that are picked up by the bipolar cells. These then activate the ganglion cells. The axons of the million or so ganglion cells in our retina converge to form the **optic nerve**. The optic nerve conducts sensory input to the brain, where it is relayed to the visual area of the occipital lobe.

As if this were not enough, the eye has additional neurons to enhance this process. Amacrine cells and horizontal cells make sideways connections at a level near the rods and cones and at another level near the ganglion cells. As a result, single bipolar cells can pick up signals from many rods and cones, and, in turn, a single ganglion cell is able to funnel information from multiple bipolar cells. In fact, rods and cones outnumber ganglion cells by more than 100 to 1.

Rods and Cones

Rods and **cones** are the photoreceptors in the retina (see Figure 3.2). About 125 million rods and 6.4 million cones are distributed across the retina. The cones are most densely packed in a small spot at the center of the retina called the **fovea** (see Figure 3.2). Visual acuity (sharpness and detail) is greatest at this spot. The fovea is composed almost exclusively of cones. Rods are most dense just outside the fovea and thin out toward the periphery of the retina.

Rods allow us to see in black and white. Cones provide color vision. Rods are more sensitive to dim light than cones are. Therefore, as light grows dim during the evening hours, objects appear to lose their color before their outlines fade from view.

In contrast to the visual acuity of the fovea is the **blind spot**, which is insensitive to visual stimulation. It is the part of the retina where the axons of the ganglion cells converge to form the optic nerve (see Figure 3.2).

Figure 3.3 will help you "view" your blind spot.

Visual acuity (sharpness of vision) is connected with the shape of the eye. People who have to be unusually close to an object to discriminate its details are *nearsighted*. People who see distant objects unusually clearly but have difficulty focusing on nearby objects are *farsighted*. Nearsightedness can result when the eyeball is elongated such that the images of distant objects are focused in front of the retina. When the eyeball is too short, the images of nearby objects are focused behind the retina, causing farsightedness. Eyeglasses or contact lenses help nearsighted people focus distant objects on their retinas. Laser surgery can correct vision by changing the shape of the cornea. Farsighted people usually see well enough without eyeglasses until they reach their middle years, when they may need glasses for reading.

Beginning in their late 30s to the mid-40s, people's lenses start to grow brittle, making it more difficult to accommodate to, or

retina
the area of the inner surface of the eye that contains rods and cones

photoreceptors
cells that respond to light

bipolar cells
neurons that conduct neural impulses from rods and cones to ganglion cells

ganglion cells
neurons whose axons form the optic nerve

optic nerve
the nerve that transmits sensory information from the eye to the brain

rods
rod-shaped photoreceptors that are sensitive only to the intensity of light

cones
cone-shaped photoreceptors that transmit sensations of color

fovea
an area near the center of the retina that is dense with cones and where vision is consequently most acute

blind spot
the area of the retina where axons from ganglion cells meet to form the optic nerve

visual acuity
sharpness of vision

FIGURE 3.3 | **The Blind Spot**

To try a "disappearing act," close your left eye, hold the book close to your face, and look at the boy with your right eye. Slowly move the book away until the pie disappears. The pie disappears because it is being projected onto the blind spot of your retina, the point at which the axons of ganglion neurons collect to form the optic nerve. Note that when the pie disappears, your brain "fills in" the missing checkerboard pattern, which is one reason that you're not usually aware that you have blind spots.

© Cengage Learning 2012

presbyopia
a condition characterized by brittleness of the lens

dark adaptation
the process of adjusting to conditions of lower lighting by increasing the sensitivity of rods and cones

complementary
descriptive of colors of the spectrum that when combined produce white or nearly white light

focus on, objects. This condition is called **presbyopia**, from the Greek words for "old man" and "eyes." Presbyopia makes it difficult to perceive nearby visual stimuli. People who had normal visual acuity in their youth often require corrective lenses to read in middle adulthood.

Light Adaptation

When we walk out onto a dark street, we may at first not be able to see people, trees, and cars clearly. But as time goes on, we are better able to discriminate the features of people and objects. The process of adjusting to lower lighting is called **dark adaptation**.

The amount of light needed for detection is a function of the amount of time spent in the dark. The cones and rods adapt at different rates. The cones, which permit perception of color, reach their maximum adaptation to darkness in about 10 minutes. The rods, which allow perception of light and dark only, are more sensitive to dim light and continue to adapt for 45 minutes or so.

Adaptation to brighter lighting conditions takes place more rapidly. For instance, when you emerge from the theater into the brilliance of the afternoon, you may at first be painfully surprised by the featureless blaze around you. But within a minute or so of entering the street, the brightness of the scene dims and objects regain their edges.

3-2c COLOR VISION

For most of us, the world is a place of brilliant colors. Color is an emotional and aesthetic part of our everyday lives. In this section, we explore some of the dimensions of color and then examine theories about how we manage to convert different wavelengths of light into perceptions of color. The perceptual dimensions of color include *hue*, *value*, and *saturation*.

The wavelength of light determines its color, or *hue*. The *value* of a color is its degree of brightness or darkness. The *saturation* refers to how intense a color appears to us. A fire-engine red is more saturated than a pale pinkish-red.

Colors also have psychological associations within various cultural settings. For example, in the United States a bride may be dressed in white

FICTION ACTUALLY, WHEN WE MIX BLUE *LIGHT* AND YELLOW *LIGHT*, WE GET GRAY, NOT GREEN LIGHT. WE GET GREEN BY MIXING BLUE AND YELLOW *PIGMENTS*, NOT LIGHTS.

as a sign of purity. In traditional India, the guests would be shocked, because white is the color for funerals. Here we mourn in black.

Warm and Cool Colors

If we bend the colors of the spectrum into a circle, we create a color wheel, as shown in Figure 3.4. Psychologically, the colors on the green–blue side of the color wheel are considered to be cool in temperature. Those colors on the yellow–orange–red side are considered to be warm.

Complementary Colors

The colors across from one another on the color wheel are labeled **complementary**. Red–green and blue–yellow are the major complementary pairs. If we mix complementary colors together, they dissolve into gray.

"But wait!" you say. "Blue and yellow cannot be complementary because by mixing pigments of blue and yellow we create green, not gray." True enough, but we have been talking about mixing *lights*, not *pigments*. Light is the source of all color. Pigments reflect and absorb different wavelengths of light selectively. The mixture of lights is an *additive* process. The mixture of pigments is *subtractive*. Figure 3.5 shows mixtures of lights and pigments of various colors.

Pigments gain their colors by absorbing light from certain segments of the spectrum and reflecting the

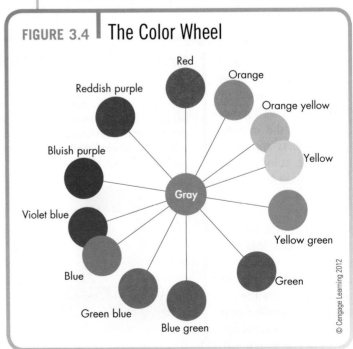

FIGURE 3.4 **The Color Wheel**

Red
Orange
Reddish purple
Orange yellow
Yellow
Bluish purple
Gray
Violet blue
Yellow green
Blue
Green
Green blue
Blue green

© Cengage Learning 2012

FIGURE 3.5

The mixture of lights is an *additive* process. The mixture of pigments is *subtractive*.

Fritz Goro/Time Life Pictures/Getty Images

rest. For example, we see most plant life as green because the pigment in chlorophyll absorbs most of the red, blue, and violet wavelengths of light. The remaining green is reflected. A red pigment absorbs most of the spectrum but reflects red. White pigments reflect all colors equally. Black pigments reflect very little light.

Afterimages

Try this experiment: Look at the strangely colored American flag on the next page for at least half a minute. Try not to blink as you are doing so. Then look at a sheet of white or light-gray paper. What has happened to the flag? If your color vision is working properly, and if you looked at the miscolored flag long enough, you should see a flag composed of the familiar red, white, and blue. The flag you perceive on the white sheet of paper is an **afterimage** of the first. (If you didn't look at the green, black, and

yellow flag long enough the first time, try it again.) In afterimages, persistent sensations of color are followed by perception of the complementary color when the first color is removed. The same holds true for black and white. Staring at one will create an afterimage of the other. The phenomenon of afterimages has contributed to one of the theories of color vision, as we will see.

3-2d THEORIES OF COLOR VISION

Adults with normal color vision can discriminate thousands of colors across the visible spectrum. Different colors have different wavelengths. Although we can vary the physical wavelengths of light in a continuous manner from shorter to longer, many changes in color are discontinuous. Our perception of a color shifts suddenly from blue to green, even though the change in wavelength may be smaller than that between two blues.

Our perception of color depends on the physical properties of an object and on the eye's transmission of different messages to the brain when lights with different wavelengths stimulate the cones in the retina. There are two main theories of color vision: the *trichromatic theory* and the *opponent-process theory* (Gegenfurtner & Kiper, 2003).

Trichromatic theory is based on an experiment conducted by the British scientist Thomas Young in the early 1800s. As in Figure 3.5, Young projected red, green, and blue-violet lights onto a screen so that they partly overlapped. He found that he could create any color in the visible spectrum by varying the intensities of the three lights. When all three lights fell on the same spot, they created white light, or the appearance of no color at all.

The German physiologist Hermann von Helmholtz saw in Young's discovery an explanation of color vision. Helmholtz suggested that the retina in the eye must have three different types of color photoreceptors or cones. Some cones must be sensitive to red light, some to green, and some to blue. We see other colors when various color receptors are stimulated simultaneously. For example, we perceive yellow when the receptors for red and green are firing.

In 1870, another German physiologist, Ewald Hering, proposed the **opponent-process theory** of color vision: There are three types of color receptors, but they are not sensitive only to red, green, and blue, as Helmholtz had

afterimage
the lingering visual impression made by a stimulus that has been removed

trichromatic theory
the theory that color vision is made possible by three types of cones, some of which respond to red light, some to green, and some to blue

opponent-process theory
the theory that color vision is made possible by three types of cones, some of which respond to red or green light, some to blue or yellow, and some to the intensity of light

FIGURE 3.6

Place a sheet of white paper beneath the book and stare at the black dot in the center of the flag for at least 30 seconds. Then remove the book. The afterimage on the paper beneath will look familiar.

© Cengage Learning 2012

claimed. Hering suggested instead that afterimages (such as that of the American flag shown in Figure 3.6) are made possible by three types of color receptors: red–green, blue–yellow, and a type that perceives differences in brightness. According to Hering, a red–green cone cannot transmit messages for red and green at the same time. Therefore, staring at the green, black, and yellow flag for 30 seconds will disturb the balance of neural activity. The afterimage of red, white, and blue would represent the eye's attempt to reestablish a balance.

Research suggests that each theory of color vision is partially correct. For example, research shows that some cones are sensitive to blue, some to green, and some to red (Pang et al., 2010). However, cones appear to be connected by bipolar and ganglion neurons such that the messages produced by the cones are transmitted to the brain in an opponent-process fashion (Yin et al., 2009).

A neural rebound effect apparently helps explain the occurrence of afterimages. That is, a green-sensitive ganglion that had been excited by green light for half a minute or so might switch briefly to inhibitory activity when the light is shut off. The effect would be to perceive red even though no red light is present (Hornstein et al., 2004).

3-2e COLOR BLINDNESS

If you can discriminate among the colors of the visible spectrum, you have normal color vision and are labeled a **trichromat**. This means that you are sensitive to red–green, blue–yellow, and light–dark. People who are totally color-blind, called **monochromats**, are sensitive only to lightness and darkness. Total color blindness is rare. Fully color-blind individuals see the world as trichromats would in a black-and-white movie.

Partial color blindness is a sex-linked trait that affects mostly males. Partially color-blind people are called **dichromats**. They can discriminate only between two colors—red and green or blue and yellow—and the colors that are derived from mixing these colors (Loop et al., 2003). Figure 3.7 shows the types of tests that are used to diagnose color blindness.

A dichromat might put on one red sock and one green sock, but would not mix red and blue socks. Monochromats might put on socks of any color. They would not notice a difference as long as the socks' colors did not differ in intensity—that is, brightness.

FIGURE 3.7 | Plates from a Test for Color Blindness

Can you see the numbers in these plates from a test for color blindness? A person with red–green color blindness would not be able to see the 6, and a person with blue-yellow color blindness would probably not discern the 12. (Caution: These reproductions cannot be used for actual testing of color blindness.)

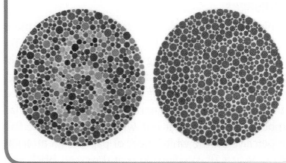

© Cengage Learning 2012

FIGURE 3.8 | Closure

Meaningless splotches of ink, or a horse and rider? This figure illustrates the Gestalt principle of closure.

© Cengage Learning 2012

(3-3) Visual Perception

What do you see in Figure 3.8—meaningless splotches of ink or a rider on horseback? If you perceive a horse and rider, it is not just because of the visual sensations provided by the drawing. Each of the blobs is meaningless in and of itself, and the pattern is vague. Despite the lack of clarity, however, you may still perceive a horse and rider.

Visual perception is the process by which we organize or make sense of the sensory impressions caused by the light that strikes our eyes. Visual perception involves our knowledge, expectations, and motivations. Whereas sensation may be thought of as a mechanical process (e.g., light stimulating the rods and cones of our retina), perception is an active process through which we interpret the world around us.

You organize bits of visual information into meaningful wholes by means of your general knowledge and your desire to fit incoming bits and pieces of information into familiar patterns. In the case of

the horse and rider, your integration of disconnected pieces of information into a meaningful whole also reflects the principle of **closure**—that is, the tendency to perceive a complete or whole figure even when there are gaps in the sensory input.

closure
the tendency to perceive a broken figure as being complete or whole

perceptual organization
the tendency to integrate perceptual elements into meaningful patterns

3-3a PERCEPTUAL ORGANIZATION

Early in the 20th century, Gestalt psychologists noted certain consistencies in the way we integrate bits and pieces of sensory stimulation into meaningful wholes. They attempted to identify the rules that govern these processes. As a group, these rules are referred to as the laws of **perceptual organization**.

Figure–Ground Perception

If you look out your window, you may see people, buildings, cars, and streets, or perhaps grass, trees, birds, and clouds. These objects tend to be perceived as figures against backgrounds. For instance, individual cars seen against the background of the street are easier to pick out than cars piled on top of one another in a junkyard.

When figure–ground relationships are *ambiguous*, or capable of being interpreted in various ways, our perceptions tend to be unstable and shift back and forth (Bull et al., 2003).

Figure 3.9 shows a Rubin vase, one of psychologists' favorite illustrations of figure–ground relationships. The figure–ground relationship in part A of the figure is ambiguous. There are no cues that suggest which area must be the figure. For this reason, our perception may shift from seeing the vase to seeing two profiles. There

FIGURE 3.9 | The Rubin Vase

A.   B.   C.

© Cengage Learning 2012

proximity

nearness; the perceptual tendency to group together objects that are near one another

similarity

the perceptual tendency to group together objects that are similar in appearance

continuity

the tendency to perceive a series of points or lines as having unity

common fate

the tendency to perceive elements that move together as belonging together

top-down processing

the use of contextual information or knowledge of a pattern in order to organize parts of the pattern

bottom-up processing

the organization of the parts of a pattern to recognize, or form an image of, the pattern they compose

is no such problem in part B. Because it seems that a blue vase has been brought forward against a colored ground, we are more likely to perceive the vase than the profiles. In part C, we are more likely to perceive the profiles than the vase, because the profiles are complete and the vase is broken against the background. Of course, if we wish to, we can still perceive the vase in part C, because experience has shown us where it is.

Other Gestalt Rules for Organization

Gestalt psychologists have noted that our perceptions are also guided by rules or laws of *proximity*, *similarity*, *continuity*, and *common fate*.

Let's try a mini-experiment. Without reading further, describe part A of Figure 3.10. Did you say it consists of six lines or of three groups of two parallel lines? If you said three sets of lines, you were influenced by the **proximity**, or nearness, of some of the lines. There is no other reason for perceiving them in pairs or subgroups: All lines are parallel and equal in length.

Now describe part B of Figure 3.10. Did you perceive the figure as a six-by-six grid, or as three columns of X's and three columns of O's? According to the law of **similarity**, we perceive similar objects as belonging together. For this reason, you may have been more likely

to describe part B in terms of columns than in terms of rows or a grid.

What of part C? Is it a circle with two lines stemming from it, or is it a (broken) line that goes through a circle? If you saw it as a single (broken) line, you were probably organizing your perceptions according to the rule of **continuity**. That is, we perceive a series of points or a broken line as having unity.

According to the law of **common fate**, elements seen moving together are perceived as belonging together. A group of people running in the same direction appears unified in purpose. Part D of Figure 3.10 provides another example of the law of closure. The arcs tend to be perceived as a circle (or a circle with gaps) rather than as just a series of arcs.

Top-Down Versus Bottom-Up Processing

Imagine that you are trying to put together a thousand-piece jigsaw puzzle. Now imagine that you are trying to accomplish it after someone has walked off with the box showing the picture formed by the completed puzzle.

If you use the picture on the box, you're engaging in **top-down processing**—using the completed image to search for the proper pieces. Similarly, we may form more lasting relationships when we search with an idea of the qualities we will find compatible in another person. Or we may make better investments when we have a retirement financial goal and date in mind. With **bottom-up processing**, we begin with bits and pieces of information and try to assemble them in a pattern—in jigsaw puzzles and, perhaps, by being thrown into a social or vocational situation. In bottom-up processing, we do not have a clear idea of where we are going, and perhaps we try to make the best of things.

FIGURE 3.10 | Some Gestalt Laws of Perceptual Organization

These drawings illustrate the Gestalt laws of proximity, similarity, continuity, and closure.

A. Proximity

B. Similarity

C. Continuity

D. Closure

© Cengage Learning 2012

In a motion picture, viewing a series of stationary images at the rate of about 16 to 22 frames per second provides an illusion of movement termed stroboscopic motion. The actual movement that is occurring is the rapid switching of stationary images.

illusions
sensations that give rise to misperceptions

stroboscopic motion
a visual illusion in which the perception of motion is generated by a series of stationary images that are presented in rapid succession

monocular cues
stimuli suggestive of depth that can be perceived with only one eye

perspective
a monocular cue for depth based on the convergence (coming together) of parallel lines as they recede into the distance

3-3b PERCEPTION OF MOTION

Imagine yourself on a train that has begun to pull out of the station while the train on the next track stays still. If your own train does not lurch as it accelerates, it might seem that the other train is moving. Or you might not be sure whether your train is moving forward or the other train is moving back.

The visual perception of movement is based on change of position relative to other objects. To early scientists, whose only tool for visual observation was the naked eye, it seemed logical that the sun circled the earth. You have to be able to imagine the movement of the earth around the sun as seen from a theoretical point in outer space; you cannot observe it directly.

How, then, can you be certain which train is moving? One way is to look for objects that you know are still, such as platform columns, houses, signs, or trees. If your position does not change in relation to them, your train is not moving. You might also try to sense the motion of the train in your body. You probably know from experience how to do these things quite well.

We have been considering the perception of real movement. Psychologists have also studied several types of apparent movement, or **illusions** of movement. One of these illusions is stroboscopic motion.

Stroboscopic Motion

So-called motion pictures do not really consist of images that move. Rather, the audience is shown 16 to 22 pictures, or *frames*, per second. Each frame differs slightly from the preceding one. Showing the frames in rapid succession provides the illusion of movement. This illusion of motion is termed **stroboscopic motion**.

At the rate of at least 16 frames per second, the "motion" in a film seems smooth and natural. With fewer than 16 or so frames per second, the movement looks jumpy and unnatural. That is why slow motion is usu-

ally achieved by filming 100 or more frames per second. When they are played back at about 22 frames per second, the movement seems slowed down, but still smooth and natural.

3-3c DEPTH PERCEPTION

Monocular and *binocular cues* help us perceive the depth of objects—that is, their distance from us.

Monocular Cues

Artists use **monocular cues** called pictorial cues to create an illusion of depth. These cues can be perceived by one eye (*mono* means "one"). They include perspective, relative size, clearness, overlapping, shadows, and texture gradient, and they cause some objects to seem more distant than others even though they are all drawn or painted on a flat surface.

Distant objects stimulate smaller areas on the retina than nearby ones, even though they may be the same size. The distances between far-off objects also appear to be smaller than equivalent distances between nearby objects. For this reason, the phenomenon known as **perspective** occurs. That is, we tend to perceive parallel lines as coming closer together, or converging, as they recede from us. As we will see when we discuss *size constancy*, however, experience teaches us that distant objects that look small are larger when they are close. In this way, their relative size also becomes a cue to their distance.

Artists normally use *relative size*—the fact that distant objects look smaller than nearby objects of the same size—to suggest depth in their works.

The *clearness* of an object suggests its distance. Experience teaches us that we sense more details of nearby objects. For this reason, artists can suggest that objects are closer to the viewer by depicting them in greater detail.

texture gradient
a monocular cue for depth based on the perception that closer objects appear to have rougher (more detailed) surfaces

motion parallax
a monocular cue for depth based on the perception that nearby objects appear to move more rapidly in relation to our own motion

binocular cues
stimuli suggestive of depth that involve simultaneous perception by both eyes

retinal disparity
a binocular cue for depth based on the difference in the image cast by an object on the retinas of the eyes as the object moves closer or farther away

We also learn that nearby objects can block our view of more distant objects. *Overlapping* is the placing of one object in front of another. Experience teaches us that partly covered objects are farther away than the objects that obscure them (see Figure 3.11).

Additional information about depth is provided by *shadowing* and is based on the fact that opaque objects block light and produce shadows. Shadows and highlights give us information about an object's three-dimensional shape and its relationship to the source of light. For example, in the right part of Figure 3.11, the left circle is perceived as a two-dimensional circle, but the right circle tends to be perceived as a three-dimensional sphere because of the highlight on its surface and the shadow underneath. In the "sphere," the highlighted central area is perceived as closest to us, with the surface receding to the edges.

Another monocular cue is **texture gradient**. (A gradient is a progressive change.) Closer objects are perceived as having rougher textures.

Motion cues are another kind of monocular cue. If you have ever driven in the country, you have probably noticed that distant objects such as mountains and stars appear to move along with you. Objects at an in-termediate distance seem to be stationary, but nearby objects such as roadside markers, rocks, and trees seem to go by quite rapidly. The tendency of objects to seem to move backward or forward as a function of their distance is known as **motion parallax**. We learn to perceive objects that appear to move with us as being at greater distances.

We noted that nearby objects cause the lens of the eye to accommodate or bend more in order to bring them into focus. The sensations of tension in the eye muscles also provide a monocular cue to depth, especially when we are within about four feet of the objects.

Binocular Cues

Binocular cues, or cues that involve both eyes, also help us perceive depth. Two binocular cues are *retinal disparity* and *convergence*.

Try an experiment. Hold your right index finger at arm's length. Now hold your left index finger about a foot closer, but in a direct line. If you keep your eyes relaxed as you do so, you will see first one finger and then the other. An image of each finger will be projected onto the retina of each eye, and each image will be slightly different because the finger will be seen from different angles. The difference between the projected images is referred to as **retinal disparity** and serves as a binocular cue for depth perception. Note that in the case of the closer finger, the "two fingers" appear to be farther apart. Closer objects have greater retinal disparity.

If we try to maintain a single image of the closer finger, our eyes must turn inward, or converge on it, mak-

---

FIGURE 3.11 | Overlapping and Shadowing as Cues for Depth

Overlapping as a Cue for Depth

The four circles are all the same size. Which circles seem closer? The complete circles or the circles with chunks bitten out of them?

Shadowing as a Cue for Depth

Shadowing makes the circle on the right look three-dimensional.

© Cengage Learning 2012

Although this woman's hand looks as though it is larger than her head, we recognize that this is an illusion created by the fact that her hand is closer to us than her head.

© Enamul Hoque/Getty Images

convergence
a binocular cue for depth based on the inward movement of the eyes as they attempt to focus on an object that is drawing nearer

size constancy
the tendency to perceive an object as being the same size even as the size of its retinal image changes according to the object's distance

color constancy
the tendency to perceive an object as being the same color even though lighting conditions change its appearance

brightness constancy
the tendency to perceive an object as being just as bright even though lighting conditions change its intensity

ing us cross-eyed. **Convergence** causes feelings of tension in the eye muscles and provides another binocular cue for depth. (After convergence occurs, try looking at the finger first with one eye closed, then the other. You will readily see how different the images are in each eye.) The binocular cues of retinal disparity and convergence are strongest when objects are close.

3-3d PERCEPTUAL CONSTANCIES

Think how confusing it would be if you believed that a door was a trapezoid and not a rectangle because it is ajar. Fortunately, perceptual constancies enable us to recognize objects even when their apparent shape or size differs.

Size Constancy

There are a number of perceptual constancies, including that of **size constancy**. The image of a dog seen from 20 feet away occupies about the same amount of space on your retina as an inch-long insect crawling on your hand. Yet you do not perceive the dog to be as small as the insect. Through your visual experiences you have acquired size constancy—that is, the tendency to *perceive* an object as the same size even though the size of its image on your retina varies as a function of its distance. Experience teaches us about perspective—that the same object seen at a distance appears to be smaller than when it is nearby.

Color Constancy

Color constancy is the tendency to perceive objects as retaining their color even though lighting conditions may alter their appearance. Your bright-yellow car may edge toward gray as the hours wend their way through twilight. But when you finally locate the car in the parking lot, you may still think of it as yellow. You expect to find a yellow car and still judge it to be "more yellow" than the (twilight-faded) red and green cars on either side of it.

Brightness Constancy

Brightness constancy is similar to color constancy. Consider Figure 3.12. The orange squares within the blue squares are equally bright, yet the one within the dark-blue square is perceived as brighter. Why? Again, consider the role of experience. If it were nighttime, we would expect orange to fade to gray. The fact that the orange within the dark square stimulates the eye with equal intensity suggests that it must be much brighter than the orange within the lighter square.

FIGURE 3.12 | Brightness Constancy

The orange squares within the blue squares are the same hue, yet the orange within the dark blue square is perceived as brighter. Why?

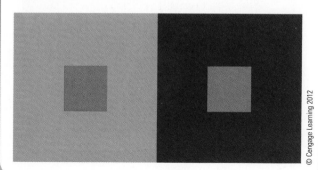

© Cengage Learning 2012

Shape Constancy

Shape constancy is the tendency to perceive objects as maintaining their shape, even if we look at them from different angles so that the shape of their image on the retina changes dramatically. You perceive the top of a coffee cup or a glass to be a circle even though it is a circle only when seen from above. When seen from an angle, it is an ellipse. When the cup or glass is seen on edge, its retinal image is the same as that of a straight line. So why do you still describe the rim of the cup or glass as a circle? Perhaps for two reasons: First, experience has taught you that the cup will look circular when seen from above. Second, you may have labeled the cup as circular or round.

Let's return to the door that "changes shape" when it is ajar. The door is a rectangle only when viewed straight on. When we move to the side or open it, the left or right edge comes closer and appears to be larger, changing the retinal image to a trapezoid. Yet we continue to think of doors as rectangles. In the photo on the previous page, we see a woman with a very large hand, but because of experience, we recognize that the hand only appears to be out of proportion to the rest of her because it is pushed toward us.

3-3e VISUAL ILLUSIONS

The principles of perceptual organization make it possible for our eyes to "play tricks" on us. That is, the perceptual constancies trick the eye through *visual illusions*.

The *Hering–Helmholtz* and *Müller–Lyer illusions* (see Figure 3.13) are named after the people who devised them. In the Hering–Helmholtz illusion (part A), the horizontal lines are straight and parallel. However, the radiating lines cause them to appear to be bent outward near the center. The two lines in the Müller–Lyer illusion (part B) are the same length, but the line on the right, with its reversed arrowheads, looks longer.

Let's try to explain these illusions. Because of our experience and lifelong use of perceptual cues, we tend to perceive the Hering–Helmholtz drawing as three-dimensional. Because of our tendency to perceive bits of sensory information as figures against grounds, we perceive the blue area in the center as a circle in front of a series of radiating lines, all of which lie in front of a blue ground. Next, because of our experience with perspective, we perceive the radiating lines as parallel. We perceive the two horizontal lines as intersecting the "receding" lines, and we know that they would have to appear bent out at the center if they were to be equidistant at all points from the center of the circle.

Experience probably compels us to perceive the vertical lines in the Müller–Lyer illusion as the corners of a building (see Figure 3.13, part B). We interpret the length of the lines based on our experience with corners of buildings.

3-4 Hearing

Consider the advertising slogan for the classic science fiction film *Alien*: "In space, no one can hear you scream." It's true. Space is an almost perfect vacuum. Hearing requires a medium through which sound can travel, such as air or water.

FIGURE 3.13 | The Hering–Helmholtz and Müller–Lyer Illusions

In the Hering–Helmholtz illusion, are the horizontal lines straight or curved? In the Müller–Lyer illusion, are the vertical lines equal in length?

A. The Hering–Helmholtz Illusion

B. The Müller–Lyer Illusion

FIGURE 3.14 | Sound Waves of Various Frequencies and Amplitudes

Which sounds have the highest pitch? Which are loudest?

Low frequency

Higher frequency

Low amplitude

Higher amplitude

© Cengage Learning 2012

The pitch of women's voices is usually higher than that of men's voices because women's vocal cords are usually shorter and therefore vibrate at a greater frequency. Also, the strings of a violin are shorter than those of a viola or double bass. Pitch detectors in the brain allow us to tell differences in pitch.

The loudness of a sound roughly corresponds to the height, or amplitude, of sound waves. Figure 3.14 shows records of sound waves that vary in frequency and amplitude. Frequency and amplitude are independent. That is, both high- and low-pitched sounds can be either high or low in loudness. The loudness of a sound is expressed in **decibels (dB)**. Zero dB is equivalent to the threshold of hearing—the lowest sound that the typical person can hear. How loud is that? It's about as

"The empty vessel makes the greatest sound."

—WILLIAM SHAKESPEARE

Sound, or *auditory stimulation*, is the vibration of molecules in a medium such as air or water. Sound travels through the medium like waves, or like ripples in a pond when you toss in a pebble. The molecules of the medium are alternately compressed and expanded like the movements of an accordion. If you were listening under water, you would also hear the splash because of changes in the pressure of the water. In either case, the changes in pressure are vibrations that approach your ears in waves. These vibrations—sound waves—can also be created by a ringing bell, your vocal cords, guitar strings, or the slam of a book thrown down on a desk. A single cycle of compression and expansion is one wave of sound. Sound waves can occur many times in one second. The human ear is sensitive to sound waves with frequencies of from 20 to 20,000 cycles per second.

3-4a PITCH AND LOUDNESS

Pitch and loudness are two psychological dimensions of sound. The pitch of a sound is determined by its frequency, or the number of cycles per second as expressed in the unit **hertz (Hz)**. One cycle per second is 1 Hz. The greater the number of cycles per second (Hz), the higher the pitch of the sound.

✳ iPods on Campus: The Sounds of Oblivion?

The majority of university students own iPods, and most others have another personal listening device (Danhauer, 2009). Because these devices can produce outputs at 130 dB and higher, listeners may be at risk for hearing loss. To combat hearing loss, Fligor and Cox (2004) recommend the "60–60 rule"—that people should listen at no more than 60% of full volume for no more than 60 minutes per day. There are other dangers, such as "iPod oblivion," in which listeners pay less attention to their environments when they are listening. Two pedestrian deaths in New York within four months were attributed to iPod oblivion (Kuntzman, 2007).

Jeffrey Danhauer (2009) surveyed students drawn from universities across the United States and found that their reasons for using iPods included listening to music (95%), avoiding bothering other people with their music (77%), relaxing (75%), fighting boredom (74%), isolating themselves from the people around them (55%), and helping them concentrate on things such as schoolwork (46%).

© Tetra Images/Corbis

cochlea
the inner ear; the bony tube that contains the basilar membrane and the organ of Corti

basilar membrane
a membrane that lies coiled within the cochlea

organ of Corti
the receptor for hearing that lies on the basilar membrane in the cochlea

auditory nerve
the axon bundle that transmits neural impulses from the organ of Corti to the brain

loud as the ticking of a watch 20 feet away in a very quiet room.

The decibel equivalents of familiar sounds are shown in Figure 3.15. Twenty-five dB is equivalent in loudness to a whisper at five feet. Thirty dB is roughly the limit of loudness at which your librarian would like to keep your college library. You may suffer hearing damage if you are exposed to sounds of 85 to 90 dB for long periods.

FIGURE 3.15 | Decibel Ratings of Familiar Sounds

Zero dB is the threshold of hearing. You may suffer hearing loss if you incur prolonged exposure to sounds of 85 to 90 dB.

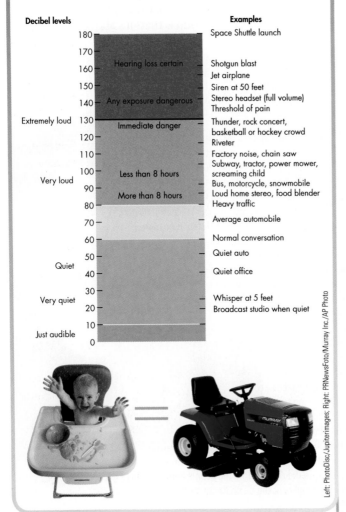

Decibel levels		Examples
	180	Space Shuttle launch
	170	
Hearing loss certain	160	Shotgun blast
	150	Jet airplane / Siren at 50 feet
Any exposure dangerous	140	Stereo headset (full volume) / Threshold of pain
Extremely loud	130	Thunder, rock concert, basketball or hockey crowd
Immediate danger	120	Riveter
	110	Factory noise, chain saw
	100	Subway, tractor, power mower, screaming child
Less than 8 hours		
Very loud	90	Bus, motorcycle, snowmobile
More than 8 hours	80	Loud home stereo, food blender / Heavy traffic
	70	Average automobile
	60	Normal conversation
	50	Quiet auto
Quiet	40	Quiet office
Very quiet	30	
	20	Whisper at 5 feet / Broadcast studio when quiet
Just audible	10	
	0	

Left: PhotoDisc/Jupiterimages; Right: PRNewsFoto/Murray Inc./AP Photo

3-4b THE EAR

The ear is shaped and structured to capture sound waves, vibrate in sympathy with them, and transmit them to the brain. In this way, you not only hear something, you can also figure out what it is. The ear has three parts: the outer ear, the middle ear, and the inner ear (see Figure 3.16).

The outer ear is shaped to funnel sound waves to the *eardrum*, a thin membrane that vibrates in response to sound waves, and thereby transmits them to the middle and inner ears. The middle ear contains the eardrum and three small bones, which also transmit sound by vibrating. These bones were given their Latin names (*malleus*, *incus*, and *stapes* [pronounced STAYpeas], which translate as "hammer," "anvil," and "stirrup") because of their shapes. The middle ear functions as an amplifier, increasing the pressure of the air entering the ear.

The stirrup is attached to another vibrating membrane, the *oval window*. The oval window works in conjunction with the round window, which balances the pressure in the inner ear (see Figure 3.16). The round window pushes outward when the oval window pushes in, and is pulled inward when the oval window vibrates outward.

The oval window transmits vibrations into the inner ear, the bony tube called the **cochlea** (from the Greek word for "snail"). The cochlea, which is shaped like a snail shell, contains two longitudinal membranes that divide it into three fluid-filled chambers. One of the membranes that lies coiled within the cochlea is called the **basilar membrane**. Vibrations in the fluids within the chambers of the inner ear press against the basilar membrane.

The **organ of Corti**, sometimes referred to as the "command post" of hearing, is attached to the basilar membrane. Some 16,000 receptor cells—called *hair cells* because they project like hair from the organ of Corti—are found in each ear. Hair cells "dance" in response to the vibrations of the basilar membrane (Hwang et al., 2010). Their movements generate neural impulses, which are transmitted to the brain via the **auditory nerve**. Auditory input is then projected onto the hearing areas of the temporal lobes of the cerebral cortex.

3-4c LOCATING SOUNDS

There is a resemblance between balancing a set of stereo speakers and locating sounds. A sound that is louder in the right ear is perceived as coming from the right. A sound coming from the right also reaches the right ear first. Both loudness and the sequence in which the sounds reach the ears provide directional cues.

FIGURE 3.16 | The Human Ear

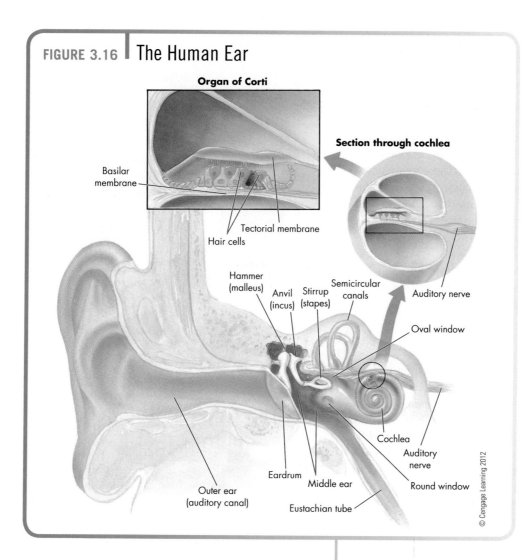

Organ of Corti

Section through cochlea

Basilar membrane

Tectorial membrane

Hair cells

Hammer (malleus)

Anvil (incus)

Stirrup (stapes)

Semicircular canals

Auditory nerve

Oval window

Cochlea

Auditory nerve

Round window

Eardrum

Middle ear

Outer ear (auditory canal)

Eustachian tube

© Cengage Learning 2012

But it may not be easy to locate a sound coming from in front or in back of you or above. Such sounds are equally distant from each ear and equally loud. So what do we do? Simple—we turn our head slightly to determine in which ear the sound increases. If you turn your head to the right and the loudness increases in your left ear, the sound is likely coming from in front.

3-4d PERCEPTION OF LOUDNESS AND PITCH

Sounds are heard because they cause vibration in parts of the ear and information about these vibrations is transmitted to the brain. The loudness and pitch of sounds appear to be related to the number of receptor neurons on the organ of Corti that fire and how often they fire. Psychologists generally agree that sounds are perceived as louder when more of these sensory neurons fire.

As discussed earlier, it takes two processes to explain perception of color: *trichromatic theory* and *opponent-process theory*. For pitch perception—that is, percep-

tion of sound waves that vary in frequency from 20 to 20,000 cycles per second—it takes three processes: *place theory, frequency theory*, and the *volley principle*.

Hermann von Helmholtz helped develop the place theory of pitch discrimination as well as the trichromatic theory of color vision. **Place theory** holds that the pitch of a sound is sensed according to the place along the basilar membrane that vibrates in response to it. In research that led to the award of a Nobel Prize, Georg von Békésy (1957) found that receptors at different sites along the membrane fire in response to tones of differing frequencies. Receptor neurons appear to be lined up along the basilar membrane like piano keys. The higher the pitch of a sound, the closer the responsive neurons lie to the oval window (Erixon et al., 2009). However, place theory appears to apply only to pitches that are at least 4,000 Hz. But what about lower pitches? That's where frequency theory comes in.

Frequency theory notes that for us to perceive lower pitches, we need to match the frequency of the sound waves with our neural impulses. That is, in response to low pitches—say 20 to 1,000 cycles per second—hair cells on the basilar membrane fire at the same frequencies as the sound waves. However, neurons cannot fire more that 1,000 times per second. Therefore, frequency theory best explains perception of pitches between 20 and 1,000 cycles per second. In actuality, frequency the-

flavor
a complex quality of food and other substances that is based on their odor, texture, and temperature as well their taste

olfactory nerve
the nerve that transmits information concerning odors from olfactory receptors to the brain

taste cells
receptor cells that are sensitive to taste

taste buds
the sensory organs for taste; they contain taste cells and are located mostly on the tongue

ory appears to account only for pitch perception between 20 and a few hundred cycles per second.

The *volley principle* accounts for pitch discrimination between a few hundred and 4,000 cycles per second (Ebeling, 2008; Machery & Carlyon, 2010). In response to sound waves of these frequencies, groups of neurons take turns firing in the way that one row of soldiers used to fire rifles while another row knelt to reload. Alternating firing—that is, volleying—appears to transmit sensory information about pitches in the intermediate range.

3-4e DEAFNESS

More than 1 in 10 Americans have a hearing impairment, and 1 in 100 cannot hear at all (Erixon et al., 2009). Two major types of deafness are *conductive deafness* and *sensorineural deafness*. *Conductive deafness* stems from damage to the structures of the middle ear—either to the eardrum or to the bones that conduct (and amplify) sound waves from the outer ear to the inner ear (Daud et al., 2010; Erixon et al., 2009). This is the hearing impairment often found among older people. Hearing aids amplify sound and often help people with conductive deafness.

Sensorineural deafness usually stems from damage to the structures of the inner ear, most often the loss of hair cells. Sensorineural deafness can also stem from damage to the auditory nerve, caused by such factors as disease or exposure to very loud sounds. In sensorineural deafness, people tend to be more sensitive to some pitches than others. In so-called Hunter's notch, the loss is limited to the frequencies of the sound waves generated by a gun firing. Prolonged exposure to 85 dB can cause hearing loss. People who attend rock concerts, where sounds may reach 140 dB, risk damaging their ears, as do workers who run pneumatic drills or drive noisy vehicles. The ringing sensation that often follows exposure to loud sounds probably means that hair cells in the inner ear have been damaged.

Cochlear implants, or "artificial ears," contain microphones that sense sounds and electronic equipment that transmits sounds past damaged hair cells to stimulate the auditory nerve. Such implants have helped many people with sensorineural deafness (Tait et al., 2010). However, they cannot assume the functions of damaged auditory nerves.

"I judge people on how they smell, not how they look."
—JENNIFER LOPEZ

3-5 The Chemical Senses: Smell and Taste

Smell and taste are the chemical senses. In vision and hearing, physical energy strikes our sensory receptors. In smell and taste, we sample molecules of substances.

3-5a SMELL

Smell has an important role in human behavior. It contributes to the **flavor** of foods, for example. If you did not have a sense of smell, an onion and an apple might taste the same to you. People's sense of smell may be deficient when compared with that of a dog, but we can detect the odor of 1 one-millionth of a milligram of vanilla in a liter of air.

The sense of smell detects odors. An odor is a sample of molecules of a substance in the air. Odors trigger firing of receptor neurons in the *olfactory membrane* high in each nostril. Receptor neurons can detect even a few molecules of the substance in gaseous form. The receptor neurons transmit information about odors to the brain via the **olfactory nerve**.

3-5b TASTE

As in the case of smell, the sense of taste samples molecules of a substance. Taste is sensed through **taste cells**—receptor neurons located on **taste buds**. You have about

What's that SCENT you're wearing?

10,000 taste buds, most of which are located near the edges and back of your tongue. Some taste buds are more responsive to sweetness, whereas others react to several tastes. Other taste receptors are found in the roof, sides, and back of the mouth, and in the throat. Buds in the mouth are evolutionarily adaptive because they can warn of bad food before it is swallowed (Brand, 2000).

Researchers generally agree on at least four primary taste qualities: sweet, sour, salty, and bitter. Many argue that more basic tastes exist, including *umami*, which is pronounced *ooh-mommy* in Japanese and means "meaty" or "savory" (Rolls, 2009; Yamamoto et al., 2009). Regardless of the number of basic tastes, the flavor of a food is more complex than taste alone. *Flavor* depends on odor, texture, and temperature as well as on taste. Apples and onions are similar in taste, but their flavors differ greatly.

Just as some people see better than others, some people taste better than others—but their superiority may be limited to one or more basic tastes. Those of us with low sensitivity for sweetness may require twice the sugar to sweeten our food as those who are more sensitive. Those of us who claim to enjoy bitter foods may actually be taste-blind to them. Sensitivities to various tastes

Apples and onions are similar in taste, but their flavors differ greatly.

have a genetic component (Bartoshuk, 2000; Snyder & Bartoshuk, 2009).

3-6 The Skin Senses

The skin senses include touch, pressure, warmth, cold, and pain. We have distinct sensory receptors for pressure, temperature, and pain, but some nerve endings may receive more than one type of sensory input. Let's focus on touch, pressure, temperature, and pain.

3-6a TOUCH AND PRESSURE

Sensory receptors embedded in the skin fire when the surface of the skin is touched. There may be several kinds of receptors for touch, some that respond to constant pressure, some that respond to intermittent pressure, as in tapping the skin. *Active touching* means continuously moving your hand along the surface of an object so that you continue to receive sensory input from the object. If you are trying to "get the feel of" a fabric or the texture of a friend's hair, you must move your hand over it. Otherwise, the sensations quickly fade. If you pass your hand over the fabric or hair and then hold it still, the sensations of touching will fade. Active touching receives information concerning pressure, temperature, texture, and feedback from the muscles involved in movements of our hands.

Different parts of the body are more sensitive to touch and pressure than others. The parts of the body that "cover" more than their fair share of somatosensory cortex are most sensitive to touch. These parts include the hands, face, and some other regions of the body. Our fingertips, lips, noses, and cheeks are more sensitive than our shoulders, thighs, and calves. Why the difference in sensitivity? First, nerve endings are more densely packed in the fingertips and face than in other locations. Second, more sensory cortex is devoted to the perception of sensations in the fingertips and face (see Figure 2.11 on page 41).

3-6b TEMPERATURE

The receptors for temperature are neurons located just beneath the skin. When skin temperature increases, the receptors for warmth fire. Decreases in skin temperature cause receptors for cold to fire.

Sensations of temperature are relative. When we are at normal body temperature, we might perceive another person's skin as warm. When we are feverish, though, the other person's skin might seem cool. We also adapt to differences in temperature. When we enter a swimming pool, the water may seem cold because it is below body temperature. Yet after a few moments an 80°F pool may seem quite warm. In fact, we may chide a newcomer for not diving right in.

3-6c PAIN

For most people, pain is a frequent visitor. Headaches, backaches, toothaches—these are only a few of the types of pain that most of us encounter from time to time. According to a national Gallup survey of more than 2,000 adults (Arthritis Foundation, 2000), 89% experience pain at least once a month. More than half (55%) of people aged 65 and above say they experience pain daily. People aged 65 and above are most likely to attribute pain to getting older (88%) and to assume they can do nothing about disabilities such as arthritis. By contrast, people aged 18 to 34 are more likely to attribute pain to tension or stress (73%), overwork (64%), or their lifestyle (51%). When we assume that there is nothing we can do about pain, we are less likely to try. Yet 43% of Americans say that pain curtails their activities, and 50% say that pain puts them in a bad mood.

Pain results when neurons called *nociceptors* in the skin are stimulated. Evolutionary psychologists would point out that pain is adaptive, if unpleasant, because it motivates us to do something about it. For some of us, however, chronic pain—pain that lasts once injuries or illnesses have cleared—saps our vitality and interferes with the pleasures of everyday life (Fenton, 2010; Gatchel & Kishino, 2010).

We can sense pain throughout most of the body, but pain is usually sharpest where nerve endings are densely packed, as in the fingers and face. Pain can also be felt deep within the body, as in the cases of abdominal pain and back pain. Even though headaches may seem to originate deep inside the head, there are no nerve endings for pain in the brain.

Pain usually originates at the point of contact, as when you bang a knee. But it reverberates throughout the nervous system. The pain message to the brain is facilitated by the release of chemicals such as prostaglandins, bradykinin, and P (yes, P stands for "pain"). *Prostaglandins* facilitate transmission of the pain message to the brain and heighten circulation to the injured area, causing the redness and swelling that we call inflammation. Inflammation attracts infection-fighting blood cells to the injury to protect it against invading germs. Pain-relieving drugs such as aspirin and ibuprofen help by inhibiting production of prostaglandins.

The pain message is relayed from the spinal cord to the thalamus and then projected to the cerebral cortex, making us aware of the location and intensity of the damage. Ronald Melzack speaks of a "neuromatrix" that includes these chemical reactions but involves other aspects of our physiology and psychology in our reaction to pain (Gatchel et al., 2012). For example, visual and other sensory inputs tell us what is happening and affect our interpretation of the situation. Our emotional response affects the degree of pain, and so do the ways in which we respond to stress. If, for instance, the pain derives from an object we fear, perhaps a knife or a needle, we may experience more pain. If we perceive that there is nothing we can do to change the situation, perception of pain may increase. If we have self-confidence and a history of successful response to stress, perception of pain may diminish.

Phantom Limb Pain

One of the more intriguing topics in the study of pain is phantom limb pain. About two out of three combat veterans with amputated limbs report feeling pain in such missing, or "phantom," limbs (Nampiaparampil, 2008). Although the pain occurs in the absence of the limb, it is real enough. The pain sometimes involves activation of nerves in the stump of the missing limb, but local anesthesia does not always eliminate the pain.

TRUTH? **FICTION?** MANY PEOPLE DO FEEL AS THOUGH THEY EXPERIENCE PAIN IN LIMBS THAT HAVE BEEN AMPUTATED (SO-CALLED *PHANTOM LIMB PAIN*). HOWEVER, THE LIMBS ARE GONE, SO THAT PAIN CANNOT ACTUALLY BE "IN" THE LIMB.

Researchers have found that many people who experience phantom limb pain have also undergone reorganization of the motor and somatosensory cortex that is consistent with the pain (Melzack & Katz, 2006).

Gate Theory

Simple remedies like rubbing a banged knee frequently help relieve pain. Why? According to the *gate theory* of pain originated by Ronald Melzack and Patrick Wall, the nervous system can process only a limited amount of stimulation at a time. Rubbing the knee transmits sensations to the brain that "compete" for the attention of neurons. Many nerves are thus prevented from transmitting pain messages to the brain. It is like shutting down a "gate" in the spinal cord, or like a switchboard being flooded with calls.

Acupuncture

Thousands of years ago, the Chinese began mapping the body to learn where pins might be placed to deaden pain. This practice is termed acupuncture. Traditional acupuncturists believe that the practice balances the body's flow of energy, but research has shown that it stimulates nerves that reach the hypothalamus and may also cause the release of endorphins and cortisol (Spelts & Gaynor, 2010). Endorphins are neurotransmitters that are similar in effect to the narcotic morphine. Cortisol is a stress hormone.

3-7 Kinesthesis and the Vestibular Sense

Try an experiment. Close your eyes and then touch your nose with your finger. If you weren't right on target, I'm sure you came close. But how? You didn't see your hand moving, and you didn't hear your arm swishing through the air. Humans and many other animals have senses that alert them to their movements and body position without relying on vision, including *kinesthesis* and the *vestibular sense*.

3-7a KINESTHESIS

Kinesthesis is the sense that informs you about the position and motion of parts of the body. The term is derived from the ancient Greek words for "motion"

(kinesis) and "perception" (aisthesis). In kinesthesis, sensory information is fed back to the brain from sensory organs in the joints, tendons, and muscles. You were able to bring your finger to your nose easily by employing your kinesthetic sense. When you make a muscle in your arm, the sensations of tightness and hardness are also provided by kinesthesis.

Imagine going for a walk without kinesthesis. You would have to watch the forward motion of each leg to be certain you had raised it high enough to clear the curb. And if you had tried the brief nose-to-finger experiment without the kinesthetic sense, you would have had no sensory feedback until you felt the pressure of your finger against your nose (or cheek, or eye, or forehead), and you probably would have missed dozens of times.

3-7b THE VESTIBULAR SENSE

It is your **vestibular sense** that provides your brain with information as to whether or not you are physically upright. Sensory organs located in the semicircular canals and elsewhere in the ears monitor your body's motion and position in relation to gravity. They tell you whether you are falling and provide cues to whether your body is changing speed, such as when you are in an accelerating airplane or automobile.

3-8 ESP: Is There Perception Without Sensation?

Imagine the wealth you could amass if you had *precognition*, that is, if you were able to perceive future events in advance. Perhaps you would check the next week's stock market reports and know what to buy or sell. Or you could bet with confidence on who would win the next Super Bowl or World Series. Or think of the power you would have if you were capable of *psychokinesis*, that is, mentally manipulating or moving objects. Precognition and psychokinesis are two concepts associated with extrasensory perception (ESP). Two other theoretical forms of ESP are *telepathy*, or direct trans-

kinesthesis
the sense that informs us about the positions and motion of parts of our bodies

vestibular sense
the sense of equilibrium that informs us about our bodies' positions relative to gravity

perception of objects or
events through means other
than the recognized sensory
organs

mission of thoughts or ideas from one person to another, and *clairvoyance*, or the perception of objects that do not stimulate the known sensory organs. An example of clairvoyance is "seeing" what card will be dealt next, even though it is still in the deck and unseen even by the dealer.

ESP—also referred to as *parapsychological* or *psi phenomena*—refers to the perception of objects or events through means other than the known sensory organs. *Para*psychological (psi) means standing alongside psychology, not being a part of psychology. Psychological communication occurs verbally or by means of body language. *Psi communication* refers to the transfer of information through an irregular or unusual process—not through the usual senses.

Many psychologists do not believe ESP is an appropriate area for scientific inquiry. Psychologist Ray Hyman (2011) argues that "It's craziness, pure craziness." Scientists study natural events, but ESP smacks of the supernatural, even the occult. Extrasensory perception also has the flavor of a nightclub act in which a blindfolded "clairvoyant" calls out the contents of an audience member's pocketbook. Other psychologists, however, believe that there is nothing wrong with investigating ESP. The issue for them is not whether ESP is sensationalistic but whether its existence can be demonstrated in the laboratory.

Perhaps the best known of the ESP researchers was Joseph Banks Rhine, who studied ESP for several decades beginning in the late 1920s (Viulli, 2008). In a typical experiment in clairvoyance, Rhine would use a pack of 25 Zener cards, which contained five sets of simple symbols. Pigeons' pecking randomly to indicate which one was about to be turned up would be "correct" 20% of the time. Rhine found that some people guessed correctly significantly more often than the 20% chance rate. He concluded that these individuals might have some degree of ESP.

A more current method for studying *telepathy* (direct communication between minds) is the *ganzfeld procedure* (Howard et al., 2009). In this method, one person acts as a "sender" and the other as a "receiver." The sender views randomly selected visual stimuli such as photographs or videotapes, while the receiver, who is in another room and whose eyes are covered and ears are blocked, tries to mentally tune in to the sender. After a session, the receiver is shown four visual stimuli and asked to select the one transmitted by the sender. A person guessing which stimulus was "trans-

FICTION THERE IS NO ADEQUATE SCIENTIFIC EVIDENCE THAT PEOPLE CAN READ OTHER PEOPLE'S MINDS.

mitted" would be correct 25% of the time (1 time in 4) by chance alone. An analysis of 28 experiments using the ganzfeld procedure, however, found that receivers correctly identified the visual stimulus 38% of the time (Honorton, 1985), a percentage unlikely to be due to chance.

An article by Daryl Bem (2011) reported the results of several experiments with more than 1,000 participants. In one experiment, the researchers showed 100 Cornell University students photos of erotic or non-erotic scenes. They were then

Image Source Pink/Jupiterimages

shown the photos again, in random order, but asked to predict whether the next photo would have erotic or non-erotic content. Since half were erotic and half were not, a chance result would be 50–50. Participants correctly predicted the erotic photos 53.1% of the time, whereas their hit rate on predicting non-erotic photos was just 50–50, a chance result. The chances that the 53.1% success rate was due to chance alone were less than 1 in 20. However, no single individual was correct every time.

Overall, there are many reasons for skepticism of ESP. First is the *file-drawer problem* (Howard et al., 2009). Buyers of supermarket magazines tend to forget "psychics'" predictions when they fail to come true (that is, they have "filed" them away). Similarly, ESP researchers are less likely to report research results that show failure. Therefore, we would expect unusual findings (for example, a subject with a high success rate at psi-communication tasks over a period of several days) to appear in the research literature. In other words, if you flip a coin indefinitely, eventually you will flip 10 heads in a row. The odds against it are high, but if you report only your success and not the weeks of failure, you appear to have unique coin-flipping ability.

Then, too, people who appear to have demonstrated ESP with one researcher have failed to do so with another researcher or have refused to participate in other studies (Howard et al., 2009). Moreover, in all of these studies, *not one person has emerged who can reliably show ESP from one occasion to another and from one researcher to another.* In sum, most psychologists do not grant ESP research much credibility. They prefer to study perception that involves sensation. After all, what is life without sensation?

By the Numbers

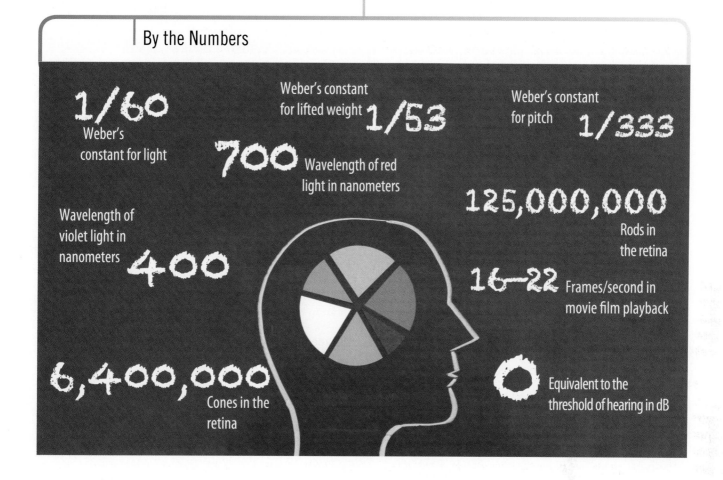

1/60 Weber's constant for light

Weber's constant for lifted weight **1/53**

Weber's constant for pitch **1/333**

700 Wavelength of red light in nanometers

Wavelength of violet light in nanometers **400**

125,000,000 Rods in the retina

16–22 Frames/second in movie film playback

6,400,000 Cones in the retina

0 Equivalent to the threshold of hearing in dB

STUDY TOOLS ▶ 3

Ready to study? In the book, you can:

- ❍ Review what you've read with Fill-Ins and Multiple Choice quizzes (below).
- ❍ Rip out Chapter Review card (in the back).

Or you can go online to CourseMate at www.cengagebrain.com for these resources:

- ❍ Complete Practices Quizzes to prepare for tests.
- ❍ Review Key Terms Flash Cards (online or print).
- ❍ Play games to master concepts.

FILL-INS

Answers can be found in the back of the book, starting on page 368.

1. _____ is the organization of sensations into an inner representation of the world; it reflects learning and expectations as well as sensations.

2. The _____ threshold for a stimulus, such as light, is the lowest intensity at which it can be detected.

3. The retina is made up of photoreceptors called _____ and _____.

4. The axons of ganglion cells make up the _____ nerve, which conducts visual information to the brain.

5. We perceive movement by sensing motion across the _____ of the eye and change of position in relation to other objects.

6. Odors are detected by the _____ membrane in each nostril.

7. The receptor neurons for taste are called _____ cells, which are located in taste buds on the tongue.

8. Kinesthesis is the sensing of bodily _____ and movement.

9. The vestibular sense is housed mainly in the _____ canals of the ears.

10. One reason for skepticism about ESP is the _____-_____ problem; that is, researchers are less likely to report research results that show failure.

1. _____ is to mechanical stimulation as perception is to mental representation.
   a. Adaptation   c. Sensation
   b. Organization   d. Cognition

2. Which of the following accommodates to an image by changing thickness and focusing light onto the retina?
   a. Sclera   c. Iris
   b. Lens   d. Cornea

3. Which of the following colors is longest in wavelength?
   a. Red   c. Violet
   b. Yellow   d. Green

4. The Gestalt rule describing the perceptual tendency to see objects that are near each other as belonging to a set is termed _____; while the tendency to see like objects as belonging together is termed _____.
   a. proximity; continuity
   b. closure; constancy
   c. continuity; similarity
   d. proximity; similarity

5. The normal human ear can hear sounds varying in frequency from _____ to _____ cycles per second (Hz).
   a. 2 to 2,000
   b. 20 to 2,000
   c. 20 to 20,000
   d. 200 to 20,000

6. Which of the following is *not* involved in explaining the perception of pitch?
   a. Place theory
   b. The volley principle
   c. Opponent-process theory
   d. Frequency theory

7. The following are considered to be basic tastes, with the exception of
   a. savory.
   b. sweet.
   c. sour.
   d. salty.

8. Because one odor can mask another, people use _____.
   a. air fresheners   c. incense burners
   b. perfumes   d. all of the above

9. The sensory receptors for kinesthesis are located in the
   a. tendons, muscles, and joints.
   b. semicircular canals.
   c. bony frame of the body.
   d. skin and hair.

10. Most psychologists do not believe in extrasensory perception because
    a. scientists have not defined what is meant by extrasensory perception.
    b. there is no evidence to support the existence of extrasensory perception.
    c. extrasensory perception would give those who have it unfair advantages.
    d. it is a sensationalistic concept.

Colin Anderson/Jupiter Images

LEARNING OUTCOMES

4-1 Define consciousness

4-2 Explain the nature of sleep and various sleep disorders

4-3 Explain the natures and uses of hypnosis, meditation, and biofeedback in altering consciousness

4-4 Define substance abuse and dependence, identify categories of psychoactive drugs, and explain their allures and dangers

STUDY TOOLS

After you read the chapter, go to the Study Tools at the end of the chapter, page 107.

Consciousness

CHAPTER 4

When you talk to yourself, who talks, and who listens?

This is the type of question posed by philosophers and scientists who study consciousness. Although it might seem that psychologists, who study the brain and mental processes, are best equipped to look into consciousness, they banished this topic from their field for many years. In 1904, for example, William James wrote an article with the intriguing title "Does Consciousness Exist?" James did not think consciousness was a proper area of study for psychologists because scientific methods could not directly observe or measure another person's consciousness.

John Watson, the "father of modern behaviorism," agreed. Watson insisted that only observable, measurable behavior is the province of psychology: "The time seems to have come when psychology must discard all references to consciousness" (1913, p. 163). When Watson became the president of the American Psychological Association in 1914, his view was further cemented in the minds of many psychologists.

But the past few decades have seen a cognitive revolution, and thousands of psychologists now believe we cannot capture the richness of human experience without referring to consciousness (Sternberg, 2009). We are flooded with studies of consciousness by psychologists, biologists, neuroscientists, physicists, even computer scientists. Yet we still cannot directly observe the consciousness of another person, and so we rely on self-reports of consciousness as we observe events such as neural activity in the brain.

4-1 What Is Consciousness?

Mental concepts such as consciousness acquire scientific status by being tied to observable behavior whenever possible. The concept of consciousness has various meanings, and psychologists use it in many ways.

When you talk to yourself, who talks, and who listens?

TRUTH OR FICTION

WHAT DO YOU THINK? FOLKLORE, COMMON SENSE, OR NONSENSE? CIRCLE THE T FOR "TRUTH" OR THE F FOR "FICTION," AND CHECK THE ACCURACY OF YOUR ANSWERS AS YOU READ THROUGH THE CHAPTER.

T	F	WE ACT OUT OUR FORBIDDEN FANTASIES IN OUR DREAMS.
T	F	INSOMNIA CAN BE CAUSED BY TRYING TOO HARD TO FALL ASLEEP.
T	F	IT IS DANGEROUS TO AWAKEN A SLEEPWALKER.
T	F	YOU CAN BE HYPNOTIZED AGAINST YOUR WILL.
T	F	YOU CAN TEACH A RAT TO RAISE OR LOWER ITS HEART RATE.
T	F	HEROIN WAS ONCE USED AS A CURE FOR ADDICTION TO MORPHINE.
T	F	MANY HEALTH PROFESSIONALS CALM DOWN HYPERACTIVE CHILDREN BY GIVING THEM A STIMULANT.
T	F	COCA-COLA ONCE "ADDED LIFE" TO ITS SIGNATURE DRINK THROUGH THE USE OF A POWERFUL—BUT NOW ILLEGAL—STIMULANT.
T	F	THE NUMBER OF PEOPLE WHO DIE FROM SMOKING-RELATED CAUSES IS GREATER THAN THE NUMBER LOST TO MOTOR-VEHICLE ACCIDENTS, ABUSE OF ALCOHOL AND ALL OTHER DRUGS, SUICIDE, HOMICIDE, AND AIDS *COMBINED*.

consciousness
a concept with many meanings, including sensory awareness of the world outside, direct inner awareness of one's thoughts and feelings, personal unity, and the waking state

selective attention
the focus of one's consciousness on a particular stimulus

direct inner awareness
knowledge of one's own thoughts, feelings, and memories without the use of sensory organs

4-1a CONSCIOUSNESS AS AWARENESS

One meaning of **consciousness** is *sensory awareness* of the environment. The sense of vision enables us to see, or be *conscious* of, the sun gleaming on the snow. The sense of hearing allows us to hear, or be conscious of, a concert. Yet sometimes we are not aware of sensory stimulation. We may be unaware, or unconscious, of sensory stimulation when we do not pay attention to it. The world is abuzz with signals, yet you are conscious of or focusing on only the words on this page (I hope).

Therefore, another aspect of consciousness is **selective attention**. Selective attention means focusing one's consciousness on a particular stimulus. Selective attention is a key to self-control. To keep your car on the road, you must pay more attention to driving conditions than to your hunger pangs or a cellphone call.

Adaptation to our environment involves learning which stimuli must be attended to and which can be safely ignored. Selective attention makes our senses keener (Kerlin et al., 2010; McLachlan & Wilson, 2010). This is why we can pick out the speech of a single per-

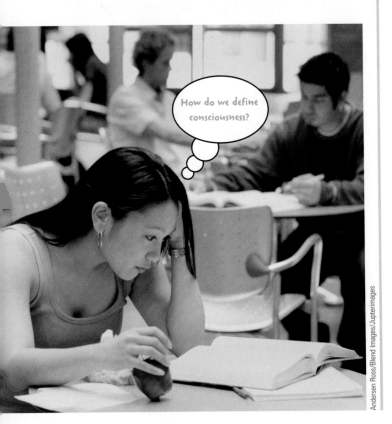

How do we define consciousness?

Andersen Ross/Blend Images/Jupiterimages

son across a room at a cocktail party, a phenomenon aptly termed the *cocktail party effect*. Selective attention also plays a role in the advertisements and marketing ploys we notice.

How do advertisers of running shoes, automobiles, or beer use these facts to get "into" our consciousness and, they hope, our pocketbooks? Think of some TV commercials that captured your attention. What kinds of stimuli made them front and center in your awareness?

Yet another meaning of consciousness is that of **direct inner awareness**. Close your eyes and imagine spilling a can of bright-red paint across a black tabletop. Watch it spread across the black, shiny surface and then spill onto the floor. Although this image may be vivid, you did not "see" it literally. Neither your eyes nor any other sensory organs were involved. You were conscious of the image through direct inner awareness.

We are conscious of—or have direct inner awareness of—our own thoughts, images, emotions, and memories. However, we may not be able to measure direct inner awareness scientifically. Nevertheless, many psychologists would argue that if you have it, you know it. Self-awareness is connected with the firing of billions of neurons hundreds of times per second. Even so, we detect psychological processes but not neural events (Roth, 2000).

4-1b CONSCIOUS, PRECONSCIOUS, UNCONSCIOUS, AND NONCONSCIOUS

Sigmund Freud, the founder of psychoanalysis, differentiated between thoughts and feelings of which we are conscious and those that are preconscious and unconscious.

> *"Consciousness comes in many flavors. Anyone who has taught an introductory psychology class, or attended one at eight o'clock Friday morning, has seen them all. There may be a couple of party-hearty frat boys in the back row, dozing after a long night spent celebrating the upcoming weekend. These two are not conscious. Up a couple of rows is the scammer checking out [someone] across the aisle and wondering if he can get a date. He is conscious, but not of you; nor are the three girls down the way who are passing notes to each other and suppressing their merriment. Another student has a tape recorder going and is finishing up a paper for another class, and he will be conscious of you later. The front-row kids are sippin' their coffee, taking notes furiously and occasionally nodding in agreement; at least they are conscious of you."*
>
> —MICHAEL S. GAZZANIGA, 2008, P. 277.

Preconscious material is not currently in awareness but is readily available. For example, if you answer the following questions, you will summon up "preconscious" information: What did you eat for breakfast? What is your phone number? You can make these preconscious bits of information conscious by directing your attention to them.

According to Freud, still other mental events are **unconscious**, or unavailable to awareness under most circumstances. Freud believed that some painful memories and sexual and aggressive impulses are unacceptable to us, so we *automatically* (unconsciously) eject them from awareness. That is, we *repress* them. **Repression** of these memories and impulses allows us to avoid feelings of anxiety, guilt, or shame.

Related, non-Freudian concepts include *suppression* and *nonconscious*. When people choose to stop thinking about unacceptable ideas or distractions, they are using **suppression**. When we consciously eject unwanted mental events from awareness, we are using suppression. We may, for example, suppress thoughts of an upcoming party when we need to study for a test. We may also try to suppress thoughts of the test while we are at the party!

Some bodily processes, such as the firing of neurons, are **nonconscious**. They cannot be experienced through sensory awareness or direct inner awareness. Growing hair and carrying oxygen in the blood are nonconscious. We can see that our hair has grown, but we have no sense receptors that provide sensations of growing. We feel the need to breathe but do not experience the exchange of carbon dioxide and oxygen.

4-1c CONSCIOUSNESS AS PERSONAL UNITY

As we develop, we differentiate ourselves from that which is not us. We develop a sense of being persons, individuals. There is a totality to our impressions, thoughts, and feelings that makes up our consciousness—our continuing sense of self in the world. That self forms intentions and guides behavior. In this usage of the word, consciousness *is* self.

4-1d CONSCIOUSNESS AS THE WAKING STATE

The word *conscious* also refers to the waking state as opposed, for example, to sleep. From this perspective, sleep, meditation, the hypnotic "trance," and the distorted perceptions that can accompany use of consciousness-altering drugs are considered *altered states of consciousness*.

The remainder of the chapter explores various altered states of consciousness, including sleep and dreams; hypnosis, meditation, and biofeedback; and, finally, the effects of psychoactive drugs.

preconscious
in psychodynamic theory, descriptive of material that is not in awareness but can be brought into awareness by focusing one's attention

unconscious
in psychodynamic theory, descriptive of ideas and feelings that are not available to awareness; also: without consciousness

repression
in psychodynamic theory, the automatic (unconscious) ejection of anxiety-evoking ideas, impulses, or images from awareness

suppression
the deliberate, or conscious, placing of certain ideas, impulses, or images out of awareness

nonconscious
descriptive of bodily processes, such as growing hair, of which we cannot become conscious; we may "recognize" that our hair is growing, but we cannot directly experience the biological process

One of the meanings of consciousness is the continuing sense of self in the world.

DEX IMAGE/Getty Images

circadian rhythm
a cycle that is connected with the twenty-four-hour period of the earth's rotation

4-2 Sleep and Dreams

Sleep is a fascinating topic. After all, we spend about one-third of our adult lives asleep. Sleep experts recommend that adults get eight hours of sleep a night, but according to the National Sleep Foundation (2009), adults in the United States typically get about 6.8 hours of sleep. About one-third get six hours or less of sleep a night during the workweek. One-third admit that lack of sleep impairs their ability to function during the day, and nearly one in five admits to falling asleep at the wheel.

Yes, we spend one-third of our lives in sleep—or would if we could. As you can see in Figure 4.1, some animals get much more sleep than we do, and some obtain much less. Why? It might have something to do with evolutionary forces. Animals that are most at risk of being hunted by predators tend to sleep less—an adaptive response to the realities of life and death.

FIGURE 4.1 | Sleep Times for Mammals

Different mammals require different amounts of sleep. Reasons remain uncertain, but evolution apparently plays a role: Animals more prone to being attacked by predators sleep less.

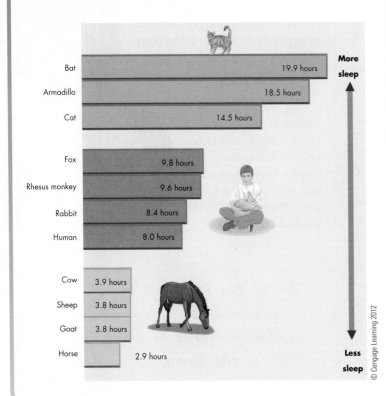

4-2a BIOLOGICAL AND CIRCADIAN RHYTHMS

We and other animals are subject to rhythms, and they are related to the rotation and revolutions of the planet. Many birds (and people who can afford it!) migrate south in the fall and north in the spring. A number of animals hibernate for the winter and emerge when buds are once again about to blossom.

Alternating periods of wakefulness and sleep reflect an internally generated *circadian rhythm*. A **circadian rhythm** is a cycle that is connected with the 24-hour period of the earth's rotation. A cycle of wakefulness and sleep is normally 24 hours long. When people are removed from cues that signal day or night, however, a cycle tends to become extended to about 25 hours, and people sleep nearly 10 of them (National Sleep Foundation, 2009). Why? We do not know. And during a night of sleep, we typically undergo a series of 90-minute cycles in which we run through the stages of sleep. In the morning, the shining sun adjusts the timing of the circadian clock by activating proteins in the retinas of the eyes. The proteins then signal tiny structures in the hypothalamus called the *suprachiasmatic nucleus (SCN)*. In turn, the SCN stimulates the pineal gland to decrease its output of the hormone melatonin, which promotes sleep.

Some of us, known as "morning people," function best in the morning; others function best in the afternoon. Some of us are "night owls," who are at our best when most neighbors are sound asleep.

Why do we sleep? Why do we dream? Let's explore the nature of sleep, dreams, and sleep disorders.

4-2b THE STAGES OF SLEEP

When we sleep, we slip from consciousness to unconsciousness. When we are conscious, our brains emit waves characterized by certain *frequencies* (numbers of waves per second) and *amplitudes* (heights—an index of strength). Brain waves are rough indicators of the activity of large numbers of neurons. The strength, or energy, of brain waves is expressed in volts (an electrical unit). When we sleep, our brain waves differ from those emitted when we are conscious. The electroencephalograph (EEG; see Figure 2.7 on page 37) has enabled researchers to measure brain waves. Figure 4.2 shows EEG patterns that reflect the frequency and strength of brain waves during the waking state, when we are relaxed, and when we are in the various stages of sleep. Brain waves, like other waves, are cyclical. The printouts in Figure 4.2 show what happens during a period of 15 seconds or so.

High-frequency brain waves are associated with wakefulness. When we move deeper into sleep, their frequency decreases and their amplitude (strength) increases. When we close our eyes and begin to relax before going to sleep, our brains emit **alpha waves**—low-amplitude brain waves of about 8 to 13 cycles per second.

Figure 4.2 shows five stages of sleep. The first four sleep stages are considered **nonrapid eye movement (NREM) sleep**. These contrast with the fifth stage, **rapid eye movement (REM) sleep**, so called because our eyes dart back and forth beneath our eyelids.

As we enter stage 1 sleep, our brain waves slow down from the alpha rhythm and enter a pattern of **theta waves**. Theta waves, with a frequency of about 6 to 8 cycles per second, are accompanied by slow, rolling eye movements. The transition from alpha waves to theta waves may be accompanied by a *hypnagogic state* dur-

ing which we may experience brief but vivid dreamlike images. Stage 1 sleep is the lightest stage of sleep. If we are awakened from stage 1 sleep, we may feel we were not sleeping at all.

After 30 to 40 minutes of stage 1 sleep, we undergo a steep descent into stages 2, 3, and 4 (see Figure 4.3). During stage 2, brain waves are medium in amplitude with a frequency of about 4 to 7 cycles per second, but these are punctuated by *sleep spindles*, brief bursts of brain activity that have a frequency of 12 to 16 cycles per second.

During deep sleep stages 3 and 4, our brains produce slower **delta waves**, which reach relatively great amplitude. During stage 3, the delta waves have a frequency of 1 to 3 cycles per second. Stage 4 is the deepest stage of sleep, from which it is the most difficult to be awakened. During

alpha waves
rapid low-amplitude brain waves that have been linked to feelings of relaxation

nonrapid eye movement (NREM) sleep
the first four stages of sleep

rapid eye movement (REM) sleep
a stage of sleep characterized by rapid eye movements, which have been linked to dreaming

theta waves
slow brain waves produced during the hypnagogic state

delta waves
strong, slow brain waves usually emitted during stage 4 sleep

---

FIGURE 4.2 | The Stages of Sleep

This figure illustrates typical EEG patterns for the stages of sleep. During REM sleep, EEG patterns resemble those of the waking state. For this reason, REM sleep is often termed *paradoxical sleep*. As sleep progresses from stage 1 to stage 4, brain waves become slower, and their amplitude increases. Dreams, including normal nightmares, are most vivid during REM sleep. More disturbing sleep terrors tend to occur during deep stage 4 sleep.

Awake — beta waves
(low amplitude, high frequency)

Awake

Drowsy — alpha waves
(higher amplitude, slower frequency)

Stage 1 sleep — theta waves
(low frequency, low amplitude)

NREM Sleep

Sleep spindle   K complex

Stage 2 sleep — sleep spindles
and the K complex

Stage 3 sleep — beginning of
delta waves (low frequency,
high amplitude)

Stage 4 sleep — delta waves
continue to increase
in amplitude

REM Sleep
Occurs when we re-enter
Stage 1, about ninety minutes
after falling asleep (frequently
called *paradoxical sleep*)

REM sleep — brain-wave
patterns are very similar
to those of initial
NREM stage 1

© Cengage Learning 2012

FIGURE 4.3 | Sleep Cycles

This figure illustrates the alternation of REM and non-REM sleep for the typical sleeper. There are about five periods of REM sleep during an 8-hour night. Sleep is deeper earlier in the night, and REM sleep tends to become prolonged toward morning.

| Sleep stage | A | 1 | 2 | 3 | 4 | 3 | 2 | REM | 1 | 2 | 3 | 4 | 3 | 2 | 3 | 2 | REM |

11 PM 12 AM 1 AM 2 AM

stage 4 sleep, the delta waves slow to about 0.5 to 2 cycles per second, and their amplitude is greatest.

After perhaps half an hour of deep stage 4 sleep, we begin a relatively rapid journey back upward through the stages until we enter REM sleep (see Figure 4.3). During REM sleep, we produce relatively rapid, low-amplitude brain waves that resemble those of light stage 1 sleep. REM sleep is also called *paradoxical sleep* because the EEG patterns observed suggest a level of arousal similar to that of the waking state (see Figure 4.2). However, it is difficult to awaken a person during REM sleep. When people are awakened during REM sleep, as is the practice in sleep research, about 80% of the time they report that they have been dreaming. (People report dreaming only about 20% of the time when awakened during NREM sleep.)

Each night we tend to undergo five cycles through the stages of sleep (see Figure 4.3). Five cycles include five periods of REM sleep. Our first journey through stage 4 sleep is usually the longest. Sleep tends to become lighter as the night wears on; periods of REM sleep lengthen and we may not enter the deepest stages of sleep. Toward morning our last period of REM sleep may last about half an hour.

4-2c THE FUNCTIONS OF SLEEP

Researchers do not have all the answers as to why we sleep, but sleep seems to serve several purposes: It rejuvenates the body, helps us recover from stress, helps us consolidate learning, and may promote development of infants' brains.

Consider the hypothesis that sleep helps rejuvenate a tired body. Most of us have had the experience of going without sleep for a night and feeling "wrecked" or "out of it" the following day. Perhaps the next evening we went to bed early to "catch up on our sleep." What happens to you if you do not sleep for one night? For several nights? Compare people who are highly sleep-deprived with people who have been drinking heavily. Sleepless people's abilities to concentrate and perform may be seriously impaired, but they may not recognize their limitations.

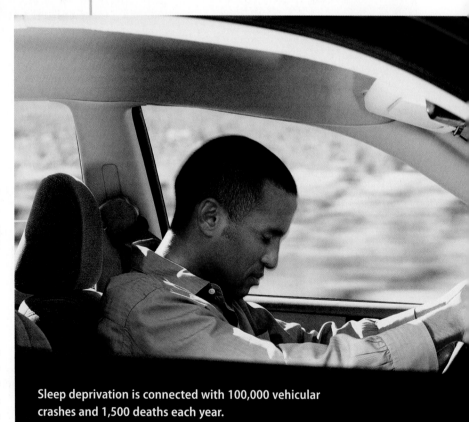

Sleep deprivation is connected with 100,000 vehicular crashes and 1,500 deaths each year.

Adam Gault/Getty Images

3 AM			4 AM				5 AM				6 AM		7 AM
2	3	2	REM	1	2	3 2 A 1	REM	A 1 A	2		REM		

© Cengage Learning 2012

Many students can pull "all-nighters" in which they cram for a test through the night and perform reasonably well the following day. But they begin to show deficits in psychological functions such as attention, learning, and memory, especially if they go sleepless for more than one night (Dubiela et al., 2010; Ward et al., 2009). Sleep deprivation also makes for dangerous driving (M. L. Jackson, 2009). It is estimated to be connected with 100,000 vehicular crashes and 1,500 deaths each year (S. Clark, 2009). To combat sleep deprivation during the week, many people sleep late or nap on their days off (National Sleep Foundation, 2009).

Why Do You Need the Amount of Sleep You Need?

The amount of sleep we need seems to be in part genetically determined (Cirelli, 2009). People also need more sleep when they are under stress, such as a change of job or an episode of depression (Mayers et al., 2009; Rosekind et al., 2010). In fact, sleep seems to help us recover from stress.

Newborn babies may sleep 16 hours a day, and teenagers may sleep 12 hours or more. It is widely believed that older people need less sleep than younger adults do, but sleep in older people is often interrupted by physical discomfort or the need to go to the bathroom. To make up for sleep lost at night, older people may "nod off" during the day.

Sleep, Learning, and Memory

REM sleep and deep sleep are both connected with the consolidation of learning and memory (Dubiela et al., 2010; Ward et al., 2009). In fact, fetuses have periods of waking and sleeping, and REM sleep may foster the development of the brain before birth (Fifer & Moon, 2003; Uhlhaas et al., 2010). In some studies, animals or people have been deprived of REM sleep. Under deprivation of REM sleep, animals and people learn more slowly and forget what they have learned more quickly. REM-sleep-deprived people and animals tend to show *REM rebound*, meaning that they spend more time in REM sleep during subsequent sleep periods. They "catch up."

4-2d DREAMS

Like memories and fantasies, dreams are imagery in the absence of external stimulation and can seem real. In college, I often had "anxiety dreams" the night before a test. I would dream that I had taken the test and it was all over. (Imagine my disappointment when I awakened and realized the test still lay before me!)

Dreams are most likely to be vivid during REM sleep, whereas images are vaguer and more fleeting during NREM sleep. If you sleep for eight hours and undergo five sleep cycles, you may have five dreams. Dreams may compress time the way a movie does, by skipping hours or days to a future time, but the actual action tends to take place in "real time." Fifteen minutes of events fills about 15 minutes of dreaming. Furthermore, your dream theater is quite flexible. You can dream in black and white or in full color.

Some dreams are nightmares. One common nightmare is that you are falling. Another is that you are trying to run away from a threat but cannot gain your footing or coordinate your legs. Nightmares, like most pleasant dreams, are products of REM sleep.

There are many theories about why we dream what we dream. Some are psychological, and others are more biologically oriented.

Dreams as "the Residue of the Day"

You may recall dreams involving fantastic adventures, but most dreams involve memories of the activities and problems of the day (Morewedge & Norton, 2009). If we are preoccupied with illness or death, sexual or aggressive urges, or moral dilemmas, we are likely to dream

activation–synthesis model
the view that dreams reflect activation of cognitive activity by the reticular formation and synthesis of this activity into a pattern

about them. The characters in our dreams are more likely to be friends and neighbors than spies, monsters, and princes—subjects that have been referred to, poetically, as "the residue of the day."

Traumatic events, however, can spawn nightmares, as reported in the aftermath of the terrorist attacks on the World Trade Center and Pentagon in 2001 (Roberts et al., 2009; Singareddy & Balon, 2002). People who have frequent nightmares are more likely than others to also suffer from anxiety, depression, and other psychological problems (Roberts et al., 2009).

Dreams as the Expression of Unconscious Desires

In the Disney film *Cinderella*, a song lyric goes, "A dream is a wish your heart makes." Freud theorized that dreams reflect unconscious wishes and urges. He argued that dreams express impulses we would censor during the

FICTION THERE IS NO EVIDENCE THAT WE ACT OUT FORBIDDEN FANTASIES IN OUR DREAMS.

day, although researchers find no evidence for this assertion. Moreover, he said that the content of dreams is symbolic of unconscious fantasized objects such as the genitals. In his method of psychoanalysis, Freud would interpret his clients' dreams.

The Activation–Synthesis Model of Dreams

There are also biological views of the "meanings" of dreams. According to the **activation–synthesis model**, acetylcholine (a neurotransmitter) and the pons (see Figure 2.11 on page 41) stimulate responses that lead to dreaming (Hobson, 2003, 2009; Stuart & Conduit, 2009). One is *activation* of the reticular formation, which arouses us, but not to waking. During the waking state, firing of these cells is linked to movement, particularly the movements in walking, running, and other physical acts. But during REM sleep, neurotransmitters tend to inhibit activity so we usually do not thrash about as we dream (Stuart & Conduit, 2009). In this way, we save ourselves—and our bed partners—some wear and tear.

Most dreams involve memories of the day gone by—or, poetically, "the residue of the day."

Blend Images/Jupiterimages

STUDY TOOLS ▶ 4

Ready to study? In the book, you can:

- ➲ Review what you've read with Fill-Ins and Multiple Choice quizzes (below).
- ➲ Rip out Chapter Review card (in the back).

Or you can go online to CourseMate at www.cengagebrain.com for these resources:

- ➲ Complete Practices Quizzes to prepare for tests.
- ➲ Review Key Terms Flash Cards (online or print).
- ➲ Play games to master concepts.

FILL-INS

Answers can be found in the back of the book, starting on page 368.

1. *Consciousness* has several meanings, including sensory awareness, the selective aspect of attention, direct inner _____, personal unity, and the waking state.

2. Because EEG patterns during REM sleep resemble those of the waking state, REM sleep is also called _____ sleep.

3. During a typical 8-hour night, we undergo (how many?) _____ trips through the different stages of sleep.

4. According to the _____–synthesis model, dreams reflect neural activity.

5. Hypnosis is an altered state of consciousness in which people are suggestible and behave as though they are in a _____.

6. In meditation, one focuses on a _____ to alter the normal person–environment relationship.

7. Substance _____ is characterized by repeated use of a substance although it is impairing functioning.

8. Physiological dependence is evidenced by tolerance or by an _____ syndrome when one discontinues use of the substance.

9. _____ is a stimulant that boosts self-confidence but also triggers rises in blood pressure and constricts the coronary arteries.

10. _____ substances distort perceptions.

1. When we say that we are "conscious of" seeing something or hearing a sound, we are referring to consciousness as

    a. a stream.
    b. a behavioral concept.
    c. the sense of personal unity.
    d. sensory awareness.

2. The notion that animals that are most at risk from predators sleep less is taken from which of the following perspectives?

    a. Behaviorist   c. Evolutionary
    b. Environmental   d. Developmental

3. Which of the following statements is correct concerning brain waves and the sleep cycle?

    a. Low-frequency brains waves are associated with being awake.
    b. High-frequency brains waves are associated with being awake.
    c. There are no recordable brain waves when we sleep.
    d. It is difficult to tell the difference between "sleep" brain waves and "awake" brain waves.

4. Allegra is said to have hypnotic suggestibility. She is likely to

    a. be prone to fantasy.
    b. have no idea as to what is expected in the trance state.
    c. attend to her own internal feelings rather than the instructions of the hypnotist.
    d. all of the above

5. In his classic study of transcendental meditation, Benson found that meditation leads to

    a. spiritual awakening.
    b. expanded consciousness.
    c. a relaxation response.
    d. more intense hypnagogic states.

6. Which of the following are children most likely to "outgrow"?

    a. Insomnia
    b. Bed-wetting
    c. Sleep apnea
    d. Narcolepsy

7. When Clay joined AA in order to stop drinking, he received a pamphlet that described the symptoms of alcohol withdrawal. These included

    a. high blood pressure and rapid pulse.
    b. restlessness and tremors.
    c. anxiety and weakness.
    d. all of the above

8. The most popular drug on college campuses is

    a. alcohol.
    b. marijuana.
    c. cocaine.
    d. LSD.

9. Elyse is a college student who has developed a tolerance to heroin and experiences withdrawal symptoms whenever she doesn't have a "fix" at least every eight hours. She feels that she has lost control and has to organize her life around her habit. She would be classified as having

    a. substance abuse.
    b. substance dependence.
    c. substance use.
    d. an anxiety disorder.

10. Which of the following is most likely to be prescribed for use with hyperactive children?

    a. Ritalin
    b. Morphine
    c. Dopamine
    d. Tranquilizers

4LTR Press solutions are designed for today's learners through the continuous feedback of students like you. Tell us what you think about PSYCH3 and help us improve the learning experience for future students.

YOUR FEEDBACK MATTERS.

Complete the Speak Up survey in CourseMate at www.cengagebrain.com

 Follow us at www.facebook.com/4ltrpress

LEARNING OUTCOMES

5-1 Define learning

5-2 Describe principles and methods of classical conditioning

5-3 Describe principles and methods of operant conditioning

5-4 Discuss cognitive factors in learning

STUDY TOOLS ▶ After you read the chapter, go to the Study Tools at the end of the chapter, page 132.

5-2d EXTINCTION AND SPONTANEOUS RECOVERY

Extinction and *spontaneous recovery* are aspects of conditioning that help us adapt by updating our expectations or revising our thinking about (representations of) the changing environment. For example, a child may learn to connect hearing a car pull into the driveway (a conditioned stimulus) with the arrival of his or her parents (an unconditioned stimulus). Thus, the child may squeal with delight (squealing is a conditioned response) when he or she hears the car.

Extinction enters the picture when times—and the relationships between events—change. After moving to a new house, the child's parents may commute by public transportation. The sound of a car in a nearby driveway may signal a neighbor's, not a parent's, homecoming. When a conditioned stimulus (such as the sound of a car) is no longer followed by an unconditioned stimulus (a parent's homecoming), the conditioned stimulus loses its ability to elicit a conditioned response. In this way, the organism adapts to a changing environment.

In classical conditioning, **extinction** is the process by which conditioned stimuli lose the ability to elicit conditioned responses because the conditioned stimuli are no longer associated with unconditioned stimuli. That is, the toddler is no longer gleeful at the sounds of the car in the driveway. From the cognitive perspective, extinction changes the child's mental representation of its environment because the conditioned stimulus no longer allows the child to make the same prediction.

In experiments on the extinction of conditioned responses, Pavlov found that repeated presentations of the conditioned stimulus (in this case, the tone) without the unconditioned stimulus (in this case, meat powder) led to extinction of the conditioned response (salivation in response to the tone). Basically, the dog stopped salivating at the sound of the tone. Interestingly, Figure 5.2 shows that after the initial conditioning, a dog's responsive salivation increased for a while and then leveled off. The dog was conditioned to begin to salivate in response to a tone after two or three pairings of the tone with meat powder. Continued pairings of the stimuli led to increased salivation (measured in number of drops of saliva). After seven or eight trials, salivation leveled off at 11 to 12 drops.

In the next series of experiments, salivation in response to the tone was extinguished through several trials in which the tone was presented without the meat powder. After about 10 extinction trials, the animal no longer salivated. That is, it no longer showed the conditioned response when the tone was sounded.

What would happen if we were to allow a day or two to pass after we had extinguished salivation in Pavlov's dog and then again sounded the tone? Where would you place your bet? Would the dog salivate or not?

If you bet that the dog would again show the conditioned response (in this case, salivation in response to the tone), you were correct. Organisms tend to show **spontaneous recovery** of extinguished conditioned responses as a function of the passage of time. For this reason, the term *extinction* may be a bit misleading. When a species of animal becomes extinct, all members of that species capable of reproducing have died. The species vanishes. But the experimental extinction of conditioned responses does not lead to their permanent eradication. Rather, extinction merely *inhibits* the response. The response remains available for the future under the "right" conditions.

extinction
the process by which stimuli lose their ability to evoke learned responses because the events that had followed the stimuli no longer occur (The learned responses are said to be *extinguished*.)

spontaneous recovery
the recurrence of an extinguished response as a function of the passage of time

FIGURE 5.2 | Learning and Extinction Curves

*Actual data from Pavlov (1927) is illustrated by the dots, and the curved lines are idealized.

© Cengage Learning 2012

generalization
in conditioning, the tendency for a conditioned response to be evoked by stimuli that are similar to the stimulus to which the response was conditioned

discrimination
in conditioning, the tendency for an organism to distinguish between a conditioned stimulus and similar stimuli that do not forecast an unconditioned stimulus

Evolutionary psychologists note that spontaneous recovery, like extinction, is adaptive. In the wild, a water hole may contain water for only a couple of months during the year. But evolution would favor the survival of animals that associate the water hole with the thirst drive from time to time so that they return to it when it again holds water. As time passes and the seasons change, things sometimes follow circular paths and arrive where they were before. Spontaneous recovery helps organisms adapt to situations that recur from time to time.

5-2e GENERALIZATION AND DISCRIMINATION

No two things are exactly alike. Traffic lights are hung at slightly different heights, and shades of red and green differ a little. The barking of two dogs differs, and the sound of the same animal differs slightly from one bark to the next. Rustling sounds in the undergrowth differ, but evolution would favor the survival of rabbits and deer that flee when they perceive any one of many possible rustling sounds. Adaptation requires us to respond similarly (or *generalize*) to stimuli that are equivalent in function and to respond differently to (or *discriminate* between) stimuli that are not.

Pavlov noted that responding to different stimuli as though they were functionally equivalent—*generalizing*—is adaptive for animals. **Generalization** is the tendency for a conditioned response to be evoked by stimuli that are similar to the stimulus to which the response was conditioned. For example, Pavlov demonstrated generalization by getting his dog to salivate when it was shown a circle. Then later the dog salivated in response to being shown closed geometric figures—even squares. The more closely the figure resembled a circle, however, the greater the *strength* of the response (as measured by drops of saliva).

But what happens if food follows the presentation of a circle but not a square? Organisms must also learn that (1) many stimuli perceived as being similar are functionally different, and (2) they must respond adaptively to each. During the first couple of months of life, for example, babies can discriminate their mother's voice from those of other women. They often stop crying when they hear their mother but not when they hear a stranger.

Pavlov showed that a dog conditioned to salivate in response to circles could be trained *not* to salivate in response to ellipses. After a while, the dog no longer salivated in response to the ellipses. Instead, it showed **discrimination**: It salivated only in response to circles. Pavlov found that increasing the difficulty of the discrimination task apparently tormented the dog. After the dog was trained to salivate in response to circles but not ellipses, Pavlov showed it a series of progressively rounder ellipses. Eventually the dog could no longer distinguish the ellipses from circles. The animal was so stressed that it urinated, defecated, barked profusely, and snapped at laboratory personnel.

How do we explain the dog's belligerent behavior? In *Frustration and Aggression*, a classic work written more than 70 years ago, a group of behaviorally oriented psychologists suggested that frustration induces aggression (Dollard et al., 1939). Why is failure to discriminate circles from ellipses frustrating? For one thing, in such experiments, rewards—such as food—are usually contingent on correct discrimination. That is, if the dog errs, it doesn't eat. Cognitive theorists, however, disagree (Rescorla, 1988). They would say that in Pavlov's experiment, the dog lost its ability to adjust its mental map of the environment as the ellipses grew more circular. Thus, it was frustrated.

Evolution would favor the survival of animals that associate a water hole with the thirst drive from time to time so that they return to it when it once more holds water.

Jeremy Woodhouse/Getty Images

Daily life requires generalization and discrimination. No two hotels are alike, but when we travel from one city to another, it is adaptive to expect to stay in a hotel. It is encouraging that a green light in Washington has the same meaning as a green light in Paris. But returning home in the evening requires the ability to discriminate between our home and those of others. Imagine the confusion that would occur if we could not discriminate among our friends, mates, or coworkers from other people.

5-2f HIGHER-ORDER CONDITIONING

Consider a child who is burned by touching a hot stove. After this experience, the sight of the stove may evoke fear. And because hearing the word *stove* may evoke a mental image of the stove, just hearing the word may evoke fear.

Recall the mini-experiment in which an adult smiles, says "kitchie-coo," and then tickles an infant's foot. After a few repetitions, just smiling at the infant may cause the infant to retract its foot. In fact, just walking into the room may have the same effect! The experiences with touching the hot stove and tickling the infant's foot are examples of *higher-order conditioning*.

In **higher-order conditioning**, a previously neutral stimulus (for example, hearing the word *stove* or seeing the adult who had done the tickling enter the room) comes to serve as a learned, or conditioned, stimulus after being paired repeatedly with a stimulus that has already become a learned, or conditioned, stimulus (for example, seeing the stove or hearing the phrase "kitchie-coo"). Pavlov demonstrated higher-order conditioning by first conditioning a dog to salivate in response to a tone. He then repeatedly paired the shining of a light with the sounding of the tone. After several pairings, shining the light (the higher-order conditioned stimulus) came to evoke the response (salivation) that had been elicited by the tone (the first-order conditioned stimulus).

5-2g APPLICATIONS OF CLASSICAL CONDITIONING

Some of the most important applications of classical conditioning involve the conditioning of fear and the counterconditioning, or extinction, of fear. The fear-reduction

methods we discuss are part of behavior therapy and are elaborated on in Chapter 13.

"Little Albert": Classical Conditioning of Emotional Responses

In 1920, John B. Watson and his future wife, Rosalie Rayner, published an article describing their demonstration that emotional reactions such as fears can be acquired through principles of classical conditioning. The subject of their demonstration was a lad known in psychological literature by the name of Little Albert. Albert was a phlegmatic fellow at the age of 11 months, not given to ready displays of emotion. But prior to the study, the infant did enjoy playing with a laboratory rat.

Using a method that some psychologists have criticized as unethical, Watson startled Little Albert by clanging steel bars behind his head when he played with the rat. After seven pairings, Albert showed fear of the rat even though clanging was suspended. Albert's fear was also generalized to objects similar in appearance to the rat, such as a rabbit and the fur collar on his mother's coat. Albert's conditioned fear of rats may never have become extinguished because extinction would have required perceiving rats (the conditioned stimuli) without painful consequences (in the absence of the unconditioned stimuli). But Albert's mother removed him from the laboratory before Watson and Rayner could attempt to countercondition the boy's acquired fear. And once outside the laboratory, fear might have prevented Albert from facing furry animals.

higher-order conditioning

a classical conditioning procedure in which a previously neutral stimulus comes to elicit the response brought forth by a *conditioned* stimulus by being paired repeatedly with that conditioned stimulus

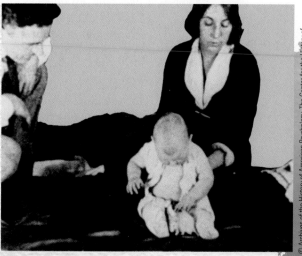

Watson and Rayner conditioned "Little Albert" to fear a rat by clanging steel bars behind his head when he played with the rat.

And as we shall see in the section on operant conditioning, avoiding furry animals might have been *reinforced* by reduction of fear.

Preparedness and the Conditioning of Fear

Little Albert developed his fear of rats easily enough, but would Watson and Rayner have been able to condition him to fear flowers or potted plants? Perhaps not. As suggested by Arne Öhman and Susan Mineka (2003), humans (and other primates) may be **biologically prepared** by evolutionary forces to rapidly develop fears of certain animals, including snakes, that could do them harm. People also seem to be prepared to fear thunder, threatening faces, sharp objects, darkness, and heights—all of which would have been sources of danger to our ancestors and which, to some degree, may still threaten us (Gerdes et al., 2009; Mineka & Oehlberg, 2008; Starratt & Shackelford, 2010).

Counterconditioning

In **counterconditioning**, an organism learns to respond to a stimulus in a way that is incompatible with a response that was conditioned earlier. For example, relaxation is incompatible with a fear response. The reasoning behind counterconditioning is this: If fears, as Watson had shown, could be conditioned by painful experiences like a clanging noise, perhaps fears could be counterconditioned by substituting pleasant experiences. In 1924, Watson's protégé Mary Cover Jones attempted to countercondition fear in a two-year-old boy named Peter.

Peter had an intense fear of rabbits.

© Michael Newman/Photo Edit

Jones had a rabbit gradually brought closer to Peter while he munched candy and cookies. Jones first placed the rabbit in a far corner of the room while Peter munched and crunched. Peter cast a wary eye, but he continued to consume the treats. Over a couple of months, the animal was brought closer until Peter simultaneously ate and touched the rabbit. Jones theorized that the joy of eating was incompatible with fear and thus counterconditioned it.

TRUTH IT IS TRUE THAT PSYCHOLOGISTS HELPED A YOUNG BOY OVERCOME HIS FEAR OF RABBITS BY HAVING HIM EAT COOKIES WHILE A RABBIT WAS BROUGHT CLOSER AND CLOSER.

Flooding and Systematic Desensitization

If Mary Cover Jones had simply plopped the rabbit on Peter's lap rather than bring it gradually closer, she would have been using the method of **flooding**. Flooding, like counterconditioning, is a behavior therapy method for reducing fears. It is based on the classical conditioning principle of extinction (Mystkowski & Mineka, 2007). In flooding, the client is exposed to the fear-evoking stimulus until fear is extinguished. Little Albert, for example, might have been placed in close contact with a rat until his fear had become extinguished. In extinction, the conditioned stimulus (in this case, the rat) is presented repeatedly in the absence of the unconditioned stimulus (the clanging of the steel bars) until the conditioned response (fear) is no longer evoked.

Although flooding is usually effective, it is unpleasant. (When you are fearful of rats, being placed in a room with one is no picnic.) For this reason, behavior therapists frequently prefer to use **systematic desensitization**, in which the client is gradually exposed to fear-evoking stimuli under circumstances in which he or she remains relaxed. For example, while feeling relaxed, Little Albert might have been given an opportunity to look at photos of rats or to see rats from a distance before they were brought closer. Systematic desensitization takes longer than flooding but is not as unpleasant.

In any event, people can learn by means of simple association. In terms of the evolutionary perspective, organisms that can learn by several routes—including conditioning and conscious reflection—would stand a greater chance of survival than organisms whose learning is limited to conditioning.

Whereas *reinforcers*—even negative reinforcers—increase the frequency of the behavior they follow, *punishments* decrease it (see Figure 5.6). Punishment can rapidly suppress undesirable behavior (Gershoff, 2002) and may be warranted in "emergencies," such as when a child tries to run into the street.

Psychologists distinguish between *positive punishments* and *negative punishments*. Both kinds of punishments are aversive events, and both decrease the frequency of the behavior they follow (see Figure 5.8). *Positive punishment* is the application of an aversive stimulus to decrease unwanted behavior, such as spanking, scolding, or a parking ticket. *Negative punishment* is the removal of a pleasant stimulus, such as removing a student's opportunity to talk with friends in class by seating them apart, or removing a student's opportunity to mentally escape from class by taking his or her iPhone or iPad. "Time out" is a form of negative punishment because it places a misbehaving child in an environment in which she or he cannot experience rewards.

5-3g DISCRIMINATIVE STIMULI

Skinner might not have succeeded in getting his pigeons into the drivers' seats of missiles, but he had no problem training them to respond to traffic lights. Imagine yourself trying the following experiment: Place a pigeon in a Skinner box with a button on the wall. Deprive it of food for a while. Drop a food pellet into the cage whenever it pecks the button. Soon it will learn to peck the button. Now you place a small green

"Education is what survives when what has been learned has been forgotten."
—B. F. SKINNER

light in the cage and turn it on and off intermittently throughout the day. Reinforce button pecking with food whenever the green light is on, but not when the light is off. It will not take long for the pigeon to learn that it will gain as much by grooming itself or cooing and flapping around as it will by pecking the button when the light is off.

The green light has become a discriminative stimulus. **Discriminative stimuli**, such as green or red lights, indicate whether behavior (in the case of the pigeon, pecking a button) will be reinforced (by a food pellet being dropped into the cage). Behaviors (or operants) that are not reinforced tend to be extinguished. For the pigeon in our experiment, the behavior of pecking the button *when the light is off* is extinguished.

A moment's reflection will suggest many ways in which discriminative stimuli influence our behavior. Isn't it more efficient to answer the telephone when it is ringing? Do you think it is wise to ask someone for a favor when she or he is displaying anger and disapproval toward you?

We noted that a pigeon learns to peck a button if food drops into its cage when it does so. What if you want the pigeon to continue to peck the button, but you're running out of food? Do not despair. As we see in the following section, you can keep that bird pecking away indefinitely, even as you hold up on most of the food.

discriminative stimulus
in operant conditioning, a stimulus that indicates that reinforcement is available

continuous reinforcement
a schedule of reinforcement in which every correct response is reinforced

partial reinforcement
one of several reinforcement schedules in which not every correct response is reinforced

5-3h SCHEDULES OF REINFORCEMENT

In operant conditioning, some responses are maintained by means of **continuous reinforcement**. You probably become warmer every time you put on heavy clothing. You probably become less thirsty every time you drink water. Yet if you have ever watched people toss their money down the maws of slot machines, you know that behavior can also be maintained by means of **partial reinforcement**.

FIGURE 5.6 | Negative Reinforcers Versus Punishments

Procedure	Behavior	Consequence	Change in behavior
Use of negative reinforcement	Behavior (Studying)	Negative reinforcer (Teacher disapproval) is *removed* when student studies	Frequency of behavior *increases* (Student studies more)
Use of punishment	Behavior (Talking in class)	Punishment (Detention) is *presented* when student talks in class	Frequency of behavior *decreases* (Student talks less in class)

© Cengage Learning 2012

fixed-interval schedule

a schedule in which a fixed amount of time must elapse between the previous and subsequent times that reinforcement is available

variable-interval schedule

a schedule in which a variable amount of time must elapse between the previous and subsequent times that reinforcement is available

fixed-ratio schedule

a schedule in which reinforcement is provided after a fixed number of correct responses

variable-ratio schedule

a schedule in which reinforcement is provided after a variable number of correct responses

Folklore about gambling is based on solid learning theory. You can get a person "hooked" on gambling by fixing the game to allow heavy winnings at first. Then you gradually space out the winnings (reinforcements) until gambling is maintained by infrequent winning—or even no winning at all. Partial reinforcement schedules can maintain gambling, like other behavior, for a great deal of time, even though it goes unreinforced (Pulley, 1998).

Responses that have been maintained by partial reinforcement are more resistant to extinction than responses that have been maintained by continuous reinforcement (Rescorla, 1999). From the cognitive perspective, we could suggest that organisms that have experienced partial reinforcement do not expect reinforcement every time they engage in a response. Therefore, they are more likely to persist in the absence of reinforcement.

There are four basic reinforcement schedules: *fixed-interval, variable-interval, fixed-ratio,* and *variable-ratio.*

Interval Schedules

In a **fixed-interval schedule**, a fixed amount of time— say, a minute—must elapse before the correct response will result in a reinforcer. With a fixed-interval schedule, an organism's response rate falls off after each reinforcement and then picks up again as the time when reinforcement will occur approaches. For example, in a one-minute fixed-interval schedule, a rat is reinforced with, say, a food pellet for the first operant—for example, the first pressing of a lever—that occurs after one minute has elapsed. After each reinforcement, the rat's rate of lever pressing slows down, but as the end of the one-minute interval draws near, lever pressing increases in frequency, as suggested in Figure 5.7. It is as if the rat has learned that it must wait awhile before it is reinforced. The resultant record on the *cumulative recorder* shows a typical series of upward waves, or scallops, which are called *fixed-interval scallops.*

Car dealers use fixed-interval reinforcement schedules when they offer in-

centives for buying up the remainder of the year's line in summer and fall. In a sense, they are suppressing buying at other times, except for consumers whose current cars are in their death throes or those with little self-control. Similarly, you learn to check your e-mail only at a certain time of day if your correspondent writes at that time each day.

Reinforcement is more unpredictable in a **variable-interval schedule**. Therefore, the response rate is lower, but it is also steadier. If the boss calls us in for a weekly report, we probably work hard to pull things together just before the report is to be given, just as we might cram the night before a weekly quiz. But if we know that the boss might call us in for a report on the progress of a certain project at any time (variable-interval schedule), we are likely to keep things in a state of reasonable readiness at all times. However, our efforts are unlikely to have the intensity they would in a fixed-interval schedule (for example, a weekly report). Similarly, we are less likely to cram for unpredictable pop quizzes than to study for regularly scheduled quizzes. But we are likely to do at least some studying on a regular basis in preparation for pop quizzes. Likewise, if you receive e-mail from your correspondent irregularly, you are likely to check your e-mail regularly for his or her communication, but with less eagerness.

Ratio Schedules

In a **fixed-ratio schedule**, reinforcement is provided after a *fixed* number of correct responses have been made. In a **variable-ratio schedule**, reinforcement is

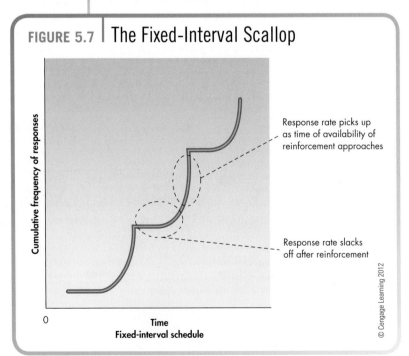

FIGURE 5.7 | The Fixed-Interval Scallop

Response rate picks up as time of availability of reinforcement approaches

Response rate slacks off after reinforcement

Cumulative frequency of responses

0

Time
Fixed-interval schedule

© Cengage Learning 2012

2001). Parental rejection and use of physical punishment further increase the likelihood of aggression in children (Eron, 1982). These family factors suggest that the parents of aggressive children may be absent or unlikely to help young children understand that the kinds of socially inappropriate behaviors they see in the media are not for them. A harsh home life may also confirm the TV viewer's or game player's vision of the world as a violent place.

If children believe violence to be inappropriate for them, they will be less likely to act aggressively, even if they have acquired aggressive skills from exposure to the media or other sources. It would be of little use to talk about learning if we couldn't remember what we learn from second to second or from day to day. In the next chapter, we turn our attention to memory. In Chapter 8, we see how learning is intertwined with thinking, language, and intelligence.

Teaching Children Not to Imitate Media Violence

Children are going to be exposed to media violence—if not in Saturday-morning cartoon shows, then in evening dramas and in the news. Or they'll hear about violence from friends or watch other children get into fights. If all those sources of violence were somehow hidden from view, they would learn about violence in *Hamlet*, *Macbeth*, and the Bible. The notion of preventing children from being exposed to violent models may be impractical.

What, then, should be done? Parents and educators can do many things to tone down the impact of media violence. Children who watch violent shows may act less aggressively when they are informed that:

- The violent behavior they observe in the media does not represent the behavior of most people.

- The apparently aggressive behaviors they watch are not real. They reflect camera tricks, special effects, and stunts.

- Most people resolve conflicts by nonviolent means.

- The real-life consequences of violence are harmful to the victim and often to the aggressor.

Despite our history of evolutionary forces, and despite the fact that in most species, successful aggression usually wins individuals the right to transmit their genes to future generations, humans are thinking beings. If children consider violence to be inappropriate for them, they will be less likely to act aggressively, even when they have acquired aggressive skills from exposure to the media or other sources.

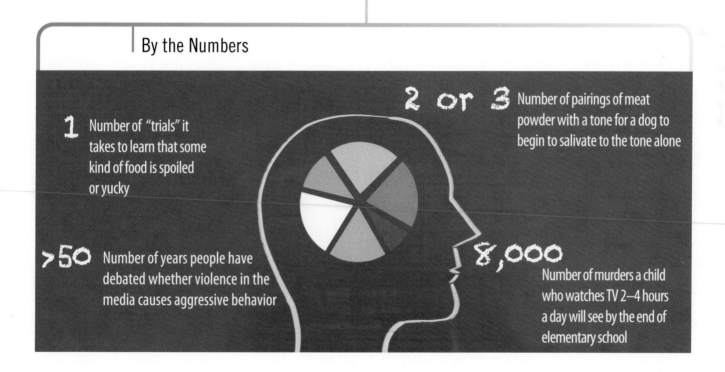

By the Numbers

1 Number of "trials" it takes to learn that some kind of food is spoiled or yucky

2 or 3 Number of pairings of meat powder with a tone for a dog to begin to salivate to the tone alone

>50 Number of years people have debated whether violence in the media causes aggressive behavior

8,000 Number of murders a child who watches TV 2–4 hours a day will see by the end of elementary school

STUDY TOOLS ▶ 5

Ready to study? In the book, you can:

- Review what you've read with Fill-Ins and Multiple Choice quizzes (below).
- Rip out Chapter Review card (in the back).

Or you can go online to CourseMate at www.cengagebrain.com for these resources:

- Complete Practices Quizzes to prepare for tests.
- Review Key Terms Flash Cards (online or print).
- Play games to master concepts.

FILL-INS

Answers can be found in the back of the book, starting on page 368.

1. A response to an unconditioned stimulus is called a(n) _____ response.

2. A response to a conditioned stimulus is termed a(n) _____ response.

3. Repeated presentation of a CS (such as a tone) without the UCS (such as meat) will_____ the CR (salivation).

4. Extinguished responses often show _____ recovery as a function of the passage of time.

5. John B. Watson and Rosalie Rayner used conditioning to teach a boy who is known as "Little _____" to fear rats.

6. In the behavior-therapy method of _____, a client is continuously exposed to a fear-evoking stimulus until the fear response is extinguished.

7. _____ reinforcers increase the probability that operants will occur when they are removed.

8. In a _____-_____ schedule, a specific amount of time must elapse since a previous correct response before reinforcement again becomes available.

9. _____ learning breaks down learning tasks into small steps and reinforces correct performance of each step.

10. According to _____ theory, learning occurs because a CS indicates that the UCS is likely to follow.

132   Learning

1. According to behaviorists, _____ is a relatively permanent change in an organism's behavior that occurs because of experience.
   a. extinction
   b. learning
   c. acquisition
   d. higher-order conditioning

2. While attempting to identify neural receptors that trigger salivary glands, Ivan Pavlov inadvertently found that responses can be learned through
   a. operant conditioning.
   b. observation.
   c. instinct.
   d. association.

3. Roberto kept seeing signs on the highway advertising Pizza Hut. He started to salivate at the possibility of having a pizza. The signs were
   a. unconditioned stimuli.
   b. unconditioned responses.
   c. conditioned stimuli.
   d. conditioned responses.

4. Johnny was tormented in the schoolyard every day by a bully with bright red frizzy hair. One day, Johnny's father brought his boss, Mr. Dale, home. The boss had bright red frizzy hair, and Johnny ran to his room, crying. Mr. Dale's hair functioned as a _____, and Johnny's fear was a _____.
   a. US; CR   c. CS; CR
   b. US; UR   d. CR; CS

5. Spotted Zebras learn to stop going to a particular water hole after approaching it several times and finding that it is dry. However, after a month or two passes, they may return to the water hole. Learning to stop going to the water hole because it is dry, but then returning to it after time passes, is an example of _____ followed by _____.
   a. extinction, spontaneous recovery
   b. shaping, successive approximations
   c. discrimination training, generalization
   d. contingency theory, latent learning

6. Which of the following best illustrates operant conditioning according to Skinner?
   a. **A dog salivates at the sound of a dinner bell.**
   b. **A cat comes running when it hears the sound of the can opener.**
   c. **A dolphin is given a fish every time it jumps through a hoop.**
   d. **The mating behavior of salmon.**

7. When a behavior is followed by negative reinforcement, the behavior is likely to
   a. be extinguished.   c. decrease.
   b. be suppressed.   d. increase.

8. Slot machines tend to keep gamblers playing by using a _____ schedule of reinforcement.
   a. fixed-interval
   b. variable-interval
   c. fixed-ratio
   d. variable-ratio

9. Professor Fournier gives a quiz every Monday. His students would then tend to _____ because they are on a _____ schedule of reinforcement.
   a. start studying immediately after the quiz; fixed-ratio
   b. study regularly through the week; fixed-interval
   c. study on Sunday nights; fixed-interval
   d. pay attention in class; variable-interval

10. Johnny watches TV violence for an hour or two a day, but he is not violent outside the home. Then one day Billy attacks him on the way home from school, and Johnny imitates the behavior he saw on TV to fight Billy off and teach Billy never to attack him again. Although Johnny had not shown violent behavior until he was attacked, we can assume that when watching TV, he was engaging in
    a. latent learning.
    b. shaping.
    c. discrimination training.
    d. operant conditioning.

LEARNING OUTCOMES

6-1 Define memory and differentiate between types of memories

6-2 Explain the processes of memory

6-3 Explain the stages of memory

6-4 Identify contributors to forgetting

6-5 Describe the biological aspects of memory

After you read the chapter, go to the Study Tools at the end of the chapter, page 158.

gabczi/Shutterstock.com

CHAPTER 6

MEMORY:
Remembrance of Things Past—and Future

Jeff would never forget his sudden loss of memory. He watched in horror as his cell phone slipped from his pocket and fell to the floor of the Blockbuster store in Boston. Before he could grab it, it shattered into pieces. A New York college student, Jeff experienced the trauma of phone loss on his winter break.

Why was the loss traumatic? Why was it a memory problem? Simple: There was no way for Jeff to retrieve his phone book. "I was at the store and it was snowing out and I suddenly realized that I had no way of getting in touch with anyone," he explains (Metz, 2005). Jeff now copies every cell-phone entry in a little black book—made of paper. Other people back up their phone books—and their pictures and downloads—on servers provided by cellular telephone operating companies or cellphone manufacturers. iPhones have backups available. Verizon's method is called Backup Assistant. Most people transfer their memories from their old cellphone to the new one when they make a change.

What's the problem with remembering all those phone numbers? The answer lies partly in their length. Psychologist George Miller (1956) researched the amount of information people can keep in mind at once, and he found that the average person is comfortable with digesting about seven digits at a time. Most people have little trouble recalling five pieces of information, as in a ZIP code. Some can remember nine, which is, for most, an upper limit. So seven pieces of information, plus or minus one or two, is the "magic" number.

This chapter is all about the "backup assistant" in your brain—your memory. Without memory, there is no past. Without memory, experience is trivial and learning is lost. Let's see what psychologists have learned about the ways in which we remember things—other than keying them into a cellphone's memory chip.

> *Without memory, there is no past.*

TRUTH OR **FICTION**

WHAT DO YOU THINK? FOLKLORE, COMMON SENSE, OR NONSENSE? CIRCLE THE T FOR "TRUTH" OR THE F FOR "FICTION," AND CHECK THE ACCURACY OF YOUR ANSWERS AS YOU READ THROUGH THE CHAPTER.

T	F	A WOMAN WHO COULD NOT REMEMBER WHO SHE WAS AUTOMATICALLY DIALED HER MOTHER'S NUMBER WHEN THE POLICE GAVE HER A TELEPHONE.
T	F	LEARNING MUST BE MEANINGFUL IF WE ARE TO REMEMBER IT.
T	F	IF YOU CAN SEE, YOU HAVE A PHOTOGRAPHIC MEMORY.
T	F	ALL OF OUR EXPERIENCES ARE PERMANENTLY IMPRINTED ON THE BRAIN, SO THE PROPER STIMULUS CAN CAUSE US TO REMEMBER THEM EXACTLY.
T	F	IT MAY BE EASIER FOR YOU TO RECALL THE NAME OF YOUR FIRST-GRADE TEACHER THAN THE NAME OF SOMEONE YOU JUST MET AT A PARTY.
T	F	YOU MAY ALWAYS RECALL WHERE YOU WERE AND WHAT YOU WERE DOING ON THE MORNING OF SEPTEMBER 11, 2001.
T	F	IF YOU STUDY WITH THE STEREO ON, YOU WOULD PROBABLY DO BETTER TO TAKE THE TEST WITH THE STEREO ON.
T	F	LEARNING SPANISH CAN MAKE IT HARDER TO REMEMBER FRENCH—AND VICE VERSA.

6-1 Kinds of Memory

Jeff remembered a thing he had personally done, like drop his cellphone in Boston on a blustery day in January. Remembering dropping one's cellphone is an *episodic memory*—a memory of an event in one's life. According to psychologists who have extensively researched memory, episodic memory is one kind of memory system (Carver & Cluver, 2009; Dickerson & Eichenbaum, 2009). And when I learned of Jeff's experience, I tried to remind myself repeatedly not to forget to jot down notes about it and write it up as soon as I could. (I was trying to jog my *prospective memory*—remembering to do something in the future.) Let's consider several memory systems.

6-1a EXPLICIT MEMORY

Explicit memory—also referred to as *declarative memory*—is memory for specific information. Things that are *explicit* are clear, or clearly stated or explained. The use of the term *declarative* indicates that these memories state or reveal (that is, *declare*) specific information. The information may be autobiographical or refer to general knowledge.

Psychologist Endel Tulving (1985) describes two kinds of explicit memories: episodic and semantic. They are identified according to the type of information they hold.

Episodic Memory (I remember . . .)

Episodic memories are types of explicit memories. They are memories of the things that happen to us or take place in our presence (Dickerson & Eichenbaum, 2009; Grillon et al., 2010). Episodic memory is also referred to as *autobiographical memory*. Your memories of what you ate for breakfast and of what your professor said in class today are episodic memories. We tend to use the phrase "I remember …" when we are referring to episodic memories, as in "I remember the blizzard of 2004."

Semantic Memory (I know . . .)

General knowledge is referred to as **semantic memory**—another kind of explicit memory. *Semantics* concerns meanings. You can "know" that the United States has 50 states without visiting them and personally adding them up. You "know" who authored *Hamlet*, although you were not looking over Shakespeare's shoulder as he did so. These are examples of semantic memory.

✳ Five Memory Challenges

Let's challenge your memory. This is not an actual memory test of the sort used by psychologists to determine whether people's memory functioning is within normal limits. Instead, it will provide you with some insight into how your memory works and may also be fun.

Directions: Find four sheets of blank paper and number them 1 through 4. Also use a watch with a second hand. Then follow these instructions:

1. Following are 10 letters. Look at them for 15 seconds. Later in the chapter I will ask you if you can write them on sheet number 1. (No cheating! Don't do it now.)

   THUNSTOFAM

2. Look at these nine figures for 30 seconds. Then try to draw them in the proper sequence on sheet number 2, right after you have finished looking at them. (We'll talk about your drawings later.)

3. Look at the following list of 17 letters for 60 seconds and then see whether you can reproduce it on sheet number 3.

   GMC-BSI-BMA-TTC-IAF-BI

4. Which of these pennies is an accurate reproduction of the Lincoln penny you see every day? This time there's nothing to draw on another sheet; just circle or put a checkmark by the penny that you think resembles the ones you throw in the back of the drawer.

   A   B   C   D   E   F

5. Examine the following drawings for 1 minute. Then copy the *names* of the figures on sheet number 4. When you're finished, just keep reading. Soon I'll be asking you to draw those figures.

   eyeglasses   hourglass   seven   gun

That's it. You'll find out about the results of these memory challenges as you read through the chapter.

Your future recollection that there are several memory systems is more likely to be semantic than episodic. That is, you are more likely to "know" that there are several types of memory than to recall where you were and how you were sitting. We are more likely to say "I know …" in reference to semantic memories, as in "I *know* about—" (or "I heard about—") "—the blizzard of 1898." Put another way, you may *remember* that you wrote to your mother, but you *know* that Shakespeare wrote *Hamlet*.

6-1b IMPLICIT MEMORY

Implicit memory—also referred to as *nondeclarative memory*—is memory of how to perform a task. It is the act itself, doing something, like riding a bike, accessing your cellphone contacts list, and texting a message (Schacter et al., 1993). Implicit memories are suggested (or implied) but not plainly stated or verbally expressed. Implicit memories are illustrated by the things that people *do* but not by the things they state clearly. Implicit memories involve procedures and skills, cognitive and physical, and are also referred to as *procedural* or *skill memories*.

Implicit memories can endure even when we have not used them for years. Getting to class "by habit"—without paying attention to landmarks or directions—is another instance of implicit memory. If someone asked you what 2 times 2 is, the number 4 would probably "pop" into mind without conscious calculation. After going over the alphabet or multiplication tables hundreds of times, our memory of them becomes automatic or implicit. We need not focus on them to use them.

Your memory of the alphabet or the multiplication tables is the result of a great deal of repetition that makes associations automatic, a phenomenon that psychologists refer to as **priming**. Studies involving brain imaging reveal that priming makes it possible for people to carry out mental tasks with less neural activity (Koenig et al., 2008; Spencer et al., 2009). Years of priming help people make complete words out of the following word fragments (Friedrich et al., 2009; Schacter et al., 2007). Even though the cues in the following fragments are limited, you might make them into words:

PYGY TXT BUFL

Sample answers are "pygmy," "text," and "buffalo." Can you think of others?

Daniel Schacter (1992) illustrates implicit memory with the story of a woman with amnesia who was wandering the streets. The police picked her up and found that she could not remember who she was and that she had no identification. After fruitless interviewing, the police hit on the idea of asking her to dial phone numbers—just any number at all. When asked for the phone numbers of people she knew, she

TRUTH IT IS TRUE THAT A WOMAN WHO COULD NOT REMEMBER WHO SHE WAS AUTOMATICALLY DIALED HER MOTHER'S NUMBER WHEN THE POLICE GAVE HER A TELEPHONE.

had no answer. She could not *declare* her mother's phone number. She could not make the number *explicit*. She could not even remember her mother's name, or whether she had a mother. But dialing her mother's phone number was a habit, and she did it "on automatic pilot." We can assume that she had been *primed* for this task by dialing the number hundreds of times. Implicit memory reveals the effects of experience when we are not specifically trying to recall information.

6-1b RETROSPECTIVE MEMORY VERSUS PROSPECTIVE MEMORY

Retrospective memory is the recalling of information that has been previously learned. *Episodic, semantic,* and *implicit memories* involve remembering things that were learned. **Prospective memory** refers to remembering to do things in the future, such as remembering to pay your bills or to withdraw some cash.

Most of us have had failures of prospective memory in which we felt we were supposed to do something but couldn't remember what. Prospective memory may fail when we are preoccupied, distracted, or "stressed out" about time (Knight & Titov, 2009).

There are various kinds of prospective memory tasks. For example, *habitual tasks* such as getting to class on time are easier to remember than occasional tasks such as meeting someone for coffee at an arbitrary time (Henry et al., 2004). But motivation also plays a role. You are more likely to remember the coffee date if the person you are meeting excites you. Psychologists also

© Ocean/Corbis

implicit memory memory that is suggested (implied) but not plainly expressed, as illustrated in the things that people *do* but do not state clearly

priming the activation of specific associations in memory, often as a result of repetition and without making a conscious effort to access the memory

retrospective memory memory for past events, activities, and learning experiences, as shown by explicit (episodic and semantic) and implicit memories

prospective memory memory to perform an act in the future, as at a certain time or when a certain event occurs

encoding
modifying information so that it can be placed in memory; the first stage of information processing

storage
the maintenance of information over time; the second stage of information processing

distinguish between event-based and time-based prospective memory tasks (Fortin et al., 2002). *Event-based tasks* are triggered by events, such as remembering to take one's medicine at breakfast or to brush one's teeth after eating. *Time-based tasks* are to be performed at a certain time or after a certain amount of time has elapsed between occurrences, such as tuning in to a favorite news program at 7:30 p.m. or taking a pill every four hours (Marsh et al., 2005).

An age-related decline takes place in retrospective and prospective memories (Old & Naveh-Benjamin, 2008). Generally speaking, the decline in older adults may be related to their speed of cognitive processing rather than the "loss" of information per se. In the case of prospective memory, older adults appear about equally aware of specific cues or reminders as young adults; however, it takes them longer to respond to the cues or reminders (Old & Naveh-Benjamin, 2008). That is, if they meet with a friend, they are likely to remember that they were supposed to ask something, but it may take longer for them to remember the particular question.

Moods and attitudes affect prospective memory (Villa & Abeles, 2000). For example, depressed people are less likely to push to remind themselves to do what they intend to do (Rude et al., 1999).

Before moving to the next section, why don't you turn to the piece of paper on which you wrote the names of the four figures—that is, sheet 4—and draw them from memory as exactly as you can. Hold on to the drawings. We'll talk about them soon.

FICTION LEARNING NEED NOT ALWAYS BE MEANINGFUL IF WE ARE TO REMEMBER IT. MAINTENANCE REHEARSAL OFTEN WORKS AS WELL.

(6-2) Processes of Memory

Both psychologists and computer scientists speak of processing information. Think of using a computer to write a term paper. Once the system is up and operating, you begin to enter information. You can enter information into the computer's memory by, for example, typing alphanumeric characters on a keyboard or—in the case of voice recognition technology—speaking. But if you were to do some major surgery on your computer and open up its memory, you wouldn't find these characters or sounds inside it. This is because the computer is programmed to change the characters or sounds—the information you have entered—into a form that can be placed in its electronic memory. Similarly, when we perceive information, we must change it into a form that can be remembered if we are to place it in our memory.

6-2a ENCODING

Information about the outside world reaches our senses in the form of physical and chemical stimuli. The first stage of information processing is changing information so that we can place it in memory: **encoding**. When we encode information, we transform it into psychological formats that can be represented mentally. To do so, we commonly use visual, acoustic, and semantic codes.

Let's illustrate the uses of coding by referring to the list of letters you first saw in the section on challenges to memory. Try to write the letters on sheet number 1. Go on, take a minute, and then come back.

If you had used a *visual code* to try to remember the list, you would have mentally represented it as a picture. That is, you would have maintained—or attempted to maintain—a mental image of the letters.

You may also have decided to read the list of letters to yourself—that is, to silently say them in sequence: "t," "h," "u," and so on. By so doing, you would have been using an *acoustic code*, or representing the stimuli as a sequence of sounds. You may also have read the list as a three-syllable word, "thun-sto-fam." This is an acoustic code, but it also involves the "meaning" of the letters, in the sense that you are interpreting the list as a word. This approach has elements of a semantic code.

Semantic codes represent stimuli in terms of their meaning. Our 10 letters were meaningless in and of themselves. However, they can also serve as an acronym—a term made up of the first letters of a phrase that is pronounced as a word—for the familiar phrase "THe UNited STates OF AMerica." This observation lends them meaning.

6-2b STORAGE

The second memory process is *storage*. **Storage** means maintaining information over time. If you were given the task of storing the list of letters—that is, told to remember it—how would you attempt to place it in storage? One way would be by **maintenance rehearsal**—by mentally repeating the list, or saying it to yourself.

You could also encode the list of letters by relating it to something that you already know. This coding is called **elaborative rehearsal**. You are "elaborating" or extending the semantic meaning of the letters you are trying to remember. For example, as mentioned above, the list of 10 letters is an acronym for "The United States of America." That is, you take the first two letters of each of the words in the phrase and string them together to make up the 10 letters of THUNSTOFAM. If you had recognized this, storage of the list of letters might have been almost instantaneous, and it would probably have been permanent. But enough maintenance rehearsal can do the job.

6-2c RETRIEVAL

The third memory process is *retrieval*. **Retrieval** of stored information means locating it and returning it to consciousness. With well-known information such as our names and occupations, retrieval is effortless and rapid. But when we are trying to remember large amounts of information, or information that is not perfectly understood, retrieval can be difficult or fail. It is easiest to retrieve information stored in a computer by using the name of the file. Similarly, retrieval of information from our memories requires knowledge of the proper *retrieval cues*.

If you had encoded THUNSTOFAM as a three-syllable word, your retrieval strategy would involve recollection of the word and rules for decoding. In other words, you would say the "word" *thun-sto-fam* and then decode it by spelling it out. You might err in that "thun" sounds like "thumb" and "sto" could also be spelled "stow." However, using the semantic code, or recognition of the acronym for "The

United States of America," could lead to flawless recollection.

I predicted that you would immediately and permanently store the list if you recognized it as an acronym. Here, too, there would be recollection (of the name of a nation) and rules for decoding. That is, to "remember" the 10 letters, you would have to envision the phrase ("The United States of America") and read off the first two letters of each word. In this case, you are actually reconstructing the list of 10 letters.

But what if you were not able to remember the list of 10 letters? What would have gone wrong? In terms of the three processes of memory, it could be that you had (a) not encoded the list in a useful way, (b) not entered the encoded information into storage, or (c) stored the information but forgotten the cues for remembering it—such as the phrase "The United States of America" or the rule for decoding the phrase.

You may have noticed that we have come a long way into this chapter, but I have not yet *defined* memory. No apologies—we weren't ready. Now that we have explored some basic concepts, let's give it a try: **Memory** is the processes by which information is encoded, stored, and retrieved.

maintenance rehearsal
mental repetition of information to keep it in memory

elaborative rehearsal
the kind of coding in which new information is related to information that is already known

retrieval
the location of stored information and its return to consciousness; the third stage of information processing

memory
the processes by which information is encoded, stored, and retrieved

6-3 Stages of Memory

William James (1890) was intrigued by the fact that some memories are unreliable. They would "go in one ear and out the other," while other memories stuck for a lifetime. The world is a dazzling array of sights and

"THE STREAM OF THOUGHT FLOWS ON, BUT MOST OF ITS ELEMENTS FALL INTO THE BOTTOMLESS PIT OF OBLIVION. OF SOME, NO ELEMENT SURVIVES THE INSTANT OF THEIR PASSAGE. OF OTHERS, IT IS CONFINED TO A FEW MOMENTS, HOURS, OR DAYS. OTHERS, AGAIN, LEAVE VESTIGES WHICH ARE INDESTRUCTIBLE, AND BY MEANS OF WHICH THEY MAY BE RECALLED AS LONG AS LIFE ENDURES."
—WILLIAM JAMES

sensory memory
the type or stage of memory first encountered by a stimulus; sensory memory holds impressions briefly, but long enough so that series of perceptions are psychologically continuous

sounds and other sources of sensory information, but only some of it is remembered. Psychologists Richard Atkinson and Richard Shiffrin (1968) suggested a model for how some information is lost immediately, other information is held briefly, and still other information is held for a lifetime. As shown in Figure 6.1, they proposed three stages of memory that determine whether (and how long) information is retained: *sensory memory*, *short-term memory* (STM), and *long-term memory* (LTM).

6-3a SENSORY MEMORY

When we look at a visual stimulus, our impressions may seem fluid enough. Actually, however, they consist of a series of eye fixations referred to as *saccadic eye movements*. These movements jump from one point to another about four times each second. Yet the visual sensations seem continuous, or streamlike, because of **sensory memory**. Sensory memory is the type or stage of memory that is first encountered by a stimulus. Although sensory memory holds impressions briefly, it is long enough so that a series of perceptions seem to be connected.

FIGURE 6.1 | Three Stages of Memory: The Atkinson–Shiffrin Model

The Atkinson–Shiffrin model proposes that there are three stages of memory: (a) sensory memory, (b) short-term memory, and (c) long-term memory. Part A shows that sensory information impacts on the registers of the sensory memory. Memory traces are held briefly in sensory memory before decaying. If we attend to the information, much of it can be transferred to short-term memory (STM). Part B: Information may be maintained in STM through maintenance rehearsal or elaborative rehearsal. Otherwise, it may decay or be displaced. Part C: Once information is transferred to long-term memory (LTM), it may be filed away indefinitely. However, if the information in LTM is organized poorly, or if we cannot find cues to retrieve it, it can be lost.

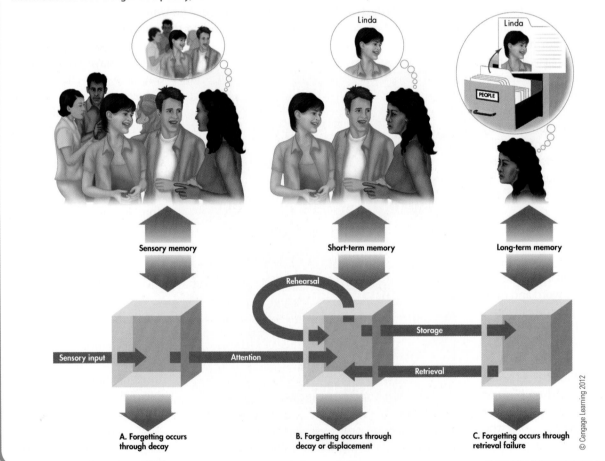

© Cengage Learning 2012

To understand the functioning of sensory memory, let's return to our list of letters: THUNSTOFAM. If the list were flashed on a screen for a fraction of a second, the visual impression, or **memory trace**, of the stimulus would also last for only a fraction of a second afterward. Psychologists speak of the memory trace of the list as being held in a visual *sensory register*.

If the letters had been flashed on a screen for, say, 1/10th of a second, your ability to remember them on the basis of sensory memory alone would be limited. Your memory would be based on a single eye fixation, and the trace of the image would vanish before a single second had passed. A century ago, psychologist William McDougall (1904) engaged in research in which he showed people one to 12 letters arranged in rows—just long enough to allow a single eye fixation. Under these conditions, people could typically remember only four or five letters. Thus, recollection of THUNSTOFAM, a list of 10 letters arranged in a single row, would probably depend on whether one had encoded it so that it could be processed further.

George Sperling (1960) modified McDougall's experimental method and showed that there is a difference between what people can see and what they can report. McDougall had used a *whole-report procedure*, in which people were asked to report every letter they saw in the array. Sperling used a modified *partial-report procedure*, in which people were asked to report the contents of one of three rows of letters. In a typical procedure, Sperling flashed three rows of letters like the following on a screen for 50 milliseconds (1/20th of a second):

A G R E

V L S B

N K B T

Using the whole-report procedure, people could report an average of four letters from the entire display (one out of three). But if immediately after presenting the display Sperling pointed an arrow at a row he wanted viewers to report, they usually reported most of the letters in the row successfully.

If Sperling presented six letters arrayed in two rows, people could usually report either row without error. If people were flashed three rows of four letters each—a total of 12—they reported correctly an average of three of four letters in the designated row, suggesting that about nine of the 12 letters had been perceived.

Sperling found that the amount of time that elapsed before he pointed to the row to be reported affected people's memory. If he delayed pointing for a few fractions of a second after showing the letters, people were less successful in reporting the letters in the row. If he allowed a full second to elapse, the arrow did not help people remember at all. Sperling concluded that the memory trace of visual stimuli *decays* within a second (see Figure 6.1). With a single eye fixation, people can *see* most of a display of 12 letters clearly, as shown by their ability to immediately read off most of the letters in a designated row. Yet as fractions of a second are elapsing, the memory trace of the letters is fading. By the time a full second elapses, the trace is gone.

"The true art of memory is the art of attention."

–DR. SAMUEL JOHNSON

Iconic Memory

Psychologists believe we possess a sensory register for each sense. The mental representations of visual stimuli are referred to as **icons**. The sensory register that holds icons is labeled **iconic memory**. Iconic memories are accurate, photographic memories. If you can see and are not neurologically impaired, you have a "photographic memory." But such memories are brief. What most of us usually think of as a photographic memory—the ability to retain exact mental representations of visual stimuli over long periods—is technically termed **eidetic imagery**. Only a few people are capable of eidetic imagery.

memory trace
an assumed change in the nervous system that reflects the impression made by a stimulus

icon
a mental representation of a visual stimulus that is held briefly in sensory memory

iconic memory
the sensory register that briefly holds mental representations of visual stimuli

eidetic imagery
the maintenance of detailed visual memories over several minutes

echo
a mental representation of an auditory stimulus (sound) that is held briefly in sensory memory

echoic memory
the sensory register that briefly holds mental representations of auditory stimuli

short-term memory
the type or stage of memory that can hold information for up to a minute or so after the trace of the stimulus decays; also called *working memory*

working memory
another term for *short-term memory*

Iconic Memory and Saccadic Eye Movements

As mentioned previously, saccadic eye movements occur about four times a second. But iconic memory holds icons for up to a second. For this reason, the flow of visual information seems smooth and continuous. Your impression that the words you are reading flow across the page, rather than jumping across in spurts, is a product of your iconic memory. Similarly, motion pictures present 16 to 22 separate frames, or still images, each second, but iconic memory allows you to perceive the imagery in the film as being seamless (Demeyer et al., 2009).

Echoic Memory

Mental representations of sounds, or auditory stimuli, are called **echoes**. **Echoic memory** is the sensory register that holds echoes.

The memory traces of auditory stimuli—echoes—can last for several seconds, many times longer than the traces of visual stimuli (icons). This difference is one of the reasons that acoustic codes aid in the retention of information that has been presented visually—or why saying the letters or syllables of THUNSTOFAM makes the list easier to remember.

6-3b SHORT-TERM MEMORY

Imagine you are completing a writing assignment, and you key or speak words and phrases into your word-processing program. They appear on your monitor as a sign that your computer has them in *memory*. Your word-processing program allows you to add words, delete words, check whether they are spelled correctly, add images, and move paragraphs from place to place. Although you can manipulate the information in your computer's memory, it isn't saved. It hasn't been entered into storage. If the program or the computer crashes, the information is gone. The computer's memory is a short-term affair. To maintain a long-term connection with the information, you have to save it. Saving it means giving it a name—hopefully, a name that you will remember so that you can later find and retrieve the information—and instructing your computer to save it (keep it in storage until told otherwise).

If you focus on a stimulus in the sensory register, you will tend to retain it in your own **short-term memory**—also referred to as **working memory**—for a minute or so after the trace of the stimulus decays. As one researcher describes it, "Working memory is the mental glue that links a thought through time from its beginning to its end" (Goldman-Rakic, 1995). When you are given a new phone number and write it down or immediately dial the number, you are retaining the number in your short-term memory. When you are told the name of someone at a party and then use that name immediately in addressing that person, you are retaining the name in short-term memory. In short-term memory, the image tends to fade significantly after 10 to 12 seconds if it is not repeated or rehearsed. It is possible to focus on maintaining a visual image in the short-term memory, but it is more common to encode visual stimuli as sounds, or auditory stimuli. Then the sounds can be rehearsed, or repeated.

These actors are memorizing a script by rehearsing echoic memories. As actors work on memorizing scripts, they first encode visual information (printed words) as echoes (their corresponding sounds within the brain). Then they commit the echoes to memory by rehearsing (repeating) them, referring back to the visual information as necessary. Eventually, the lines of other actors become cues that trigger memory of an actor's own lines.

Once information is in our short-term memories, we can work on it. Like the information in the word-processing program, we can manipulate it. But it isn't necessarily saved. If we don't do something to save—such as write down a new telephone number or key it into your cellphone's contact list—it can be gone forever. You need to rehearse new information to "save" it, but you may need only the proper cue to retrieve information from long-term memory.

Let's now return to the task of remembering the first list of letters in the challenges to memory at the beginning of the chapter. If you had encoded the letters as the three-syllable "word" THUN-STO-FAM, you would probably have recalled them by mentally rehearsing (saying to yourself) the three-syllable "word" and then spelling it out from the sounds. A few minutes later, if someone asked whether the letters had been uppercase (THUNSTOFAM) or lowercase (thunstofam), you might not have been able to answer with confidence. You used an acoustic code to help recall the list, and uppercase and lowercase letters sound alike.

Because it can be pronounced, THUNSTOFAM is not too difficult to retain in short-term memory. But what if the list of letters had been TBXLFNTSDK? This list of letters cannot be pronounced as it is. You would have to find a complex acronym to code these letters, and do so within a fraction of a second—most likely an impossible task. To aid recall, you would probably choose to try to repeat the letters rapidly—to read each one as many times as possible before the memory trace fades. You might visualize each letter as you say it and try to get back to it (that is, to run through the entire list) before it decays.

Let's assume that you encoded the letters as sounds and then rehearsed the sounds. When asked to report the list, you might mistakenly say T-V-X-L-F-N-T-S-T-K. This would be an understandable error because the incorrect V and T sounds are similar, respectively, to the correct B and D sounds.

The Serial-Position Effect

If asked to recall the list of letters TBXLFNTSDK, you would be likely to recall the first and last letters in the series, T and K, more accurately than the others. The tendency to recall the first and last items in a series is known as the **serial-position effect**. This effect may occur because we pay more attention to the first and last stimuli in a series. They serve as the visual or auditory boundaries for the other stimuli. In addition, the first items are likely to be rehearsed more frequently (repeated more times) than other items. The last items are likely to have been rehearsed most recently and hence are most likely to be retained in short-term memory.

Chunking

Rapidly rehearsing 10 meaningless letters is not an easy task. With TBXLFNTSDK there are 10 discrete elements, or **chunks**, of information that must be kept in short-term memory. When we encode THUNSTOFAM as three syllables, there are only three chunks to memorize at once—a memory task that is much easier on the digestion.

As noted earlier, psychologist George Miller (1956) found that the average person is comfortable with remembering about seven integers at a time, the number of integers in a telephone number. Businesses pay the phone company hefty premiums so that they can attain numbers with two or three zeroes or repeated digits—for example, 592-2000 or 272-3333. These numbers include fewer chunks of information and so are easier to remember. Customer recollection of business phone numbers increases sales. A financial services company might use the toll-free number CALL-IRA, which reduces the task to two chunks of information that also happen to be meaningfully related (semantically coded) to the nature of the business.

Return to the third challenge to memory presented earlier. Were you able to remember the six groups of letters (GMC-BSI-BMA-TTC-IAF-BI)? Would your task have been simpler if you had grouped them differently? How about moving the dashes forward by a letter, so that they read GM-CBS-IBM-ATT-CIA-FBI? If we do this, we have the same list of letters, but we also have six chunks of information that can be coded semantically (according to what they mean). You may have also been able to generate the list by remembering a rule, such as "big corporations and government agencies."

Reconsider the second challenge to memory presented earlier. You were asked to remember nine chunks of visual information. Perhaps you could have used the acoustic codes "L" and "Square" for chunks three and five, but no obvious codes are available for the seven other chunks. Now look at Figure 6.2. If you had recognized that the elements in the challenge could be arranged as the familiar tic-tac-toe grid, remembering the nine elements might have required two chunks of information. The first would have been the mental image of the grid, and the second would have been the rule for decoding: Each element corresponds to the shape of a section of the grid if read like words on a page (from upper left to lower right). The number sequence 1 through 9 would not in itself present a problem, because you learned this series by rote many years ago and have rehearsed it in countless calculations since then.

displace
in memory theory, to cause information to be lost from short-term memory by adding new information

long-term memory
the type or stage of memory capable of relatively permanent storage

repression
in Freud's psychodynamic theory, the ejection of anxiety-evoking ideas from conscious awareness

FIGURE 6.2 | A Familiar Grid

The nine drawings in the second challenge to memory form this familiar tic-tac-toe grid when the numbers are placed inside them and they are arranged in order. This method for recalling the shapes collapses nine chunks of information into two. One is the tic-tac-toe grid. The second is the rule for decoding the drawings from the grid.

© Cengage Learning 2012

Interference in Short-Term Memory

In a classic experiment with college students, Lloyd and Margaret Peterson (1959) demonstrated how prevention of rehearsal can wreak havoc with short-term memory. They asked students to remember three-letter combinations such as HGB—normally, three easy chunks of information. They then had the students count backward from an arbitrary number, such as 181, by threes (that is, 181, 178, 175, 172, and so on). The students were told to stop counting and to report the letter sequence after the intervals of time shown in Figure 6.3. The percentage of correctly recalled letter combinations fell dramatically within seconds. Counting backward for 18 seconds had dislodged the letter sequences in almost all of these bright students' memories.

Psychologists say that the appearance of new information in short-term memory **displaces** the old information. Remember: Only a few bits of information can be retained in short-term memory at the same time.

6-3c LONG-TERM MEMORY

Long-term memory is the third stage of information processing (refer back to Figure 6.1). Think of your long-term memory as a vast storehouse of information containing names, dates, places, what Johnny did to you in second grade, and what Susan said about you when you were 12.

Some psychologists (Freud was one) believed that nearly all of our perceptions and ideas are stored permanently. We might not be able to retrieve all of them, however. Some memories might be "lost" because of lack of proper cues. Still others might be kept unconscious by the forces of **repression**. Adherents to this view often pointed to the work of neurosurgeon Wilder Penfield (1969). When parts of their brains were electrically stimulated, many of Penfield's patients reported the appearance of images that had something of the feel of memories.

Today, most psychologists view this notion as exaggerated. Memory researcher Elizabeth Loftus, for example, notes that the "memories" stimulated by Penfield's probes lacked detail and were sometimes incorrect (e.g., Bernstein & Loftus, 2009). Therefore, it has *not* been

FIGURE 6.3 | The Effect of Interference on Short-Term Memory

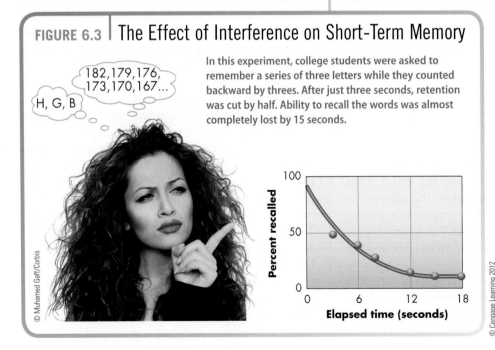

In this experiment, college students were asked to remember a series of three letters while they counted backward by threes. After just three seconds, retention was cut by half. Ability to recall the words was almost completely lost by 15 seconds.

© Muhamed Gaff/Corbis

© Cengage Learning 2012

shown that all of our experiences are permanently imprinted on the brain. Now let's consider some other questions about long-term memory.

How Accurate Are Long-Term Memories?

Psychologist Elizabeth Loftus notes that memories are distorted by our biases and needs—by the ways in which we conceptualize our worlds. We represent much of our world in the form of **schemas**. A *schema* is a way of mentally representing the world, such as a belief or expectation, that can influence our perception of persons, objects, and situations.

FICTION — NOT ALL EXPERIENCES ARE PERMANENTLY IMPRINTED ON THE BRAIN.

Now, retrieve sheet number 4. You drew the figures "from memory" according to instructions on page 136. Now look at Figure 6.4. Are your drawings closer in form to those in group 1 or to those in group 2? I wouldn't be surprised if they were more like those in group 1—if, for example, your first drawing looked more like eyeglasses than a dumbbell. After all, they were labeled like the drawings in group 1. The labels serve as *schemas* for the drawings—ways of organizing your knowledge of them—and these schemas may have influenced your recollections. By the way, take out a penny and look at it. Did you pick the correct penny when you answered the challenges to memory?

How Much Information Can Be Stored in Long-Term Memory?

How many terabytes of storage are there in your most personal computer—your brain? Unlike a computer, the human ability to store information is, for all practical purposes, unlimited (Voss, 2009; Y. Wang et al., 2009). Even the largest hard drives fill up when we save Web pages, pictures, or videos. Yet how many "movies" of the past have you saved in your own long-term memory? How many thousands of scenes and stories can you rerun at will? And, assuming that you have an intact sensory system, the movies in your personal storage bins not only have color and sound but also aromas, tactile sensations, and more. *Your long-term memory is a biochemical "hard drive" with no known limits on the amount of information it can store.*

New information may replace older information in short-term memory, but there is no evidence that long-term memories—those in "storage"—are lost by displacement. Long-term memories may endure a lifetime. Now and then, it may seem that we have forgotten, or "lost," a long-term memory such as the names of elementary-school classmates, yet it may be that we

schema
a way of mentally representing the world, such as a belief or an expectation, that can influence perception of persons, objects, and situations

FIGURE 6.4 | Memory as Reconstructive

Figures shown	Group 1	Group 2
	Eyeglasses	Dumbbell
	Hourglass	Table
	Seven	Four
	Gun	Broom

In their classic experiment, Carmichael, Hogan, and Walter (1932) showed people the figures in the left box and made remarks as suggested in the other boxes. For example, the experimenter might say, "This drawing looks like eyeglasses [or a dumbbell]." When people later reconstructed the drawings, they were influenced by the labels.

© Cengage Learning 2012

cannot find the proper cues to retrieve them. However, if you drive by your elementary school (a cue) you might suddenly recall the long-lost names of schoolteachers.

Levels of Processing Information

People who use elaborative rehearsal (the kind of coding in which new information is related to information that is already known) to remember things are *processing information at a deeper level* than people who use maintenance rehearsal (mental repetition of information to keep it in memory). Fergus Craik and Robert Lockhart (2008) pioneered the *levels-of-processing model of memory*, which holds that memories tend to endure when information is processed *deeply*—attended to, encoded carefully, pondered, and related to things we already know. Remembering relies on how carefully they attend to information and how *deeply* they process it, not on whether memories are transferred from one *stage* of memory to another. If you are bombarded by one name after another at a cocktail party, it may be easier for you to recall the name of your first-grade teacher—someone with whom you had countless interactions—than the name of someone you just met.

TRUTH IT IS TRUE THAT IT MAY BE EASIER TO RECALL THE NAME OF YOUR FIRST GRADE TEACHER THAN THOSE OF PEOPLE YOU HAVE JUST MET. YOU LEARNED THEIR NAMES MORE RECENTLY, BUT YOU HAD COUNTLESS MEANINGFUL INTERACTIONS WITH YOUR FIRST GRADE TEACHER.

Think of all the math problems we solved in high school. Each problem is an application of a procedure and, perhaps, of certain formulas. By repeatedly applying the procedures and formulas in slightly different contexts, we rehearse them elaboratively. As a result, we are more likely to remember them.

There is also a good deal of biologically oriented research that connects deep processing with activity in certain parts of the brain, notably the prefrontal area of the cerebral cortex (Barbey & Barsalou, 2009; Luo & Craik, 2009). One reason that older adults show memory loss is that they tend not to process information quite as deeply as younger people do (Craik & Bialystok, 2006; Schneider-Garces et al., 2010). Deep processing requires sustained attention, and older adults, along with people who have suffered brain injuries and strokes, are apparently not capable of focusing their attention as well as they had previously (Willmott et al., 2009).

Flashbulb Memories

Why are some events, like the attack of September 11, 2001, etched in memory for a lifetime? It appears that we tend to remember events that are surprising, important, and emotionally stirring more clearly. Such events can create *flashbulb memories*, which preserve experiences in detail (Hirst et al., 2009) even if those details are sometimes reconstructed, as is the case with other memories (Kvavilashvili et al., 2009). Why is the memory etched when the "flashbulb" goes off? One factor is the distinctness of the memory. It is easier to discriminate stimuli that stand out. Such events are striking in themselves. The feelings caused by them are also special. It is thus relatively easy to pick them out from the storehouse of memories. Major events such as the assassination of a president or the loss of a close relative also tend to have important effects on our lives. We are likely to dwell on them and form networks of associations. That is, we are likely to rehearse them elaboratively. Our rehearsal may include great expectations, or deep fears, for the future. Therefore, you may always recall where you were and what you were doing on the morning of September 11, 2001, when terrorists attacked the World Trade Center and the Pentagon.

Why is it that some events, such as the terrorist attack of September 11, 2001, can be etched in memory for a lifetime?

AP Photo/Carmen Taylor

TRUTH IT IS TRUE THAT THE "FLASHBULB" IN YOUR MEMORY PROBABLY WENT OFF ON SEPTEMBER 11, 2001, EVEN THOUGH YOU WERE QUITE A BIT YOUNGER THAN YOU ARE NOW AND THAT EVENT OCCURRED MORE THAN 10 YEARS AGO. YOU MAY RECALL WHERE YOU WERE AND WHAT YOU WERE DOING AT THE TIME FOR DECADES TO COME.

Biology is intimately connected with psychology. Strong feelings are connected with the secretion of stress hormones, and stress hormones help carve events into memory—"as almost to leave a scar upon the cerebral tissues," as noted by William James.

Organization in Long-Term Memory

The storehouse of long-term memory is usually well organized. Items are not just piled on the floor or thrown into closets. We tend to gather information about rats and cats into a certain section of the storehouse, perhaps the animal or mammal section. We put information about oaks, maples, and eucalyptus into the tree section. Such categorization of stimuli is a basic cognitive function. It allows us to make predictions about specific instances and to store information efficiently.

We tend to organize information according to a *hierarchical structure*, as shown in Figure 6.5. A *hierarchy* is an arrangement of items (or chunks of information) into groups or classes according to common or distinct features. As we work our way up the hierarchy shown in the figure, we find more encompassing, or *superordinate*, classes to which the items below them belong. For example, all mammals are animals, but there are many types of animals other than mammals.

When items are correctly organized in long-term memory, you are more likely to recall—or know—accurate information about them. For example, do you "remember" whether whales breathe underwater? If you did not know that whales are mammals (or in Figure 6.5, *subordinate* to mammals), or if you knew nothing about mammals, a correct answer might depend on some remote instance of rote learning. That is, you might be depending on chancy episodic memory rather than on reliable semantic memory. For example, you might recall some details from a TV documentary on whales. If you *did* know that whales are mammals, however, you would also know—or remember—that whales do not breathe underwater. How? You would reconstruct information about whales from knowledge about mammals, the group to which whales are subordinate. Similarly, you would know, or remember, that because they are mammals, whales are warm-blooded, nurse their young, and are a good deal more intelligent than, say, tunas and sharks, which are fish. Had you incorrectly classified whales as fish, you might have searched your memory and constructed the incorrect answer that they do breathe underwater.

Your memory is thus organized according to a remarkably complex filing system that has a certain inter-

FIGURE 6.5 | The Hierarchical Structure of Long-Term Memory

Where are whales filed in the hierarchical cabinets of your memory? Your classification of whales may influence your answers to these questions: Do whales breathe underwater? Are they warm-blooded? Do they nurse their young? A note to biological purists: This figure is not intended to represent phyla, classes, orders, and so on accurately. Rather, it shows how an individual's classification scheme might be organized.

Living Things — Animals, Plants
Animals — Mammals, Fish
Plants — Shrubs, Trees
Mammals — Monkeys, Whales?, Rats
Fish — Tuna, Whales?, Sticklebacks
Trees — Eucalyptus, Oaks, Maples

© Cengage Learning 2012

tip-of-the-tongue (TOT) phenomenon
the feeling that information is stored in memory although it cannot be readily retrieved; also called the *feeling-of-knowing experience*

context-dependent memory
information that is better retrieved in the context in which it was encoded and stored, or learned

nal logic. If you place a piece of information into the wrong file, it is probably not the fault of the filing system itself. Nevertheless, you may "lose" the information in the sense of not being able to find the best cues to retrieve it.

"It's **déjà vu** all over again."
—YOGI BERRA

The Tip-of-the-Tongue Phenomenon

Having something on the tip of your tongue can be a frustrating experience. Psychologists term this experience the **tip-of-the-tongue (TOT) phenomenon**, or the *feeling-of-knowing experience*.

Research provides insight into the TOT phenomenon (Brown & McNeill, 1966; Galdo-Alvarez et al., 2009; Schwartz, 2008). In classic research, Brown and McNeill (1966) defined some rather unusual words for students, such as *sampan*, a small riverboat used in China and Japan. The students were then asked to recall the words they had learned. Some of the students often had the right word "on the tip of their tongue" but reported words with similar meanings such as *junk, barge,* or *houseboat*. Still other students reported words that sounded similar, such as *Saipan, Siam, sarong,* and *sanching*. Why?

To begin with, the words were unfamiliar, so elaborative rehearsal did not take place. The students did not have an opportunity to relate the words to other things they knew. Brown and McNeill also suggested that our storage systems are indexed according to cues that include both the sounds and the meanings of words—that is, according to both acoustic and semantic codes. By scanning words similar in sound and meaning to the word on the tip of the tongue, we sometimes find a useful cue and retrieve the word for which we are searching.

Sometimes an answer seems to be on the tip of our tongue because our learning of the topic is incomplete. We may not know the exact answer, but we know something. (As a matter of fact, if we have good writing skills, we may present our incomplete knowledge so forcefully that we earn a good grade on an essay question on the topic!) At such times, the problem lies not in retrieval but in the original processes of learning and memory—that is, encoding and storage.

Context-Dependent Memory

The context in which we acquire information can also play a role in retrieval. I remember walking down the halls of the apartment building where I had lived as a child. Cooking odors triggered a sudden assault of images of playing under the staircase, of falling against a radiator, of the shrill voice of a former neighbor calling for her child at dinnertime. Odors, it turns out, are particularly likely to trigger related memories (Lee et al., 2009).

My experience was an example of a **context-dependent memory**. My memories were particularly clear in the context in which they were formed. It could also be helpful, if possible, to study in the same room in which a test will be given. Being in the proper context—for example, studying in the exam room or under the same conditions—can dramatically enhance recall (Isarida & Isarida, 2006).

According to a study with 20 bilingual Cornell students, the "context" for memory extends to language (Marian & Neisser, 2000). The students emigrated from Russia at an average age of 14 and were an average of about 22 years old at the time of the experiment. They were asked to recall the details of experiences in Russia and the United States. When they were interviewed in Russian, they were better able to retrieve experiences from their lives in Russia. Similarly, when they were interviewed in English, they were better able to recall events that happened in the United States.

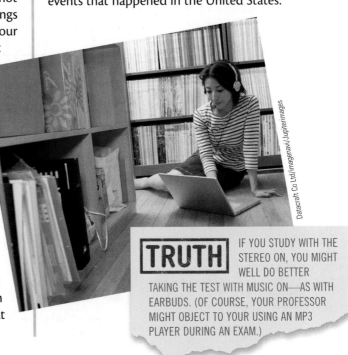

Datacraft Co Ltd/imagenavi/Jupiterimages

TRUTH IF YOU STUDY WITH THE STEREO ON, YOU MIGHT WELL DO BETTER TAKING THE TEST WITH MUSIC ON—AS WITH EARBUDS. (OF COURSE, YOUR PROFESSOR MIGHT OBJECT TO YOUR USING AN MP3 PLAYER DURING AN EXAM.)

6-5b BRAIN STRUCTURES AND MEMORY

Memory does not reside in a single structure of the brain. Memory relies on complex neural networks that draw on various parts of the brain (Nyberg et al., 2000). However, some parts of the brain play more specific roles in memory. The hippocampus is vital in storing new information even if we can retrieve old information without it (Squire, 2009). But the hippocampus is not a storage bin. Rather, it is involved in relaying sensory information to parts of the cortex.

Where are the storage bins? The brain stores parts of memories in the appropriate areas of the sensory cortex. Sights are stored in the visual cortex, sounds in the auditory cortex, and so on. The limbic system is largely responsible for integrating these pieces of information when we recall an event.

However, the frontal lobes apparently store information about where and when events occur (Chafee & Goldman-Rakic, 2000; C. R. E. Wilson et al., 2008).

But what of the decision to try to recall something? What of the spark of consciousness that drives us to move backward in time or to strive to remember to do something in the future? The prefrontal cortex (see

✳ Can We Trust Eyewitness Testimony?

Jean Piaget, the investigator of children's cognitive development, distinctly remembered an attempt to kidnap him from his baby carriage as he was being wheeled along the Champs Élysées. He recalled the excited throng, the abrasions on the face of the nurse who rescued him, the police officer's white baton, and the flight of the assailant. Although they were graphic, Piaget's memories were false. Years later, the nurse admitted that she had made up the tale. Piaget had fallen victim to an example of what psychologists term the **misinformation effect**. The false information provided by his nurse became implanted in his own memory.

Can eyewitness testimony be trusted? Is there reason to believe that the statements of eyewitnesses are any more factual than Piaget's?

One problem with eyewitness testimony is that the words chosen by an experimenter—and those chosen by a lawyer interrogating a witness—have been shown to influence the reconstruction of memories (Cutler & Kovera, 2010). For example, as in the experiment described earlier, an attorney for the plaintiff might ask the witness, "How fast was the defendant's car going when it *smashed into* the plaintiff's car?" In such a case, the car might be reported as going faster than if the question had been: "How fast was the defendant's car going when the accident occurred?" (Loftus & Palmer, 1974). Could the attorney for the defendant claim that the use of the word *smashed* biased the witness? What about jurors who heard the word *smashed*? Would they be biased toward assuming that the driver had been reckless?

Children tend to be more suggestible witnesses than adults, and preschoolers are more suggestible than older children (Ceci et al., 2007;

© Rubberball/Corbis

How trustworthy is eyewitness testimony? Memories are reconstructive rather than photographic. The wording of questions also influences the content of the memory. Attorneys therefore are sometimes instructed not to phrase questions in such a way that they "lead" the witness.

Cutler & Kovera, 2010; Krähenbühl et al., 2009). But when questioned properly, even young children may provide accurate and useful testimony (Ceci et al., 2007; Krähenbühl et al., 2009).

There are also problems in the identification of criminals by eyewitnesses. For one thing, witnesses may pay more attention to the suspect's clothing than to more meaningful characteristics such as facial features, height, and weight. In one experiment, viewers of a videotaped crime incorrectly identified a man as the criminal because he wore the eyeglasses and T-shirt that had been worn by the perpetrator on the tape. The man who had actually committed the crime was identified less often (Sanders, 1984).

Other problems with eyewitness testimony include the following (Cutler & Kovera, 2010):

• Identification is less accurate when suspects belong to ethnic or racial groups that differ from that of the witness.

• Identification of suspects is compromised when interrogators make misleading suggestions.

• Witnesses are seen as more credible when they claim to be certain in their testimony, but there is little evidence that claims of certainty are accurate.

Thus, there are many problems with eyewitness testimony. Yet even Elizabeth Loftus (e.g., Wright & Loftus, 2008), who has extensively studied the accuracy of eyewitness testimony, agrees that it is a valuable tool in the courtroom. After all, identifications made by eyewitnesses are frequently correct, and what, Loftus asks, would be the alternative to the use of eyewitnesses? If we were to prevent eyewitnesses from testifying, how many criminals would go free?

✳ The Relationships Among the Various Kinds of Memories

Memories can address past events (*retrospective memories*) or future events (*prospective memories*). Memories of the past can be *explicit* (declarative) or *implicit* (nondeclarative). Explicit memories include memories of personal episodes (which are called *episodic or autobiographical memories*) or of general information (*semantic memories*).

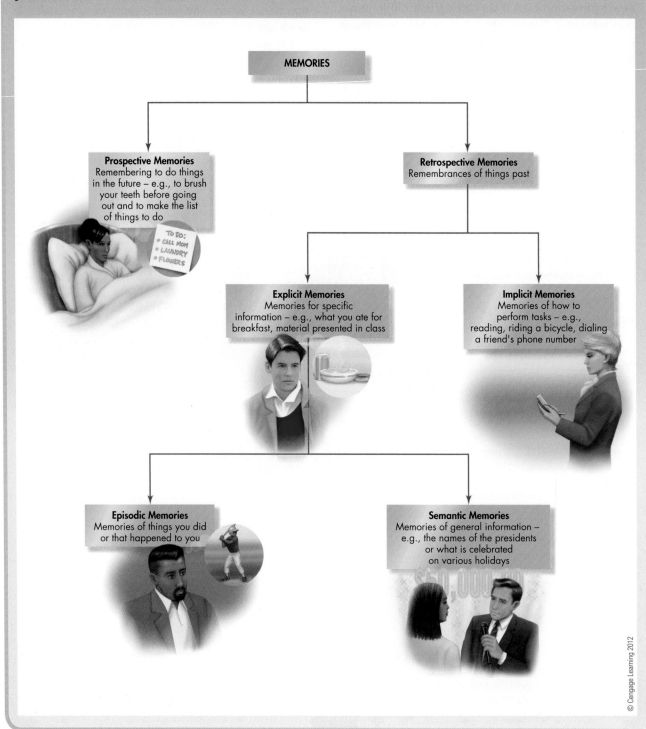

MEMORIES

Prospective Memories
Remembering to do things in the future – e.g., to brush your teeth before going out and to make the list of things to do

TO DO:
• CALL MOM
• LAUNDRY
• FLOWERS

Retrospective Memories
Remembrances of things past

Explicit Memories
Memories for specific information – e.g., what you ate for breakfast, material presented in class

Implicit Memories
Memories of how to perform tasks – e.g., reading, riding a bicycle, dialing a friend's phone number

Episodic Memories
Memories of things you did or that happened to you

Semantic Memories
Memories of general information – e.g., the names of the presidents or what is celebrated on various holidays

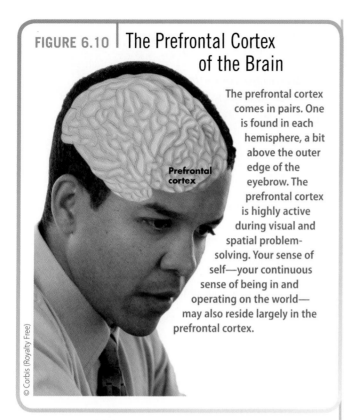

FIGURE 6.10 | The Prefrontal Cortex of the Brain

Prefrontal cortex

The prefrontal cortex comes in pairs. One is found in each hemisphere, a bit above the outer edge of the eyebrow. The prefrontal cortex is highly active during visual and spatial problem-solving. Your sense of self—your continuous sense of being in and operating on the world—may also reside largely in the prefrontal cortex.

© Corbis (Royalty Free)

Figure 6.10) is the executive center in memory (Christ et al., 2009; Wheeler & Treisman, 2002). It appears to empower people with consciousness—the ability to mentally represent and become aware of experiences that occur in the past, present, and future. It enables people to mentally travel back in time to reexperience the personal, autobiographical past. It enables people to focus on the things they intend to do in the future, such as mail a letter on the way to class or brush their teeth before going to bed.

The hippocampus is also involved in the where and when of things (Eichenbaum & Fortin, 2003). The hippocampus does not become mature until we are about two years old. Immaturity may be connected with infantile amnesia. Adults with hippocampal damage may be able to form new procedural memories, even though they cannot form new episodic ("where and when") memories (Fields, 2005). They can develop new skills even though they cannot recall the practice sessions (Squire & Kandel, 2008).

The thalamus is involved in the formation of verbal memories. Part of the thalamus of an Air Force cadet known as N. A. was damaged in a fencing accident. Afterward, N. A. could no longer form verbal memories, but he could form visual memories (Squire, 2004). (One might measure visual memory by showing people pictures, allowing time to pass, and then asking them to point out those they have been shown.)

The encoding, storage, and retrieval of information thus involve biological activity. As we learn, new synapses are developed, and changes occur at existing synapses. Parts of the brain are also involved in the formation of memories. In the next chapter, we see how people manipulate information they have stored to adapt to the environment or create new environments.

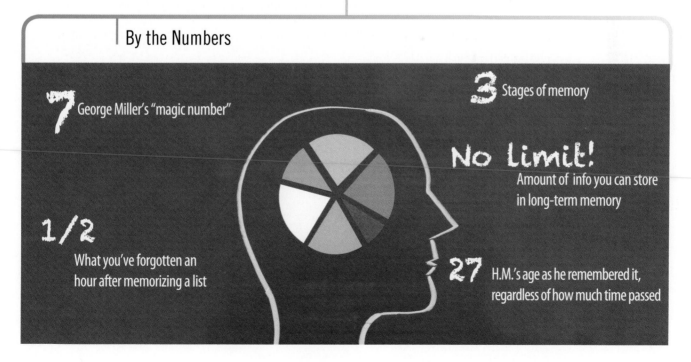

By the Numbers

7 George Miller's "magic number"

3 Stages of memory

No Limit! Amount of info you can store in long-term memory

1/2 What you've forgotten an hour after memorizing a list

27 H.M.'s age as he remembered it, regardless of how much time passed

STUDY TOOLS ▶ 6

Ready to study? In the book, you can:

- ❍ Review what you've read with Fill-Ins and Multiple Choice quizzes (below).
- ❍ Rip out Chapter Review card (in the back).

Or you can go online to CourseMate at www.cengagebrain.com for these resources:

- ❍ Complete Practices Quizzes to prepare for tests.
- ❍ Review Key Terms Flash Cards (online or print).
- ❍ Play games to master concepts.

FILL-INS

Answers can be found in the back of the book, starting on page 368.

1. Memories of the events that happen to a person are _____ memories.

2. _____ memories concern generalized knowledge.

3. One way of storing information is by _____ rehearsal, or by mentally repeating it.

4. Another way of storing information is by _____ rehearsal, when we relate new information to things we already know.

5. The Atkinson–Shiffrin model hypothesizes three stages of memory: _____, _____-_____, and _____-_____.

6. _____ imagery is the ability to retain exact mental representations of visual stimuli over long periods of time.

7. Detailed memories of surprising, important, and emotional events are termed _____ memories.

8. In _____ interference, new learning interferes with the retrieval of old learning.

9. In _____ interference, older learning interferes with the capacity to retrieve more recently learned material.

10. Experience enhances the avenues of communication among brain cells by development of dendrites and _____.

1. Remembering what you had for dinner is an example of _____. memory.
   a. implicit
   b. episodic
   c. dependent
   d. semantic

2. Hamilton told himself to remember to get three things at the corner deli. On the way to the store, he ran into Jason and chatted for a few minutes. Afterward, he could only remember two of the items. Chatting with Jason had apparently interfered with Hamilton's
   a. episodic memory.
   b. semantic memory.
   c. prospective memory.
   d. implicit memory.

3. You recall what you ate for breakfast this morning, but you know who wrote Hamlet. Your knowledge that Shakespeare wrote Hamlet is an example of
   a. episodic memory.
   b. prospective memory.
   c. implicit memory.
   d. semantic memory.

4. Breaking THUNSTOFAM into three syllables THUN-STO-FAM and then repeating them many times in an effort to remember the ten letters is an example of using the techniques of
   a. chunking and maintenance rehearsal.
   b. encoding and elaborative rehearsal.
   c. sensory memory and short-term memory.
   d. working memory and semantic memory.

5. Tracy took tennis lessons when she was very young but had not played tennis for years when she decided to enroll in a tennis class at college. A moment after she picked up her racket, she realized with surprise that she had shifted it to the correct forehand grip without even thinking. Tracy's _____. memory made this possible.
   a. implicit
   b. episodic
   c. psychomotor
   d. semantic

6. If you learn how to do something once, and then forget it, what is most likely to happen if you attempt to relearn it?
   a. Anxiety will interfere with your ability to relearn it.
   b. The original learning will be on the tip of your tongue.
   c. Your hippocampus will be flooded with dopamine.
   d. You will relearn it more quickly than you originally learned it.

7. The process of modifying information so that we can place it in memory is called
   a. storing.
   b. memorizing.
   c. encoding.
   d. programming.

8. Mentally repeating a list or saying it to yourself refers to
   a. metamemory.
   b. elaborative rehearsal.
   c. retrospective memory.
   d. maintenance rehearsal.

9. Evan met Lesley at a party three weeks ago. He bumps into her on the way to class. He feels as though he knows her name but he just can't retrieve the information. This experience is referred to as
   a. mnemonic failure.
   b. tip-of-the-tongue phenomenon.
   c. consolidation.
   d. déjà vu.

10. From the clinical evidence on brain injury, it appears that storage bins for long-term memories are located in
    a. the hippocampus.
    b. one specific brain area.
    c. different brain areas.
    d. the frontal lobe and thalamus.

LEARNING OUTCOMES

7-1 Define thinking and the various concepts involved in thinking

7-2 Describe how language develops

7-3 Identify the concept of intelligence and the techniques used to measure intelligence

7-4 Describe the controversy surrounding intelligence testing

After you read the chapter, go to the Study Tools at the end of the chapter, page 187.

CHAPTER 7

Thinking, Language, and Intelligence

What form of life is so adaptive that it can survive in desert temperatures of 120°F or Arctic climes of −40°F? What form of life can run, walk, climb, swim, live underwater for months on end, and fly to the moon and back? I won't keep you in suspense any longer. We are that form of life. Yet our unclad bodies do not allow us to adapt to these extremes of temperature. Brute strength does not allow us to live underwater or travel to the moon. Rather, it is our cognitive processes of thinking, language, and intelligence that permit us to adapt to these conditions and surpass our physical limitations.

Our cognitive processes are the key assets that have enabled humans to survive and prosper. Other species may be stronger, run faster, smell more keenly, even live longer, but only humans have produced literature, music, mathematics, and science. Our cognitive processes have made these achievements possible. In this chapter, we look at these three related areas of **cognition**: thinking, language, and intelligence.

7-1 Thinking

The Greek philosopher Aristotle pointed out that people differ from lower organisms in their capacity for rational thinking. *What is thinking?* **Thinking** means paying attention to information, representing it mentally, reasoning about it, and making judgments and decisions about it. Thinking refers to conscious, *planned* attempts to make sense of and change the world. By contrast, mental processes such as dreaming and daydreaming do not represent thinking; they may be unplanned and proceed more or less on their own.

We begin with concepts, which provide many of the building blocks for thinking.

7-1a CONCEPTS

Concepts are mental categories used to group together objects, relations, events, abstractions, or qualities that have common properties. Concepts are crucial to cog-

> *Intelligence may be the most controversial topic in psychology.*

TRUTH OR *FICTION*

WHAT DO YOU THINK? FOLKLORE, COMMON SENSE, OR NONSENSE? CIRCLE THE T FOR "TRUTH" OR THE F FOR "FICTION," AND CHECK THE ACCURACY OF YOUR ANSWERS AS YOU READ THROUGH THE CHAPTER.

T	F	ONLY HUMANS CAN USE INSIGHT TO SOLVE PROBLEMS.
T	F	CRYING IS A CHILD'S FIRST USE OF LANGUAGE.
T	F	YOUNG CHILDREN SAY THINGS LIKE "DADDY GOED AWAY" AND "MOMMY SITTED DOWN" BECAUSE THEY *DO* UNDERSTAND RULES OF GRAMMAR.
T	F	"STREET SMARTS" ARE A SIGN OF INTELLIGENCE.
T	F	CREATIVE PEOPLE ARE HIGHLY INTELLIGENT.
T	F	HIGHLY INTELLIGENT PEOPLE ARE CREATIVE.
T	F	TWO CHILDREN CAN ANSWER EXACTLY THE SAME ITEMS ON AN INTELLIGENCE TEST CORRECTLY, YET ONE CHILD CAN OBTAIN AN ABOVE AVERAGE IN IQ, AND THE OTHER CAN OBTAIN A BELOW AVERAGE IQ.
T	F	INTELLIGENCE TESTS MEASURE MANY THINGS OTHER THAN INTELLIGENCE.

cognition

mental activity involved in understanding, processing, and communicating information

thinking

paying attention to information, mentally representing it, reasoning about it, and making decisions about it

concept

a mental category that is used to class together objects, relations, events, abstractions, ideas, or qualities that have common properties

prototype

a concept of a category of objects or events that serves as a good example of the category

exemplar

a specific example

nition. They can represent objects, events, and activities—and visions of things that never were or cannot be measured, such as Middle Earth in *The Lord of the Rings* or the land of Oz in *The Wizard of Oz.*

Labels for objects depend on experience with them and on one's cultural setting (Sloman et al., 2002). Concepts such as *square, circle,* and *triangle* are not all that common in nature, and some peoples who do not construct houses with these shapes, such as the Himba of northern Namibia, have no words for them (Davidoff et al., 2008; Roberson et al., 2002). But these shapes are concepts that are basic to geometry. Much thinking has to do with categorizing new concepts and manipulating relationships among concepts, as in problems in geometry.

We tend to organize concepts in *hierarchies* (see Figure 7.1). For example, the newspaper category includes objects such as your school paper and the *Los Angeles Times.* Newspapers, college textbooks, and catalogs can be combined into higher-order categories such as *printed matter* or *printed devices that store information.* If you add iPods, hard drives, and DVDs, you can create a still higher category—*objects that store information.* Now consider a question that requires categorical thinking: How are a newspaper and a DVD alike? Answers to such questions entail supplying the category that includes both objects. In this case, we can say that both objects store information. Their functions are alike, even if their technology differs.

Prototypes are good examples. They best match the key features of categories (Machery, 2009). Which animal seems more birdlike to you: a robin or an ostrich? Why? Which better fits the prototype of a fish: a sea horse or a tuna? Why?

Many simple prototypes, such as *dog* and *red*, are taught by means of examples, or **exemplars**. Research suggests that it is more efficient for most of us to learn what *fruits* and *vegetables* are from experience with

FIGURE 7.1 | Organization of Concepts into Hierarchies

People may have a concept, "objects that store information." This concept may include concepts such as iPod, DVD, and printed matter. Within the concept of printed matter, people may include newspapers, college textbooks (certainly the most important object that stores information!), novels, and catalogs. The concept of newspaper may include one's school newspaper and various commercial newspapers.

OBJECTS THAT STORE INFORMATION

Printed matter   iPod   DVDs

Newspapers   College textbooks   Novels   Catalogs

© Cengage Learning 2014

exemplars of each, rather than by working from definitions of them (Freund, 2009; Voorspoels et al., 2008). We point to a dog and tell a child "dog" or "This is a dog." Dogs are *positive instances* of the dog concept. *Negative instances*—things that are *not* dogs—are then shown to the child while we say, "This is *not* a dog." Negative instances of one concept may be positive instances of another. So, in teaching a child, we may be more likely to say, "This is not a dog—it's a cat" than simply, "This is not a dog."

Children may at first include horses and other four-legged animals within the dog concept until the differences between dogs and horses are pointed out. In language development, such overinclusion of instances in a category (reference to horses as dogs) is labeled *overextension*. Children's prototypes become refined after they are shown positive and negative instances and given explanations. Abstract concepts such as *bachelor* or *square root* tend to be formed through explanations that involve more basic concepts.

7-1b PROBLEM SOLVING

Problem solving is an important aspect of thinking. Here's a problem for you to solve. What are the next two letters in this series?

O T T F F S S E _ _ ?

How did you try to find the answer? Did you search your personal memory banks and ask yourself what O can stand for, then T, and so on? Did you try to think of some phrase the letters might represent? Perhaps the first letters of the stars in a constellation? [If you don't resort to a search engine answer and do not arrive at the answer on your own, I'll be discussing it within a few pages.]

7-1c UNDERSTANDING THE PROBLEM

Successful understanding of a problem generally requires three features:

- *The parts or elements of our mental representation of the problem relate to one another in a meaningful way.* If we are trying to solve a problem in geometry, our mental triangles, like actual triangles, should have angles that total 180 degrees.

How Do You Go about Understanding a Problem? This student is apparently seeking to boost her storehouse of background knowledge. Will doing so help her focus on the answer efficiently?

- *The elements of our mental representation of the problem correspond to the elements of the problem in the outer world.* If we are assessing a patient in the emergency room of a hospital, we want to arrive at a diagnosis of what might be wrong before we make a treatment plan. To do so, we take the patient's vital signs, including heart rate, temperature, and blood pressure, so that our mental picture of the patient conforms to what is going on in his or her body.

- *We have a storehouse of background knowledge that we can apply to the problem.* We have the necessary experience or course work to solve the problem.

algorithm
a systematic procedure for solving a problem that works invariably when it is correctly applied

The Use of Algorithms

An **algorithm** is a specific procedure for solving a type of problem. An algorithm invariably leads to the solution—if it is used properly, that is. Mathematical formulas like the Pythagorean theorem are examples of algorithms. They yield correct answers to problems *as long as the right formula is used*. Finding the right formula to solve a problem may require scanning one's memory for all formulas that contain variables that represent one or more of the elements in the problem. The Pythagorean theorem concerns right triangles. Therefore, it is appropriate to consider using this formula for problems concerning right triangles, but not others.

If you are going to be meeting someone for the first time and want to make a good impression, you consider the nature of the encounter (for example, a job interview or a blind date) and then consider how to dress and behave for the encounter. If it's a job interview, the algorithm may be to dress neatly, to be well groomed, and not to wear too much cologne or perfume. If it's a date, you may ditch the suit but hike up the cologne or perfume a notch. In either case, smile and make eye contact—it's all part of the formula.

Anagrams are scrambled words. *Korc* is an anagram for *rock* or *cork*. The task in anagram problems is to try to reorganize jumbles or groups of letters into words. Some anagram problems require us to use every letter from the pool of letters; others allow us to use only some of the letters. How many words can you make from the pool of letters *DWARG*? If you were to use the

systematic random search algorithm, you would list every possible letter combination, using from one to all five letters. You could use a dictionary or a spell-checking program to see whether each result is, in fact, a word. The method might take awhile, but it would work.

The Use of Heuristic Devices

Sometimes people use shortcuts to "jump to conclusions"—and these are often correct conclusions. The shortcuts are called **heuristics**, or heuristic devices—rules of thumb that help us simplify and solve problems. Heuristics are often based on strategies that worked in the past (Mair et al., 2009).

In contrast to algorithms, heuristics do not guarantee a correct solution. But when they work, they permit more rapid solutions. A heuristic device for solving the anagram problem would be to look for familiar letter combinations and then check the remaining letters for words that include these combinations. In *DWARG*, for example, we find some familiar combinations: *dr* and *gr*. We may then quickly find *draw, drag,* and *grad.* The drawback to this method is that we might miss some words.

One type of heuristic device is the **means–end analysis**. In using this heuristic device, we assess the difference between our current situation and our goals and do what we can to reduce this difference. Let's say that you are out in your car and have gotten lost. One heuristic device based on analysis of what you need to do to get to where you want to go might be to ask for directions. This approach requires no "sense of direction." An algorithm might be more complicated and require some scientific knowledge. For example, if you know your destination is west of your current location you might try driving toward the setting sun.

The Use of Analogies

An *analogy* is a partial similarity among things that are different in other ways. The analogy heuristic applies the solution of an earlier problem to the solution of a new one. We use the analogy heuristic whenever we try to solve a new problem by referring to a previous problem (Mair et al., 2009; Wang & Chiew, 2010).

Let's see whether you can use the analogy heuristic to your advantage in the following number-series problem. Look at the following series of numbers and find the rule that governs their order:

8, 5, 4, 9, 1, 7, 6, 3, 2, 0

This is rather abstract and mathematical. Actually, you use the analogy heuristic regularly. For example, when you begin a new term with a new instructor, you probably consider who the instructor reminds you of. Then, perhaps, you recall the things that helped you get along with the analogous instructor and try them on the new one. We tend to look for things—analogies—that have helped us in similar situations. When we considered OTTFFSSENT, we used the first letters of the numbers one through ten. When we consider the first 10 digits in the following order—8, 5, 4, 9, 1, 7, 6, 3, 2, and 0—we can again think of their first letters when they are spelled out. It happens that they are in alphabetical order (*eight, five, four,* and so on).

Factors That Affect Problem Solving

The way you approach a problem is central to how effective you are at solving it. Other factors also influence your effectiveness. Three factors that can make it easier or harder to solve problems reside within you: your level of expertise, whether you fall prey to a mental set, and whether you develop insight into the problem.

Expertise   To appreciate the role of expertise in problem solving, unscramble the following anagrams, taken from Novick and Coté (1992). In each case use all of the letters to form an actual English word:

DNSUO

RCWDO

IASYD

How long did it take you to unscramble each anagram ("sound," "crowd," and "daisy")? Would a person whose native language is English—that is, an "expert"—unscramble each anagram more efficiently than a bilingual person who spoke another language in the home? Why or why not?

Experts solve problems more efficiently and rapidly than novices do. Generally speaking, people who are experts at solving a certain kind of problem share the following characteristics (Bassok & Novick, 2012; Mair et al., 2009; Nokes & VanLehn, 2008):

- They know the particular area well.
- They have a good memory for the elements in the problems.
- They form *mental images* or representations that facilitate problem solving.
- They relate the problem to similar problems.
- They are more goal-directed and have efficient methods for problem solving.

These factors are interrelated. Art historians, for example, acquire a database that permits them to understand the intricacies of paintings. As a result, their memory for details of paintings mushrooms.

Novick and Coté (1992) found that the solutions to the anagram problems seemed to "pop out" in under two seconds among experts. The experts apparently used more efficient methods than the novices. Experts seemed to use *parallel processing*. That is, they dealt simultaneously with two or more elements of the problems. In the case of DNSUO, for example, they may have played with the order of the vowels (*UO* or *OU*) at the same time that they tested which consonant (D, N, or S) was likely to precede them, arriving quickly at *sou* and *sound*. Novices were more likely to engage in *serial processing*—that is, to handle one element of the problem at a time.

Mental Sets   The tendency to respond to a new problem with the same approach that helped solve similar problems is termed a **mental set.** Mental sets usually make our work easier, but they can mislead us when the similarity between problems is illusory.

Insight   To gain insight into the role of **insight** in problem solving, consider the following problem, posed by Metcalfe (1986):

> *A stranger approached a museum curator and offered him an ancient bronze coin. The coin had an authentic appearance and was marked with the date 544 BCE. The curator had happily made acquisitions from suspicious sources before, but this time he promptly called the police and had the stranger arrested. Why?*

I'm not going to give you the answer to this problem. But I'll make a guarantee. When you arrive at the solution, it will hit you all at once. You'll think "Of course!" It will seem as though the pieces of information in the problem have suddenly been reorganized so that the solution leaps out—in a flash.

Bismarck, one of psychologist N. R. F. Maier's rats, appeared to suddenly reorganize the pieces of information in a problem with which he was presented, showing evidence of insight in his species (Maier & Schneirla, 1935). Bismarck had been trained to climb a ladder to a tabletop where food was placed. On one occasion, Maier used a mesh barrier to prevent the rat from reaching his goal. But, as shown in Figure 7.2, a second ladder was provided and was visible to the animal. At first Bismarck sniffed and scratched and tried to find a path through the mesh. Then he spent some time washing his face, an activity that may signal frustration in rats. Suddenly he jumped into the air, turned, ran down the familiar ladder and around to the new ladder, ran up the new ladder, and claimed his just desserts. Did Bismarck suddenly perceive the relationships between the elements of the problem so that the solution occurred by insight? He seems to have had what Gestalt psychologists have termed an "Aha! experience."

FICTION   IT APPEARS THAT HUMANS ARE NOT THE ONLY SPECIES WHO USE INSIGHT TO SOLVE PROBLEMS, AS SHOWN IN MAIER'S RESEARCH WITH "BISMARCK."

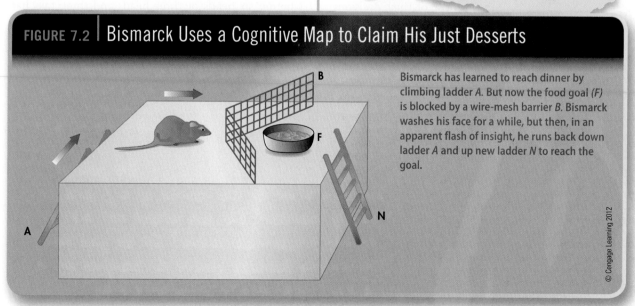

FIGURE 7.2 | Bismarck Uses a Cognitive Map to Claim His Just Desserts

Bismarck has learned to reach dinner by climbing ladder *A*. But now the food goal *(F)* is blocked by a wire-mesh barrier *B*. Bismarck washes his face for a while, but then, in an apparent flash of insight, he runs back down ladder *A* and up new ladder *N* to reach the goal.

© Cengage Learning 2012

Incubation An incubator warms chicken eggs so that they will hatch. **Incubation** in problem solving refers to standing back from the problem for a while as some process within may continue to work on it. Later, the answer may come to us in a flash of insight. Standing back from the problem may help by distancing us from unprofitable but persistent mental sets (Kohn & Smith, 2009; Sio & Ormerod, 2009).

Functional Fixedness **Functional fixedness** may hinder problem solving. For example, first ask yourself what a pair of pliers is. Is it a tool for grasping, a paperweight, or a weapon?

A pair of pliers could function as any of these, but your tendency to think of it as a grasping tool is fostered by your experience with it. You have probably used pliers only for grasping things. Functional fixedness is the tendency to think of an object in terms of its name or its familiar function. It can be similar to a mental set in that it makes it difficult to use familiar objects to solve problems in novel ways.

7-1d JUDGMENT AND DECISION MAKING

You might like to think that people are so rational that they carefully weigh the pros and cons when they make judgments or decisions. Or you might think that they insist on finding and examining all the relevant information. Actually, people make most of their decisions on the basis of limited information. They take shortcuts. They use heuristic devices—rules of thumb—in judgments and decision making just as they do in problem solving (Gigerenzer et al.,

2008). For example, they may let a financial advisor select stocks for them rather than research the companies themselves. Or they may see a doctor recommended by a friend rather than look at the doctor's credentials. In this section we consider various factors in judgment and decision making.

Heuristics in Decision Making

Imagine that you flip a coin six times. In the following three possible outcomes, H stands for heads and T for tails. Circle the most likely sequence:

H H H H H H

H H H T T T

T H H T H T

Did you select T H H T H T as the most likely sequence of events? Most people do. Why? There are two reasons. First, people recognize that the sequence of six heads in a row is unlikely. (The probability of achieving it is $1/2 \times 1/2 \times 1/2 \times 1/2 \times 1/2 \times 1/2$, or 1/64th.) Three heads and three tails are more likely than six heads (or six tails). Second, people recognize that the sequence of heads and tails ought to appear random. T H H T H T has a random look to it, whereas H H H T T T does not.

People tend to select T H H T H T because of the **representativeness heuristic**. According to this decision-making heuristic, people make judgments about events (samples) according to the populations of events that they appear to represent (Nilsson et al., 2008). In this case, the sample of events is six coin tosses. The "population" is an infinite number of random coin tosses. But guess what? *Each* sequence is equally likely (or unlikely). If the question had been whether six heads or three heads and three tails had been more likely, the correct answer would have been three and three.

If the question had been whether heads and tails would be more likely to be consecutive or in random order, the correct answer would have been random order. But each of the three sequences is a *specific* sequence. What is the probability of attaining the spe-

How Do You Choose a Doctor? Do you go by reputation or the advice of a friend or family member? Do you check out his or her credentials online? Or do you have no choice because you're on campus or in a particular health insurance plan?

cific sequence T H H T H T? The probability that the first coin toss will result in a tail is 1/2. The probability that the second will result in a head is 1/2, and so on. Thus, the probability of attaining the exact sequence T H H T H T is identical to that of achieving any other specific sequence: $1/2 \times 1/2 \times 1/2 \times 1/2 \times 1/2 \times 1/2 = 1/64$th. (Try this out on a friend.)

Another heuristic device used in decision making is the **availability heuristic**. According to this heuristic, our estimates of frequency or probability are based on how easy it is to find examples of relevant events. Let me ask you whether there are more art majors or sociology majors at your college. Unless you are familiar with the enrollment statistics, you will probably answer on the basis of the numbers of art majors and sociology majors that you know.

The **anchoring and adjustment heuristic** suggests that there can be a good deal of inertia in our judgments. In forming opinions or making estimates, we have an initial view, or presumption. This is the anchor. As we receive additional information, we make adjustments, sometimes grudgingly. That is, if you grow up believing that one religion or one political party is the "right" one, that belief serves as a cognitive anchor. When inconsistencies show up in your religion or political party, you may adjust your views of them, but perhaps not very willingly.

Let's illustrate further by means of a math problem. Write each of the following multiplication problems on a separate piece of paper:

A. $8 \times 7 \times 6 \times 5 \times 4 \times 3 \times 2 \times 1$

B. $1 \times 2 \times 3 \times 4 \times 5 \times 6 \times 7 \times 8$

Show problem A to a few friends. Give them each 5 seconds to estimate the answer. Show problem B to some other friends and give them 5 seconds to estimate the answer.

The answers to the multiplication problems are the same because the order of quantities being multiplied does not change the outcome. However, when Amos Tversky and Daniel Kahneman (1982, 2003) showed these problems to high-school students, the average estimate given by students who were shown version A was significantly higher than that given by students who were shown version B. Students who saw 8 in the first position offered an average estimate of 2,250. Students who saw 1 in the first position gave an average estimate of 512. That is, the estimate was larger when 8 served as the anchor. By the way, what is the correct answer to the multiplication problems? Can you use the anchoring and adjustment heuristic to explain why both groups were so far off?

The Framing Effect

The **framing effect** refers to the way in which wording, or the context in which information is presented, affects decision making (Li & Chapman, 2009; Tetlock & McGraw, 2005). Political groups, like advertisers, are aware of the framing effect and choose their words accordingly. For example, proponents of legalized abortion refer to themselves as "pro-choice" and opponents refer to themselves as "pro-life." Each group frames itself in a positive way ("pro" something) and refers to a popular value (freedom or life).

Overconfidence

Whether our decisions are correct or incorrect, most of us tend to be overconfident about them. We also tend to view our situations with 20-20 hindsight. When we are proven wrong, we frequently find a way to show that we "knew it all along." We also become overconfident that we would have known the actual outcome if we had had access to the information that became available after the event. For example, if we had known that a key player would pull a hamstring muscle, we would have predicted a different outcome for the football game. If we had known that it would be blustery on Election Day, we would have predicted a smaller voter turnout and a different outcome. There are several reasons for overconfidence, even when our judgments are wrong:

- We tend to be unaware of how flimsy our assumptions may be.

- We tend to focus on examples that confirm our judgments and ignore those that do not.

- Because our working memories have limited space, we tend to forget information that runs counter to our judgments.

- We work to bring about the events we believe in, so they sometimes become self-fulfilling prophecies.

7-2 Language

Oscar Wilde, the Irish playwright, wrote "It is only by language that we rise above [the lower animals]—by language, which is the parent, not the child, of thought."

availability heuristic
a decision-making heuristic in which our estimates of frequency or probability of events are based on how easy it is to find examples

anchoring and adjustment heuristic
a decision-making heuristic in which a presumption or first estimate serves as a cognitive anchor; as we receive additional information, we make adjustments but tend to remain in the proximity of the anchor

framing effect
the influence of wording, or the context in which information is presented, on decision making

He gave us quite a bit to think about. Are humans the only species to use language? We'll grapple with that question in a moment. And then, which comes first: language or thinking? Can you think without using language? (Give it a try.) We'll come back to that question later too. For the moment, let's consider whether apes can use language, and also whether language is for the birds—more specifically, the African Grey parrot.

"MAN INVENTED LANGUAGE TO SATISFY HIS DEEP NEED TO COMPLAIN."

—LILY TOMLIN

7-2a COMMUNICATION BY NONHUMANS

In recent years, the exclusive human claim to language has been brought into question by studies of communication with various animal species. The African Grey parrot, like many other parrots, can mimic human speech, but it is also suspected of being intelligent enough to understand some of the words it imitates. It has long been suspected that spontaneous language development occurs among many species of dolphins and whales, but we lack solid scientific evidence. Monkeys signal the peril of nearby predators with characteristic hoots. But none of these sounds contains *symbols*.

A language is a system of symbols along with rules that are used to manipulate the symbols. Symbols such as words stand for or represent other objects, events, or ideas. Because chimpanzees and gorillas have been taught to communicate by making signs with their hands, the question as to whether or not they are actually using language in the way that humans do is much more complex.

Chimpanzees are our closest genetic relatives, sharing an estimated 98.42% of their genetic code with humans (Zimmer, 2002–2003). Magnetic resonance imaging (MRI) studies with chimpanzees and gorillas show that most of them, like humans, show enlargement in the left hemisphere of the cerebral cortex, in part of Broca's area (Cantalupo & Hopkins, 2001; Keller et al., 2009). The differences that remain between humans and chimps are at least in part associated with capabilities such as fine control of the mouth and larynx that are not found in apes (Sherwood et al., 2008). The genetic differences between chimps and humans probably explain why chimps cannot articulate speech but also apparently give chimps and other apes some meaningful ability to use language (Sherwood et al., 2008).

Do Apes Really Use Language?

Although apes do not speak, they have been taught to use American Sign Language and other symbol systems. For example, a chimpanzee named Washoe, who was a pioneer in the effort to teach apes to use language, was using 181 signs by the age of 32 (King, 2008). Loulis, a baby chimp adopted by Washoe, gained the ability to use signs just by observing Washoe and some other chimps that had been trained in sign language. Other chimps have used plastic symbols or pressed keys on a computer keyboard to communicate.

Sue Savage-Rumbaugh and her colleagues (Segerdahl et al., 2006; Washburn et al., 2007) believe that pygmy chimpanzees can understand some of the *semantic* subtleties of language. She claims that one chimp, Kanzi, picked up language from observing another chimp being trained and has the grammatical abilities of a 2½-year-old child. Kanzi also understands several words spoken by humans. Kanzi held a toy snake to a toy dog's mouth when asked to make the dog bite the snake.

Critics of the view that apes can learn to produce language, such as Herbert Terrace (Terrace & Metcalfe, 2005) and Steven Pinker (1994a, 2011), note that:

- Apes can string together signs in a given sequence to earn rewards, but animals lower on the evolutionary ladder, such as pigeons, can also peck buttons in a certain sequence to obtain a reward.
- It takes apes longer to learn new signs than it takes children to learn new words.
- Apes are unreliable in their sequencing of signs, suggesting that by and large they do not comprehend rules of grammar.
- People observing apes signing may be subject to *observer bias*—that is, they may be seeing what they want to see.

Scientists will continue to debate how well chimpanzees and gorillas understand and produce language, but there is little doubt that they have learned to use symbols to communicate (Segerdahl et al., 2006).

7-2b WHAT IS LANGUAGE?

As you can see from the discussion of apes and language, the way in which one defines language is no small matter. If we define language simply as a system of communication, many animals have language, including the birds and the bees. Through particular chirps and shrieks, birds may communicate that they have taken possession of a tree or bush. The waggle dances of bees inform other bees of the location of a food source or a predator. All of these are instinctive communication patterns but not what we mean by language.

With language, sounds or signs are symbols for objects and actions. Apes have been taught to use symbols to communicate, but is such usage an adequate definition of language? Many language experts require one more piece. They define **language** as the communication of thoughts and feelings by means of symbols *that are arranged according to rules of grammar*. Instinctive waggle dances and shrieks have no symbols and no grammar. By these rigorous rules, only humans use language. Whether apes can handle rules of grammar is under debate.

Language makes it possible for one person to communicate knowledge to another and for one generation to communicate to another. It creates a vehicle for recording experiences. It allows us to put ourselves in the shoes of other people, to learn more than we could learn from direct experience. Language also provides many units of thinking.

True language is distinguished from the communication systems of lower animals by properties such as semanticity, infinite creativity, and displacement (Hoff, 2005):

- **Semanticity**: The sounds (or signs) of a language have meaning. Words serve as symbols for actions, objects, relational concepts (*over, in, more*, and so on), and other ideas. The communication systems of the birds and the bees do not use words and symbols. Therefore, they lack semanticity.

- **Infinite creativity**: The capacity to create rather than imitate sentences.
- **Displacement**: The capacity to communicate information about events and objects in another time or place. Language makes it possible to transmit knowledge from one person to another and from one generation to another, furthering human adaptation.

7-2c LANGUAGE AND COGNITION

The relationships between language and thinking are complex and not always obvious. For example, can you think *without* using language? Would you be able to solve problems without using words or sentences?

Jean Piaget (Inhelder & Piaget, 1958) believed that language reflects knowledge of the world but that much knowledge can be acquired without language. For example, it is possible to understand the concepts of roundness or redness even when we do not know or use the words *round* or *red*.

language
the communication of information by means of symbols arranged according to rules of grammar

semanticity
meaning; the quality of language in which words are used as symbols for objects, events, or ideas

infinite creativity
the capacity to combine words into original sentences

displacement
the quality of language that permits one to communicate information about objects and events in another time and place

Joyce Butler of Columbia University shows chimpanzee "Nim Chimpsky"— named humorously after linguist Noam Chomsky— the sign for "drink," and Nim imitates her.

Susan Kuklin/Photo Researchers, Inc.

7-2d LANGUAGE AND CULTURE

Different languages have different words for the same concepts, and concepts do not necessarily overlap. As noted earlier, concepts expressed in our own language (such as *square* and *triangle)* may not exist in the language of another culture—and vice versa. Is it possible for English speakers to share the thoughts experienced by people who speak other languages? The answer is probably yes in many or most cases, but in some cases, no. In any event, the question brings us to the linguistic-relativity hypothesis.

The Linguistic-Relativity Hypothesis

The **linguistic-relativity hypothesis** was proposed by Benjamin Whorf (1956). Whorf believed that language structures the way we perceive the world. That is, the categories and relationships we use to understand the world are derived from our language. Therefore, speakers of various languages conceptualize the world in different ways.

Thus, most English speakers' ability to think about snow may be limited compared with that of the Inuit (Eskimos). We have only a few words for snow, whereas the Inuit have many. The Inuit's words differ according to whether the snow is hard packed, falling, melting, covered by ice, and so on. When we think about snow, we have fewer words to choose from and have to search for descrip-

tive adjectives. The Inuit, however, can readily find a single word that describes a complex weather condition. Is it therefore easier for them to think about this variety of snow? Similarly, the Hanunoo people of the Philippines use 92 words for rice depending on whether the rice is husked or unhusked and on how it is prepared. And whereas we have one word for camel, Arabs have more than 250.

In English, we have hundreds of words to describe colors. There is about a 95% overlap in perception and labeling of colors among English speakers and Chinese people (Moore et al., 2002). It has been pointed out, however, that Shona-speaking people use only three words for colors, and Bassa speakers use only two corresponding to light and dark. Nevertheless, studies of languages spoken in nonindustrialized societies find overlaps for white, black, red, green, yellow, and blue (Regier, 2005; Tohidian, 2009). Moreover, people who use only a few words to distinguish among colors seem to perceive the same color variations as people with more words. For example, the Dani of New Guinea have just two words for colors: one that refers to yellows and reds and one that refers to greens and blues. Yet performance on matching and memory tasks shows that the Dani can discriminate the many colors of the spectrum.

Most cognitive scientists no longer accept the linguistic-relativity hypothesis (Pinker, 2007, 2011). For one thing, adults use images and abstract logical propositions, as well as words, as units of thought. Infants, moreover, display considerable intelligence before they have learned to speak. Another criticism is that a language's vocabulary suggests the range of concepts that the speakers of the language have traditionally found important, not their cognitive limits. For example, people who were magically lifted from the 19th century and placed inside an airplane probably would not think they were flying inside a bird or a large insect, even if their language lacked a word for airplane.

7-2e LANGUAGE DEVELOPMENT: THE TWO-YEAR EXPLOSION

Languages around the world develop in a specific sequence of steps, beginning with the *prelinguistic* vocalizations of

How many words do you know for snow?

crying, cooing, and babbling. These sounds are not symbols. That is, they do not represent objects or events. Therefore, they are *prelinguistic*, not linguistic.

Prelinguistic Vocalizations

As parents are well aware, newborn children have one inborn, highly effective form of verbal expression: crying—and more crying. But crying does not represent language; it is a prelinguistic event. During the second month, babies begin *cooing*, another form of prelinguistic expression that appears to be linked to feelings of pleasure. By the fifth or sixth month, children begin to *babble*. Children babble sounds that occur in many languages, including the throaty German *ch*, the clicks of certain African languages, and rolling *r*'s. Babies' babbling frequently combines consonants and vowels, as in "ba," "ga," and, sometimes, the much-valued "dada" (McCardle et al., 2009). "Dada" at first is purely coincidental (sorry, dads), despite the family's delight over its appearance.

Babbling, like crying and cooing, is inborn and prelinguistic. Deaf children babble, and children from cultures whose languages sound very different all seem to babble the same sounds (Hoff, 2005). But children single out the sounds used in the home within a few months. By the age of 9 or 10 months, they are repeating the sounds regularly, and foreign sounds are dropping out. In fact, early experience in acquiring the phonemes (that is, meaningful units of sound) native to one's own language can make it difficult to pronounce and even discriminate the phonemes used in other languages later in life (Iverson et al., 2003).

Children tend to utter their first word at 11 to 13 months, but a range of 8 to 18 months is normal (McCardle et al., 2009; Tamis-LeMonda et al., 2006). Parents often miss the first word because it is not pronounced clearly. The growth of vocabulary is slow at first. It may take children 3 to 4 months to achieve a 10-word vocabulary after they have spoken their first word. By about 18 months, children are producing

FICTION CRYING DOES *NOT* REPRESENT LANGUAGE; IT IS A PRELINGUISTIC EVENT.

Although crying can effectively communicate discomfort and the desire to have a caregiver present—now—cries do not possess symbols and are thus not an example of true language.

a couple of dozen words.

holophrase
a single word used to express complex meanings

Development of Grammar

The first linguistic utterances of children around the globe are single words that can express complex meanings. These initial utterances of children are called **holophrases**. For example, *mama* may be used by the child to signify meanings as varied as "There goes Mama," "Come here, Mama," and "You are my Mama." Similarly, *cat* can signify "There is a cat," "That stuffed animal looks just like my cat," or "I want you to give me my cat right now!" Most children show their parents what they intend by augmenting their holophrases with gestures and intonations. That is, they act delighted when parents do as requested and howl when they do not.

Toward the end of the second year, children begin to speak two-word sentences. These sentences are termed *telegraphic speech* because they resemble telegrams. Telegrams cut out the "unnecessary" words. "Home Tuesday" might stand for "I expect to be home on Tuesday." Two-word utterances seem to appear at about the same time in the development of all languages (Saffran, 2009; Slobin, 1983). Two-word utterances are brief but grammatically correct. The child says, "Sit chair" to tell a parent to sit in a chair, not "Chair sit." The child says, "My shoe," not "Shoe my," to show possession. "Mommy go" means Mommy is leaving. "Go Mommy" expresses the wish for Mommy to go away.

There are different kinds of two-word utterances. Some, for example, contain nouns or pronouns and verbs ("Daddy sit"). Others contain verbs and objects ("Hit ball"). The sequence of emergence of the various kinds of two-word utterances is also apparently the same in all languages—languages as diverse as English, Luo (an African tongue), German, Russian, and Turkish (Slobin, 1983). The invariance of this sequence has implications for theories of language development, as we will see.

Mike Kemp/Rubberball

overregularization
the application of regular grammatical rules for forming inflections (e.g., past tense and plurals) to irregular verbs and nouns

Overregularization

Overregularization is an important development for understanding the roles of nature and nurture in language development (E. V. Clark & Nikitina, 2009). In English, we add *d* or *ed* to make the past tense of regular verbs and *s* or *z* sounds to make regular nouns plural. Thus, *walk* becomes *walked*, and *look* becomes *looked*. *Cat* becomes *cats*, and *doggy* becomes *doggies*. There are also irregular verbs and nouns. For example, *see* becomes *saw*, *sit* becomes *sat*, and *go* becomes *went*. *Sheep* remains *sheep* (plural) and *child* becomes *children*.

At first children learn irregular verbs and nouns by imitating older people. Two-year-olds tend to form them correctly—at first! Then they become aware of the grammatical rules for forming the past tense and plurals. As a result, they tend to make charming errors (Pinker, 2011). A three- to five-year-old, for example, may be more likely to say "I seed it" than "I saw it," and more likely to say "Mommy sitted down" than "Mommy sat down." They are likely to talk about the "gooses" and "sheeps" they "seed" on the farm and about all the "childs" they ran into at the playground. This tendency to regularize the irregular is what is meant by overregularization.

Should parents be concerned about overregularization? Not at all. Overregularization reflects knowledge of grammar, not faulty language development. In another year or two, *mouses* will be boringly transformed into *mice*, and Mommy will no longer have *sitted* down. Parents might as well enjoy overregularization while they can.

Other Developments

By the age of six, children's vocabularies have expanded to 10,000 words, give or take a few thousand. By seven to nine, most children realize that words can have more than one meaning, and they are entertained by riddles and jokes that require some sophistication with language.

TRUTH YOUNG CHILDREN SAY THINGS LIKE "DADDY GOED AWAY" AND "MOMMY SITTED DOWN" BECAUSE THEY *DO* UNDERSTAND RULES OF GRAMMAR.

"Since all normal humans talk but no house pets or house plants do, no matter how pampered, heredity must be involved in language. But since a child growing up in Japan speaks Japanese whereas the same child brought up in California would speak English, the environment is also crucial."

—STEVEN PINKER,
THE LANGUAGE INSTINCT

Between the elementary school and high school years, language grows more complex, and children rapidly add to their vocabularies. Vocabulary, in fact, can grow for a lifetime, especially in one's fields of specialization and interest.

7-2f NATURE AND NURTURE IN LANGUAGE DEVELOPMENT

Billions of children have acquired the languages spoken by their parents and passed them down, with minor changes, from generation to generation. Language development, like many other areas of development, apparently reflects the interactions between nature and nurture.

Learning Theory and Language Development

Learning theorists see language as developing according to laws of learning (Hoff, 2005). They usually refer to the concepts of imitation and reinforcement. From a social-cognitive perspective, parents serve as *models*. Children learn language, at least in part, through observation and imitation. Many words, especially nouns and verbs (including irregular verbs), are apparently learned by imitation.

Children initially repeat the irregular verb forms they have heard accurately, apparently as a result of modeling. Modeling, however, does not explain all of the events in language learning. As noted previously, children later overregularize irregular verb forms because they have developed an understanding of grammar. Nor can learning by imitation explain how children come to utter phrases and sentences they have *not* observed. Parents, for example, are unlikely to model utterances such as "Bye-bye sock" and "All gone Daddy," but children say them.

Learning theory cannot account for the unchanging sequence of language development and the spurts in children's language acquisition. Even the types of two-word utterances emerge in a consistent pattern in diverse cultures. Although timing differs from one child to another, the types of questions used, passive versus active sentences, and so on, all emerge in the same order.

The Nativist Approach to Language Development

The nativist theory of language development holds that the innate factors—which make up children's *nature*—cause children to attend to and acquire language in certain ways. From this perspective, children bring neurological "prewiring" to language learning (A. Clark & Misyak, 2009; Pinker, 2011).

According to **psycholinguistic theory**, language acquisition involves the interaction of environmental influences—such as exposure to parental speech and reinforcement—and the inborn tendency to acquire language. Noam Chomsky (see Cherniak, 2009) refers to the inborn tendency as a **language acquisition device (LAD)**. Evidence for an LAD is found in the universality of human language abilities and in the specific sequence of language development (Cherniak, 2009; A. Clark & Misyak, 2009).

The LAD prepares the nervous system to learn grammar. On the surface, languages differ a great deal. However, the LAD serves children all over the world because languages share what Chomsky refers to as a "universal grammar"—an underlying set of rules for turning ideas into sentences (Pinker, 2011).

psycholinguistic theory
the view that language learning involves an interaction between environmental factors and an inborn tendency to acquire language

language acquisition device (LAD)
in psycholinguistic theory, neural "prewiring" that facilitates the child's learning of grammar

---

✱ "Motherese"—Of "Yummy Yummy" and "Kitty Cats"

One way that adults attempt to prompt the language development of children is by using baby talk, or "motherese," referred to more technically as *infant-directed speech (IDS)* (Meltzoff & Brooks, 2009; Singh et al., 2009). Motherese is a limiting term because grandparents, fathers, siblings, and unrelated people have also been observed using IDS (Braarud & Stormark, 2008). Moreover, women (but usually not men) often talk to their pets as if they were infants (Prato-Previde et al., 2006). Infant-directed speech is used in languages as diverse as Arabic, English, Comanche, Italian, French, German, Xhosa (an African tongue), Japanese, Mandarin Chinese, and even a Thai sign language (Lee et al., 2010; Nonaka, 2004).

IDS has the following characteristics (Matsuda et al., 2011; Meltzoff & Brooks, 2009):

- It is spoken more slowly, at a higher pitch, and includes pauses between ideas.

- Sentences are brief, and the focus is on nouns, verbs, and just a few modifiers.

- Key words are placed at the ends of sentences and spoken in a higher, louder voice.

- The diminutive *y* is frequently added to nouns. *Dad* becomes *Daddy*; *horse* becomes *horsey*.

- Adults repeat sentences, sometimes using minor variations, as in "Show me your nose." "Where is your nose?"

- It includes duplication. *Yummy* becomes *yummy-yummy*. *Daddy* may alternate with *Da-da*.

- Much IDS focuses on naming objects (Meltzoff & Brooks, 2009). Vocabulary is concrete and refers to the child's environment. For example, stuffed lions may be called "kitties."

- Objects may be overdescribed with compound labels. Rabbits may become "bunny rabbits," and cats may become "kitty cats." Users of IDS try to ensure they are using at least one label the child will recognize.

- Parents speak for the children, as in "Is baby tired?" "Oh, we're so tired." Parents seem to be helping children express themselves by offering them models of sentences they can use.

Does IDS encourage communication and foster language development? Research supports its use. Infants as young as two days old prefer IDS to adult talk (N. A. Smith & Trainor, 2008). The short, simple sentences and high pitch are more likely to produce a response from the child and enhance vocabulary development than complex sentences and those spoken in a lower pitch (Matsuda et al., 2011). Repetition of children's vocalizations appears to encourage vocalizing.

© Rubberball

intelligence
a general mental capability that involves the ability to reason, plan, solve problems, think abstractly, comprehend complex ideas, learn quickly, and learn from experience

g
Spearman's symbol for general intelligence, which he believed underlay more specific abilities

s
Spearman's symbol for *specific* factors, or *s factors*, which he believed accounted for individual abilities

primary mental abilities
according to Thurstone, the basic abilities that make up intelligence examples include word fluency and numerical ability

In the following section, we see that some aspects of language development—particularly vocabulary development—are strongly related to intelligence. Numerous researchers suggest that language learning occurs during one or more *sensitive periods*, which begin at about 18 to 24 months and last until puberty (Bates, 2001). During these sensitive periods, neural development (as in the differentiating of brain structures) provides plasticity that facilitates language learning.

7-3 Intelligence

The concept of intelligence is closely related to thinking. Whereas thinking involves the understanding and manipulating of information, **intelligence** is the underlying ability to understand the world and cope with its challenges (Cornoldi, 2006; Sternberg et al., 2005). That is, intelligence is seen as making thinking possible. Although these concepts overlap, psychologists tend to be concerned with *how* we think, but laypeople and psychologists are often concerned with *how much* intelligence we have. Although intelligence, like thinking, cannot be directly seen or touched, psychologists tie the concept to achievements such as school performance and occupational status (Nisbett, 2009).

7-3a THEORIES OF INTELLIGENCE

Although psychologists have engaged in thousands of studies on intelligence, they do not quite agree on what intelligence is. Psychologists have therefore developed theories to help them understand and define intelligence.

Factor Theories

Many investigators have viewed intelligence as consisting of one or more *factors*. Factor theories argue that intelligence is made up of a number of mental abilities, ranging from one kind of ability to hundreds.

In 1904, British psychologist Charles Spearman suggested that the behaviors we consider intelligent have a common underlying factor that he labeled **g**, for "general intelligence" or broad reasoning and problem-solving abilities. Spearman supported his view by noting that people who excel in one area (such as vocabulary) are also likely to excel in others (such as math). But he also noted that even the most capable people are relatively superior in some areas—such as music or business or poetry. For this reason, he suggested that specific, or **s**, factors account for specific abilities.

Contemporary psychologists continue to use the term *g* in research, speaking, for example, of the extent to which they believe a particular kind of test, such as the SATs, measure *g* (Lubinski & Benbow, 2006).

American psychologist Louis Thurstone (1938) analyzed tests of specific abilities and concluded that Spearman had oversimplified intelligence. Thurstone's data suggested the presence of eight specific factors, which he labeled **primary mental abilities** (see Table 7.1). Thurstone's primary mental abilities contain the types of items measured on the most widely used intelligence tests today. The question remains as to whether his primary mental abilities are distinct or whether they are different ways of assessing *g*.

The Theory of Multiple Intelligences

Thurstone wrote about various factors or components of intelligence. Howard Gardner's (1983/1993, 2009) *theory of multiple intelligences* proposes, instead, that there are a number of *intelligences*, not just one. Gardner

TABLE 7.1

Primary Mental Abilities, According to Thurstone

ABILITY	DEFINITION
Visual and spatial abilities	Visualizing forms and spatial relationships
Perceptual speed	Grasping perceptual details rapidly, perceiving similarities and differences between stimuli
Numerical ability	Computing numbers
Verbal meaning	Knowing the meanings of words
Memory	Recalling information (e.g., words and sentences)
Word fluency	Thinking of words quickly (e.g., rhyming and doing crossword puzzles)
Deductive reasoning	Deriving examples from general rules
Inductive reasoning	Inferring general rules from examples

© Cengage Learning 2012

refers to each kind of intelligence in his theory as "an intelligence" because they can differ so much. Two of these "intelligences" are familiar ones: language ability and logical–mathematical ability. Gardner also refers, however, to bodily–kinesthetic talents (of the sort shown by dancers and athletes), musical talent, spatial–relations skills, and two kinds of personal intelligence: awareness of one's own inner feelings and sensitivity to other people's feelings. Gardner (2001) more recently added "naturalist intelligence" and "existential intelligence." Naturalist intelligence refers to the ability to look at natural events, such as kinds of animals and plants, or the stars above, and to develop insights into their nature and the laws that govern their behavior. Existential intelligence means dealing with the larger philosophical issues of life. According to Gardner, one can compose symphonies or advance mathematical theory yet be average in, say, language and personal skills.

Critics of Gardner's view agree that people function more intelligently in some aspects of life than in others. They also agree that many people have special talents, such as bodily–kinesthetic talents, even if their overall intelligence is average. But these critics question whether such talents are best thought of as "intelligences" or special talents (Neisser et al., 1996). Language skills, reasoning ability, and ability to solve math problems seem to be more closely related than musical or gymnastic talent to what most people mean by intelligence.

The Triarchic Theory of Intelligence

Psychologist Robert Sternberg (2000; 2006) has constructed a three-pronged or *triarchic theory of intelligence* that resembles a view proposed by the Greek philosopher Aristotle (Tigner & Tigner, 2000). The three prongs include *analytical*, *creative*, and *practical intelligence* (see Figure 7.3).

Analytical intelligence is similar to Aristotle's "theoretical intelligence" and can be defined as academic ability. It enables us to solve problems and acquire new knowledge. It is the type of intelligence measured by standard intelligence tests. Problem-solving skills include encoding information, combining and comparing bits of information, and generating a solution. Consider Sternberg's analogy problem:

Washington is to *1* as *Lincoln* is to
(a) 5, (b) 10, (c) 15, (d) 50?

TRUTH IT IS TRUE THAT STREET SMARTS ARE A SIGN OF INTELLIGENCE—AT LEAST ACCORDING TO ARISTOTLE AND STERNBERG.

To solve the analogy, we must first correctly *encode* the elements—*Washington*, *1*, and *Lincoln*—by identifying them and comparing them to other information. We can first encode *Washington* and *Lincoln* as the names of presidents and then try to combine *Washington* and *1* in a meaningful manner. (There are other possibilities: Both are also the names of memorials and cities, for example.) If we do encode the names as presidents, two possibilities quickly come to mind. Washington was the first president, and his picture is on the $1 bill. We can then generate two possible solutions and try them out. First, was Lincoln the 5th, 10th, 15th, or 50th president? Second, on what bill is Lincoln's picture found? (Do you need to consult a history book or peek into your wallet at this point?) The answer is (a) 5, because Lincoln's likeness is found on the $5 bill. (He was the nation's 16th president, not 15th president.)

Creative intelligence is similar to Aristotle's "productive intelligence" and is defined by the ability to cope with novel situations and generate many possible solutions to problems. It is creative to quickly relate novel situations to familiar situations (that is, to perceive similarities and differences). Psychologists who consider creativity to be separate from analytical intelligence or academic ability note that there is only a moderate relationship between academic ability and creativity (Simonton, 2009). To Sternberg, however, creativity *is* a form of intelligence.

Aristotle and Sternberg both speak of practical intelligence ("street smarts"). Practical intelligence enables people to deal with other people, including difficult people, and to meet the demands of their environment. For example, keeping a job by adapting one's behavior to the employer's requirements is adaptive. But if the employer is making unreasonable demands, finding a more suitable job is also adaptive. Street smarts appear to help people get by in the real world, especially with other people, but are not particularly predictive of academic success (Heng, 2000).

Emotional Intelligence

Psychologists Peter Salovey and John Mayer developed the theory of emotional intelligence, which was popularized by psychologist Daniel Goleman (1995). The theory holds that social and emotional skills, like academic skills, are a form of intelligence (Mayer et al., 2008; Salovey et al., 2008). Emotional intelligence resembles two of Gardner's "intelligences"—intrapersonal

FIGURE 7.3 | Sternberg's Theory of Intelligence

According to Robert Sternberg, there are three types of intelligence: analytical (academic ability), creative, and practical ("street smarts"). Psychologists discuss the relationships between intelligence and creativity, but within Sternberg's model, creativity is a *type* of intellectual functioning.

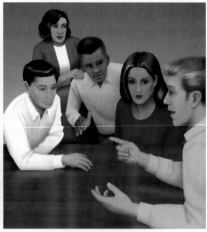

Analytical intelligence
(Academic ability)
Abilities to solve problems, compare and contrast, judge, evaluate, and criticize

Creative intelligence
(Creativity and insight)
Abilities to invent, discover, suppose, or theorize

Practical intelligence
("Street smarts")
Abilities to adapt to the demands of one's environment and apply knowledge in practical situations

© Cengage Learning 2012

skills and interpersonal skills (including insight into the feelings of other people). It also involves self-insight and self-control—the abilities to recognize and regulate one's moods (Salovey et al., 2008). Failure to develop emotional intelligence is connected with poor ability to cope with stress, depression, and aggressive behavior (Brackett et al., 2011).

But *is* emotional intelligence a form of intelligence? Psychologist Ulric Neisser (1997b) says that "the skills that Goleman describes … are certainly important for determining life outcomes, but nothing is to be gained by calling them forms of intelligence."

There are thus many views of intelligence—what intelligence is and how many kinds of intelligence there may be. We do not yet have the final word on the nature of intelligence, but I would like to share psychologist Linda Gottfredson's definition: Intelligence is "a very general mental capability that, among other things, involves the ability to reason, plan, solve problems, think abstractly, comprehend complex ideas, learn quickly and learn from experience. It is not merely book learning, a narrow academic skill, or test-taking smarts. Rather it reflects a broader and deeper capability for comprehending our surroundings—'catching on,' 'making sense,' of things, or 'figuring out what to do'" (in Nisbett, 2009, p. 4).

7-3b CREATIVITY AND INTELLIGENCE

Think of artists, musicians, poets, scientists who innovate research methods, and other creative individuals. Like the concept of intelligence, the concept of creativity has been difficult to define. One issue is whether creativity is distinct from intelligence, or is, as Sternberg suggests, a type of intelligence. For example, we would not ask the question, "Do creative people tend to be intelligent?" unless we saw creativity as distinct from intelligence. If you consider creativity to be an aspect of intelligence, then the two concepts—intelligence and creativity—overlap. But if you think of intelligence as more closely related to academic ability, it is not always true that a highly intelligent person is creative or that a creative person is highly intelligent. Research findings suggest that the relationship between intelligence test

TRUTH **FICTION** (DEPENDS)

THE ANSWER TO WHETHER AN INTELLIGENT PERSON IS CREATIVE OR A CREATIVE PERSON IS INTELLIGENT PARTLY DEPENDS ON DEFINITIONS OF THE TERMS. WHICH PSYCHOLOGIST CONSIDERS CREATIVITY TO BE A KIND OF INTELLIGENCE?

scores and standard measures of creativity is only moderate (Simonton, 2009).

Within his triarchic theory, Sternberg defines **creativity** as the ability to do things that are novel and useful (Sternberg et al., 2012). Creative people can solve problems to which there are no preexisting solutions and no proven formulas. Creative people share a number of qualities (Sternberg et al., 2012): They take chances. They refuse to accept limitations. They appreciate art and music. They use common materials to make unique things. They challenge social norms and take unpopular stands. They challenge ideas that other people accept at face value.

Creative problem solving demands divergent rather than convergent thinking. In **convergent thinking**, thought is limited to present facts; the problem-solver narrows his or her thinking to find the best solution. (You use convergent thinking to arrive at the right answer to a multiple-choice question.) In **divergent thinking**, the problem-solver associates freely to the elements of the problem, allowing "leads" to run a nearly limitless course. (You may use divergent thinking when you are trying to generate ideas to answer an essay question on a test.) Problem solving can involve both kinds of thinking. At first, divergent thinking helps generate many possible solutions. Convergent thinking is then used to select likely solutions and reject others.

Intelligence test questions usually require analytical, convergent thinking to focus in on the one right answer. Tests of creativity determine how flexible a person's thinking is (Simonton, 2009). Here is an item from a test used by Getzels and Jackson (1962) to measure associative ability, a factor in creativity: "Write as many meanings as you can for each of the following words: (a) duck; (b) sack; (c) pitch; (d) fair." Those who write several meanings for each word, rather than only one, are rated as potentially more creative.

Now that we have begun speaking of scores on intelligence tests, let's see how psychologists go about measuring intelligence. We will also see how psychologists attempt to *validate* their measures of intelligence—that is, how they try to demonstrate that they are in fact measuring intelligence.

7-3c THE MEASUREMENT OF INTELLIGENCE

Although psychologists disagree about the nature of intelligence, laypeople and educators are concerned with "how much" intelligence people have, because the issue affects educational and occupational choices. In this section we consider two of the most widely used intelligence tests.

The Stanford–Binet Intelligence Scale

Many of the concepts of psychology have their origins in common sense. The commonsense notion that academic achievement depends on children's intelligence led Alfred Binet and Theodore Simon to invent measures of intelligence.

Early in the 20th century, the French public school system was looking for a test that could identify children who were unlikely to benefit from regular classroom instruction. If these children were identified, they could be given special attention. The first version of that test, the Binet–Simon scale, came into use in 1905. Since that time it has undergone extensive revision and refinement. The current version is the Stanford–Binet Intelligence Scale (SBIS).

Binet assumed that intelligence increases with age, so older children should get more items right than younger children. Binet therefore included a series of age-graded questions, as in Table 7.2, arranged in order of difficulty.

The Binet–Simon scale yielded a score called a **mental age (MA)**. The MA shows the intellectual level at which a child is functioning. For example, a child with an MA of six is functioning intellectually like the average six-year-old. In taking the test, children earned "months" of credit for each correct answer. Their MA was determined by adding up the years and months of credit they attained.

Louis Terman adapted the Binet–Simon scale for use with American children at Stanford University. The first version of the resultant Stanford–Binet Intelligence Scale was published in 1916. The SBIS included more items than the original test and was used with children aged 2 to 16. The SBIS also yielded an **intelligence quotient (IQ)** rather than an MA. As a result, American educators developed interest in learning the IQs of their pupils. The SBIS is used today with children from the age of two upward and with adults.

The IQ reflects the relationship between a child's mental age and his or her actual or chronological age (CA). Use of this ratio reflects the fact that the same MA score has different implications for children of dif-

creativity
the ability to generate novel and useful solutions to problems

convergent thinking
a thought process that narrows in on the single best solution to a problem

divergent thinking
a thought process that attempts to generate multiple solutions to problems

mental age (MA)
the accumulated months of credit that a person earns on the Stanford–Binet Intelligence Scale

intelligence quotient (IQ)
(a) originally, a ratio obtained by dividing a child's score (or mental age) on an intelligence test by chronological age. (b) generally, a score on an intelligence test

TABLE 7.2

Items Similar to Those on the Stanford–Binet Intelligence Scale

LEVEL (YEARS)	ITEM
2	1. Children show knowledge of basic vocabulary words by identifying parts of a doll, such as the mouth, ears, and hair.
	2. Children show counting and spatial skills along with visual–motor coordination by building a tower of four blocks to match a model.
4	1. Children show word fluency and categorical thinking by filling in the missing words when they are asked questions such as: "Father is a man; mother is a _____?" "Hamburgers are hot; ice cream is_____ ?"
	2. Children show comprehension by answering correctly when they are asked questions such as: "Why do people have automobiles?" "Why do people have medicine?"
9	1. Children can point out verbal absurdities, as in this question: "In an old cemetery, scientists unearthed a skull which they think was that of George Washington when he was only five years of age. What is silly about that?"
	2. Children display fluency with words, as shown by answering these questions: "Can you tell me a number that rhymes with snore?" "Can you tell me a color that rhymes with glue?"
Adult	1. Adults show knowledge of the meanings of words and conceptual thinking by correctly explaining the differences between word pairs like "sickness and misery," "house and home," and "integrity and prestige."
	2. Adults show spatial skills by correctly answering questions like: "If a car turned to the right to head north, in what direction was it heading before it turned?"

© Cengage Learning 2012

Rubberball/Mike Kemp/Jupiterimages

ferent ages. That is, an MA of 8 is an above-average score for a 6-year-old but below average for a 10-year-old. In 1912, German psychologist Wilhelm Stern suggested the IQ as a way to deal with this problem. Stern computed IQ using the formula

$$IQ = \frac{\text{Mental age (MA)}}{\text{Chronological age (CA)}} \times 100.$$

According to this formula, a child with an MA of 6 and a CA of 6 would have an IQ of 100. Children who can handle intellectual problems as well as older children do have IQs above 100. For example, an 8-year-old who does as well on the SBIS as the average 10-year-old would attain an IQ of 125. Children who do not answer as many items correctly as other children of the same age attain MAs lower than their CAs. Thus, their IQ scores are below 100.

IQ scores on the SBIS today are derived by comparing their results to those of other people of the same age. People who answer more items correctly than the average for people of the same age attain IQ scores above 100. People who answer fewer items correctly than the average for their age attain scores below 100. Therefore, two children can answer exactly the same items on an intelligence test correctly, yet one can be above average in IQ. This is because the ages of the children may differ. The more intelligent child would be the younger of the two.

The Wechsler Scales

In contrast to the SBIS, David Wechsler developed a series of scales for use with children and adults. The Wechsler scales group test questions into a number of separate subtests (see Figure 7.4). Each subtest measures a different intellectual task. For this reason, the test shows how well a person does on one type of task (such as defining words) as compared with another (such as using blocks to construct geometric designs). In this way, the Wechsler scales highlight children's relative strengths and weaknesses, as well as measure overall intellectual functioning.

Wechsler described some of his scales as measuring *verbal* tasks and others as assessing *performance* tasks. In general, verbal subtests re-

TRUTH TWO CHILDREN CAN ANSWER EXACTLY THE SAME ITEMS ON AN INTELLIGENCE TEST CORRECTLY, YET ONE CAN BE ABOVE AVERAGE AND THE OTHER BELOW AVERAGE IN IQ.

quire knowledge of verbal concepts, whereas performance subtests require familiarity with spatial–relations concepts. Wechsler's scales permit the computation of verbal and performance IQs. Nontechnically oriented college students often attain higher verbal than performance IQs. Less-well-educated people often obtain higher performance than verbal IQs.

Wechsler also introduced the concept of the *deviation IQ.* Instead of dividing mental age by chronological age to compute an IQ, he based IQ scores on how a person's answers compared with those attained by people in the same age group. The average test result at any age level is defined as an IQ score of 100. Wechsler distributed IQ scores so that the middle 50% were defined as the "broad average range" of 90 to 110. As you can see in Figure 7.5, IQ scores cluster around the average. Only 4% of the population have IQ scores of above 130 or below 70.

FIGURE 7.4 | Items Similar to Those on the Wechsler Adult Intelligence Scale

Picture arrangement

These pictures tell a story, but they are in the wrong order. Put them in the right order so that they tell a story.

Picture completion

What part is missing from this picture?

Block design

Put the blocks together to make this picture.

Object assembly

Put the pieces together as quickly as you can.

© Cengage Learning 2012

Group Tests

The SBIS and Wechsler scales are administered to one person at a time. This one-to-one ratio is optimal because it allows the examiner to observe the test taker closely. Examiners are alerted to factors that impair performance, such as language difficulties, illness, or a noisy or poorly lit room. But large institutions with few trained examiners, such as the public schools and armed forces, require tests that can be administered simultaneously to large groups.

Group tests for children were first developed during World War I. At first these tests were hailed as remarkable instruments because they helped school administrators place children. As the years passed, however, group tests came under attack because many administrators relied on them exclusively and did not seek other sources of information about children's abilities.

At their best, intelligence tests provide only one source of information about individual children. Numbers alone, and especially IQ scores, cannot adequately define children's special abilities and talents.

The Reliability and Validity of Intelligence Tests

Over the years, the SBIS and the Wechsler scales have been shown to be reliable and valid. In terms of *reliability*, the scores are rather consistent from testing to testing. This kind of reliability is called *test–retest reliability*. The tests also show *validity* in that the scores correlate moderately to highly with the variables they are supposed to predict, such as school performance, even though motivation and adjustment to the school setting are also involved (Kaplan & Saccuzzo, 2008; Roid & Tippin, 2009).

FIGURE 7.5 | Approximate Distribution of IQ Scores

Many studies of IQ confuse the factors of social class and ethnicity because disproportionate numbers of African Americans, Latin Americans, and Native Americans are found among the lower socioeconomic classes (Helms, 2006; Nisbett, 2009). When we limit our observations to particular ethnic groups, we still find an effect for social class. That is, middle-class European Americans outscore poorer European Americans. Middle-class African Americans, Latin Americans, and Native Americans outscore poorer members of their own ethnic groups. *Washington Post* columnist Eugene Robinson (2011) notes that "a gap has opened up between an educated middle-class Black America and a poor, undereducated Black America." In other words, it would be a mistake to lump all African Americans together.

There may also be intellectual differences between Asians and Caucasians. Asian Americans, for example, frequently outscore European Americans on the math portion of the Scholastic Aptitude Test. Students in China (Taiwan) and Japan also outscore European Americans on achievement tests in math and science (Nisbett, 2009). In the United States, moreover, people of Asian Indian, Korean, Japanese, Filipino, and Chinese descent are more likely than European Americans, African Americans, and Latin Americans to graduate from high school and complete college (Sternberg, 2007; Xie & Goyette, 2003; Yeh & Chang, 2004). They are also overrepresented in competitive colleges and universities (Knapp et al., 2011; Liu, 2009). For example, Asian Americans make up 12% of the population of California, but they comprise 41% of the student population of the state's highest-ranked public university: the University of California at Berkeley.

Most psychologists believe that such ethnic differences reflect cultural attitudes toward education rather than inborn racial differences (Nisbett, 2009). That is, the Asian children may be more motivated to work in school. Research shows that Chinese and Japanese students and their mothers tend to attribute academic

7-3d DIFFERENCES IN INTELLECTUAL FUNCTIONING

The average IQ score in the United States is very close to 100. Yet for some socioeconomic and ethnic groups in the United States, the average is higher, and for others, it is lower. Questions have also been raised about whether males or females are more intelligent overall, and whether there are gender differences in the kinds of intellectual or cognitive skills valued in society. Tests of intellectual functioning have thus been seen as divisive and as maintaining a class system or social order that is based on prejudices and "tradition" as much as on science. In this section we discuss (a) socioeconomic and ethnic differences and (b) gender differences in cognitive skills.

Socioeconomic and Ethnic Differences

There is a body of research suggestive of differences in intelligence—or, more precisely, intelligence test scores—between socioeconomic and ethnic groups. Lower-class U.S. children obtain IQ scores some 10 to 15 points lower than those obtained by middle- and upper-class children. African American children tend to obtain IQ scores some 15 points lower than those obtained by their European American age-mates (Helms, 2006; Neisser et al., 1996). Latin American and Native American children also tend to score below the norms for European Americans (Neisser et al., 1996; Sternberg, 2007).

Ready to study? In the book, you can:

- ○ Review what you've read with Fill-Ins and Multiple Choice quizzes (below).
- ○ Rip out Chapter Review card (in the back).

Or you can go online to CourseMate at www.cengagebrain.com for these resources:

- ○ Complete Practices Quizzes to prepare for tests.
- ○ Review Key Terms Flash Cards (online or print).
- ○ Play games to master concepts.

FILL-INS

Answers can be found in the back of the book, starting on page 368.

1. _____ are mental categories used to class objects, relations, or events with common properties.

2. A(n) _____ is a specific procedure for solving a type of problem.

3. _____ devices are rules of thumb that serve as shortcuts to rapid solutions.

4. A _____ set is the tendency to respond to a new problem with the same approach that helped solve similar problems.

5. According to the _____-relativity hypothesis, language structures the way we perceive the world.

6. Children's use of sentences such as "I standed up" and "Mommy sitted down" are examples of _____.

7. Spearman suggested that intelligent behaviors have a common underlying factor, which he labeled _____, and specific factors that account for specific abilities.

8. Gardner proposes the existence of _____ intelligences, each of which is based in a different area of the brain.

9. Sternberg constructed a "triarchic" model of intelligence, including analytical, creative, and _____ intelligence.

10. The Stanford–Binet Intelligence Scale yields a score called a(n) _____ _____ (IQ).

1. Eight-year-old Stephanie understands that her dog Boodles is a dog and that all dogs are animals. Stephanie's concept of animal is best characterized as

   a. intuitive.   c. overextended.
   b. ideational.   d. hierarchical.

2. Algorithms are usually time consuming, whereas _____ provide a more rapid solution when they work.

   a. anagrams
   b. formulas
   c. systematic random searches
   d. heuristics

3. What conclusion may be drawn about problem solving from Maier's studies with Bismarck?

   a. Only humans can solve problems by means of insight.
   b. A rat has demonstrated insight under laboratory conditions.
   c. A rat has demonstrated trial-and-error learning under laboratory conditions.
   d. Rats are capable of insight under a variety of conditions.

4. One plausible explanation of the incubation effect is

   a. the tendency to allow the unconscious to free up insights.
   b. distancing problem solvers from persistent but unproductive mental sets.
   c. conscious searching for heuristic devices.
   d. spontaneous means-end analysis.

5. True language is distinguished from the communications systems of lower animals by all of the following except

   a. infinite creativity.
   b. displacement.
   c. making sounds.
   d. semanticity.

6. When reading the sentences, "The chicken is ready for dinner," and "The lion is ready for dinner," if you understand which is ready to eat and which is ready to be eaten, you are using the phrase "is ready to eat" with different _____ in each case.

   a. morphemes   c. factors
   b. phonemes   d. semanticity

7. Jamie's mother was concerned that her 4-year-old daughter overregularized plurals and tenses. She took Jamie to Dr. Acton, a noted learning theorist, who advised her to

   a. wait for Jamie's speech to correct itself.
   b. take her to a speech therapist.
   c. correct her grammar through imitation and repetition.
   d. begin instruction in another language.

8. According to Robert Sternberg, the three types of intelligence are

   a. logical, musical, emotional.
   b. experimental, logical, verbal.
   c. verbal, performance, problem solving.
   d. analytical, creative, practical.

9. The ability to do things that are unique and beneficial and to generate novel combinations out of existing elements describes

   a. insight.   c. intelligence.
   b. creativity.   d. expertise.

10. According to the text, Janet Hyde and her colleagues studied the performance of some 7 million children in second through eleventh grades in mathematics and found that

    a. boys obtained higher scores than girls.
    b. girls obtained higher scores than boys.
    c. there were no overall gender differences in scores.
    d. European Americans obtained higher scores than any other racial or ethnic group.

THE IN-CROWD

Share your 4LTR Press story on Facebook at
www.facebook.com/4ltrpress for a chance to win.

To learn more about the
In-Crowd opportunity 'like'
us on Facebook.

© age fotostock / SuperStock

LEARNING OUTCOMES

8-1 Define motivation including needs, drives, and incentives

8-2 Identify the theories of motivation

8-3 Describe the biological and psychological contributions to hunger

8-4 Explain the role of sex hormones and the sexual response cycle in human sexuality

8-5 Describe achievement motivation

8-6 Identify the theoretical explanations of emotions

STUDY TOOLS ▶ After you read the chapter, go to the Study Tools at the end of the chapter, page 214.

CHAPTER 8

Motivation and EMOTION

The Seekers had received word that the world was coming to an end on December 21st. A great flood would engulf their city and the rest of the Earth. Now they were gathered around their leader, Marian Keech, in her home, as she recorded messages that she said were sent to her by the Guardians from outer space. The messages were received through "automatic writing"; that is, the Guardians communicated through Ms. Keech, who wrote down their words without awareness. Another message brought good news, however. Because of their faith, the Seekers would be saved by flying saucers at the stroke of midnight on the 21st.

In their classic observational study, Leon Festinger and his colleagues (1956) described how they managed to be present in Ms. Keech's household at the fateful hour by pretending to belong to the group. Their purpose was to observe the behavior of the Seekers during and following the prophecy's failure. The cognitive theory of motivation that the researchers were working on—*cognitive-dissonance theory*—suggested that there would be a discrepancy or conflict between two key cognitions: (1) Ms. Keech is a prophet, and (2) Ms. Keech is wrong.

How might the conflict be resolved? One way would be for the Seekers to lose faith in Ms. Keech. But the researchers expected that according to their theory, the Seekers could also be motivated to resolve the conflict by going out to spread the word and find additional converts. Otherwise, the group would be painfully embarrassed.

Let's return to the momentous night. Many members of the group had quit their jobs and gone on spending sprees before the anticipated end. Now, as midnight approached, they fidgeted, awaiting the flying saucers. Midnight came, but there were no saucers. Anxious glances were exchanged. There was silence, and then some coughs. Minutes passed, torturously slowly. Watches were checked, more glances exchanged.

At 4:00 a.m., a bitter and frantic Ms. Keech complained that she sensed that members of the group were doubting her. At 4:45 a.m., however, she seemed suddenly relieved. Another message was arriving, and Ms. Keech was spelling it out through automatic writ-

When a prophecy fails, how do its believers respond? Why?

TRUTH OR FICTION

WHAT DO YOU THINK? FOLKLORE, COMMON SENSE, OR NONSENSE? CIRCLE THE T FOR "TRUTH" OR THE F FOR "FICTION," AND CHECK THE ACCURACY OF YOUR ANSWERS AS YOU READ THROUGH THE CHAPTER.

T	F	GETTING AWAY FROM IT ALL BY GOING ON A VACATION FROM ALL SENSORY INPUT FOR A FEW HOURS IS RELAXING.
T	F	PEOPLE FEEL HUNGER DUE TO CONTRACTIONS ("PANGS") IN THE STOMACH.
T	F	FASHION MAGAZINES CAN CONTRIBUTE TO EATING DISORDERS AMONG WOMEN.
T	F	MONEY CAN'T BUY YOU HAPPINESS.
T	F	YOU MAY BE ABLE TO FOOL A LIE DETECTOR BY BITING YOUR TONGUE OR SQUIGGLING YOUR TOES.

ing! The Seekers, it turned out, had managed to save the world through their faith. The universal powers had decided to let the world travel on along its sinful way for a while longer. Why? Because of the faith of the Seekers, there was hope!

With their faith restored, the followers called wire services and newspapers to spread the word. The three psychologists from the University of Minnesota went home, weary but enlightened. They wrote a book enti-

motivation
the state in which an organism experiences an inducement or incentive to do something

motive
a hypothetical state within an organism that propels the organism toward a goal

need
a state of deprivation

drive
a condition of arousal in an organism that is associated with a need

incentive
an object, person, or situation perceived as capable of satisfying a need or as desirable for its own sake

instinct
an inherited disposition to activate specific behavior patterns that are designed to reach certain goals

tled *When Prophecy Fails,* which serves as one of the key documents of their theory.

8-1 The Psychology of Motivation

The psychology of **motivation** is concerned with the *why* of behavior. Why do we eat? Why do some of us strive to get ahead? Why do some of us ride motorcycles at breakneck speeds? Why are some people aggressive? Why were the Seekers in a state of discomfort when the prophecy failed?

To answer these questions, psychologists use concepts such as *motives, needs, drives,* and *incentives.* **Motives** are hypothetical states that activate behavior, propelling us toward goals. We call them "hypothetical states" because motives are not seen and measured directly. They are inferred from behavior. Motives may take the form of *needs, drives,* and *incentives,* which are also inferred from behavior.

Psychologists speak of physiological and psychological **needs**. We must meet physiological needs to survive. Examples include the needs for oxygen, food, drink, pain avoidance, proper temperature, and elimination of waste products. Some physiological needs, such as hunger and thirst, are states of physical deprivation. When we have not eaten or drunk for a while, we develop needs for food and water. The body also needs oxygen, vitamins, and so on.

Psychological needs include needs for achievement, power, self-esteem, social approval, and belonging. Psychological needs are not necessarily based on states of deprivation. A person with a need for achievement may already have a history of successful achievements. Because people's biological makeups are similar, we share similar physiological needs. But because we are influenced by our cultural settings, our needs may be expressed in different ways. We all need food, but some prefer a vegetarian diet whereas others prefer meat. Because learning enters into psychological needs, they can differ markedly from one person to another.

Needs give rise to **drives**. Depletion of food gives rise to the hunger drive, and depletion of liquids gives rise to

the thirst drive. *Physiological drives* are the counterparts of physiological needs. When we have gone without food and water, our body may *need* these substances. However, our *experience* of the drives of hunger and thirst is psychological. Drives arouse us to action and tend to be stronger when we have been deprived longer. We are hungrier when we haven't eaten for 10 hours than 1 hour.

Psychological needs for approval, achievement, and belonging also give rise to drives. We can have a drive to get ahead in the business world just as we have a drive to eat. Psychologists are working to learn more about the origins of these drives. We do know that we can also be driven to obtain *incentives.* An **incentive** is an object, a person, or a situation that can satisfy a need or is desirable for its own sake. Money, food, a sexually attractive person, social approval, and attention can all act as incentives.

8-2 Theories of Motivation

Although psychologists agree that it is important to understand why humans and lower animals do things, they do not agree about the precise nature of motivation. Let's consider various theoretical perspectives on motivation.

8-2a THE EVOLUTIONARY PERSPECTIVE

The evolutionary perspective notes that many animals are neurally "prewired"—that is, born with preprogrammed tendencies—to respond to certain situations in certain ways (Burghardt, 2009; Confer et al., 2010). Spiders spin webs instinctively. Bees "dance" instinctively to communicate the location of food to other bees.

These instinctive behaviors are found in particular species. They are *species-specific.* Species-specific behaviors are also called **instincts** and are inborn. They are genetically transmitted from generation to generation.

Psychologists have asked whether humans have instincts, and if so, how many. More than a

In the presence of another male, Siamese fighting fish *(Betta splendens)* assume stereotypical threatening postures in which they extend their fins and gills and circle one another. If neither male retreats, there will be conflict.

© George Diebold/Photodisc/Getty Images

century ago, psychologists William James (1890) and William McDougall (1908) argued that humans have instincts that foster survival and social behavior. James numbered love, sympathy, and modesty as social instincts. McDougall compiled 12 "basic" instincts, including hunger, sex, and self-assertion. Other psychologists have made longer lists, and still others deny that people have instincts. The question of whether people have instincts—and what they might be—remains unresolved.

8-2b DRIVE-REDUCTIONISM AND HOMEOSTASIS

Sigmund Freud believed that tension motivates us to behave in ways that restore us to a resting state. His views are similar to those of the **drive-reduction theory** of learning, as set forth by psychologist Clark Hull in the 1930s.

According to Hull, *primary drives* such as hunger, thirst, and pain trigger arousal (tension) and activate behavior. We learn to engage in behaviors that reduce the tension. We also acquire drives—called *acquired drives*—through experience. We may acquire a drive for money because money enables us to obtain food, drink, and homes, which protect us from crime and extremes of temperature. We might acquire drives for social approval and affiliation because other people, and their goodwill, help us reduce primary drives, especially when we are infants. In all cases, reduction of tension is the goal. Yet some people appear to acquire what could be considered excessive drives for money or affiliation. They gather money long after their material needs have been met, and some people find it difficult to be alone, even briefly.

Primary drives like hunger are triggered when we are in a state of deprivation. Sensations of hunger motivate us to act in ways that will restore the bodily balance. This tendency to maintain a steady state is called **homeostasis** Homeostasis works like a thermostat. When the temperature in a room drops below the *set point*, the heating system turns on. The heat stays on until the set point is reached. Similarly, most animals eat until they are no longer hungry. But many people eat "recreationally"—as when they see an appealing dessert—suggesting there is more to eating than drive reduction.

8-2c THE SEARCH FOR STIMULATION

Physical needs give rise to drives like hunger and thirst. In such cases, we are motivated to *reduce* the tension or stimulation that impinges on us. However, in the case of *stimulus motives*, organisms seek to *increase* stimulation.

A classic study conducted at McGill University in Montreal during the 1950s suggests the importance

> "Such is the state of life, that none are happy but by the anticipation of change: the change itself is nothing; when we have made it, the next wish is to change again."
>
> —DR. SAMUEL JOHNSON

of sensory stimulation and activity. Some "lucky" students were paid $20 a day (which, with inflation, would now be more like $200) for doing nothing—literally. Would you like to "work" by doing nothing for $200 a day? Don't answer too quickly. According to the results of this study you might not like it at all.

In this experiment, student volunteers were placed in quiet cubicles and blindfolded (Bexton et al., 1954). Their arms were bandaged so that they felt little if anything with their hands. They could hear nothing but the dull, continuous hum of air conditioning. Many slept for a while, but after a few hours of sensory-deprived wakefulness, most felt bored and irritable. As time went on, many grew more uncomfortable. Many students quit the experiment during the first day despite the financial incentive. Many of those who remained for a

Do organisms have innate drives to obtain sensory stimulation, manipulate objects (like these young rhesus monkeys), and explore the environment?

self-actualization

according to Maslow and other humanistic psychologists, self-initiated striving to become what one is capable of being

FICTION GENERALLY, IT IS NOT TRUE THAT GETTING AWAY FROM IT ALL BY GOING ON A VACATION FROM ALL SENSORY INPUT FOR A FEW HOURS IS RELAXING.

few days found it hard to concentrate on simple problems for days afterward. For many, the experiment did not provide a relaxing vacation. Instead, it produced boredom, discomfort, and disorientation.

Humans and other animals appear motivated to seek novel stimulation. Even when they have been deprived of food, rats may explore unfamiliar arms of mazes rather than head straight for the food source. Animals that have just copulated and thereby reduced their primary sex drives often show renewed interest in sex when presented with a novel sex partner. People (and nonhumans) take in more calories at buffets and smorgasbords than when fewer kinds of food are available (Szentirmai et al., 2010). Children spend hour after hour playing video games for the pleasure of zapping virtual people or monsters.

Stimulus motives provide an evolutionary advantage. Animals that are active and motivated to explore and manipulate their environment are more likely to survive. If you know where the nearest tall tree is, you're more likely to escape a leopard and transmit your genes to future generations.

But note that survival is more or less a question of defending oneself or one's group against dangers of one kind or another. In the following section, we see that many psychologists believe people are also motivated to develop their unique potentials, even in the absence of any external threat.

8-2d HUMANISTIC THEORY

Humanistic psychologists such as Abraham Maslow (1908–1970) suggest that human behavior is not just mechanical and aimed toward survival and the reduction of tension. Maslow believed that people are also motivated by a conscious desire for personal growth. Humanists note that people tolerate pain, hunger, and many other kinds of tension to obtain personal fulfillment.

Maslow believed that we are separated from other animals by our capacity for **self-actualization**, or self-initiated striving to become what we believe we are capable of being. Maslow considered self-actualization to be as important a need in humans as hunger. The need for self-actualization pushes people to strive to

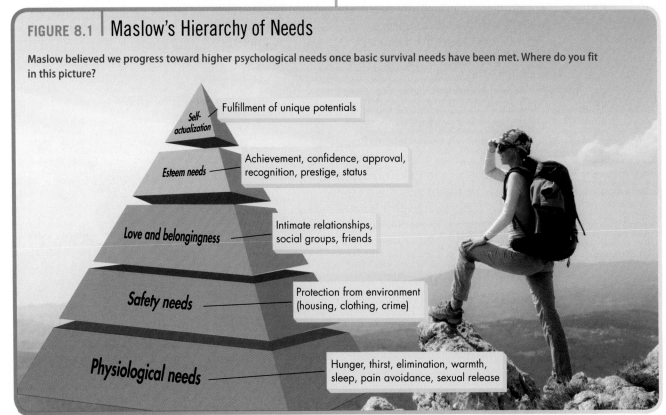

FIGURE 8.1 | **Maslow's Hierarchy of Needs**

Maslow believed we progress toward higher psychological needs once basic survival needs have been met. Where do you fit in this picture?

- *Self-actualization* — Fulfillment of unique potentials
- *Esteem needs* — Achievement, confidence, approval, recognition, prestige, status
- *Love and belongingness* — Intimate relationships, social groups, friends
- *Safety needs* — Protection from environment (housing, clothing, crime)
- *Physiological needs* — Hunger, thirst, elimination, warmth, sleep, pain avoidance, sexual release

iStockphoto.com/gaspr13

become concert pianists, chief executive officers, or best-selling authors—even when they have plenty of money to live on.

Maslow (1970) organized human needs into a hierarchy. Maslow's **hierarchy of needs** ranges from physiological needs such as hunger and thirst, through self-actualization (see Figure 8.1). He believed that we naturally strive to climb this hierarchy.

Critics of Maslow's theory argue that there is too much individual variation for the hierarchy of motives to apply to everyone (Cooke, 2008). Some people whose physiological, safety, and love needs are met show little interest in achievement and recognition. And some artists devote themselves fully to their craft, even if they have to pass up the comforts of a warm home or alienate their families.

8-2e COGNITIVE PERSPECTIVES ON MOTIVATION

Cognitive theorists note that people represent their worlds mentally. As in Piaget's cognitive developmental theory, they see people as natural scientists who strive to understand the world so that they can predict and control events. Therefore, people try to eliminate inconsistencies—or, as we saw in the case of the Seekers at the beginning of the chapter—discrepancies in information so that their ability to make sense of the world remains whole.

Children also attempt to create consistency between their own gender and what experience teaches them that boys and girls are expected to do in their cultural settings. As soon as they come to understand whether they are male or female, they begin to imitate the behavior of older people of the same gender (Ruble et al., 2006). According to *cognitive-dissonance theory*, people are generally motivated to hold consistent beliefs and to justify their behavior. That is why we are generally more likely to appreciate what we must work to obtain.

Each theory of motivation may have something to offer. Drive-reduction theory may explain why we drink when thirsty, but stimulus motives might explain why we go clubbing and drink alcohol. Each theory might apply to certain aspects of behavior. As the chapter progresses, we will describe research that lends support to each theory.

"IN GENERAL MY CHILDREN REFUSE TO EAT ANYTHING THAT HASN'T DANCED ON TELEVISION."
—ERMA BOMBECK

8-3 Hunger

We need food to survive, but for many of us, food means more than survival. Food is a symbol of family togetherness and caring. We associate food with the nurturance of the parent–child relationship and with visits home on holidays. Friends and relatives offer us food when we enter their homes, and saying no may be viewed as a personal rejection. Bacon and eggs, coffee with cream and sugar, meat and mashed potatoes—all seem to be part of sharing American values and abundance.

8-3a BIOLOGICAL INFLUENCES ON HUNGER

In considering the bodily mechanisms that regulate hunger, let's begin with the mouth, where we get signals of **satiety** that regulate our eating. We also get signals of satiety from the digestive tract, although it takes longer for these signals to reach the brain. Therefore, if we did not receive signals of satiety from chewing and swallowing, we might eat for a long time after we had taken in enough food.

What triggers your hunger drive? Are you only interested in eating when your blood sugar level falls, or do the sights and aromas of foods stimulate you to eat?

© Alloy Photography/Veer

ventromedial nucleus (VMN)
a central area on the underside of the hypothalamus that appears to function as a stop-eating center

hyperphagic
characterized by excessive eating

lateral hypothalamus
an area at the side of the hypothalamus that appears to function as a start-eating center

To demonstrate that chewing and swallowing provide feelings of satiety, researchers conducted classic "sham feeding" experiments with dogs. They implanted a tube in the animals' throats so that any food swallowed fell out of the body. Even though no food reached the stomach, the animals stopped feeding after a while (Janowitz & Grossman, 1949). Thus, sensations of chewing and swallowing must provide some feelings of satiety. However, the dogs in the study resumed feeding sooner than animals whose food did reach the stomach. Let's proceed to the stomach, too, as we seek further regulatory factors in hunger.

An empty stomach leads to stomach contractions, which we call *hunger pangs*. Classic research suggested that stomach contractions are crucial to hunger. A man (A. L. Washburn) swallowed a balloon that was inflated in his stomach. His stomach contractions squeezed the balloon, so the contractions could be recorded by observers. Washburn also pressed a key when he felt hungry, and the researchers found a correspondence between his stomach contractions and his feelings of hunger (Cannon & Washburn, 1912).

Medical observations and classic research find that humans and nonhumans whose stomachs have been removed still regulate food intake so as to maintain a normal weight (Tsang, 1938). (Food is absorbed through their intestines.) This finding led to the discovery of other mechanisms that regulate hunger, including the hypothalamus, blood sugar level, and receptors in the liver. When we are deprived of food, the level of sugar in the blood drops. The drop in blood sugar is communicated to the hypothalamus, which stokes the hunger drive.

The hypothalamus is a pea-sized structure in the brain that's involved in many aspects of motivation, including sex, aggression, and hunger. Two parts of it that involve the hunger drive are of particular interest. When a researcher destroys the **ventromedial nucleus (VMN)** of a rat's hypothalamus during surgery, the rat will grope toward food as soon as its eyes open (Fetissov & Meguid, 2010). Then it eats vast quantities of Purina Rat Chow or whatever is available. Investigators have concluded that the VMN functions like a "stop-eating center" in the rat's brain. If the VMN is electri-

"There is no sincerer love than the love of food."
—GEORGE BERNARD SHAW

cally stimulated—that is, "switched on"—the rat stops eating until the current is turned off. When the VMN is destroyed, the rat becomes **hyperphagic** (see Figure 8.2). That is, it continues to eat until it has about doubled its normal weight. Then it will level off its eating rate and maintain the higher weight. It is as if the set point of the stop-eating center has been raised to a higher level, like turning up the thermostat in a house from 65°F to 70°F. Some people develop tumors near the base of the brain that damage the VMN and apparently cause them to overeat and grow obese (Chance et al., 2007).

By contrast, the **lateral hypothalamus** may function like a "start-eating center." If you electrically stimulate the lateral hypothalamus, the rat starts to eat (N. E. Miller, 1995). If you destroy the lateral hypothala-

---

FIGURE 8.2 | A Hyperphagic Rat

This rodent winner of the basketball look-alike contest went on a binge after it received a lesion in the ventromedial nucleus (VMN) of the hypothalamus. It is as if the lesion pushed the "set point" for the body weight up several notches; the rat's weight is now about five times normal. But now it eats only enough to maintain its pleasantly plump figure, so you need not be concerned that it will eventually burst. If the lesion had been made in the lateral hypothalamus, the animal might have become the Calista Flockhart of the rat world.

Dr. Neal Miller/Yale University

mus, the rat may stop eating altogether—that is, become **aphagic**. If you force-feed an aphagic rat for a while, however, it begins to eat on its own and levels off at a relatively low body weight. It is as if you have lowered the rat's set point. It is like turning down the thermostat from, say, 70°F to 40°F.

8-3b PSYCHOLOGICAL INFLUENCES ON HUNGER

Although many areas of the body work in concert to regulate the hunger drive, this is only part of the story. In human beings, the hunger drive is more complex. Psychological as well as physiological factors play an important role. How many times have you been made hungry by the sight or aroma of food? How many times have you eaten not because you were hungry but because you were at a relative's home or hanging around a cafeteria or coffee shop? Or because you felt anxious or depressed? Or simply because you were bored?

TRUTH IT IS TRUE THAT PANGS IN THE STOMACH ARE CONNECTED WITH FEELINGS OF HUNGER, *BUT* STOMACH CONTRACTIONS ARE NOT AS INFLUENTIAL AS FORMERLY THOUGHT.

One study confirmed what most of us already assumed—that watching television increases the amount of food we eat (Higgs & Woodward, 2009). One reason is that watching television can distract us from bodily changes that signal fullness and from cognitive awareness of how much we have already eaten. The same reason seems to hold true for gorging on popcorn, candy, and soft drinks at the movies. Watching television also interferes with memory formation of how much we have eaten, making us vulnerable to overeating at subsequent meals.

8-3c BEING OVERWEIGHT: A SERIOUS AND PERVASIVE PROBLEM

Consider some facts about being overweight (Flegal et al., 2010):

- More than two out of three adult Americans are overweight, according to the national *body mass index (BMI)* guidelines, and one in three are obese.
- Problems with unhealthy weight gain have been on the upswing in the United States; for example, 68% of Americans were overweight in 2008 as compared with 60% in 1988–1994.
- More than 78% of African American women and 81% of Latina Americans, age 40 and older, are overweight, and about half are obese.
- Obesity is a risk in various chronic medical conditions including type 2 diabetes, hypertension (high blood pressure), high cholesterol levels, stroke, heart disease, some cancers, and arthritis.
- Weight control is elusive for most people, who regain most of the weight they have lost, even when they have dieted "successfully" (Apovian, 2010; Heber, 2010).

Studies using data obtained by the federal government find that extremely obese people, whose BMIs are greater than or equal to 40, live shorter lives than people who are normal in weight (Finkelstein et al., 2010; see Table 8.1). With all the health problems connected to obesity, why are so many people obese?

Factors in Becoming Overweight

Many biological and psychological factors are involved in obesity. Being overweight runs in families. A study of Scandinavian adoptees by Albert Stunkard and his colleagues (1990) found that children bear a closer resemblance in weight to their biological parents than to their adoptive parents. Today, it is widely accepted that heredity plays a role in obesity in humans (Bouchard, 2010) and other animals, including monkeys and rats (Felsted et al., 2010).

The efforts of overweight people to maintain a slender profile may be sabotaged by an adaptive mechanism that would help preserve life in times of famine—*adaptive thermogenesis*. This mechanism causes the body to produce less energy (burn fewer calories) when someone goes on a diet (Apovian, 2010; Heber, 2010). This does not mean that overweight people will not lose weight by dieting; it means that it will take longer than expected.

aphagic
characterized by undereating

TABLE 8.1

Years of Life Lost by an Extremely Obese, Non-smoking 40-Year-Old, Compared with a Normal-Weight Person of the Same Age

	EUROPEAN AMERICAN	AFRICAN AMERICAN
Male	9	8
Female	7	5

Source of data: Finkelstein, E. A., Brown, D. S., Wrage, L. A., Allaire, B. T., & Hoerger, T. J. (2010). Individual and Aggregate Years-of-life-lost Associated with Overweight and Obesity. *Obesity*, *18*(2), 333–339.

anorexia nervosa
a life-threatening eating disorder characterized by dramatic weight loss and a distorted body image

Fatty tissue in the body also metabolizes (burns) food more slowly than muscle does. For this reason, a person with a high fat-to-muscle ratio metabolizes food more slowly than a person of the same weight with more muscle (Apovian, 2010; Heber, 2010). That is, two people of the same weight may metabolize food at different rates, depending on their distribution of muscle and fat. Meanwhile, the normal distribution of fat cells is different for men and women. The average man is 40% muscle and 15% fat. The average woman is 23% muscle and 25% fat. If a man and a woman with typical distributions of muscle and fat are of equal weight, therefore, the woman—who has more fat cells—must eat less to maintain that weight.

We also live in an "obesogenic environment" (Apovian, 2010; Heber, 2010). Foods high in sugar and fat are everywhere. Children in the United States are exposed to an average of 10,000 food commercials a year. More than nine of ten of these commercials are for fast foods, sugared cereals, candy, and soft drinks (Harris et al., 2009; Sixsmith & Furnham, 2010). Psychological factors, such as observational learning, stress, and emotional

© Mike Kemp/Rubberball/Getty Images

states, also "bombard" us and play a role in obesity (Apovian, 2010). Situations contribute as well. Family celebrations, watching television, arguments, and tension at work can all lead to overeating or going off a diet. Efforts to diet may also be impeded by negative emotions such as depression and anxiety, which can lead to binge eating (Ricca et al., 2009).

8-3d EATING DISORDERS

Consider some facts about eating and eating disorders in the United States, as reported by the National Eating Disorders Association (2010):

- More than half of teenage girls and nearly one third of teenage boys use unhealthful methods to try to control their weight, including fasting, skipping meals, smoking cigarettes, vomiting, and using laxatives.

- About two out of five first- through third-grade girls would like to be thinner.

- More than four out of five 10-year-old girls report fear of being fat.

- Nearly half of 9- to 11-year old girls are "sometimes" or "very often" dieting.

- More than 90% of college women have dieted at some time.

Eating disorders are characterized by persistent, gross disturbances in eating patterns. In this section, we focus on an eating disorder in which individuals are too thin, *anorexia nervosa*, and one in which the person may be normal in weight, but certainly not in the methods used to maintain that weight—*bulimia nervosa*.

Anorexia Nervosa

Anorexia nervosa is a life-threatening eating disorder characterized by extreme fear of being too heavy, dramatic weight loss, a distorted body image, and resistance to eating enough to reach or maintain a healthful weight. Anorexia nervosa mostly afflicts women during adolescence and young adulthood (Ackard et al., 2007). The typical person with anorexia is a young European American female of higher socioeconomic status. Affluent females have greater access to fitness centers and health clubs and are more likely to subscribe to the magazines that idealize slender bodies and shop in the boutiques that cater to svelte women. They are regularly confronted with unrealistic standards of slimness that make them dissatisfied with their own figures (Ackard et al., 2007).

Females with anorexia nervosa can drop 25% or more of their weight within a year. Severe weight loss can prevent ovulation and cause respiratory and cardiovascular problems (Andersen & Ryan, 2009; Gardini et al., 2009; Papadopoulos et al., 2009). Females with anorexia are also at risk for premature development of osteoporosis, a condition characterized by loss of bone density that usually afflicts people in late adulthood (Andersen & Ryan, 2009). Given these problems, the mortality rate for females with anorexia nervosa is approximately 5%.

In one common pattern, the girl sees that she has gained some weight after reaching puberty, and she resolves that she must lose it. But even after the weight is gone, she maintains her pattern of dieting and, in many cases, exercises at a fever pitch. This pattern continues as she plunges below her "desirable" weight. Girls with the disorder are in denial about health problems; some point to feverish exercise routines as evidence of strength. Distortion of the body image—seeing oneself as heavier than one is—is a major feature of the disorder (Hrabosky et al., 2009; Miyake et al., 2010).

Bulimia Nervosa

Bulimia nervosa entails repeated cycles of binge eating and purging. Like anorexia, it tends to afflict women during adolescence and young adulthood (Bravender et al., 2010). Binge eating often follows on the heels of food restriction—as in dieting (Cifani et al., 2009; White et al., 2009). There are various methods of purging. Some people vomit. Other avenues include strict dieting or fasting, the use of laxatives, and engaging in demanding, prolonged exercise regimens. Individuals with eating disorders tend to be perfectionists about their bodies. They will not settle for less than their idealized body shape and weight (Franco et al., 2009; Watson et al., 2011). Bulimia, like anorexia, triggers hormonal imbalances: Many women with bulimia nervosa have irregular menstrual cycles (Mendelsohn, & Warren, 2010). Eating disorders are upsetting and dangerous in themselves, of course, but they are also often connected with deep depression (Wilson et al., 2010).

Origins of the Eating Disorders

Health professionals have done a great deal of research into the origins of eating disorders, but they admit that many questions about them remain unanswered.

Many parents are obsessed with getting their children—especially their infants—to eat. Thus, some psychologists suggest that children now and then refuse to eat as a way of engaging in warfare with their parents. ("You have to eat something!" "I'm not hungry!") It often seems that warfare does occur in the families of adolescents with eating disorders. Parents in such families are often unhappy with the family's functioning. They frequently have issues with eating and dieting themselves. They also "act out" against their daughters—letting them know that they consider them unattractive and, prior to the development of the eating disorder, letting them know that they think they should lose weight (Cooper et al., 2001; Crittenden & Dallos, 2009).

A particularly disturbing risk factor for eating disorders in adolescent females is a history of child abuse, particularly sexual abuse (Leung et al., 2010; Maniglio, 2009). One study found a history of childhood sexual abuse in about half of women with bulimia nervosa, as opposed to a rate of about 7% among women without the disorder (Deep et al., 1999).

The sociocultural climate also affects eating behavior. Slimness is idealized in the United States. When you check out current fashion magazines and catalogs, you are looking at models who, on average, are 9% taller and 16% thinner than the typical female—and who still manage to have ample bust lines. Miss America, the annually renewed American role model, has also been slenderizing across the years. Over the past 80 years, the winner has added only 2% in height but has lost 12 pounds in weight. In the 1920s, Miss America's weight relative to her height yielded a body mass index (BMI) of 20 to 25, which is considered normal by the World Health Organization (WHO). The WHO labels people as malnourished when their BMIs are lower than 18.5. Recent Miss Americas, however, come in at a BMI near 17 (Ludescher et al., 2009). As the cultural ideal slenderizes, women with average body weights according to the health charts feel overweight, and more-than-average women feel gargantuan.

bulimia nervosa
an eating disorder characterized by repeated cycles of binge eating and purging

Kristian Dowling/Getty Images

The Model Figure for the 2010s?
The great majority of women who compare themselves to the idealized embodiment of the tall, slender model are likely to be disappointed. The models' body mass index (BMI) is about 17, and nearly two of three American women have a BMI in excess of 25.

activating effect
the arousal-producing effects of sex hormones that increase the likelihood of sexual behavior

estrus
the periodic sexual excitement of many female mammals as governed by levels of sex hormones

sexual response cycle
Masters and Johnson's model of sexual response, which consists of four stages or phases: excitement, plateau, orgasm, and resolution

vasocongestion
engorgement of blood vessels with blood, which swells the genitals and breasts during sexual arousal

myotonia
muscle tension

excitement phase
the first phase of the sexual response cycle, which is characterized by muscle tension, increases in the heart rate, and erection in the male and vaginal lubrication in the female

8-4 Sexual Motivation and Sexual Orientation

In a TV comedy, a mother referred to her teenage son as "a hormone with feet." She recognized that her son had become obsessed with sex, which is normal enough for adolescents in our culture. It is also now widely understood that the adolescent preoccupation with sex is strongly related to the surge in sex hormones that occurs at puberty. The phrase "a hormone with feet" implies movement as well as motivation, and movement means direction. We will see that sex hormones tend to propel us in certain directions as well as provide the driving force.

8-4a HORMONES AND SEXUAL MOTIVATION

Sex hormones can be said to fuel the sex drive. Research with men who produce little testosterone—due to age or health problems—shows that their sex drive increases when they receive testosterone replacement therapy (Muraleedharan & Jones, 2010). The most common sexual problem among women is lack of sexual desire or interest, and the sex drive in women is also connected to testosterone levels (Downey, 2009). Although men produce 7 to 10 times the testosterone produced by women, women produce androgens ("male" sex hormones) in the adrenal glands and the ovaries. Testosterone injections, patches, or pills can heighten the sex drive in women who do not produce enough of the hormone (Brand & van der Schouw, 2010).

Sex hormones promote the development of male and female sex organs and regulate the menstrual cycle. They also have *activating* and *organizing* effects on sexual behavior. They affect the sex drive and promote sexual response; these are **activating effects**. Female mice, rats, cats, and dogs are receptive to males only during **estrus**, when female sex hormones are plentiful.

During estrus, female rats respond to males by hopping, wiggling their ears, and arching their backs with their tails to one side, thus enabling males to penetrate them.

8-4b SEXUAL RESPONSE AND SEXUAL BEHAVIOR

Men show more interest in sex than women do (Fisher et al., 2012; Schmitt et al., 2012). A survey of more than 1,000 undergraduates found that men reported being more interested than women in casual sex and multiple sex partners (Schmitt et al., 2012). Women are more likely to want to combine sex with a romantic relationship (Fisher et al., 2012).

Although we may be more culturally attuned to focus on sex differences rather than similarities, William Masters and Virginia Johnson (1966) found that the biological responses of males and females to sexual stimulation are quite similar. Masters and Johnson use the term **sexual response cycle** to describe the changes that occur in the body as men and women become sexually aroused. They divide the sexual response cycle into four phases: *excitement, plateau, orgasm,* and *resolution.*

The sexual response cycle is characterized by *vasocongestion* and *myotonia*. **Vasocongestion** is the swelling of the genital tissues with blood, causing erection of the penis and swelling of the area surrounding the vaginal opening. The testes and the nipples swell as blood vessels dilate in these areas. **Myotonia** is muscle tension, which causes grimaces, spasms in the hands and feet, and the spasms of orgasm.

Erection, vaginal lubrication, and orgasm are all reflexes. That is, they occur automatically in response to adequate sexual stimulation.

Excitement Phase

Vasocongestion during the **excitement phase** cause erection in men. The scrotal skin thickens, becoming less baggy. The testes increase in size and become elevated.

In the female, excitement is characterized by vaginal lubrication, which may start 10 to 30 seconds after sexual stimulation begins. Vasocongestion swells the clitoris, flattens and spreads the vaginal lips, and expands the inner part of the vagina. The breasts enlarge, and blood vessels near the surface become more prominent. The nipples may erect in both men and women. Heart rate and blood pressure increase.

Plateau Phase

The level of sexual arousal remains somewhat stable during the **plateau phase** of the cycle. Because of vasocongestion, the circumference of the head of the penis increases somewhat. The testes are elevated into position for **ejaculation** and may reach one-and-a-half times their unaroused size.

In women, vasocongestion swells the outer part of the vagina and the inner vagina expands further. The clitoris withdraws beneath the clitoral hood and shortens. Breathing becomes rapid, like panting. Heart rate may increase to 100 to 160 beats per minute. Blood pressure continues to rise.

Orgasmic Phase

During **orgasm** in the male, muscle contractions propel semen from the body. Sensations of pleasure tend to be related to the strength of the contractions and the amount of seminal fluid. The first three to four contractions are generally most intense and occur at 0.8-second intervals (five contractions every four seconds). Additional contractions occur more slowly.

Orgasm in the female is manifested by three to fifteen contractions of the pelvic muscles that surround the vaginal barrel. As with males, the contractions first occur at 0.8-second intervals. Weaker and slower contractions follow.

Blood pressure and heart rate reach a peak, with the heart beating up to 180 times per minute. Respiration may increase to 40 breaths per minute.

Resolution Phase

In the **resolution phase**, after orgasm, the body returns to its unaroused state. Men enter a **refractory period** during which they cannot experience another orgasm or ejaculate. Women do not undergo a refractory period and therefore can become quickly rearoused to the point of repeated (multiple) orgasm if they desire and receive continued sexual stimulation.

The sexual response cycle describes what happens when females and males are exposed to sexual stimulation. But what kinds of sexual experiences do people seek? How many sex partners do they have? Who are their partners? What do we know about the sex lives of people in the United States?

8-4c SURVEYS OF SEXUAL BEHAVIOR

The well-known Kinsey reports (Kinsey et al., 1948, 1953) interviewed 5,300 males and 5,940 females in the United States between 1938 and 1949. Interviewers asked about sexual experiences including masturbation, oral sex, and premarital sex. The nation was astounded to learn that most males masturbated and had had sexual intercourse prior to marriage. Moreover, significant minorities of females reported these behaviors. But Kinsey had not obtained a random sample of the population. His samples underrepresented people of color, people in rural areas, older people, poor people, Catholics, and Jews. There is thus no way of knowing whether or not Kinsey's results accurately mirrored general American sexual behavior at the time. But the *relationships* Kinsey uncovered, such as the positive link between level of education and premarital sex, may be accurate enough.

If you're trying to report accurately on sex in the United States, you have to give everyone in the country an equal chance of participating. That never happens perfectly. What if you want to interview college students and use listed phone numbers to reach them? In doing so, you've just left out all students who use cellphones only. The researchers who published the recent National Survey of Sexual Health and Behavior (NSSHB) took measures to prevent that type of thing from happening (Reece et al., 2010). All in all, they surveyed 5,865 adolescents and adults, aged 14 to 94, and derived what most researchers believe is a reasonably accurate snapshot of

plateau phase
the second phase of the sexual response cycle, which is characterized by increases in vasocongestion, muscle tension, heart rate, and blood pressure in preparation for orgasm

ejaculation
the process of propelling seminal fluid (semen) from the penis

orgasm
the height or climax of sexual excitement, involving involuntary muscle contractions, release of sexual tensions, and usually, subjective feelings of pleasure

resolution phase
the fourth phase of the sexual response cycle, during which the body gradually returns to its prearoused state

refractory period
in the sexual response cycle, a period of time following orgasm during which an individual is not responsive to sexual stimulation

FIGURE 8.3 | Percentage of Americans Performing Certain Sexual Behaviors in the Past Year (N=5865)

Sexual Behaviors	Age Groups																			
	14-15		16-17		18-19		20-24		25-29		30-39		40-49		50-59		60-69		70+	
	Men	Women	Men	Women	Men	Women	Men	Women	Men	Women	Men	Women	Men	Women	Men	Women	Men	Women	Men	Women
Masturbated Alone	62%	40%	75%	45%	81%	60%	83%	64%	84%	72%	80%	63%	76%	65%	72%	54%	61%	47%	46%	33%
Masturbated with Partner	5%	8%	16%	19%	42%	36%	44%	36%	49%	48%	45%	43%	38%	35%	28%	18%	17%	13%	13%	5%
Received Oral from Women	12%	1%	31%	5%	54%	4%	63%	9%	77%	3%	78%	5%	62%	2%	49%	1%	38%	1%	19%	2%
Received Oral from Men	1%	10%	3%	24%	6%	58%	6%	70%	5%	72%	6%	59%	6%	52%	8%	34%	3%	25%	2%	8%
Gave Oral to Women	8%	2%	18%	7%	51%	2%	55%	9%	74%	3%	69%	4%	57%	3%	44%	1%	34%	1%	24%	2%
Gave Oral to Men	1%	12%	2%	22%	4%	59%	7%	74%	5%	76%	5%	59%	7%	53%	8%	36%	3%	23%	3%	7%
Vaginal Intercourse	9%	11%	30%	30%	53%	62%	63%	80%	86%	87%	85%	74%	74%	70%	58%	51%	54%	42%	43%	22%
Received Penis in Anus	1%	4%	1%	5%	4%	18%	5%	23%	4%	21%	3%	22%	4%	12%	5%	6%	1%	4%	2%	1%
Inserted Penis into Anus	3%		6%		6%		11%		27%		24%		21%		11%		6%		2%	

Source: Center for Sexual Health Promotion. (2011). *National Survey of Sexual Health and Behavior (NSSHB)*. Indiana University, Bloomington: School of Health, Physical Education, and Recreation. http://www.nationalsexstudy.indiana.edu/graph.html (Accessed February 22, 2012)

the American population—or at least a reasonably accurate picture of what people are willing to report.

You'll find a quick overview of some of the researchers' results in Figure 8.3. The kinds of sexual behaviors they surveyed are listed in the first column. The ages of the respondents are indicted in the row at the top. Respondents are broken down by sex (men and women) as well as by age. Let's take a look at the first sexual behavior in the list, masturbation, and see what we find.

For every age group, men are more likely to report masturbating alone in the past year than women are. Why do you think that is so? Also, the incidence of masturbation alone generally rises through the late twenties and then begins to decline. How would you explain that?

Despite the availability of methods of contraception and disease prevention, and despite the widespread portrayal of casual sex in the media, a survey by the Centers for Disease Control and Prevention (Martinez et al., 2011) finds that fewer teenagers are having unmarried sex now than they did in the 1980s through the early 2000s (see Figure 8.4). According to the survey, 43% of unmarried female teens and 42% of unmarried male teens have had sex at least one time in the years 2006–2010, whereas the percentages were 52% for girls and 60% for boys as recently as 2002. Teenage pregnancy has also been undergoing a steady decline as unmarried teens have also become more likely to use condoms.

FIGURE 8.4 | Teenagers Who Have Had Sex at Least Once

Source: Martinez, G., Copen, C. E., & Abma, J. C. (2011). *Teenagers in the United States: Sexual activity, contraceptive use, and childbearing, 2006–2010.* National Survey of Family Growth. National Center for Health Statistics. Vital Health Statistics, 23(31).

8-4d SEXUAL ORIENTATION

Earlier we discussed that sex hormones have *activating* effects. However, they also have

"Bisexuality immediately doubles your chances for a date on Saturday night."

—WOODY ALLEN

directional or **organizing effects**. That is, they predispose lower animals toward stereotypical masculine or feminine mating patterns. Sex hormones are thus likely candidates for influencing the development of sexual orientation (De Rooij et al., 2009).

One's **sexual orientation** refers to the direction of his or her sexual and romantic interests—toward people of the other sex or toward people of the same sex. The great majority of people have a **heterosexual** orientation; they are sexually attracted to and interested in forming romantic relationships with people of the other sex. Some people, however, have a **homosexual** orientation; they are attracted to and interested in forming romantic relationships with people of their own sex. Males with a homosexual orientation are referred to as *gay males*. Homosexual females are referred to as *lesbians*. *Bisexual* people are attracted to both females and males.

About 7% of American men and women define themselves as being "other than heterosexual," but as noted earlier, the behavior of the other 93% doesn't exactly match up with the way people label themselves. For example, nearly twice as many people—about 14%—say they have had oral sex with a person of the same gender (Herbenick et al., 2010a, 2010b, 2010c; Reece et al., 2010). Estimates of the prevalence of various sexual orientations in our culture remain somewhat speculative.

Theories of the Origins of Sexual Orientation

Theories of the origins of sexual orientation look both at nature and nurture—the biological makeup of the individual and environmental influences. Several theories bridge the two.

Social-cognitive theorists look for the roles of factors such as reinforcement and observational learning. From this perspective, reinforcement of sexual behavior with members of one's own gender—as in reaching orgasm with them when members of the other gender are unavailable—might affect one's sexual orientation. Similarly, childhood sexual abuse by someone of the same gender could lead to fantasies about sex with people of one's own gender and affect sexual orientation. Observation of others en-

organizing effect
the directional effect of sex hormones—for example, along typical male or female patterns of mating

sexual orientation
the directionality of one's sexual and romantic interests; that is, whether one is sexually attracted to, and desires to form a romantic relationship with, members of the other gender or of one's own gender

heterosexual
referring to people who are sexually aroused by, and interested in forming romantic relationships with, people of the other gender

homosexual
referring to people who are sexually aroused by, and interested in forming romantic relationships with, people of the same gender

gaged in enjoyable male–male or female–female sexual encounters could also affect the development of sexual orientation. But critics point out that most individuals become aware of their sexual orientation before they have sexual contacts with other people of either gender (Savin-Williams & Cohen, 2007). Moreover, in a society that generally condemns homosexuality, young people are unlikely to believe that male–male or female–female contacts will have positive effects for them.

There is evidence for genetic factors in sexual orientation (Dawood et al., 2009; Ramagopalan et al., 2010). About 52% of identical (MZ) twin pairs, whose genetic codes are completely the same, share a gay male sexual orientation as compared with 22% of fraternal (DZ) twins, whose genetic codes overlap only 50%, and 11% for adoptive brothers (Dawood et al., 2009).

In many families of animals, such as rodents, there is little room for thinking about sex and deciding whether an individual will pursue sexual relationships with males or females. Sexual motivation comes under the governance of sex hormones (Henley et al., 2010; Piffer et al., 2009). Furthermore, much sexual motivation is determined by whether the brains and sex organs of fetuses are bathed in large doses of testosterone in the uterus. In male fetuses, testosterone is normally produced by the developing testes. Yet female fetuses are exposed to testosterone when they share the uterus with many male siblings. Researchers have also injected male sex hormones into the uteruses of rodents. When they do, the sex organs of females become masculinized in appearance, and they show a tendency toward masculine-type behavior patterns at maturity, including mating with other females (Phoenix, 2009).

It has been shown, then, that sex hormones predispose nonhumans to stereotypical masculine or feminine mating patterns. Do sex hormones influence the developing human embryo and fetus as they affect rodents (Garcia-Falgueras & Swaab, 2010)? The evidence is somewhat mixed, and this possibility continues to receive intensive study (Dawood et al., 2009). And if prenatal hormones affect the sexual orientation of the fetus, what causes the fluctuation in hormone levels? Hormone levels in utero can be influenced by genetic factors, maternal stress, drinking alcohol, and other factors. We must confess that much about the development of sexual orientation remains speculative.

8-5 | Achievement Motivation

Many students persist in studying despite being surrounded by distractions. Many people strive relentlessly to get ahead, to "make it," to earn large sums of money,

to invent, to accomplish the impossible. Psychological research has pointed to these people having something called *achievement motivation*.

Psychologist David McClelland (1958) helped pioneer the assessment of achievement motivation through evaluation of fantasies. One method involves the Thematic Apperception Test (TAT), developed by Henry Murray. The test contains cards with pictures and drawings that are subject to various interpretations. Individuals are shown one or more test cards and asked to construct stories about the pictured theme: to indicate what led up to it, what the characters are thinking and feeling, and what is likely to happen.

One test card is similar to that in Figure 8.5. The meaning of the card is ambiguous—unclear. Is the girl sleeping, thinking about the book, wishing she were out with friends?

Consider two stories that could be told about this card:

- *Story 1:* "She's upset that she's got to read the book because she's behind in her assignments and doesn't particularly like to work. She'd much rather be out with her friends, and she may very well sneak out to do just that."

- *Story 2:* "She's thinking, 'Someday I'll be a great scholar. I'll write books like this, and everybody will be proud of me.' She reads all the time."

The second story suggests more achievement motivation than the first. Classic studies find that people

FIGURE 8.5 | A Drawing Similar to Those on TAT Cards

© Cengage Learning 2012

with high achievement motivation earn higher grades than people with comparable learning ability but lower achievement motivation. They are more likely to earn high salaries and be promoted than less motivated people with similar opportunities (Story et al., 2009; E. A. Turner et al., 2009).

McClelland (1965) used the Thematic Apperception Test to sort college students into groups—students with high achievement motivation and students with low achievement motivation. He found that 83% of college graduates with high achievement motivation found jobs in occupations characterized by risk, decision-making, and the chance for great success, such as business management, sales, or self-employment. Most (70%) of the graduates who chose nonentrepreneurial positions showed low achievement motivation. People with high achievement motivation seem to prefer challenges and are willing to take moderate risks to achieve their goals.

8-5a EXTRINSIC VERSUS INTRINSIC MOTIVES

Do you want to do well in this course? If you do, why? Carol Dweck (2009; Dweck & Master, 2008) finds that achievement motivation can be driven by performance or learning goals, or both. For example, are you motivated mainly by performance goals, such as your grade in the course? If so, it may be in part because your motives concern tangible rewards such as getting into graduate school, landing a good job, reaping approval from your parents or your instructor, or avoiding criticism. Performance goals are usually met through *extrinsic rewards* such as praise and income. Parents of children who develop performance goals are likely to respond to good grades with rewards such as toys or money and to respond to poor grades with anger and removal of privileges.

Or is it learning goals that mainly motivate you to do well? That is, is your central motive the enhancing of your knowledge and skills—your ability to understand and master the subject matter? Learning goals usually lead to *intrinsic rewards*, such as self-satisfaction. Students who develop learning goals often have parents with strong achievement motivation who encourage their children to think and act independently. Parents and teachers help children develop learning goals by showing warmth and praising them for their efforts to

"When I was young I thought that **money was the most important** thing in life; now that I am old I know that it is."

—OSCAR WILDE

learn, exposing them to novel and stimulating experiences, and encouraging persistence (Dweck, 2006, 2009). Children who are stimulated in this way tend to set high standards for themselves, associate their achievements with self-worth, and attribute their achievements to their own efforts rather than to chance or to the intervention of others.

Many of us strive to meet both performance and learning goals in our courses as well as in other areas of life. Grades are important because they are connected with tangible benefits, but learning for its own sake is also of value and can provide great pleasure.

8-6 Emotion

Emotions color our lives. We are green with envy, red with anger, blue with sorrow. Positive emotions such as love and desire can fill our days with pleasure. Negative emotions such as fear, depression, and anger can fill us with dread and make each day a chore. Sometimes our emotions "lurk in the background." Sometimes they seize control of the day. And *emotion* can be hard to define (Solomon, 2008).

An emotion can be a response to a situation, in the way that fear is a response to a threat. An emotion can motivate behavior, as anger can motivate aggression. An emotion can also be a goal in itself. We may behave in ways that will lead us to experience happiness or love. Emotions are thus intertwined with motivation. We are driven by emotions, and meeting—or failing to meet—our needs can have powerful emotional results.

Emotions are defined as feeling states with physiological, cognitive, and behavioral components (Solomon, 2008). Strong emotions are associated with arousal of the **autonomic nervous system (ANS)** (LeDoux & Phelps, 2008). The greater the arousal, the more intense the emotion. It also appears that the type of arousal affects the emotion being experienced. Although the word *emotion* might seem to be about feeling and not about thinking, cognitions—particularly interpretations of the meanings of events—are impor-

emotion
a state of feeling that has cognitive, physiological, and behavioral components

autonomic nervous system (ANS)
the division of the peripheral nervous system that regulates glands and activities such as heartbeat, respiration, digestion, and dilation of the pupils

sympathetic nervous system

the branch of the autonomic nervous system that is most active during processes that spend body energy from stored reserves, such as in a fight-or-flight reaction to a predator or when you are anxious about a big test

parasympathetic nervous system

the branch of the autonomic nervous system that is most active during processes that restore reserves of energy to the body, such as relaxing and eating

TABLE 8.2	Components of Emotions		
EMOTION	**PHYSIOLOGICAL**	**COGNITIVE**	**BEHAVIORAL**
Fear	Sympathetic arousal	Belief that one is in danger	Avoidance tendencies
Anger	Sympathetic and para-sympathetic arousal	Frustration or belief that one is be-ing mistreated	Attack tendencies
Depression	Parasympathetic arousal	Thoughts of helplessness, hope-lessness, worthlessness	Inactivity, possible self-destructive tendencies

© Cengage Learning 2012

tant aspects of emotions. *Fear*, which usually occurs in response to a threat, involves cognitions that one is in danger as well as arousal of the **sympathetic nervous system** (e.g., rapid heartbeat and breathing, sweating, muscle tension).

Emotions also involve behavioral tendencies. Fear is connected with behavioral tendencies to avoid or escape a situation (see Table 8.2). As a response to a social provocation, *anger* involves cognitions that the provocateur should be paid back, arousal of both the sympathetic and **parasympathetic nervous systems**, and tendencies to attack (Carver & Harmon-Jones, 2009). *Depression* usually involves cognitions of helplessness and hopelessness, parasympathetic arousal, and tendencies toward inactivity—or sometimes self-destruction. *Happiness, grief, jealousy, disgust, embarrassment, liking*—all have cognitive, physiological, and behavioral components.

8-6a THE EXPRESSION OF EMOTIONS

Happiness and sadness are found in all cultures, but do people around the world express emotions in the same way? It turns out that the expression of many emotions may be universal (Ekman, 2003). Smiling is apparently a universal sign of friendliness and approval. Baring the teeth, as noted by Charles Darwin (1872) in the 19th century, may be a universal sign of anger. As the originator of the theory of evolution, Darwin believed that the universal recognition of facial expressions would have survival value. For example, in the absence of language, facial expressions could signal the approach of enemies (or friends).

Most investigators agree that certain facial expressions suggest the same emotions in people who are reared in diverse cultures (Matsumoto et al., 2008; Sebe et al., 2007). Moreover, people in diverse cultures recognize the emotions indicated by certain facial expressions. Paul Ekman (1980) took photographs of people exhibiting anger, disgust, fear, happiness, sadness, and surprise

FIGURE 8.6	Photographs Used in Research by Paul Ekman

Ekman's research suggests that the facial expressions connected with several important emotions such as happiness, anger, surprise, and fear are universally recognized.

©1976 Paul Ekman/Human Interaction Laboratory

(see Figure 8.6). He then asked people around the world to say what emotions were being depicted. Those queried ranged from European college students to members of the Fore, a tribe that dwells in the New Guinea highlands.

All groups, including the Fore, who had almost no contact with Western culture, agreed on the emotions. The Fore also displayed familiar facial expressions when asked how they would respond if they were the characters in stories that called for basic emotional responses. Ekman and his colleagues (1987) obtained similar results in a study of 10 cultures.

On the other hand, there is no perfect one-to-one relationship between facial expressions and emotions (Matsumoto et al., 2008). Facial expressions sometimes occur in the absence of the emotion they are thought to accompany (Porter & ten Brinke, 2008). The voice, posture, and gestures also provide clues to what people are feeling and are about to do (Campos, 2000).

Happy people
• believe in their ability to effect change
• are open to new experience
• are willing to risk developing new relationships

8-6b POSITIVE PSYCHOLOGY

Ted Lewis, the Great Depression–era bandleader, used to begin his act by asking, "Is evvvvrybody happy?" Well, everybody is not happy, but surveys do suggest that most people in developed nations are reasonably satisfied with their lives (Cummins & Nistico, 2002). Many people might think that psychologists are interested only in negative emotions such as anxiety, depression, and anger. Not at all. An area of psychology called **positive psychology** deals with positive emotions such as happiness and love, optimism and hope, and joy and sensual pleasures.

Are some people just "born happy," or do life experiences determine happiness? What factors interfere with happiness? Some psychologists, such as David Lykken (Lykken & Csikszentmihalyi, 2001), believe that genetic factors play a powerful role in happiness. They note that happiness tends to run in families and that we tend to have a more or less stable level of happiness throughout much of our lives (W. Johnson & Krueger, 2006). Positive events such as learning that the person we love also loves us or receiving recognition for our work can certainly raise our level of happiness at the moment (Feeney, 2004). Similarly, negative life events, such as the loss of a loved one, financial reverses, or injuries can depress us—and un-

derstandably so. Yet we may tend to bounce back to a more or less characteristic level of happiness, as did the actor Christopher Reeve following the accident—being thrown from a horse—that paralyzed him.

Which life experiences contribute to happiness? Despite the saying "Money can't buy you happiness," people tend to be happier when they live in affluent societies and earn decent incomes (W. Johnson & Krueger, 2006). Perhaps money doesn't make people happy in itself, but people who have it at least do not have to worry about money. Money aside, Chinese students tend to think of happiness in terms of feelings of contentment, inner harmony, personal achievement, physical wellness, spiritual enhancement, hopefulness about the future, generosity, and self-development (Lu, 2001). People who are married or in enduring relationships tend to be happier than loners (Waite et al., 2009; Wienke & Hill, 2009). Happy people are also more open to new experiences and new relationships (Demir & Weitekamp, 2007).

Then there are the attitudinal aspects of happiness. People at any income level can make themselves miserable when they compare themselves to people with more (Cheung & Leung, 2008). Happiness also tends to be accompanied by optimism—a cognitive bias toward assuming that things will work out (Ho et al., 2010; Wilhelm et al., 2010). But the "bias" is not groundless, because happy people often believe in their ability to effect change and then try harder. They are also willing to pat themselves on the back for their successes and are not quick to blame themselves when things go wrong—attitudes that contribute to self-esteem, another factor in happiness.

FICTION DESPITE THE SAYING THAT "MONEY CAN'T BUY YOU HAPPINESS," SURVEYS IN THE UNITED STATES, RUSSIA, CHINA, AND LATIN AMERICA SUGGEST THAT PEOPLE TEND TO BE HAPPIER WHEN THEY LIVE IN AFFLUENT SOCIETIES OR EARN DECENT INCOMES.

8-6c THE FACIAL-FEEDBACK HYPOTHESIS

The face has a special place among visual stimuli. Social animals like humans need to be able to differentiate and recognize members of their group, and in people, the face is the most distinctive key to identity (Parr et al., 2000). Faces are also a key to social communication. Facial expressions reflect emotional states, and our ability to "read" these expressions enables us to interact appropriately with other people.

It is known that various emotional states give rise to certain patterns of electrical activity in the facial muscles and in the brain (Davis et al., 2009; Porter & ten Brinke, 2008). But can it work the other way around? The **facial-feedback hypothesis** argues that facial expressions can also affect our emotional state; that is, the causal relationship between emotions and facial expressions can also work in the opposite direction.

Smiling is usually a response to feeling good within, but experimental research into the facial-feedback hypothesis suggests that the act of smiling can also enhance our moods.

Psychological research has yielded some interesting findings concerning the facial-feedback hypothesis. Inducing people to smile, for example, leads them to report more positive feelings and to rate cartoons as more humorous (Soussignan, 2002). When induced to frown, they rate cartoons as more aggressive. When people exhibit pain through facial expressions, they rate electric shocks as more painful.

What are the possible links between facial feedback and emotion? One is arousal. Intense contraction of facial muscles such as those used in signifying fear heightens arousal, which, in turn, boosts emotional response. Feedback from the contraction of facial muscles may also induce emotions. Engaging in the "Duchenne smile," characterized by "crow's feet wrinkles around the eyes and a subtle drop in the eye cover fold so that the skin above the eye moves down slightly toward the eyeball" can induce pleasant feelings (Ekman, 2003; Soussignan, 2002; see Figure 8.7).

You may have heard the British expression "Keep a stiff upper lip" as a recommendation for handling stress. It might be that a "stiff" lip suppresses emotional response—as long as the lip is relaxed rather than quivering with fear or tension. But when the lip is stiffened through strong muscle tension, facial feedback may heighten emotional response.

8-6d THEORIES OF EMOTION

David, 32, is not sleeping well. He wakes before dawn and cannot get back to sleep. His appetite is off, his energy level is low, and he has started smoking again. He has a couple of drinks at lunch and muses that it's lucky that any more alcohol makes him sick to his stomach—otherwise, he'd probably be drinking too much, too. Then he thinks, "So what difference would it make?" Sometimes he is sexually frustrated; at other times he wonders whether he has any sex drive left. Although he's awake, each day it's getting harder to drag himself out of bed in the morning. This week he missed one day of work and was late twice. His supervisor has suggested in a nonthreatening way that he "do something about it." David knows that her next warning will not be nonthreatening. It's been going downhill since Sue walked out. Suicide has even crossed David's mind. He wonders if he's going crazy.

David is experiencing the emotion of depression, and seriously so. Depression is to be expected following a loss, such as the end of a relationship, but David's feelings have lingered. His friends tell him that he should get out and do things, but David is so down that he

FIGURE 8.7 | We May Smile When We Are Pleased, but Can Smiling Make Us Feel Good about Things?

According to the facial-feedback hypothesis, smiling just might have that effect. When people are compelled to smile because they are holding a pen between their teeth, they are more likely to rate comic strips as funny (see part A). Holding the pen between their lips forces a frown, and the rating of the cartoons plummets (part B).

A.

B.

© Kathleen Olson/Kofoto

hasn't the motivation to do much at all. After much prompting by family and friends, David consults a psychologist who ironically also pushes him to get out and do things—the things he used to enjoy. The psychologist also shows David that part of his problem is that he sees himself as a failure who cannot make meaningful changes.

The "commonsense theory" of emotions is that something happens (a situation) that is cognitively appraised (interpreted) by the person, and the feeling state (a combination of arousal and thoughts) follows. For example, you meet someone new, you appraise that person as delightful, and feelings of attraction follow. Or, as in the case of David, a social relationship comes to an end, you recognize your loss, feel powerless to change it, and feel down in the dumps.

However, both historic and contemporary theories of how the components of emotions interact are at variance with this commonsense view. Let's consider a number of theories and see whether we can arrive at some useful conclusions.

The James–Lange Theory

A century ago, William James suggested that our emotions follow, rather than cause, our behavioral responses to events. At about the same time this view was also proposed by the Danish physiologist Karl G. Lange. It is therefore termed the *James–Lange theory of emotion*.

According to James and Lange, certain external stimuli instinctively trigger specific patterns of arousal and action, such as fighting or fleeing (see Figure 8.8, part A). We then become angry *because* we are acting aggressively or become afraid *because* we are running away. Emotions are simply the cognitive representations (or by-products) of automatic physiological and behavioral responses.

The James–Lange theory is consistent with the facial-feedback hypothesis. That is, smiling apparently can induce pleasant feelings, even if the effect may not be strong enough to overcome deep feelings of sadness. The theory also suggests that we may be able to change our feelings by changing our behavior. Changing one's behavior to change one's feelings is one aspect of behavior therapy. When David's psychologist urges him to get out and do things, she is assuming that by changing his behavior, David can have a positive effect on the way he feels.

Walter Cannon (1927) criticized the James–Lange assertion that each emotion has distinct physiological correlates. He argued that the physiological arousal associated with emotion A is not as distinct from the arousal associated with emotion B as the theory asserts. Note that the James–Lange view downplays the importance of human cognition; it denies the roles of cognitive appraisal, personal values, and personal choice in our behavioral and emotional responses to events.

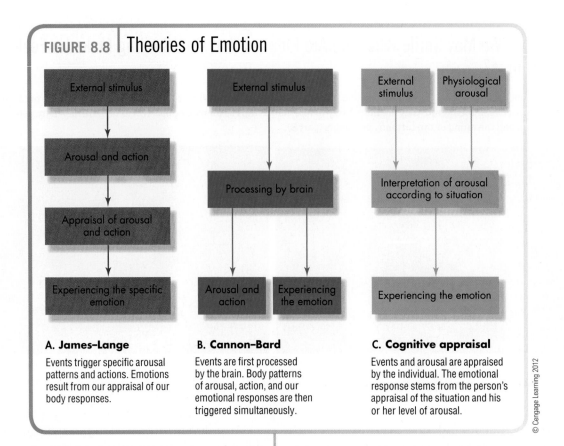

FIGURE 8.8 | Theories of Emotion

A. James–Lange

External stimulus → Arousal and action → Appraisal of arousal and action → Experiencing the specific emotion

Events trigger specific arousal patterns and actions. Emotions result from our appraisal of our body responses.

B. Cannon–Bard

External stimulus → Processing by brain → Arousal and action / Experiencing the emotion

Events are first processed by the brain. Body patterns of arousal, action, and our emotional responses are then triggered simultaneously.

C. Cognitive appraisal

External stimulus / Physiological arousal → Interpretation of arousal according to situation → Experiencing the emotion

Events and arousal are appraised by the individual. The emotional response stems from the person's appraisal of the situation and his or her level of arousal.

© Cengage Learning 2012

The Cannon–Bard Theory

Walter Cannon (1927) and Philip Bard (1934) suggested that an event might *simultaneously* trigger bodily responses (arousal and action) and the experience of an emotion. As shown in Figure 8.8 (part B), when an event is perceived (processed by the brain), the brain stimulates autonomic and muscular activity (arousal and action) *and* cognitive activity (experience of the emotion). Thus, according to the *Cannon–Bard theory of emotion*, emotions *accompany* bodily responses. They are not *produced by* bodily changes, as in the James–Lange theory.

The central criticism of the Cannon–Bard theory focuses on whether bodily responses (arousal and action) and emotions are in fact stimulated simultaneously. For example, pain or the perception of danger may trigger arousal before we begin to feel distress or fear. Also, many of us have had the experience of having a "narrow escape" and becoming aroused and shaky afterward, when we have had time to consider the damage that might have occurred. What is needed is a theory that allows for an ongoing interaction of external events, physiological changes (such as autonomic arousal and muscular activity), and cognitive activities.

The Theory of Cognitive Appraisal

More recent theoretical approaches to emotion stress cognitive factors. For example, Stanley Schachter asserts that many emotions have similar patterns of bodily arousal but that the labels we give them depend largely on our cognitive appraisal of our situations. Cognitive appraisal is based on many factors, including our perception of events and the ways other people respond to those events (see Figure 8.8, part C). When other people are present, we engage in social comparison to arrive at a response.

In a classic experiment, Schachter and Singer (1962) showed that arousal can be labeled quite differently, depending on the situation. The investigators told participants they wanted to determine the effects of a vitamin on vision. Half the participants received an injection of adrenaline, a hormone that stimulates the sympathetic branch of the autonomic nervous system. A control group received an injection of a placebo. Those who had been given adrenaline received one of three "cognitive manipulations." Group 1 was told nothing about possible emotional effects of the "vitamin." Group 2 was deliberately misinformed; members of this group were led to expect itching, numbness, or other irrelevant symptoms. Group 3 was informed accurately about the increased arousal they would experience. Group 4 was a control group injected with a placebo and given no information about its effects.

After receiving injections and cognitive manipulations, the participants were asked to wait in pairs while the experimental apparatus was being set up. The participants did not know that the person with whom they were waiting was a confederate of the experimenter. The confederate's purpose was to respond in a way that the participant would believe was caused by the injection.

Some participants waited with a confederate who acted happy-go-lucky. He flew paper airplanes about the room and tossed paper balls into a wastebasket. Other participants waited with a confederate who acted angry. He complained about the experiment, tore up a questionnaire, and stormed out of the room. As the confederates worked for their Oscar awards, the real participants were observed through a one-way mirror.

The people in groups 1 and 2 were likely to imitate the behavior of the confederate. Those who were exposed to the happy-go-lucky confederate acted jovial and content. Those who were exposed to the angry confederate imitated that person's complaining, aggressive behavior. But those in groups 3 and 4 were less influenced by the confederate's behavior.

Schachter and Singer concluded that participants in groups 1 and 2 were in an ambiguous situation. Members of these groups felt arousal from the adrenaline injection but couldn't label it as a specific emotion. Social comparison with a confederate led them to attribute their arousal either to happiness or to anger. Members of group 3 expected arousal from the injection, but no particular emotional consequences. These participants did not imitate the confederate's display of happiness or anger because they were not in an ambiguous situation; they knew their arousal was caused by adrenaline. Members of group 4 had no arousal for which they needed an

attribution, except perhaps for some arousal induced by observing the confederate. Nor did they imitate the behavior of the confederate.

Now, happiness and anger are very different emotions. Yet Schachter and Singer suggest that the bodily differences between these two emotions are slight enough that different views of the situation can lead one person to label arousal as happiness and another person to label it as anger. The Schachter–Singer view could not be further removed from the James–Lange theory, which holds that each emotion is associated with specific and readily recognized body sensations. The truth, it happens, may lie somewhere in between.

In science, it must be possible to replicate experiments and attain identical or similar results; otherwise, a theory cannot be considered valid. The Schachter and Singer study has been replicated, but with *different* results (Ekman, 1993). For example, some studies found that participants were less likely to imitate the behavior of the confederate and were likely to perceive unexplained arousal negatively, attributing it to nervousness or anger (Zimbardo et al., 1993).

The connections between arousal and emotions have led to the development of many kinds of lie detection, as we see in the following section.

The Polygraph: Just What Do Lie Detectors Detect?

Lying, for better or worse, is a part of life. People admit to lying in 14% of their emails, 27% of their face-to-face interactions, and 37% of their phone calls (Hancock, 2007). Political leaders lie to get elected. When people communicate with online "matches," men are most likely to lie about their personal assets and their goals for a relationship (Hall et al., 2010). Women are most likely to lie about their weight (Hall et al., 2010). Most people lie to their lovers, usually about other relationships (Toma et al., 2008). People also lie about their qualifications to get jobs, and of course, some people lie about whether or not they have committed a crime.

Facial expressions often offer clues to deceit, but some people can lie with a straight face—or a smile. As Shakespeare pointed out in Hamlet, "One may smile, and smile, and be a

© Blend Images / SuperStock

One way to fool a lie detector test is to bite your tongue—less obviously than this, perhaps.

villain." The use of devices to detect lies has a long if not laudable history:

> The Bedouins of Arabia ... until quite recently required conflicting witnesses to lick a hot iron; the one whose tongue was burned was thought to be lying. The Chinese, it is said, had a similar method for detecting lying: Suspects were forced to chew rice powder and spit it out; if the powder was dry, the suspect was guilty (Kleinmuntz & Szucko, 1984, pp. 766–767).

These methods may sound primitive, even bizarre, but they are broadly consistent with modern psychological knowledge. Anxiety about being caught in a lie is linked to arousal of the sympathetic division of the autonomic nervous system. One sign of sympathetic arousal is lack of saliva, or dryness in the mouth. The emotions of fear and guilt are also linked to sympathetic arousal and hence to dryness in the mouth.

Polygraphs, or lie detectors, monitor indicators of sympathetic arousal during an interrogation: heart rate, blood pressure, respiration rate, and electrodermal response (sweating). But questions have been raised about the validity of assessing truth or fiction by means of polygraphs (Iacono, 2008).

The American Polygraph Association claims that use of the polygraph is 85% to 95% accurate. Critics find polygraph testing to be less accurate and claim that it is sensitive to more than lies (Iacono, 2008). Factors such as tense muscles, drugs, and previous experience with polygraph tests can significantly reduce their accuracy rate. In one experiment, people were able to reduce the accuracy of polygraph-based judgments to about 50% by biting their tongues (to produce pain) or pressing their toes against the floor (to tense muscles) while being interrogated (Honts & Handler, 2011). You might thus give the examiner the impression that you are lying even when you are telling the truth, throwing off the test's results.

It appears that no specific pattern of bodily responses pinpoints lying (Honts & Handler, 2011). Because of validity problems, results of polygraph examinations are no longer admitted as evidence in many courts.

Evaluation

What can we make of all this? Research suggests that the patterns of arousal connected with various emotions are more specific than suggested by Schachter and Singer—although less so than suggested by James and Lange (Larsen et al., 2008). Research with brain imaging suggests that different emotions, such as happiness and sadness, involve different structures in the brain (Lane et al., 2009; Pollatos et al., 2007; Suslow et al., 2010). Even so, researchers have not found brain cells that respond to but a single emotion. The emotion of disgust apparently has the most specific location, the primary taste cortex. It makes sense that an emotion related to "distasteful" experiences would be centered here.

Regarding the Schachter and Singer study, Zimbardo and his colleagues (1993) note that lack of control over our feelings and lack of understanding what is going on are disturbing experiences. Thus, our cognitive appraisal of situations does affect our emotional responses, but perhaps not as Schachter and Singer believed.

In sum, various components of an experience—cognitive, physiological, and behavioral—contribute to our emotional responses. Our bodies may become aroused in a given situation, but people also appraise those situations; arousal in itself does not appear to directly cause one emotion or another. The fact that none of the theories of emotion we have discussed applies to all people in all situations is comforting. Apparently our emotions are not quite as easily understood, manipulated, or—as in the case of the polygraph—even detected, as some theorists have suggested.

TRUTH IT IS TRUE THAT YOU MIGHT BE ABLE TO FOOL A LIE DETECTOR BY BITING YOUR TONGUE OR WIGGLING YOUR TOES.

By the Numbers

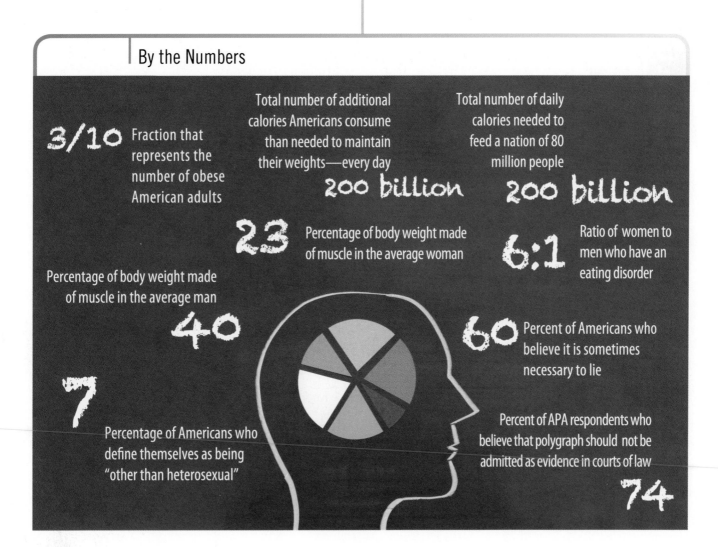

3/10 Fraction that represents the number of obese American adults

Total number of additional calories Americans consume than needed to maintain their weights—every day
200 billion

Total number of daily calories needed to feed a nation of 80 million people
200 billion

23 Percentage of body weight made of muscle in the average woman

6:1 Ratio of women to men who have an eating disorder

Percentage of body weight made of muscle in the average man
40

60 Percent of Americans who believe it is sometimes necessary to lie

7 Percentage of Americans who define themselves as being "other than heterosexual"

Percent of APA respondents who believe that polygraph should not be admitted as evidence in courts of law
74

Ready to study? In the book, you can:

- ➲ Review what you've read with Fill-Ins and Multiple Choice quizzes (below).
- ➲ Rip out Chapter Review card (in the back).

Or you can go online to CourseMate at www.cengagebrain.com for these resources:

- ➲ Complete Practices Quizzes to prepare for tests.
- ➲ Review Key Terms Flash Cards (online or print).
- ➲ Play games to master concepts.

FILL-INS

Answers can be found in the back of the book, starting on page 368.

1. _____ are hypothetical states that activate behavior and direct organisms toward goals.

2. A(n) _____ is an object, person, or situation that is perceived as capable of satisfying a need.

3. Drives help the body maintain a steady state, a tendency that is called _____.

4. Maslow argued that people have a hierarchy of needs, the highest of which is the need for _____.

5. _____ nervosa is a life-threatening eating disorder characterized by dramatic weight loss and a distorted body image.

6. Masters and Johnson divide the sexual response cycle into four phases: the _____, plateau, orgasm, and resolution phases.

7. Sex hormones have activating and _____ effects on sexual behavior.

8. McClelland used the Thematic _____ Test to measure achievement motivation.

9. Students with _____ goals are mainly motivated by factors such as good grades, rewards from parents, and the prospect of landing a good job.

10. According to the James–Lange theory, emotions have specific patterns of arousal and _____.

1. Money, food, and a sexually attractive person can all be viewed as
   a. drives.
   b. physiological.
   c. incentives.
   d. psychological.

2. Drive-reduction theory defines hunger, pain, and thirst as
   a. primary drives.
   b. instincts.
   c. secondary drives.
   d. acquired motives.

3. The _____ is signaled when there is a drop in blood sugar due to food deprivation.
   a. hypothalamus
   b. basilar membrane
   c. corpus callosum
   d. medulla

4. Whenever Farah eats, she immediately excuses herself and goes to the rest room and vomits. Farah is most likely to be diagnosed with
   a. anorexia nervosa.
   b. bulimia nervosa.
   c. aphagia.
   d. a disorder in the thyroid gland.

5. Performance goals are to _____ rewards as learning goals are to _____ rewards.
   a. intrinsic; extrinsic
   b. satisfaction with self; prestige
   c. extrinsic; intrinsic
   d. none of these

6. According to the text, which of the following hormones is most strongly connected with the sex drive in women?
   a. Estrogen   c. Oxytocin
   b. Prolactin   d. Testosterone

7. Identical (MZ) twins have the same sexual orientation about _____ percent of the time.
   a. 12   c. 52
   b. 32   d. 72

8. Fear involves activation of the _____ nervous system, but depression involves activation of the _____ nervous system.
   a. peripheral; somatic
   b. somatic; peripheral
   c. parasympathetic; sympathetic
   d. sympathetic; parasympathetic

9. Which of the following quotes supports the research regarding socioeconomic factors and happiness?
   a. "Money can't buy you love."
   b. "Good nature is worth more than money."
   c. "Happiness is a warm puppy."
   d. "Having money is better than poverty if for only financial reasons."

10. Which of the following is correct concerning relationships and happiness?
   a. People who are married or in enduring relationships report the highest level of happiness.
   b. People who are divorced or separated are happiest.
   c. People who are single are happiest.
   d. People who have a series of casual sexual relationships are happiest.

LEARNING OUTCOMES

9-1 Explain prenatal development and the role that sex hormones play

9-2 Explain the physical, cognitive, moral, social, and emotional development of children

9-3 Explain the physical, cognitive, moral, social, and emotional development of adolescents

9-4 Explain the features of emerging adulthood

9-5 Explain the physical, cognitive, moral, social, and emotional development of adults

STUDY TOOLS ▶ After you read the chapter, go to the Study Tools at the end of the chapter, page 240.

CHAPTER 9

The Voyage Through the LIFE SPAN

We have a story to tell. An important story. A fascinating story about the remarkable voyage you have already taken through childhood and adolescence. It is about the unfolding of your adult life. Billions have made this voyage before. Yet you are unique, and things will happen to you that have never happened before.

Developmental psychologists are interested in studying our voyage through the life span for several reasons. The discovery of early influences and developmental sequences helps psychologists understand adults. Psychologists are also interested in the effects of genetic factors, early interactions with parents and siblings, and the school and community on traits such as aggressiveness and intelligence.

Developmental psychologists also seek to learn the causes of developmental abnormalities. For example, should pregnant women abstain from smoking and drinking? (Yes.) What factors contribute to child abuse? Other developmental psychologists focus on adult development. For example, what can we expect as we voyage through our 30s, 40s, 50s, and beyond? The information developmental psychologists acquire can help us make decisions about how we rear our children and lead our own lives.

Let's now turn to prenatal developments—the changes that occur between conception and birth. They are spectacular, but they occur "out of sight."

> *"There is no cure for life or death save to enjoy the interval."*
> —GEORGE SANTAYANA

> ⌈ *Billions make the voyage, yet each is unique.* ⌉

TRUTH OR FICTION

WHAT DO YOU THINK? FOLKLORE, COMMON SENSE, OR NONSENSE? CIRCLE THE T FOR "TRUTH" OR THE F FOR "FICTION," AND CHECK THE ACCURACY OF YOUR ANSWERS AS YOU READ THROUGH THE CHAPTER.

T	F	YOUR HEART STARTED BEATING WHEN YOU WERE ONLY ONE-FIFTH OF AN INCH LONG AND WEIGHED A FRACTION OF AN OUNCE.
T	F	PRIOR TO SIX MONTHS OR SO OF AGE, "OUT OF SIGHT" IS LITERALLY "OUT OF MIND."
T	F	THE ARCHITECT FRANK LLOYD WRIGHT DESIGNED NEW YORK'S INNOVATIVE SPIRAL-SHAPED GUGGENHEIM MUSEUM WHEN HE WAS 65 YEARS OLD.
T	F	ALZHEIMER'S DISEASE IS A NORMAL PART OF AGING.
T	F	MOST PARENTS SUFFER FROM THE "EMPTY-NEST SYNDROME" WHEN THEIR YOUNGEST CHILD LEAVES HOME.

9-1 Prenatal Development

The most dramatic gains in height and weight occur during prenatal development. Within nine months, the newly conceived organism develops from a nearly microscopic cell to a *neonate* (newborn) about 20 inches long. Its weight increases a billionfold!

During the months following conception, the single cell formed by the union of sperm and egg—the **zygote**—multiplies, becoming two cells, then four, then eight, and so on. Following conception (which takes place in the fallopian tube), the zygote divides repeatedly as it proceeds on its 3- to 4-day voyage to

zygote
a fertilized ovum (egg cell)

germinal stage
the first stage of prenatal development, during which the dividing mass of cells has not become implanted in the uterine wall

amniotic sac
a sac within the uterus that contains the embryo or fetus

placenta
a membrane that permits the exchange of nutrients and waste products between the mother and her developing child but does not allow the maternal and fetal bloodstreams to mix

umbilical cord
a tube between the mother and her developing child through which nutrients and waste products are conducted

the uterus. The ball-like mass of multiplying cells wanders about the uterus for another three to four days before beginning to implant in the uterine wall. Implantation takes another week or so. The period from conception to implantation is called the **germinal stage**.

The *embryonic stage* lasts from implantation until about the eighth week of development. During this stage, the major body organ systems take form. As you can see from Figure 9.1, the growth of the head precedes that of other parts of the body. The growth of the organs—heart, lungs, and so on—also precedes the growth of the extremities. The relatively early *maturation* of the brain and the organ systems allows them to participate in the nourishment and further development of the embryo. The heart will continue to beat without rest every minute of every day for most of a century, perhaps longer.

During the second month, the nervous system begins to transmit messages. By five to six weeks, the embryo is only a quarter-inch to a half-inch long, yet nondescript sex organs have formed. By about the sev-

enth week, the genetic code (XY or XX) begins to assert itself, causing the sex organs to differentiate. If a Y sex chromosome is present, testes form and begin to produce *androgens* (male sex hormones), which further masculinize the sex organs. In the absence of these hormones, the embryo develops sex organs typical of the female, regardless of its genetic code. By the end of the second month, the head has become rounded and the facial features distinct—all in an embryo that is about one inch long and weighs 1/30th of an ounce.

As it develops, the embryo is suspended within a protective **amniotic sac** in the mother's uterus. The sac is surrounded by a clear membrane and contains amniotic fluid. The fluid is a sort of natural air bag, allowing the child to move or even jerk around without injury. It also helps maintain an even temperature.

From now until birth, the embryo exchanges nutrients and wastes with the mother through the **placenta**. The embryo is connected to the placenta by the **umbilical cord**. The placenta is connected to the mother by blood vessels in the uterine wall.

The *fetal stage* lasts from the beginning of the third month until birth. By the end of the third month, the major organ systems and the fingers and toes have formed. In the middle of the fourth month, the mother usually detects the first fetal movements. By the end of the sixth month, the fetus moves its limbs so vigorously that mothers often feel that they are being kicked. The fetus opens and shuts its eyes, sucks its thumb, and alternates between periods of wakefulness and sleep.

FIGURE 9.1

A Human Fetus at Twelve Weeks

By the end of the first trimester, formation of all the major organ systems is complete. Fingers and toes are fully formed, and the sex of the fetus can be determined visually.

Claude Edelmann/Photo Researchers, Inc.

A Human Fetus at Four Months

At this midway point between conception and birth, the fetus is covered with fine, downy hair, called *lanugo*.

Petit Format/Photo Researchers, Inc.

During the three months prior to birth, the organ systems of the fetus continue to mature. The heart and lungs become increasingly capable of sustaining independent life. The fetus gains about 5½ pounds and doubles in length. Newborn boys average about 7½ pounds and newborn girls about 7 pounds.

TRUTH DURING THE FOURTH WEEK, A PRIMITIVE HEART BEGINS TO BEAT AND PUMP BLOOD—IN AN ORGANISM THAT IS ONE-FIFTH OF AN INCH LONG.

9-2 Childhood

Childhood begins with birth. When my children are enjoying themselves, I kid them and say, "Stop having fun. You're a child, and childhood is the worst time of life." I get a laugh because they know that childhood is supposed to be the best time of life—a time for play and learning and endless possibilities. In this section we see that childhood is an exciting time of physical, cognitive, and social and emotional developments.

9-2a PHYSICAL DEVELOPMENT

During infancy—the first two years of childhood—dramatic gains in height and weight continue. Babies usually double their birth weight in about five months and triple it by their first birthday (Kuczmarski et al., 2000). Their height increases by about 10 inches in the first year. Children grow another four to six inches during the second year and gain some four to seven pounds. After that, they gain about two to three inches a year until they reach the adolescent growth spurt. Weight gains also remain fairly even at about four to six pounds per year until the spurt. Other aspects of physical development in childhood include reflexes and perceptual development.

Reflexes

Soon after you were born, a doctor or nurse probably pressed her fingers against the palms of your hands. Most likely you grasped the fingers firmly—so firmly that you could have been lifted from your cradle! Grasping at birth is inborn, an example of the importance of nature in human development. Grasping is one of the baby's reflexes. **Reflexes** are simple, inborn responses elicited by specific stimuli. Reflexes are essential to survival and occur automatically—that is, without thinking about them.

Newborn children do not know that it is necessary to eat to survive. Fortunately, rooting and sucking reflexes cause them to eat. They turn their head toward stimuli that prod or stroke the cheek, chin, or corner of the mouth. This

is termed **rooting**. They also automatically suck objects that touch their lips.

Newborns use the *withdrawal reflex* to avoid painful stimuli. In the *startle*, or *Moro*, *reflex*, they draw up their legs and arch their backs in response to sudden noises, bumps, or loss of support while being held. They grasp objects that press against the palms of their hands (the *grasp*, or *palmar*, *reflex*). They fan their toes when the soles of their feet are stimulated (the *Babinski reflex*). Pediatricians test these reflexes to assess babies' neural functioning. Babies also breathe, sneeze, cough, yawn, blink, defecate, and urinate reflexively.

Motor Development

The motor development of the child refers to the progression from simple acts like lifting the head to running around. Maturation and experience both play key roles in motor development (Brown et al., 2009; Spittle et al., 2009). Maturation of the brain is a key to motor development. Motor development provides some of the most fascinating changes in infants, in part because so much seems to happen so quickly—and so much of it during the first year. Children go through a sequence that includes rolling over, sitting up, crawling, creeping, walking, and running. The ages at which infants first engage in these activities vary, but the sequence generally remains the same (see Figure 9.2). Invariant sequences suggest an unfolding of the genetic code (maturation).

The role of maturation in areas such as physical development (for example, gains in height and weight and the effects of puberty), language development, and motor development is clear. But environmental factors are also involved. Children may have certain genetic potentials for body size and growth rates, but they do not reach them unless environmental factors such as nutrition, relatively clean air, and so on are available. Children do not understand or produce language until their genetic codes spark the development of certain structures and processes in the brain. But the environment is also involved. Children learn the languages used in their homes and communities. They do not speak foreign tongues without being exposed to them.

Perceptual Development

Newborn children spend about 16 hours a day sleeping and do not have much opportunity to learn about the world. Yet they perceive the world reasonably well soon after birth. Within a couple of days, infants can follow, or

reflex
a simple inborn response to a stimulus

rooting
the turning of an infant's head toward a touch, such as by the mother's nipple

fixation time
the amount of time spent looking at a visual stimulus

"track," a moving light with their eyes. By three months, they can discriminate most colors. Newborns are nearsighted (that is, they focus better on nearby than distant objects), but by about four months, infants focus on distant objects about as well as adults do.

The visual preferences of infants are measured by the amount of time, termed **fixation time**, they spend looking at one stimulus instead of another. In classic research by Robert Fantz (1961), two-month-old infants preferred visual stimuli that resembled the human face to newsprint, a bull's-eye, and featureless red, white, and yellow disks (see Figure 9.3).

Classic research has shown that infants tend to respond to cues for depth by the time they are able to crawl (at about six to eight months). Most also have the good sense to avoid crawling off ledges and tabletops into open space (Campos et al., 1978).

Normal newborns hear well. Most newborns reflexively turn their heads toward unusual sounds. This finding, along with findings about visual tracking, suggests that infants are preprogrammed to survey their environments. Speaking or singing softly in a low-pitched tone soothes infants. This is why lullabies help infants fall asleep.

Research indicates that neonates prefer their mother's voice to those of other women, but they do not show a preference for their father's voice (DeCasper & Prescott, 1984; Freeman et al., 1993). Babies, of course, have had months of "experience" in the uterus. For at least two or three months before birth, they have been able to hear. Because they are predominantly exposed to sounds produced by their mother, learning may contribute to newborn preferences. Neonates can also discriminate distinct odors, and their preferences are quite similar to those of older children and adults (Werner & Bernstein, 2001).

9-2b COGNITIVE DEVELOPMENT

This section explores the ways in which children mentally represent and think about the world—that is, their *cognitive development*. Because cognitive functioning develops over many years, young children have ideas about the

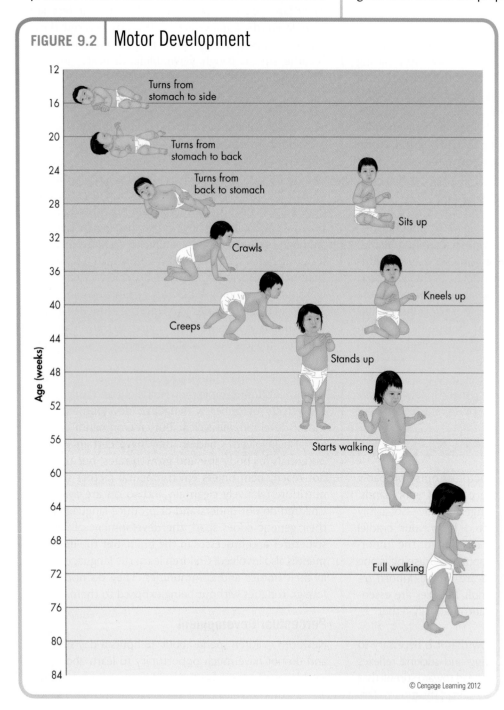

FIGURE 9.2 | Motor Development

Age (weeks): 12, 16, 20, 24, 28, 32, 36, 40, 44, 48, 52, 56, 60, 64, 68, 72, 76, 80, 84

Turns from stomach to side
Turns from stomach to back
Turns from back to stomach
Sits up
Crawls
Kneels up
Creeps
Stands up
Starts walking
Full walking

© Cengage Learning 2012

when separated from them. Harlow conducted a series of experiments to find out why (Harlow, 1959).

In one study, Harlow placed infant rhesus monkeys in cages with two surrogate mothers, as shown in Figure 9.6. One "mother" was made of wire mesh from which a baby bottle was extended. The other surrogate mother was made of soft, cuddly terry cloth. The infant monkeys spent most of their time clinging to the cloth mother, even though "she" did not gratify their need for food. Harlow concluded that monkeys—and perhaps humans—have an inborn need for **contact comfort** that is as basic as the need for food. Gratification of the need for contact comfort, rather than food, might be why infant monkeys (and humans) cling to their mothers.

Other researchers, such as **ethologist** Konrad Lorenz, argue that for many animals, attachment is an instinct—inborn. (Ethologists study the behavioral characteristics of various species of animals.) Attachment, like other instincts, is theorized to occur in the presence of a specific stimulus and during a **critical period** of life—that is, a period during which the animal is sensitive to the stimulus.

Some animals become attached to the first moving object they encounter. The formation of an attachment in this manner is therefore called **imprinting**. Lorenz (1981) became well known when pictures of his "family" of goslings were made public. How did Lorenz acquire his following? He was present when the goslings hatched and during their critical period, and he allowed them to follow him. The critical period for geese and some other animals is bounded, at the younger end, by the age at which they first walk and, at the older end, by the age at which they develop fear of strangers. The goslings followed Lorenz persistently, ran to him when frightened, honked with distress at his departure, and tried to overcome barriers between them. If you substitute crying for honking, it all sounds rather human.

Ainsworth and Bowlby (1991) consider attachment to be instinctive in humans. However, among humans attachment is less related to issues such as locomotion and fear of strangers (which is not universal). Moreover, the critical period with humans is quite extended.

Parenting Styles

Many psychologists have been concerned about the relationships between parenting styles and the personality development of the child. Diana Baumrind (1989; 2005) has been particularly interested in the connections between parental behavior and the development of children's *instrumental competence*—the ability to manipulate the environment to achieve one's goals. Baumrind has focused largely on four aspects of parental behavior: (1) restrictiveness; (2) demands for the child to achieve intellectual, emotional, and social maturity; (3) communication ability; and (4) warmth and involvement. She labeled the three parenting styles the *authoritative*, *authoritarian*, and *permissive* styles. Other researchers also speak of the *uninvolved* style. These four styles are defined in the following ways:

1. *Authoritative parents.* The parents of the most competent children rate high in all four areas of behavior. Such **authoritative parents** are strict (restrictive) and demand mature behavior. However, they temper their strictness with a desire to reason with their children and with love and support. They expect much, but they explain why and offer help.

2. *Authoritarian parents.* **Authoritarian parents** have strict guidelines about what is right and wrong, and they demand that their children follow those guidelines. Both authoritative and authoritarian parents adhere to strict standards of conduct, but authoritative parents explain their demands and are supportive, whereas authoritarian parents rely on force and

contact comfort
a hypothesized primary drive to seek physical comfort through contact with another

ethologist
a scientist who studies the characteristic behavior patterns of species of animals

critical period
a period of time when an instinctive response can be elicited by a particular stimulus

imprinting
a process occurring during a critical period in the development of an organism, in which that organism responds to a stimulus in a manner that will afterward be difficult to modify

authoritative parents
parents who are strict and warm; authoritative parents demand mature behavior but use reason rather than force in discipline

authoritarian parents
parents who are rigid in their rules and who demand obedience for the sake of obedience

Konrad Lorenz and His Family of Goslings

permissive parents
parents who impose few, if any, rules and who do not supervise their children closely

uninvolved parents
parents who generally leave their children to themselves

adolescence
the period of life bounded by puberty and the assumption of adult responsibilities

puberty
the period of physical development during which sexual reproduction first becomes possible

secondary sex characteristics
characteristics that distinguish females from males, such as distribution of body hair and depth of voice, but that are not directly involved in reproduction

communicate poorly with their children. Authoritarian parents do not respect their children's points of view, and they may be cold and rejecting.

3. *Permissive parents.* **Permissive parents** are generally easygoing with their children. As a result, the children do pretty much what the children want. Permissive parents are warm and supportive, but poor at communicating.

4. *Uninvolved parents.* **Uninvolved parents** tend to leave their children on their own. They make few demands and show little warmth or encouragement.

Research shows that the children of warm parents are more likely to be socially and emotionally well adjusted (Lau et al., 2006; Murray et al., 2009). They are also more likely to internalize moral standards—that is, to develop a conscience (Bender et al., 2007; Lau et al., 2006).

"CHILDREN BEGIN BY LOVING THEIR PARENTS; AS THEY GROW OLDER THEY JUDGE THEM; SOMETIMES THEY FORGIVE THEM."
—OSCAR WILDE

Strictness seems to pay off, provided it is tempered with reason and warmth. Children of authorit*ative* parents have greater self-reliance, self-esteem, social competence, and achievement motivation than other children (Grusec, 2006). Children of authorit*arian* parents are often withdrawn or aggressive and usually do not do as well in school as children of authoritative parents (Paulussen-Hoogeboom et al., 2007; Rudy & Grusec, 2006). Children of permissive parents seem to be less mature. They are often impulsive, moody, and aggressive. In adolescence, lack of parental monitoring

is often linked to delinquency and poor academic performance. Children of uninvolved parents tend to obtain poorer grades than children whose parents make demands on them. The children of uninvolved parents also tend to be more likely to hang out with crowds who "party" a good deal and use drugs. The message? Children profit when parents make reasonable demands, show warmth and encouragement, and spend time with them.

RubberBall Photography/Veer

9-3 Adolescence

Perhaps no other period of life is as exciting—and as bewildering—as adolescence. **Adolescence** is bounded by puberty and the assumption of adult responsibilities. Except for infancy, more changes occur during adolescence than during any other time. Like childhood, adolescence entails physical, cognitive, social, and emotional changes.

9-3a PHYSICAL DEVELOPMENT

One of the most noticeable physical developments of adolescence is a growth spurt that lasts two to three years and ends the gradual changes in height and weight that characterize most of childhood. Within this short span of years, adolescents grow some 8 to 12 inches. Most boys wind up taller and heavier than most girls.

Puberty: More Than "Just a Phase"?
Puberty is the period during which the body becomes sexually mature. It heralds the onset of adolescence. Puberty begins with the appearance of **secondary sex characteristics** such as body hair, deepening of the voice in males, and rounding of the breasts and hips in females. In boys, pituitary hormones stimulate the testes to increase the output of testosterone, which in turn causes enlargement of the penis and testes and the appearance of body hair. By the early teens, erections become common, and boys may ejaculate. Ejaculatory

ability usually precedes the presence of mature sperm by at least a year. Ejaculation thus is not evidence of reproductive capacity.

In girls, a critical body weight in the neighborhood of 100 pounds is thought to trigger a cascade of hormonal secretions in the brain that cause the ovaries to secrete higher levels of the female sex hormone, estrogen (Frisch, 1997). Estrogen stimulates the growth of breast tissue and tissue in the hips and buttocks. The pelvis widens, rounding the hips. Small amounts of androgens produced by the adrenal glands, along with estrogen, spur the growth of pubic and underarm hair. Estrogen and androgens also stoke the development of female sex organs. Estrogen production becomes cyclical during puberty and regulates the menstrual cycle. The beginning of menstruation, or **menarche**, usually occurs between 11 and 14. Girls cannot become pregnant until they ovulate, however, and ovulation may begin two years after menarche.

Brain Development

What happens to the brains of adolescents who spend hours a day practicing the piano or the violin? Their learning translates physically into increases in the thickness of the parts of the cerebral cortex that are being used (Bermudez et al., 2009; Johnson et al., 2008). The gains in thickness of the cerebral cortex represent increases in gray matter, which consists of associative neurons that transmit messages back and forth in the brain when we are engaged in thought and sensorimotor activities.

Many adolescents show poor judgment, at least from time to time, and take risks that most adults would avoid, such as excessive drinking, reckless driving, violence, disordered eating behavior, and unprotected sexual activity (Berten & Rossem, 2009). Brain immaturity may play a role. Deborah Yurgelun-Todd and her colleagues (Sava & Yurgelun-Todd, 2008) showed pictures of people with fearful expressions to adolescents ranging in age from 11 to 17 while the adolescents' brains were scanned by functional magnetic resonance imaging (fMRI). Compared to adults, the adolescents' frontal lobes (the seat of executive functioning) were less active, and their amygdalas (a part of the limbic system involved in discriminating emotions, including fear) were more active. The adolescents often misread the facial expressions, with those younger than 14 more often inferring sadness, anger, or confusion rather than fear. The researchers suggest that one reason many adolescents fail to show the judgment, insight, and reasoning ability of adults is immaturity of the frontal lobes (Yurgelun-Todd, 2007).

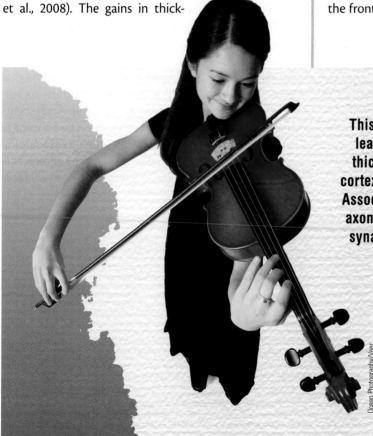

Ocean Photography/Veer

This adolescent musician is not only learning to play the violin but also thickening the parts of her cerebral cortex that are being used in the effort. Associative neurons are sprouting new axon tips and dendrites, creating new synapses, and enhancing the flow of information.

formal operational stage
Piaget's fourth stage, characterized by abstract logical thought and deduction from principles

imaginary audience
an aspect of adolescent egocentrism; the belief that other people are as concerned with our thoughts and behaviors as we are

9-3b COGNITIVE DEVELOPMENT

The adolescent thinker approaches problems differently from the elementary school child. A younger child sticks to the facts, to concrete reality. Speculating about abstract possibilities and what might be is very difficult. The adolescent, on the other hand, is able to deal with the abstract and the hypothetical. In this section, we explore some of the cognitive developments of adolescence by referring to the views of Piaget and Kohlberg.

The Stage of Formal Operations

According to Piaget, children undergo three stages of cognitive development prior to adolescence: sensorimotor, preoperational, and concrete operational. The stage of **formal operations** is the final stage in Piaget's theory, and it represents cognitive maturity. For many children in Western societies, formal operational thought begins at about the beginning of adolescence—the age of 11 or 12. Some people enter this stage later, however, and some never do.

The major achievements of the stage of formal operations involve classification, logical thought, and the ability to hypothesize. Central features are the ability to think about ideas as well as objects and to group and classify ideas—symbols, statements, entire theories. Adolescents can generally follow arguments from premises to conclusions and back again. They can generally appreciate both the outer environment and the world of the imagination: they engage in hypothetical thinking and deductive reasoning.

Formal operational adolescents (and adults) think abstractly. They solve geometric problems about circles and squares without reference to what the circles and squares may represent in the real world. Adolescents in this stage derive rules for behavior from general principles and can focus, or center, on multiple aspects of a situation at once to solve problems.

During the stage of formal operations, adolescents become capable of dealing with hypothetical situations. They realize that situations can have different outcomes, and they think ahead, imagining those outcomes. Adolescents also conduct social "experiments" to test their hypotheses. They may try out various tones of voice and ways of treating others to see what works best for them.

Adolescent Egocentrism

Adolescents in the formal operational stage can reason deductively. They classify objects or people and then draw conclusions about them. Adolescents can be proud of their new logical abilities, leading to a new sort of egocentrism: They demand acceptance of their logic without recognizing the exceptions or practical problems that may be considered by adults. Consider this example: "It is wrong to hurt people. Company A hurts people (perhaps through pollution). Therefore, Company A must be severely punished or shut down." This thinking is logical. But by impatiently demanding major changes or severe penalties, one may not fully consider various practical problems such as the thousands of workers who might be laid off if the company were shut down. Adults have often had life experiences that encourage them to see shades of gray rather than black and white.

The thought of preschoolers is characterized by egocentrism in which they cannot take another's point of view. Adolescent thought is marked by an egocentrism in which they can understand the thoughts of others but still have trouble separating things that are of concern to others and those that are of concern only to themselves (Elkind, 1967, 1985). Adolescent egocentrism gives rise to two interesting cognitive developments: the *imaginary audience* and the *personal fable*.

The concept of the **imaginary audience** refers to the belief that other people are as concerned with our thoughts and behavior as we are. Adolescents thus see themselves as the center of attention and assume that other people are also preoccupied with their appearance and behavior (Milstead et al., 1993). Adolescents may feel onstage with all eyes on them. The concept of the imaginary audience may drive the intense adolescent desire for privacy. It helps explain why adolescents are so self-conscious, why they worry about every facial blemish and spend hours grooming. Self-consciousness seems to peak at about 13 and then decline. Girls tend to be more self-conscious than boys (Elkind & Bowen, 1979).

The **personal fable** is the belief that our feelings and ideas are special, even unique, and that we are invulnerable. The personal fable seems to underlie adolescent showing off and risk taking (Alberts et al., 2007).

The Postconventional Level of Moral Reasoning

Kohlberg's theory of moral reasoning involves three levels: preconventional, conventional, and postconventional. Individuals can arrive at the same decision as to whether Heinz should save his wife by taking the drug without paying for it for different reasons. Deciding not to steal the drug for fear of punishment is less cognitively complex than deciding not to because of the belief that doing could have negative consequences for the social order.

None of Kohlberg's levels is tied to a person's age. Although postconventional reasoning is the highest level, most adolescents and adults never reach it. But if postconventional reasoning emerges, it usually does so in adolescence. Kohlberg's (1969) research found postconventional moral judgments were absent among 7- to 10-year-olds. But by age 16, stage 5 reasoning is shown by about 20% of adolescents, and stage 6 reasoning by about 5%.

At the **postconventional level**, moral reasoning is based on the person's own moral standards. Moral judgments are derived from personal values, not from conventional standards or authority figures. In the contractual, legalistic orientation characteristic of stage 5, it is recognized that laws stem from agreed-upon procedures and that the rule of law is in general good for society; therefore, laws should not be violated except under pressing circumstances. (Although it is illegal for Heinz to steal the drug, in this case it is the right thing to do.)

Stage 6 moral reasoning demands adherence to supposedly universal ethical principles such as the sanctity of human life, individual dignity, justice, and the Golden Rule ("Do unto others as you would have them do unto you"). If a law is unjust or contradicts the rights of the individual, it is wrong to obey it.

People at the postconventional level see their conscience as the highest moral authority. This point has created confusion. To some it suggests that it is right to break the law when it is convenient, but this interpretation is wrong. Kohlberg means that people at this level feel they must do what they think is right even if they break the law or must sacrifice themselves.

9-3c SOCIAL AND EMOTIONAL DEVELOPMENT

In terms of social and emotional development, adolescence has been associated with turbulence. In the 19th century, psychologist G. Stanley Hall described adolescence as a time of *Sturm und Drang*—storm and stress. Current views challenge the assumption that "storm and stress" is the norm (Griffin, 2001). Many adolescents experience a rather calm and joyous period of development. We need to consider individual differences and cultural variations (Arnett, 1999).

Certainly, many American teenagers abuse drugs, get pregnant, contract sexually transmitted infections, get involved in violence, fail in school, even attempt suicide (Miniño, 2010). The U.S. Centers for Disease Control and Prevention (Miniño, 2010) reported that 73% of all deaths among people aged 12 to 19 years result from three causes: motor vehicle and other accidents (48%), homicide (13%), and suicide (12%). Nevertheless, the majority of Americans make it through adolescence quite well.

Relationships with Parents and Peers

Adolescents spend much less time with their parents than they did as children (Halpern, 2005; Staff et al., 2004). Adolescents interact more with their mothers than their fathers and thus have more conflict with their mothers. But they also view their mothers as more supportive and more likely to accept their opinions (Costigan et al., 2007; Sheeber et al., 2007).

The decrease in time spent with family may reflect a striving for independence, yet most adolescents maintain love, loyalty, and respect for their parents (Collins & Laursen, 2006). And adolescents who feel close to their parents are more likely to show greater independence, higher self-esteem, better school performance, and fewer psychological problems (Costigan et al., 2007; Flouri & Buchanan, 2003).

"The best way to keep children home is to make the home atmosphere pleasant—and let the air out of the tires."

—DOROTHY PARKER

ego identity
Erikson's term for a firm sense of who one is and what one stands for

role diffusion
Erikson's term for lack of clarity in one's life roles (due to failure to develop ego identity)

emerging adulthood
period of development, roughly spanning the ages of 18 to 25, during which time many young people in affluent nations attend college and graduate school, sort out identity issues, and create life plans

Parent–adolescent conflict is greatest during puberty and declines in later adolescence (Smetana et al., 2003, 2006). Conflicts typically center on the everyday details of family life, such as chores, homework, curfews, personal appearance, finances, and dating, but parents and adolescents are usually similar in their beliefs regarding social, political, religious, and economic issues (Collins & Laursen, 2006).

Although relationships with parents generally remain positive, the role of peers as a source of activities, influence, and support increases during the teen years (Kirke, 2009). Adolescents stress the importance of acceptance, self-disclosure, mutual understanding, and loyalty in their friendships (Gonzalez et al., 2004). Adolescents and their friends are typically the same age and the same race (Castelli et al., 2009). Friends are also often alike in their school attitudes, educational aspirations, school achievement, and attitudes about drinking, drug use, and sexual activity (Snijders et al., 2007).

Parents often worry that their teenagers will fall in with the wrong crowd and engage in behavior that is self-destructive or goes against parental wishes. But research shows that most adolescents' friends are not bad influences (Allen & Antonishak, 2008; Reis & Youniss, 2004). Many peers reinforce positive behaviors, such as academic achievement (Allen & Antonishak, 2008).

Ego Identity Versus Role Diffusion

According to Erik Erikson (1963), we undergo eight stages of psychosocial development, each of which is characterized by a certain "crisis." Four of them, beginning with trust versus mistrust, occur in childhood. The fifth, that of *ego identity versus role diffusion*, occurs in adolescence. **Ego identity** is a firm sense of who one is and what one stands for. It can carry one through difficult times and lend meaning to achievements. Adolescents who do not develop ego identity may experience **role diffusion.** They spread themselves too thin, running down one blind alley after another and placing themselves at the mercy of leaders who promise to give them the sense of identity they cannot find for themselves.

In Western society, in which adolescents generally have a good deal of choice in determining what they will become, the creation of an adult identity is a key challenge. Much of this challenge involves learning about one's interests and abilities and connecting them

with an occupation or a role in life. But identity also involves sexual, political, and religious beliefs and commitments. Will the individual be monogamous or sexually active with several people? Will he or she lean left or right along the political spectrum? What role will be played by religion?

9-4 Emerging Adulthood

In earlier days, adolescents made a transition directly into adulthood. Now many of them in affluent nations spend time in what some theorists consider a new period of development, roughly spanning the ages of 18 to 25: **emerging adulthood**. During this time, many young people attend college and graduate school, sort out identity issues, and create meaningful life plans. But even in the United States, of course, many people cannot afford the luxury of sojourning in emerging adulthood.

Jeffrey Arnett (2012; Tanner & Arnett, 2011) hypothesizes that five features distinguish the stage of emerging adulthood that is sandwiched between the stages of adolescence, which precedes it, and young adulthood, which follows it:

- *The age of identity exploration.* Many people of the ages from 18 or 20 to about 25 or 30 are on the path to making vital choices in terms of their love lives and their career lives. They are experimenting with romantic partners and career possibilities.

- *The age of instability.* Americans today average about seven different jobs between 20 and 29. They frequently change romantic partners—sometimes by choice, sometimes because the partner decides to move on. They may move from place to place with little if any furniture. And they frequently change educational directions, finding what they like, finding what they can do, finding what is available.

- *The age of self-focus.* People are exceptionally self-focused during emerging adulthood (Arnett, 2012; Tanner & Arnett, 2011). They are freer to make decisions than they are as children or adolescents; they are more mature, more independent from parental influences, and usually have more resources.

- *The age of feeling in-between.* Emerging adults are similar to adolescents in one way: Whereas adolescents may feel that they exist somewhere between childhood and adulthood, emerging adults are likely to think that they are swimming between adolescence and "real" adulthood. They are likely to be out of school—that is, high school or undergraduate college—but obtaining further training or educa-

The woman pushing this wheelchair may be thought of as being in the "sandwich generation." She is "sandwiched" between the needs of her adolescent children and those of her aging parents.

Eric Lowenbach/Flickr/Getty Images

Late Adulthood

Generativity does not end with middle age. Research suggests that many individuals in late adulthood continue to be creative and also to maintain a firm sense of who they are and what they stand for (Webster, 2003). The Greek philosopher Plato was so optimistic about late adulthood that he argued that one could achieve great plea- sure in one's later years, engage in meaningful public service, and also achieve wisdom.

According to psychologist Erik Erikson, late adulthood is the stage of *ego integrity versus despair*. The basic challenge is to maintain the belief that life is meaningful and worthwhile as one ages and faces the inevitability of death. Erikson, like Plato, spoke of the importance of wisdom. He believed that ego integrity derives from wisdom, which can be defined as expert knowledge about the meaning of life, balancing one's own needs and those of others, and pushing toward excellence in one's behavior and achievements (Baltes & Staudinger, 2000; Sternberg, 2000). Erikson also believed that wisdom enables people to accept their life span as occurring at a certain point in the sweep of history and as being limited. We spend most of our lives accumulating objects and relationships, and Erikson argues that adjustment in the later years requires the ability to let go of them. Other views of late adulthood stress the importance of creating new challenges; however, biological and social realities may require older people to become more selective in their pursuits.

The American poet William Cullen Bryant is best known for his poem "Thanatopsis," which he composed at the age of 18. "Thanatopsis" expresses Erik Erikson's goal of ego integrity—optimism that we can maintain a sense of trust through life. By meeting squarely the challenges of our adult lives, perhaps we can take our leave with dignity. And when our time comes to "join the innumerable caravan"—the billions who have died before us—perhaps we can depart life with integrity as well.

> "Live," wrote the poet, so that
> . . . *when thy summons comes to join*
>
> *The innumerable caravan that moves*
> *To that mysterious realm, where each shall take*
>
> *His chamber in the silent halls of death,*
> *Thou go not, like the quarry-slave at night,*
>
> *Scourged to his dungeon, but, sustained and soothed*
> *By an unfaltering trust, approach thy grave*
>
> *Like one that wraps the drapery of his couch*
> *About him, and lies down to pleasant dreams.*

Bryant, of course, wrote "Thanatopsis" at age 18, not at 85, the age at which he died. At that advanced age, his feelings—and his verse—might have differed. But literature and poetry, unlike science, need not perfectly mirror reality. They can serve to inspire and warm us.

Ready to study? In the book, you can:

- ⊃ Review what you've read with Fill-Ins and Multiple Choice quizzes (below).
- ⊃ Rip out Chapter Review card (in the back).

Or you can go online to CourseMate at www.cengagebrain.com for these resources:

- ⊃ Complete Practices Quizzes to prepare for tests.
- ⊃ Review Key Terms Flash Cards (online or print).
- ⊃ Play games to master concepts.

FILL-INS

Answers can be found in the back of the book, starting on page 368.

1. Neonates show _____, which are simple, unlearned, stereotypical responses elicited by specific stimuli.

2. Piaget's _____-operational period is characterized by conservation and reversibility.

3. Vygotsky used the concepts of scaffolding and the _____ of proximal development to explain cognitive development.

4. Ainsworth identified three stages of attachment: The _____ phase, the attachment-in-the-making phase, and the clear-cut-attachment phase.

5. Puberty begins with the appearance of _____ sex characteristics, such as the deepening of the voice in males and rounding of the breasts and hips in females.

6. _____-operational thought is characterized by hypothetical thinking and deductive logic.

7. Adolescent egocentrism gives rise to the _____ audience and the personal fable.

8. Erik Erikson considers the life crisis of adolescence to be ego identity versus role _____.

9. _____ intelligence is mental flexibility as shown by the ability to solve new kinds of problems.

10. Research shows that most parents (do or do not?) suffer from the empty-nest syndrome.

1. A newborn shows a preference for his/her mother's voice rather than the father's voice. This is most likely the result of

   a. an inability to hear until after birth.
   b. learning to recognize the mother's voice because of more exposure to these sounds before birth.
   c. an inability to hear lower pitched tones as in a male's voice.
   d. liking mom more than they like dad.

2. Piaget's stages of cognitive development are, in order of increasing age,

   a. sensorimotor, preoperational, concrete operational, formal operational.
   b. sensorimotor, concrete operational, formal operational, preoperational.
   c. preoperational, operational, postoperational, formal operational.
   d. assimilation, adaptation, accommodation.

3. An adult who chooses not to park in a handicap space because they want to avoid a ticket and fine, is operating at the _____ level of Kohlberg's theory.

   a. nonconventional   c. preconventional
   b. postconvention   d. conventional

4. According to Ainsworth, babies who demonstrate proximity to their mother and separation anxiety when apart are showing indications of

   a. socialization.   c. association.
   b. neuroticism.   d. attachment.

5. Harry Harlow (1959) demonstrated that attachment in rhesus monkeys was related to

   a. feeding only.   c. learning experiences.
   b. contact comfort.   d. insecurity.

6. Menarche is the term used to describe

   a. adolescence.
   b. the beginning of adolescent growth spurts.
   c. the first menstruation.
   d. the onset of male secondary sex characteristics.

7. Formal operations allow adolescents to think

   a. symbolically.
   b. in terms of cause and effect.
   c. concretely.
   d. hypothetically.

8. An adolescent's belief that other people are as concerned with their thoughts and behavior as they are is called the

   a. personal fable.
   b. imaginary audience.
   c. pretend view.
   d. personal fantasy.

9. Intelligence associated with the intellectual attainments of a lifetime or acquired knowledge is called

   a. fluid intelligence.
   b. creative intelligence.
   c. crystallized intelligence.
   d. flexible intelligence.

10. Erikson labeled the life crisis of the middle years as

   a. trust versus mistrust.
   b. generativity versus stagnation.
   c. identity versus stagnation.
   d. midlife transition versus despair.

© Andrew Adolphus

LEARNING OUTCOMES

10-1 Describe the psychoanalytical perspective and how it contributed to the study of personality

10-2 Explain the trait perspective and the "Big Five" trait model

10-3 Identify the contributions of learning theory to understanding personality

10-4 Describe the humanistic-existential perspective on personality

10-5 Describe the sociocultural perspective on personality

10-6 Describe the different kinds of tests psychologists use to measure personality

After you read the chapter, go to the Study Tools at the end of the chapter, page 264.

CHAPTER 10

PERSONALITY:

Theory and Measurement

Nearly 1,000 years ago, an Islamic poet, Rumi, wrote of the fable of *The Blind Men and the Elephant*:

Once upon a time, a group of blind men heard that an unusual animal called an elephant had come to their country. Since they had no idea what an elephant looked like and had never even heard its name, they resolved that they would obtain a "picture" of sorts, and the knowledge they sought, by feeling the animal. After all, that was the only possibility available to them. They sought out the elephant, and its handler kindly permitted them to touch the beast. One blind man stroked its leg, the other a tusk, the third an ear, and believing that they now had knowledge of the elephant, they returned home satisfied. But when they were questioned by others, they provided very different descriptions. The one who had felt the leg said that the elephant was firm, strong, and upright, like a pillar. The one who had felt the tusk disagreed. He described the elephant as hard and smooth, clearly not as stout as a pillar, and sharp at the end. Now spoke the third blind man, who had held the ear of the elephant. "By my faith," he asserted, "the elephant is soft and rough." It was neither pillar-like nor hard and smooth. It was broad, thick, and leathery. And so the three argued about the true nature of the beast. Each was right in part, but none grasped the real nature of the elephant. Yet each was fervent in his belief that he knew the animal.

Each of the blind men had come to know the elephant from a different angle. Each was bound by his first experience and blind to the beliefs of his fellows and to the real nature of the beast—not just because of his physical limitations, but also because his initial encounter led him to think of the elephant in a certain way.

Can there ever be one true portrait of human personality?

WHAT DO YOU THINK? FOLKLORE, COMMON SENSE, OR NONSENSE? CIRCLE THE T FOR "TRUTH" OR THE F FOR "FICTION," AND CHECK THE ACCURACY OF YOUR ANSWERS AS YOU READ THROUGH THE CHAPTER.

T	F	BITING ONE'S FINGERNAILS OR SMOKING CIGARETTES IS A SIGN OF CONFLICT EXPERIENCED DURING EARLY CHILDHOOD.
T	F	BLOODLETTING AND VOMITING WERE ONCE RECOMMENDED AS WAYS OF COPING WITH DEPRESSION.
T	F	TWENTY-FIVE HUNDRED YEARS AGO, A GREEK PHYSICIAN DEVISED A WAY OF LOOKING AT PERSONALITY THAT—WITH A LITTLE "TWEAKING"—REMAINS IN USE TODAY.
T	F	ACTUALLY, THERE ARE NO BASIC PERSONALITY TRAITS. WE ARE ALL CONDITIONED BY SOCIETY TO BEHAVE IN CERTAIN WAYS.
T	F	THE MOST WELL-ADJUSTED IMMIGRANTS ARE THOSE WHO ABANDON THE LANGUAGE AND CUSTOMS OF THEIR COUNTRY OF ORIGIN AND BECOME LIKE MEMBERS OF THE DOMINANT CULTURE IN THEIR NEW HOST COUNTRY.
T	F	PSYCHOLOGISTS CAN DETERMINE WHETHER A PERSON HAS TOLD THE TRUTH ON A PERSONALITY TEST.
T	F	THERE IS A PSYCHOLOGICAL TEST MADE UP OF INKBLOTS, AND TEST-TAKERS ARE ASKED TO SAY WHAT THE BLOTS LOOK LIKE TO THEM.

personality

the reasonably stable patterns of emotions, motives, and behavior that distinguish one person from another

psychodynamic theory

Sigmund Freud's perspective, which emphasizes the importance of unconscious motives and conflicts as forces that determine behavior

Our own conceptions about people, and about ourselves, may be similarly bound up with our own perspectives and initial beliefs. Some think of personality as consisting of the person's most striking traits, as in "This person has an outgoing personality" or "That person has an agreeable personality." But many psychological theorists look deeper.

Those schooled in the Freudian tradition look at personality as consisting of underlying mental structures that jockey for supremacy outside the range of our ordinary awareness. Other theorists focus on how personality is shaped by learning. And to the humanistic theorists, personality is not something people *have* but rather something they *create* to give meaning and direction to their lives. Then, too, sociocultural theorists remind us that we must always consider the influences of culture, race, and ethnicity on personality.

Sometimes even psychologists prefer the first theory of personality they learn about. The Islamic theologian taught his pupils the legend of the blind men and the elephant to illustrate that no person can have a complete view of religious truths; we must therefore remain flexible in our thinking and open to new ideas. It may also be that none of the views of personality presented in this chapter will offer the one true portrait of human personality, but each may have something to contribute to our understanding. So let's approach our study with an open mind, because years from now psychologists may well be teaching new ideas about personality.

While the blind men could touch the elephant, researchers cannot touch a personality; therefore, personality is even harder to describe and understand. Before we discuss psychologists' various approaches to personality, let's define our subject matter: psychologists define **personality** as the reasonably stable patterns of emotions, motives, and behavior that distinguish one person from another.

10-1 The Psychodynamic Perspective

There are several **psychodynamic theories** of personality, each of which owes its origin to Sigmund Freud. Each teaches that personality is characterized by con-

flict. At first the conflict is external: Drives like sex, aggression, and the need for superiority come into conflict with laws, social rules, and moral codes. But at some point laws and social rules are brought inward—that is, *internalized*. The conflict is then between opposing *inner* forces. At any given moment our behavior, our thoughts, and our emotions represent the outcome of these inner contests.

10-1a SIGMUND FREUD'S THEORY OF PSYCHOSEXUAL DEVELOPMENT

Sigmund Freud (1856–1939) was a mass of contradictions. Some have lauded him as one of the greatest thinkers of the 20th century. Others have criticized him as overrated. He preached liberal views on sexuality but was himself a model of sexual restraint. He invented a popular form of psychotherapy but experienced lifelong psychologically related problems such as migraine headaches, fainting under stress, and hatred of the telephone. He smoked 20 cigars a day and could not break the habit even after he developed cancer of the jaw.

SIGMUND FREUD

id
the psychic structure, present at birth, that represents physiological drives and is fully unconscious

Freud was trained as a physician. Early in his practice, he was surprised to find that some people apparently experienced loss of feeling in a hand or paralysis of the legs even though they had no medical disorder. These odd symptoms often disappeared once the person recalled and discussed stressful events and feelings of guilt or anxiety that seemed to be related to the symptoms. Although these events and feelings lay hidden beneath the surface of awareness, they could influence behavior.

From this sort of clinical evidence, Freud concluded that the human mind is like an iceberg. Only the tip of an iceberg rises above the surface of the water; the great mass of it lies hidden in the depths (see Figure 10.1). Freud came to believe that people, similarly, are aware of only a small part of the ideas and impulses that dwell within their minds. He argued that a much greater portion of the mind—one that contained our deepest images, thoughts, fears, and urges—remains beneath the surface of conscious awareness, where little light illumines them.

Freud labeled the region that pokes into the light of awareness the *conscious* part of the mind. He called the regions below the surface the *preconscious* and the *unconscious*. The preconscious mind contains ideas that are out of awareness but can be made conscious by focusing on them. The unconscious mind is shrouded in mystery. It contains primitive instincts such as sex and aggression. Some unconscious urges cannot be experienced consciously because mental images and words cannot portray them in all their color and fury. Other unconscious urges may be kept below the surface by repression because they would create anxiety.

Repression is defined as the automatic ejection of anxiety-evoking ideas from awareness. People forget many ugly experiences, and some research evidence suggests that people *might* repress them (Furnham et al., 2003; Myers & Brewin, 1994). Other investigators allow that forgetting and distortion of memory occurs, but view the concept of repression as nothing but a myth (Kihlstrom, 2002).

In the unconscious mind, primitive drives seek expression, while learned values try to keep them in check. The conflict can arouse emotional outbursts and psychological problems. To explore the unconscious mind, Freud used a form of mental detective work called *psychoanalysis*. For this reason, his theory of personality is also referred to as *psychoanalytic theory*. In psychoanalysis, people are encouraged to talk about anything that pops into their mind while they remain comfortable and relaxed.

The Structure of Personality

Freud spoke of mental or *psychic structures* to describe the clashing forces of personality. Psychic structures cannot be seen or measured directly, but their presence is suggested by behavior, expressed thoughts, and emotions. Freud believed that there are three psychic structures: the *id*, the *ego*, and the *superego*.

The **id** is present at birth. It represents biological drives and is entirely unconscious. Freud described the id as "a chaos, a cauldron of seething excitations" (1927/1964, p. 73). The conscious mind might find it inconsistent to love and hate the same person, but such conflicting emotions can dwell side by side in the id. In the id, one can hate one's mother for failing to gratify immediately all of one's needs while also loving her. The id follows what Freud termed the *pleasure principle*. It demands instant gratification without consideration for law, social custom, or other people.

FIGURE 10.1 | The Human Iceberg According to Freud

According to psychodynamic theory, only the tip of human personality rises above the surface of the mind into conscious awareness. Material in the preconscious can become conscious if we direct our attention to it. Unconscious material tends to remain shrouded in mystery.

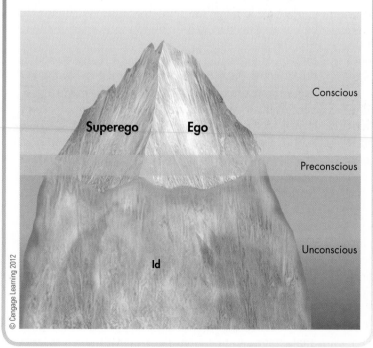

© Cengage Learning 2012

ego

the second psychic structure to develop, characterized by self-awareness, planning, and delay of gratification

superego

the third psychic structure, which functions as a moral guardian and sets forth high standards for behavior

psychosexual development

in psychodynamic theory, the process by which libidinal energy is expressed through different erogenous zones during different stages of development

oral stage

the first stage of psychosexual development, during which gratification is hypothesized to be attained primarily through oral activities

anal stage

the second stage of psychosexual development, when gratification is attained through anal activities

The **ego** begins to develop during the first year of life, largely because a child's demands for gratification cannot all be met immediately. The ego stands for reason and good sense, for rational ways of coping with frustration. The ego is guided by the *reality principle*. It curbs the appetites of the id and seeks ways to find gratification yet avoid social disapproval. The id informs you that you are hungry, but the ego decides to microwave enchiladas. The ego takes into account what is practical along with what is urged by the id. The ego also provides the conscious sense of self.

Although most of the ego is conscious, some of its business is carried out unconsciously. For example, the ego also acts as a censor that screens the impulses of the id. When the ego senses that improper impulses are rising into awareness, it may use psychological defenses to prevent them from surfacing. Repression is one such psychological defense, or *defense mechanism*.

The **superego** develops as the child incorporates the moral standards and values of parents and other members of the community. The child does so through *identification*, by trying to become like these people. The superego functions according to the *moral principle*. It holds up shining models of an ideal self and monitors the intentions of the ego, handing out judgments of right and wrong. It floods the ego with feelings of guilt and shame when the verdict is negative.

Freud believed that a healthy personality has found ways to gratify most of the id's demands without seriously offending the superego. Most of these demands are contained or repressed. If the ego is not a good problem solver, or if the superego is too stern, the ego will have a hard time of it.

Stages of Psychosexual Development

Freud stirred controversy by arguing that sexual impulses are a central factor in personality development, even among children. He believed that sexual feelings are closely linked to children's basic ways of relating to the world, such as nursing and moving their bowels.

Freud believed that a major instinct, *eros*, aims to preserve and perpetuate life. Eros is fueled by psycho-

Freud believed that the first year of life is the oral stage of development. During this time, if it fits, into the mouth it goes.

logical, or psychic, energy, which Freud labeled *libido*. Libidinal energy involves sexual impulses, so Freud considered it to be *psychosexual*. As the child develops, this energy is expressed through sexual feelings in different parts of the body, or *erogenous zones*. To Freud, human development involves the transfer of libidinal energy from one erogenous zone to another. He hypothesized five periods of **psychosexual development**: oral, anal, phallic, latency, and genital.

During the first year of life, a child experiences much of her or his world through the mouth. If it fits, into the mouth it goes. This is the **oral stage**. Freud argued that oral activities such as sucking and biting give the child sexual gratification as well as nourishment.

Freud believed that children encounter conflict during each stage of psychosexual development. During the oral stage, conflict centers on the nature and extent of oral gratification. Early weaning (cessation of breastfeeding) can lead to frustration. Excessive gratification, on the other hand, can lead an infant to expect that it will routinely get anything it wants. Insufficient or excessive gratification in any stage could lead to *fixation* in that stage and to the development of traits that are characteristic of the stage. Oral traits include dependency, gullibility, and excessive optimism or pessimism (depending on the child's experiences with gratification).

Freud theorized that adults with an *oral fixation* could experience exaggerated desires for "oral activities," such as smoking, overeating, alcohol abuse, and nail biting. Like the infant whose survival depends on the mercy of an adult, adults with oral fixations may desire clinging, dependent relationships.

The anal stage begins in the second year. During the **anal stage**, gratification is attained through contraction and relaxation of the muscles that control elimination of waste products. Elimination, which is reflexive during most of the first year, comes under voluntary muscular control, even if such control is not reliable at first. During the anal stage, children learn to delay the gratification that comes from eliminating whenever they feel the urge. The general issue of self-control may bring conflict between parent and child. *Anal fixations* may stem from this conflict and lead to either of two sets of traits in adulthood. *Anal-retentive* traits involve excessive use of self-control: perfectionism, a strong need for order, and exaggerated neatness and cleanliness. *Anal-expulsive* traits, on the other hand, "let it all hang out": they include carelessness, messiness, even sadism.

Children enter the **phallic stage** during the third year. The major erogenous zone is the phallic region (the penis in boys and the clitoris in girls). Parent–child conflict is likely to develop over masturbation, to which parents may respond with threats or punishment. During this stage children may develop strong sexual attachments to the parent of the other gender and begin to view the parent of the same gender as a rival for the other parent's affections.

Children have difficulty dealing with feelings of lust and jealousy. These feelings, therefore, remain unconscious, but their influence is felt through fantasies about marriage with the parent of the other gender and hostility toward the parent of the same gender. In boys, this conflict is labeled the **Oedipus complex**, after the legendary Greek king who unwittingly killed his father and married his mother. Similar feelings in girls give rise to the **Electra complex**. According to Greek legend, Electra was the daughter of the king Agamemnon. She longed for him after his death and sought revenge against his slayers—her mother and her mother's lover.

The Oedipus and Electra complexes are resolved by about the ages of five or six. Children repress their hostilities toward the parent of the same gender and begin to identify with her or him. In psychoanalytic theory, identification is the key to gender-typing: It leads children to play the gender roles of the parent of the same gender and to internalize his or her values. Sexual feelings toward the parent of the other gender are repressed for several years. When the feelings reemerge during adolescence, they are displaced, or transferred, to socially appropriate members of the other gender.

Freud believed that by the age of five or six, children have been in conflict with their parents over sexual feelings for several years. The pressures of the Oedipus and Electra complexes cause them to repress all sexual urges. In so doing, they enter a period of **latency**, during which their sexual feelings remain unconscious, they prefer playmates of their own gender, and they focus on schoolwork.

Freud believed that we enter the final stage of psychosexual development, the **genital stage**, at puberty. Adolescent males again experience sexual urges toward their mother, and adolescent females experience such urges toward their father. However, the *incest taboo* causes them to repress these impulses and displace them onto other adults or adolescents of the other gender. Boys might seek girls "just like the girl that married dear old Dad." Girls might be attracted to boys who resemble their fathers.

People in the genital stage prefer to find sexual gratification through intercourse with a member of the other gender. In Freud's view, oral or anal stimulation, masturbation, and sexual activity with people of the same gender all represent *pregenital* fixations and immature forms of sexual conduct.

10-1b NEO-FREUDIANS

Several personality theorists—*neo-Freudians*—are among Freud's intellectual heirs. Their theories, like his, include conflict and defense mechanisms. In other respects, they differ considerably.

Carl Jung

Carl Jung (1875–1961) was a Swiss psychiatrist who had been a member of Freud's inner circle. He fell into disfavor with Freud when he developed his own psychodynamic theory—**analytical psychology**. In contrast to Freud, Jung downplayed the importance of sex, which he saw as just one of several important instincts.

Jung, like Freud, was intrigued by unconscious processes. He believed that we not only have a *personal* unconscious that contains repressed memories and impulses, but also a **collective unconscious** containing primitive images, or *archetypes*, that reflect the history of our species. Examples of archetypes are the all-powerful God, the young hero, the fertile and nurturing mother, the wise old man, the hostile brother—even fairy godmothers, wicked witches, and themes of rebirth or resurrection. Arche-

phallic stage
the third stage of psychosexual development, characterized by a shift of libido to the phallic region

Oedipus complex
a conflict of the phallic stage in which the boy wishes to possess his mother sexually and perceives his father as a rival in love

Electra complex
a conflict of the phallic stage in which the girl longs for her father and resents her mother

latency
a phase of psychosexual development characterized by repression of sexual impulses

genital stage
the mature stage of psychosexual development, characterized by preferred expression of libido through intercourse with an adult of the other gender

analytical psychology
Jung's psychodynamic theory, which emphasizes the collective unconscious and archetypes

collective unconscious
Jung's hypothesized store of vague memories that represent the history of humankind

inferiority complex
feelings of inferiority hypothesized by Adler to serve as a central motivating force

creative self
according to Adler, the self-aware aspect of personality that strives to achieve its full potential

individual psychology
Adler's psychoanalytic theory, which emphasizes feelings of inferiority and the creative self

types themselves remain unconscious, but Jung believed they affect our thoughts and feelings and cause us to respond to cultural themes in the media.

Alfred Adler

Alfred Adler (1870–1937), another follower of Freud, also felt that Freud had placed too much emphasis on sex. Adler believed that people are basically motivated by an **inferiority complex**. In some people, feelings of inferiority may be based on physical problems and the need to compensate for them. Adler believed, however, that all of us encounter some feelings of inferiority because of our small size as children, and that these feelings give rise to a *drive for superiority*. As a child, Adler was crippled by rickets and suffered from pneumonia, and it may be that his theory developed in part from his own striving to overcome bouts of illness.

Adler believed that self-awareness plays a major role in the formation of personality. He spoke of a **creative self**, a self-aware aspect of personality that strives to overcome obstacles and develop the person's potential. Because each person's potential is unique, Adler's views have been termed **individual psychology**.

Karen Horney

Karen Horney (1885–1952) was criticized by the New York Psychoanalytic Institute because she took issue with the way in which psychoanalytic theory portrayed

Science Source/Photo Researchers

KAREN HORNEY

Horney, like many of Freud's intellectual descendants, took issue with Freud on many issues. For one thing, Horney did not believe that little girls had penis envy or felt inferior to boys in any other way. She also believed that children's social relationships are more important in their development than unconscious sexual and aggressive impulses.

women. Early in the 20th century, psychoanalytic theory taught that a woman's place was in the home. Women who sought to compete with men in the business world were assumed to be suffering from unconscious *penis envy*. Psychoanalytic theory taught that little girls feel inferior to boys when they learn that boys have a penis and

---

✳ Why Do We Need to Have Sports Heroes?

What have psychologists learned about the appeal of celebrities, and especially sports celebrities? Many people form deep and enduring bonds of attachment with athletes and sports teams. Once they identify with a team, their self-esteem rises and falls with the team's wins and losses (Wann et al., 2011a, 2011b). Wins lead to a surge of testosterone in males (Winegard, 2010; Wood & Stanton, 2011), which is connected with aggressiveness and self-confidence. Wins increase the optimism of both males and females.

Psychodynamic theory suggests that children identify with parents and other "big" people in their lives because big people seem to hold the keys to the resources they need for sustenance and stimulation or excitement. Athletes and entertainers—the rich and famous—have their fan clubs, filled with people who tie their own lights to the brilliant suns of their stars.

Teams and sports heroes provide both entertainment and the kind of gutsy competition that evolutionary psychologists believe whispers to us from our genes, pushing us toward aggression and dominance. If we can't do it on our own, we can do it *through* someone else. In some kind of psychological sense, we can *be* someone who is more effective at climbing the heap of humankind into the sun.

Michael Regan/Getty Images

they do not. But Horney argued that little girls do *not* feel inferior to boys and that these views were founded on Western cultural prejudice, not scientific evidence.

Horney agreed with Freud that childhood experiences are important in psychological development. Like other neo-Freudians, however, she asserted that unconscious sexual and aggressive impulses are less important than social relationships. She also believed that genuine and consistent love can alleviate the effects of a traumatic childhood.

Erik Erikson

Like many other modern psychoanalysts, Erik Erikson (1902–1994) believed that Freud had placed undue emphasis on sex. Like Horney, he believed that social relationships (such as that between a parent and child) are more important determinants of personality than sexual urges. Erikson also believed that to a large extent we are the conscious architects of our own personalities.

Erikson, like Freud, is known for devising a comprehensive theory of personality development. But whereas Freud proposed stages of psycho*sexual* development, Erikson proposed stages of psycho*social* development. Rather than label stages for various erogenous zones, Erikson labeled them for the traits that might be developed during the stages. The first stage of **psychosocial development** is labeled the stage of trust versus mistrust because two outcomes are possible: (1) a warm, loving relationship with the mother and others during infancy might lead to a sense of basic trust in people and the world; or (2) a cold, ungratifying relationship with the mother and others might generate a general sense of mistrust. For Erikson, the goal of adolescence is the attainment of **ego identity**, not genital sexuality. The focus is on who we see ourselves as being and what we stand for, not on sexual interests.

Like other modern-day analysts, Erikson believed that Freud had placed too much emphasis on sex and unconscious conflict. Erikson believed that social relationships were the key to healthful development.

Ted Streshinsky/Time Life Pictures/Getty Images

psychosocial development
Erikson's theory of personality and development, which emphasizes social relationships and eight stages of growth

ego identity
a firm sense of who one is and what one stands for

10-1c EVALUATION OF THE PSYCHODYNAMIC PERSPECTIVE

Psychodynamic theories have tremendous appeal. They are rich in concepts and seem to explain many human traits. Today, concepts such as the *id* and *libido* strike many psychologists as unscientific, but Freud was fighting for the idea that human personality and behavior are subject to scientific analysis. He developed his theory at a time when many people viewed psychological problems as signs of possession by the devil or evil spirits. Freud argued that psychological disorders stem from psychological problems—not evil spirits. His views contributed to the development of compassion for people with psychological disorders and to methods of psychotherapy.

"Freud found sex an outcast in the outhouse, and left it in the living room an honored guest."
—W. BERTRAM WOLFE

Psychodynamic theory also focused attention on the far-reaching effects of childhood events and suggested that parents respond to the emotional needs of their children. Freud has helped us recognize that sexual and aggressive urges are common, and that recognizing them is not the same as acting on them. As W. Bertram Wolfe put it, "Freud found sex an outcast in the outhouse, and left it in the living room an honored guest." On the other hand, his views of girls and women have been seen as sexist, as noted by Karen Horney.

Critics note that "psychic structures"— id, ego, and superego—are too vague to measure scientifically (Hergenhahn, 2009). Nor can they be used to predict behavior. Nor have the stages of psychosexual development escaped criticism. Children begin to masturbate as early as the first year, not in the phallic stage. As parents know from discovering their children playing "doctor," the

trait
a relatively stable aspect of personality that is inferred from behavior and assumed to give rise to consistent behavior

latency stage is not as sexually latent as Freud believed. Much of Freud's thinking about the Oedipus and Electra complexes remains little more than speculation.

The evidence for Erikson's developmental views seems sturdier. For example, people who fail to develop ego identity in adolescence seem to have problems with intimate relationships later on.

Freud's clinical method of gathering evidence is also suspect (Hergenhahn, 2009). Therapists may subtly guide clients into producing memories and feelings they expect to find. Also, most psychodynamic theorists restricted their evidence gathering to case studies with individuals who sought help, particularly people from the middle and upper classes. People who seek therapy differ from the general population.

Psychoanalytic theory focused on reasons that people develop certain traits. We next discuss trait theory, which is not so much concerned with the origins of traits as with their description and categorization.

10-2 The Trait Perspective

The notion of *traits* is familiar enough. If I asked you to describe yourself, you would probably do so in terms of traits such as bright, sophisticated, and witty. (That is you, is it not?) We also describe other people in terms of traits.

Traits are reasonably stable elements of personality that are inferred from behavior. If you describe a friend as "shy," it may be because you have observed anxiety or withdrawal in that person's social encounters. Traits are assumed to account for consistent behavior in different situations. You probably expect your "shy" friend to be retiring in most social confrontations. The concept of traits is also found in other approaches to personality. Freud linked the development of cer-

"In most of us by the age of thirty, the character has set like plaster, and will never soften again."
—WILLIAM JAMES

tain traits to children's experiences in each stage of psychosexual development.

10-2a FROM HIPPOCRATES TO THE PRESENT

The trait perspective dates at least to the Greek physician Hippocrates (ca. 460–377 BCE). Hippocrates believed that traits were embedded in bodily fluids. In his view, a person's personality depends on the balance of four basic fluids, or "humors," in the body. Yellow bile is associated with a choleric (quick-tempered) disposition; blood with a sanguine (warm, cheerful) one; phlegm with a phlegmatic (sluggish, calm, cool) disposition; and black bile with a melancholic (gloomy, pensive) temperament. Disease was believed to reflect an imbalance among the humors. Depression, for example, represented an excess of black bile. Methods such as bloodletting and vomiting were recommended to restore the balance (Lander & Pritchett, 2009). Although Hippocrates' theory was speculative, the terms *choleric, sanguine,* and so on are still used in descriptions of personality.

TRUTH METHODS SUCH AS BLOODLETTING AND VOMITING WERE IN FACT ONCE RECOMMENDED TO RESTORE THE BALANCE OF BODILY HUMORS.

More contemporary trait theories assume that traits are heritable and are embedded in the nervous system. These theories rely on the mathematical technique of *factor analysis*, developed by Charles Spearman to study intelligence, to determine which traits are basic to others.

Early in the 20th century, Gordon Allport and a colleague (Allport & Oddbert, 1936) catalogued some 18,000 human traits from a search through word lists like dictionaries. Some were physical traits such as *short, weak,* and *brunette.* Others were behavioral traits such as *shy* and *emotional.* Still others were moral traits such as *honest.* This exhaustive list has served as the basis for personality research by many other psychologists.

10-2b HANS EYSENCK'S TRAIT THEORY

British psychologist Hans J. Eysenck (1916–1997) focused much of his research on the relationships between two personality traits: **introversion–extraversion** and emotional stability–instability (Eysenck & Eysenck, 1985). (Emotional *in*stability is also called *neuroticism*.) Carl Jung was the first to distinguish between introverts and extraverts. Eysenck added the dimension of emotional stability–instability to introversion–extraversion. He catalogued various personality traits according to where they are situated along these dimensions (see Figure 10.2). For example, an anxious person would be high in both introversion

TRUTH IT IS TRUE THAT SOME 2,500 YEARS AGO, HIPPOCRATES, THE GREEK PHYSICIAN, DEVISED A WAY OF LOOKING AT PERSONALITY THAT COULD BE SAID TO REMAIN IN USE TODAY.

and neuroticism—that is, preoccupied with his or her own thoughts and emotionally unstable.

Eysenck acknowledged that his scheme is similar to Hippocrates'. According to Eysenck's dimensions, the choleric type would be extraverted and unstable; the sanguine type, extraverted and stable; the phlegmatic type, introverted and stable; and the melancholic type, introverted and unstable.

FIGURE 10.2 | Eysenck's Personality Dimensions and Hippocrates' Personality Types

Various personality traits shown in the outer ring fall within the two major dimensions of personality suggested by Hans Eysenck, The inner circle shows how Hippocrates' four major personality types—choleric, sanguine, phlegmatic, and melancholic—fit within Eysenck's dimensions.

Unstable

Moody
Anxious
Rigid
Sober
Pessimistic
Reserved
Unsociable
Quiet

Touchy
Restless
Aggressive
Excitable
Changeable
Impulsive
Optimistic
Active

Melancholic | Choleric

Introverted   **Extraverted**

Phlegmatic | Sanguine

Passive
Careful
Thoughtful
Peaceful
Controlled
Reliable
Even-tempered
Calm

Sociable
Outgoing
Talkative
Responsive
Easygoing
Lively
Carefree
Leadership

Stable

©2010 Mike Kemp/Jupiterimages Corporation

10-2c THE "BIG FIVE": THE FIVE-FACTOR MODEL

More recent research suggests that there may be five basic personality factors, not two. These include the two found by Eysenck—*extraversion* and *neuroticism*—along with *conscientiousness*, *agreeableness*, and *openness to experience* (see Table 10.1).

Many personality theorists, especially Robert McCrae and Paul T. Costa, Jr., played a role in the development of the *five-factor model*. Cross-cultural research has found that these five factors appear to define the personality structure of American, German, Portuguese, Israeli, Chinese, Korean, Japanese, and Philippine people (Katigbak et al., 2002; McCrae & Costa, 1997). A study

Rubberall/Jupiterimages

TABLE 10.1

The "Big Five": The Five-Factor Model

FACTOR NAME	TRAITS
I. Extraversion	Contrasts talkativeness, assertiveness, and activity with silence, passivity, and reserve
II. Agreeableness	Contrasts kindness, trust, and warmth with hostility, selfishness, and distrust
III. Conscientiousness	Contrasts organization, thoroughness, and reliability with carelessness, negligence, and unreliability
IV. Neuroticism	Contrasts nervousness, moodiness, and sensitivity to negative stimuli with coping ability
V. Openness to experience	Contrasts imagination, curiosity, and creativity with shallowness and lack of perceptiveness

of more than 5,000 German, British, Spanish, Czech, and Turkish people suggests that the factors are related to people's basic temperaments, which are considered to be largely inborn (McCrae et al., 2000). The researchers interpreted the results to suggest that our personalities tend to mature over time rather than be shaped by environmental conditions, although the expression of personality traits is certainly affected by culture.

The five-factor model—also known as the *Big Five model*—is fueling a great deal of research now. Hundreds of studies have correlated scores on the five factors—according to a psychological test constructed by Costa and McCrae (the *NEO Five-Factor Inventory*)—with various behavior patterns, psychological disorders, and kinds of "personalities." Consider driving. Significant negative correlations have been found between the numbers of traffic citations people receive and the accidents they get into, on the one hand, and the factor of agreeableness on the other (Cellar et al., 2000). In other words, it's safer to share the freeway with agreeable people. People who are not judgmental—who will put up with your every whim—tend to score low on conscientiousness (they don't examine you closely) and high on agreeableness (you can be yourself) (Bernardin et al., 2000). Despite the stereotype that older people, especially men, are "crotchety," assessment of 65- to 100-year-olds using the *NEO Five-Factor Inventory* suggests that people, especially men, become more agreeable as they grow older (Weiss et al., 2005). People who are anxious or depressed tend to score higher on the trait of neuroti-

FICTION ACTUALLY, THERE MAY BE SEVERAL BASIC PERSONALITY TRAITS, AS SUGGESTED BY TRAIT THEORY.

cism (Bienvenu et al., 2005). Introverts are more likely than extraverts to fear public gatherings and public speaking (Bienvenu et al., 2005).

10-2d BIOLOGY AND TRAITS

Researchers have also been investigating biological factors that are connected with, and may give rise to, personality traits. For example, researchers estimate that the heritability of the extraverted personality is 40% to 60% (Smillie et al., 2009). Research suggests that brain levels of the neurotransmitter dopamine are involved with extraversion and that levels tend to be higher in extraverts than in introverts (Smillie et al., 2009; Wacker et al., 2009).

Jerome Kagan and other researchers (Dai et al., 2003; Kagan & Saudino, 2001) have also found evidence that genetic factors are part of a child's basic temperament and are involved in shyness and behavioral inhibition. The *antisocial personality*—characterized by frequent conflict with society and lack of feelings of guilt or anxiety—is the other side of the coin when it comes to personality. Whereas shy children readily acquire fears and are highly reactive to stress, children who are on the path to developing antisocial personalities show low responses to threats and stressors (Gao et al., 2010b; Isen et al., 2010). As children, they show a pattern of deceit, callous disregard for the feelings of others, and lack of interest in conforming their behavior to social rules (Raine, 2008). As adults, they are likely to become involved in criminal activity.

Adrian Raine (2008) has extensively studied the intersection of biology and the antisocial personality. In a review of the literature, he found a number of brain impairments that are related to the development of an antisocial personality in the ventral prefrontal cortex (part of the so-called executive center of the brain) and the amygdala (part of the limbic system).

10-2e EVALUATION OF THE TRAIT PERSPECTIVE

Trait theorists have focused much attention on the development of personality tests. They have also given rise to theories about the fit between personality and certain kinds of jobs (Gottfredson, 2009). The qualities that suit a person for various kinds of work can be expressed in terms of abilities, personality traits, and interests.

One limitation of trait theory is that it has tended to be more descriptive than explanatory. It has historically focused on describing traits rather than on tracing their origins or seeking ways to modify maladaptive personality traits and behavior.

10-3 Learning-Theory Perspectives

Trait theory focused on enduring personality characteristics that were generally presumed to be embedded in the nervous system. Learning theorists tend not to theorize in terms of traits. They focus instead on behaviors and presume that those behaviors are largely learned.

That which is learned is also, in principle, capable of being unlearned. As a result, learning theory and personality theory may not be a perfect fit. Nevertheless, learning theorists—both behaviorists and social cognitive theorists—have contributed to the discussion of personality.

10-3a BEHAVIORISM

At Johns Hopkins University in 1924, John B. Watson sounded the battle cry of the behaviorist movement:

Give me a dozen healthy infants, well-formed, and my own specified world to bring them up in, and I'll guarantee to take any one at random and train him to become any type of specialist I might suggest—doctor, lawyer, merchant-chief and, yes, even beggar-man and thief, regardless of his talents, penchants, tendencies, abilities, vocations, and the race of his ancestors. (p. 82)

This proclamation underscores the behaviorist view that personality is plastic—that situational or environmental influences, not internal, individual variables, are the key shapers of personality. In contrast to the psychoanalysts and structuralists of his day, Watson argued that unseen, undetectable mental structures must be rejected in favor of that which can be seen and measured. In the 1930s, Watson's flag was carried onward by B. F. Skinner, who agreed that psychologists should avoid trying to see into the "black box" of the organism and instead emphasize the effects of reinforcements on behavior.

The views of Watson and Skinner largely ignored the notions of personal freedom, choice, and self-direction. Most of us assume that our wants originate within us. Watson and Skinner suggested that environmental influences such as parental approval and social customs shape us into *wanting* certain things and *not wanting* others.

In his novel *Walden Two*, Skinner (1948) described a Utopian society in which people are happy and content because they are allowed to do as they please. From early childhood, however, they have been trained or conditioned to be cooperative. Because of their reinforcement histories, they *want* to behave in decent, kind, and unselfish ways. They see themselves as free because society makes no effort to force them to behave in particular ways. The American poet Robert Frost wrote, "You have freedom when

✳ Virtuous Traits: Positive Psychology and Trait Theory

Trait theory has found applications within positive psychology, an approach that studies character strengths and virtues such as those just listed. Psychologists are also developing psychological methods that help people increase their happiness and life satisfaction (Sheldon, 2009; Shyrack et al., 2010). Psychologists list six major virtues (see the table below) that were found in countries as different as Azerbaijan and Venezuela, along with the United States and other developed nations (Peterson & Seligman, 2004; Snyder et al., 2010).

The *Character Strengths and Virtues: A Handbook and Classification (the CSV)* was partly developed as a counterpoint to the *DSM*, which is the *Diagnostic and Statistical Manual of the Mental Disorders* of the American Psychiatric Association (2000). Whereas the *DSM* is a catalogue of (nearly) everything that can go wrong with people, the *CSV* is a catalogue of things that go right. Fortunately, there are many of them.

VIRTUE	CORRESPONDING CHARACTER STRENGTHS
Wisdom and knowledge	Creativity, curiosity, open-mindedness, love of learning, perspective (ability to provide other people with sound advice)
Courage	Authenticity (speaking one's mind), bravery, persistence, zest
Humanity	Kindness, love, social intelligence
Justice	Fairness, leadership, teamwork
Temperance	Forgiveness, modesty, prudence, self-regulation
Transcendence	Appreciation of beauty and excellence, gratitude (when appropriate), hope, humor, religiosity (having a belief system about the meaning of life)

Source: Peterson & Seligman, 2004.

social cognitive theory

a cognitively oriented learning theory in which observational learning and person variables such as values and expectancies play major roles in individual differences

gender-typing

the process by which males and females come to display behavior patterns consistent with stereotypical masculine and feminine gender roles

gender-schema theory

a cognitive view of gender-typing that proposes that once girls and boys become aware of their anatomic sex, they begin to blend their self-expectations and self-esteem with the ways in which they fit the gender roles prescribed in a given culture

you're easy in your harness." Society in Skinner's *Walden Two* made children "easy" in their "harnesses," but the harnesses were very real.

Some object to behaviorist notions because they play down the importance of consciousness and choice. Others argue that humans are not blindly ruled by reinforcers (that is, rewards and punishments). In some circumstances, people have rebelled against the so-called necessity of survival by choosing pain and hardship over pleasure, or death over life. Many people have sacrificed their own lives to save those of others. The behaviorist "defense" might be that the apparent choice of pain or death is forced on some just as conformity to social custom is forced on others.

10-3b SOCIAL COGNITIVE THEORY

Social cognitive theory was developed by Albert Bandura (1986, 2008) and other psychologists. In contrast to behaviorism, which focuses on observable behavior and the situations in which behavior occurs, social cognitive theory focuses on learning by observation and on the cognitive processes that underlie personal differences. Social cognitive theorists differ from behaviorists in that they see people as influencing their environment just as their environment affects them. Social cognitive theorists agree with behaviorists that discussions of human nature should be tied to observable behavior, but they assert that variables within people—*person variables*—must also be considered if we are to understand people. *Situational variables* include rewards and punishments. Person variables include

FIGURE 10.3 | Person Variables and Situational Variables in Social-Cognitive Theory

According to social-cognitive theory, person variables and situational variables interact to influence behavior.

© Rubberball

knowledge and skills, ways of interpreting experience, expectancies, emotions, and self-regulatory systems and plans (Bandura, 2008; Rodin et al., 2009; Sherman et al., 2009; see Figure 10.3).

We cannot predict behavior from situational variables alone. Whether a person will behave in a certain way also depends on the person's *expectancies* about the outcomes of that behavior and the perceived or *subjective values* of those outcomes. There are various kinds of expectancies. Some are predictions about what will follow what. For example, people might predict other people's behavior on the basis of body language such as "tight lips" or "shifty eyes." *Self-efficacy expectations* are beliefs that we can accomplish certain things, such as doing a backflip into a swimming pool or solving math problems (Bandura & Locke, 2003). People with positive self-efficacy expectations tend to have high self-esteem (Sanna & Meier, 2000) and achievement motivation (Heimpel

"It is **our attitude** at the beginning of a difficult task which, more than anything else, will affect its successful outcome."

—WILLIAM JAMES

Biology, Social Cognition, and Gender-Typing

Gender-typing is the process by which males and females come to develop personality traits and behavior patterns that society considers to be consistent with their gender, male or female—at least most of the time. Researchers who investigate people's perceptions of gender differences in personality traits tend to find groups of "masculine" and "feminine" traits, such as those shown in Table 10.2. According to evolutionary psychologists, gender differences were fashioned by natural selection in response to problems in adaptation that were repeatedly encountered over thousands of generations (Buss, 2009; Schmitt, 2008). Men, who have generally been the hunters, breadwinners, and warriors, are more likely to be seen as *adventurous, aggressive,* and *assertive* (Amanatullah & Morris, 2010; Guzzetti, 2010; Lippa, 2010). Women, who have more often been the homemakers and caretakers, are more likely to be seen as *affectionate, agreeable,* and *emotional.*

Biology and Gender-Typing
Other researchers suggest that the development of gender differences in personality, along with the development of anatomic gender differences, may be related to prenatal levels of sex hormones. Although results of many studies attempting to correlate prenatal sex hormone levels with subsequent gender-typed play have been mixed, a study of 212 pregnant women conducted by Bonnie Auyeung and her colleagues (2009) found that fetal testosterone was related to masculine or feminine-typed play at the age of 8½ years. Other studies show that children display gender-typed preferences—with boys preferring transportation toys and girls preferring dolls—as early as the age of 13 months (Knickmeyer et al., 2005). Another study investigated the gender-typed visual preferences of 30 human infants at the early ages of three to eight months (Alexander et al., 2009). The researchers assessed interest in a toy truck and a doll by using eye-tracking technology to indicate the direction of visual attention. Girls showed a visual preference for the doll over the truck (that is, they made a greater number of visual fixations on the doll), and boys showed a visual preference for the truck.

Social Cognition and Gender-Typing
Social cognitive theorists find roles for learning in gender-typing, and they suggest that children learn what is considered masculine or feminine in their societies by means of observational learning and socialization (Golombok et al., 2008; Zosuls et al., 2009). Children observe the behavior of adult role models and may come to assume that their behavior should conform to that of adults of the same gender. In social-cognitive theory, rewards and punishments influence children to imitate adult models of the same gender. The child not only imitates

Hill Street Studios/Blend Images/Jupiterimages

What do this mother's female and male twins have to look forward to in terms of gender-role stereotypes?

the behavior of the model but also tries to become broadly like the model—that is, she or he *identifies* with the model.

Almost from the moment a baby comes into the world, she or he is treated in ways that are consistent with gender stereotypes. Parents tend to talk more to baby girls, and fathers especially engage in more roughhousing with boys. When children are old enough to speak, caregivers and even other children begin to tell them how they are expected to behave. Parents may reward children for behavior they consider gender appropriate and punish (or fail to reinforce) them for behavior they consider inappropriate. Girls are encouraged to practice caregiving, which is intended to prepare them for traditional feminine adult roles. Boys are handed LEGOS® or doctor sets to help prepare them for traditional masculine adult roles.

The Gender-Schema Theory of Gender-Typing
Gender-schema theory emphasizes the role of cognition in gender-typing (Martin et al., 2002; Martin & Ruble, 2004). Gender-schema theory proposes that children develop a **gender schema** as a means of organizing their perceptions of the world. A gender schema is a cluster of ideas about masculine and feminine physical traits. Gender becomes important because of society's emphasis on it. According to gender-schema theory, once children come to see themselves as female or male, they begin to seek information concerning gender-typed traits and try to live up to them (Grace et al., 2008; Most et al., 2007; Tenenbaum et al., 2010). Jack will retaliate when provoked because boys are expected to do so. Jill will be "sugary and sweet" if such is expected of little girls.

Today, most scholars would agree that both biology and social cognition interact to affect most areas of behavior and mental processes—including the complex processes involved in gender-typing.

TABLE 10.2 | Stereotypical Masculine and Feminine Traits

MASCULINE		FEMININE	
Adventurous	Determined	Affectionate	Fickle
Aggressive	Hardheaded	Agreeable	Gentle
Assertive	Independent	Cautious	Kind
Capable	Intelligent	Dependent	Patient
Confident	Pleasure-seeking	Emotional	Sensitive
Courageous	Rational	Fearful	Talkative

Sources: Amanatullah & Morris, 2010; Guzzetti, 2010; Lippa, 2010; Schmitt et al., 2008.

humanism
the view that people are capable of free choice, self-fulfillment, and ethical behavior

existentialism
the view that people are completely free and responsible for their own behavior

self-actualization
in humanistic theory, the innate tendency to strive to realize one's potential

et al., 2002). Psychotherapy often motivates people to try new things by changing their self-efficacy expectations from "I can't" to "Perhaps I can" (Bandura, 1999).

Observational Learning

Observational learning (also termed *modeling* or *cognitive learning*) is one of the foundations of social cognitive theory. It refers to acquiring knowledge by observing others. For operant conditioning to occur, an organism must first engage in a response, and that response must be reinforced. However, observational learning occurs even when the learner does not perform the observed behavior. Direct reinforcement is not required either. Observing others extends to reading about them or seeing what they do and what happens to them in books, TV, film, and the Internet.

10-3c EVALUATION OF THE LEARNING PERSPECTIVE

Learning theorists have contributed to the scientific understanding of behavior, but they have left some psychologists dissatisfied. Psychodynamic theorists and trait theorists propose the existence of psychological structures that cannot be seen and measured directly. Learning theorists—particularly behaviorists—have dramatized the importance of referring to publicly observable variables, or behaviors, if psychology is to be accepted as a science.

Similarly, psychodynamic theorists and trait theorists focus on internal variables such as unconscious conflict and traits to explain and predict behavior. Learning theorists emphasize the importance of environmental conditions, or situational variables, as determinants of behavior. They have also elaborated on the conditions that foster learning, including automatic kinds of learning. They have shown that we can learn to do things because of reinforcements and that many behaviors are learned by observing others.

Social cognitive theory does not account for self-awareness, and, like its intellectual forebear, behaviorism, it may not pay enough attention to genetic variation in explaining individual differences in behavior.

"Always remember that you are absolutely unique. Just like everyone else."
—MARGARET MEAD

10-4 The Humanistic-Existential Perspective

Humanists and existentialists dwell on the meaning of life. Self-awareness is the hub of the humanistic–existential search for meaning. The term **humanism** has a long history and many meanings. As a counterpoint (or "third force") to the predominant psychodynamic and behavioral models, it puts self-awareness at the center of consideration and argues that people are capable of free choice, self-fulfillment, and ethical behavior. Humanism also represented a reaction to the "rat race" spawned by industrialization and automation. The humanistic views of Abraham Maslow and Carl Rogers emerged from these concerns.

Existentialism in part reflects the horrors of mass destruction of human life through war and genocide, frequent events in the 20th century. The European existentialist philosophers Jean-Paul Sartre and Martin Heidegger saw human life as trivial in the grand scheme of things. But psychiatrists like Viktor Frankl, Ludwig Binswanger, and Medard Boss argued that seeing human existence as meaningless could give rise to withdrawal and apathy—even suicide. Psychological salvation therefore requires giving personal meaning to things and making personal choices (McDonald, 2008).

10-4a ABRAHAM MASLOW AND THE CHALLENGE OF SELF-ACTUALIZATION

Freud wrote that people are basically motivated to gratify biological drives and that their perceptions are distorted by their psychological needs. The humanistic psychologist Abraham Maslow—whose hierarchy of needs we described in Chapter 8—argued that people also have a conscious need for **self-actualization**, or to become all that they can be. Because people are unique, they must follow unique paths to self-actualization. People are not at the mercy of unconscious, primitive impulses. Rather, the main threat to individual personality development is control by other people. We must each be free to get in touch with and actualize our selves. But self-actualization requires taking risks. Many people are more comfortable with the familiar. But people who adhere to the "tried and true" may find their lives slipping into monotony and mediocrity.

10-4b CARL ROGERS'S SELF THEORY

The humanistic psychologist Carl Rogers (1902–1987) wrote that people shape themselves through free choice and action. Rogers defined the *self* as the center of experience. Your self is your ongoing sense of who and what you are, your sense of how and why you react to the environment and how you choose to act on the environment. Your choices are made on the basis of your values, and your values are also part of your self. Rogers's self theory focuses on the nature of the self and the conditions that allow the self to develop freely. Two of his major concerns are the self-concept and self-esteem.

The Self-Concept and Frames of Reference

Our *self-concepts* consist of our impressions of ourselves and our evaluations of our adequacy. Rogers believed that we all have unique ways of looking at ourselves and the world—that is, unique *frames of reference*. It may be that we each use a different set of dimensions in defining ourselves and that we judge ourselves according to different sets of values. To one person, achievement–failure may be the most important dimension. To another person, the most important dimension may be decency–indecency. A third person may not even think in these terms.

Self-Esteem and Positive Regard

Rogers assumed that we all develop a need for self-regard, or self-esteem. At first, self-esteem reflects the esteem in which others hold us. Parents help children develop self-esteem when they show them **unconditional positive regard**—that is, when they accept them as having intrinsic merit regardless of their behavior at

the moment. Rogers was optimistic about human nature. He believed that people are basically good, and that when they develop in an atmosphere of unconditional positive regard, they will become generous and loving—not selfish. But when parents show children **conditional positive regard**—that is, when they accept them only when they behave in a desired manner—children may develop **conditions of worth**. Therefore, children may come to think that they have merit only if they behave as their parents wish them to behave.

Because each individual has a unique potential, children who develop conditions of worth must be somewhat disappointed in themselves. They cannot fully live up to the wishes of others and be true to themselves. Children in some families learn that it is bad to have ideas of their own, especially about sexual, political, or religious matters. When they perceive their caregivers' disapproval, they may come to see themselves as rebels and label their feelings as selfish, wrong, or evil. If they wish to retain a consistent self-concept and self-esteem, they may have to deny their feelings or disown parts of themselves. In this way, their self-concept becomes distorted. According to Rogers, anxiety often stems from recognition that people have feelings and desires that are inconsistent with their distorted self-concept. Because anxiety is unpleasant, people may deny the existence of their genuine feelings and desires.

Rogers believed that the path to self-actualization requires getting in touch with our genuine feelings, accepting them, and acting on them. This is the goal of Rogers's method of psychotherapy, *client-centered therapy*. Rogers also be-

unconditional positive regard a persistent expression of esteem for the value of a person, but not necessarily an unqualified acceptance of all of the person's behaviors

conditional positive regard judgment of another person's value on the basis of the acceptability of that person's behaviors

conditions of worth standards by which the value of a person is judged

ASP via Getty Images

JUST DOING IT

Many males tie their self-esteem to prowess in athletics. What are the roots of your self-esteem?

lieved that we have mental images of what we are capable of becoming. These are termed *self-ideals*. We are motivated to reduce the difference between our self-concepts and our self-ideals.

Gabriela Medina/Blend Images/Jupiterimages

"You are unique, and if that is not fulfilled, then something has been lost."

—MARTHA GRAHAM

10-4c EVALUATION OF THE HUMANISTIC–EXISTENTIAL PERSPECTIVE

Humanistic–existential theories have tremendous appeal for college students because of their focus on the importance of personal experience. We tend to treasure our conscious experiences (our "selves"). For most nonhumans, to live is to move, to process food, to exchange oxygen and carbon dioxide, and to reproduce. But for humans, an essential aspect of life is conscious experience—the sense of oneself as progressing through space and time.

Ironically, the primary strength of the humanistic–existential approaches—their focus on conscious experience—is also their main weakness. Conscious experience is private and subjective. Therefore, the validity of formulating theories in terms of consciousness has been questioned.

Humanistic–existential theories, like learning theories, have little to say about the development of traits and personality types. They assume that we are all unique, but they do not predict the sorts of traits, abilities, and interests we will develop.

10-5 The Sociocultural Perspective

Thirteen-year-old Hannah brought her lunch tray to the table in the cafeteria. Her mother, Julie, eyed with horror the French fries, the plate of mashed potatoes in gravy, the bag of potato chips, and the large paper cup brimming with soda. "You can't eat that!" she said. "It's garbage!"

"Oh come on, Mom! Chill, okay?" Hannah rejoined before taking her tray to sit with some friends rather than with us.

I used to spend Saturdays with my children at the Manhattan School of Music. Not only did they study voice and piano, they—and I—widened our cultural perspective by relating to families and students from all parts of the world.

Julie and Hannah are Korean Americans. Flustered, Julie shook her head and said, "I've now been in the United States longer than I was in Korea, and I still can't get used to the way children act here. When she talks that way, it's embarrassing." I vaguely recall making some unhelpful comments about the ketchup on the French fries having antioxidants and some slightly helpful comments about what is typical of teenagers in the United States. But as I thought about Hannah, I realized that in our multicultural society, personality cannot be understood without reference to the **sociocultural perspective**. Different ethnic groups within the United States have different attitudes, beliefs, norms, self-definitions, and values (Phinney & Baledelomar, 2011; Schwartz et al., 2010).

Hannah was strongly influenced by her peers—she was completely at home with blue jeans and French fries. She was also a daughter in an Asian American immigrant group that views education as the key to success in our culture (Leppel, 2002; Magno, 2010). Belonging to this ethnic group had contributed to her ambition and her hard work in school and on her violin, but had not prevented her from becoming an outspoken American teenager. Behavior that struck me as typical and inoffensive had struck her mother as brazen and inappropriate.

Let's consider how sociocultural factors can affect one's sense of self.

10-5a INDIVIDUALISM VERSUS COLLECTIVISM: WHO AM I (IN THIS CULTURAL SETTING)?

One could say that Julie's complaint was that Hannah saw herself as an individual and an artist to a greater extent than as a family member and a Korean girl. Cross-cultural research reveals that people in the United States and many northern European nations tend to be individualistic. **Individualists** tend to define themselves in terms of their personal identities and to give priority to their personal goals (Brewer & Chen, 2007; Triandis, 2006). When asked to complete the statement "I am . . . ," they are likely to respond in terms of their personality traits ("I am outgoing," "I am artistic") or their occupations ("I am a nurse," "I am a systems analyst") (Triandis & Suh, 2005).

In contrast, many people from cultures in Africa, Asia, and Central and South America tend to be collectivistic (Brewer & Chen, 2007; Triandis, 2006). **Collectivists** tend to define themselves in terms of the groups to which they belong and to give priority to the group's goals (Triandis, 2006). They feel complete in terms of their relationships with others (see Figure 10.4). They are more likely than individualists to conform to group norms and judgments (Brewer & Chen, 2007; Triandis & Suh, 2002). When asked to complete the statement "I am . . . ," collectivists are more likely to respond in terms of their families, gender, or nation ("I am a father," "I am a Buddhist," "I am a Japanese") (Triandis, 2001).

The seeds of individualism and collectivism are found in the culture in which a person grows up. The capitalist system fosters individualism to some degree.

sociocultural perspective
the view that focuses on the roles of ethnicity, gender, culture, and socioeconomic status in personality formation, behavior, and mental processes

individualist
a person who defines herself or himself in terms of personal traits and gives priority to her or his own goals

collectivist
a person who defines herself or himself in terms of relationships to other people and groups and gives priority to group goals

FIGURE 10.4 | The Self in Relation to Others from the Individualist and Collectivist Perspectives

To an individualist, the self is separate from other people (part A). To a collectivist, the self is complete only in terms of relationships to other people (part B). (Based on Markus & Kitayama, 1991).

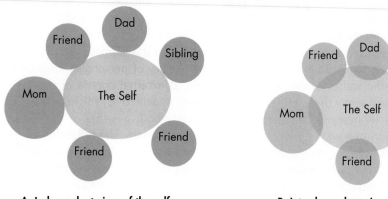

A. Independent view of the self

B. Interdependent view of the self

acculturation
the process of adaptation in which immigrants and native groups identify with a new, dominant culture by learning about that culture and making behavioral and attitudinal changes

validity
in psychological testing, the degree to which a test measures what it is supposed to measure

reliability
in psychological testing, the consistency or stability of test scores from one testing to another

The traditional writings of the East have exalted people who resist personal temptations to do their duty and promote the welfare of the group.

Another issue from the sociocultural perspective is *acculturation.* Just how much acculturation is good for you?

10-5b ACCULTURATION, ADJUSTMENT, AND SELF-ESTEEM

Self-esteem is connected with patterns of **acculturation** among immigrants (Phinney & Baledelomar, 2011). Those patterns take various forms. Some immigrants are completely assimilated by the dominant culture. They lose the language and customs of their country of origin and identify with the dominant culture in the new host country. Others maintain almost complete separation. They retain the language and customs of their country of origin and never acclimate to those of the new country. Still others become bicultural. They remain fluent

OSCAR RIVERA/AFP/Getty Images

in the language of their country of origin but also become conversant in the language of their new country. They blend the customs and values of both cultures (Schwartz et al., 2010). They can switch "mental gears"; they apply the values of one culture under some circumstances and apply the values of the other culture under others (Phinney, 2006). Perhaps they relate to other people in one way at work or in school, and in another way at home or in the neighborhood. Research evidence suggests that bicultural people have relatively higher self-esteem than people who completely surrender their traditional backgrounds (David et al., 2009; Schwartz et al., 2010).

FICTION ACTUALLY, RESEARCH EVIDENCE SUGGESTS THAT PEOPLE WHO DO NOT FULLY SURRENDER THEIR TRADITIONAL BACKGROUNDS HAVE HIGHER SELF-ESTEEM THAN THOSE WHO DO.

10-5c EVALUATION OF THE SOCIOCULTURAL PERSPECTIVE

The sociocultural perspective provides valuable insights into the roles of ethnicity, gender, culture, and socioeconomic status in personality formation. It enhances our sensitivity to cultural differences and expectations and allows us to appreciate the richness of human behavior and mental processes.

(10-6) Measurement of Personality

Physicians have an easy time of it measuring heart rate and blood pressure. Psychologists, biologists, and neuroscientists find it easier to measure electricity in the brain or substances in the blood than to measure psychological concepts such as intelligence, depression, extraversion, or emotional stability. It may take time, money, and expertise to develop and operate the proper instruments, but once you have them, the measurements tend to be accurate enough.

In Chapter 7 we saw that many critics argue that intelligence tests measure many things other than intelligence, including motivation and familiarity with European American middle-class culture. In Chapter 8 we saw that lie detectors measure four physiological variables and detect much more than lies. The reliability and validity of intelligence tests and lie detectors have been brought into question. So too have the reliability and validity of personality tests.

The **validity** of a test is the extent to which it measures what it is supposed to measure. We usually assess the validity of personality tests by comparing test results to external criteria or standards. For example, a test of hyperactivity might be compared with teachers' reports about whether or not children in their classes are hyperactive. The **reliability** of a test is the stability of one's test results from one testing to another. We usually determine the reliability of tests by comparing testing results on different occasions or at different ages. A reliable IQ test should provide scores during childhood that remain reasonably similar in adolescence and adulthood. Test **standardization** is a process that checks out the scores, validity, and reliability of a test with people of various ages and from various groups. We cannot assess the intellectual functioning of an individual without relating it to other people in the same age group. Such information is made available when tests are professionally developed and scored.

Behavior-rating scales assess behavior in settings such as classrooms or mental hospitals. With behavior-rating scales, trained observers usually check off each occurrence of a specific behavior within a certain time frame—say, 15 minutes. Behavior-rating scales are growing in popularity, especially for use with children (Kamphaus et al., 2000). However, standardized objective and projective tests are used more frequently, and we focus on them in this section.

Measures of personality are used to make important decisions, such as whether a person is suited for a certain type of work, a particular class in school, or a drug to reduce agitation. As part of their admissions process, graduate schools often ask professors to rate prospective students on scales that assess traits such as intelligence, emotional stability, and cooperation. Students may take tests to measure their *aptitudes* and interests to gain insight into whether they are suited for certain occupations. It is assumed that students who share the aptitudes and interests of people who function well in certain positions are also likely to function well in those positions.

Let's consider the two most widely used types of personality tests: objective tests and projective tests.

10-6a OBJECTIVE TESTS

Objective tests present respondents with a standardized group of test items in the form of a questionnaire. Respondents are limited to a specific range of answers. One test might ask respondents to indicate whether items are true or false for them. Another might ask respondents to select the preferred activity from groups of three.

Some tests have a *forced-choice format*, in which respondents are asked to indicate which of two or more statements is more true for them or which of several activities they prefer. The respondents are not usually given the option of answering "none of the above." Forced-choice formats are frequently used in interest inventories, which help predict whether the person would function well in a certain occupation. They are typically the only means of responding to online assessments because the test-taker is usually required to "click" the chosen answer. The following item is similar to those found in occupational interest inventories:

I would rather
   a. be a forest ranger.
   b. work in a busy office.
   c. play a musical instrument.

The Minnesota Multiphasic Personality Inventory (MMPI)[1] contains hundreds of items presented in a true–false format. The MMPI is designed for use by clinical and counseling psychologists to help diagnose psychological disorders. Accurate measurement of an individual's problems should point to appropriate treatment. The MMPI is the most widely used psychological test in clinical work and is widely used in psychological research.

The MMPI scales were constructed *empirically*—that is, on the basis of actual clinical data rather than psychological theory. A test-item bank of several hundred items was derived from questions that are often asked in clinical interviews. Here are some examples of the kinds of items that were used:

My father was a good man.	T F
I am very seldom troubled by headaches.	T F
My hands and feet are usually warm enough.	T F
I have never done anything dangerous for the thrill of it.	T F
I work under a great deal of tension.	T F

The items were administered to people with previously identified symptoms, such as depressive or schizophrenic symptoms. Items that successfully set these people apart were included on scales named for these conditions. Confidence in the MMPI has developed because of its extensive use.

10-6b PROJECTIVE TESTS

Projective tests have no clear specified answers. People are shown ambiguous stimuli such as inkblots or ambiguous drawings and asked to say what they look like or to tell stories about them. Or they are asked to

FICTION IT IS NOT TRUE THAT PSYCHOLOGISTS CAN GUARANTEE THAT THEY CAN DETECT DECEPTION ON A PERSONALITY TEST.

standardization
in psychological testing, the process by which one obtains and organizes test scores from various population groups, so that the results of a person's completing a test can be compared to those of others of his or her gender, in his or her age group, and so on

objective tests
tests whose items must be answered in a specified, limited manner; tests whose items have concrete answers that are considered correct

projective test
a psychological test that presents ambiguous stimuli onto which the test-taker projects his or her own personality in making a response

---

[1]Currently the updated MMPI-2.

complete sentences or to draw pictures of persons. There is no one correct response. It is assumed that people *project* their own personalities into their responses. The meanings they attribute to these stimuli are assumed to reflect their personalities as well as the drawings or blots themselves.

The Rorschach Inkblot Test

There are a number of psychological tests made up of inkblots, and test-takers are asked to say what the blots look like to them. The best known of these is the Rorschach inkblot test, named after its originator, Hermann Rorschach (Archer et al., 2006).

In the Rorschach test, people are given the inkblots, one by one, and are asked what they look like or what they could be. A response that reflects the shape of the blot is considered a sign of adequate *reality testing*. A response that richly integrates several features of the blot is considered a sign of high intellectual functioning. Supporters of the Rorschach believe that it provides insight

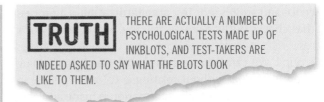

TRUTH THERE ARE ACTUALLY A NUMBER OF PSYCHOLOGICAL TESTS MADE UP OF INKBLOTS, AND TEST-TAKERS ARE INDEED ASKED TO SAY WHAT THE BLOTS LOOK LIKE TO THEM.

into a person's intelligence, interests, cultural background, personality traits, psychological disorders, and many other variables. Critics argue that there is little empirical evidence to support the test's validity (Garb et al., 2005). Even when the Rorschach is being severely challenged as a method of obtaining diagnoses of psychological disorders, researchers continue to claim that it has uses

FIGURE 10.5 | An Inkblot Test

Of all the inkblot tests, the Rorschach is the most widely used projective personality test. What does this inkblot look like to you? What could it be?

Masterfile (Royalty-Free Div.)

in many other areas, including the hiring and selection of personnel in organizations (Del Giudice, 2010), determination of whether individuals are suitable to have child custody (Weiner, 2006), and even in the assessment of children in schools (Hojnoski et al., 2006).

Although there is no single "correct" response to the inkblot shown in Figure 10.5, some responses are not in keeping with the features of the blots and reveal to the examiner that the test-taker is projecting his or her personality onto the test stimuli. The shape of the inkblot in Figure 10.5 might commonly suggest a butterfly or a flower, or many other things. A test-taker who makes unusual or uncommon responses to the features of the blot may be revealing personality problems.

The Thematic Apperception Test

The Thematic Apperception Test (TAT) was developed in the 1930s by Henry Murray and Christiana Morgan. It consists of drawings, like the one shown in Figure 8.5 (see p. 204), that are open to various interpretations. Individuals are given the cards one at a time and asked to make up stories about them.

The TAT is widely used in research on motivation and in clinical practice (Archer et al., 2006; Hojnoski et al., 2006). The assumption is that we are likely to project our own needs into our responses to ambiguous situations, even if we are unaware of them or reluctant to talk about them. The TAT is also widely used to assess attitudes toward other people, especially parents and intimate partners.

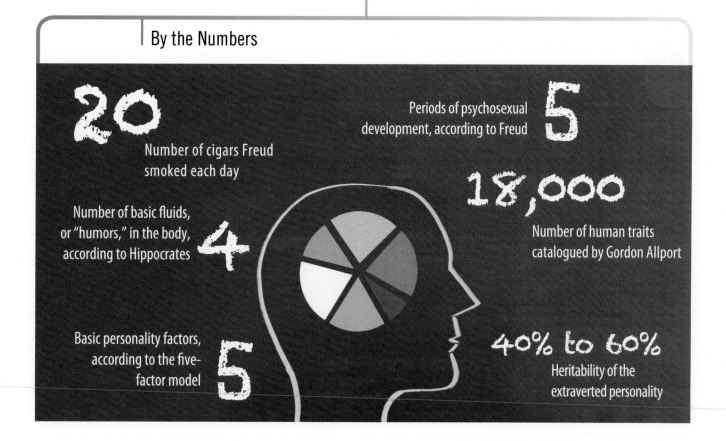

By the Numbers

20 Number of cigars Freud smoked each day

4 Number of basic fluids, or "humors," in the body, according to Hippocrates

5 Basic personality factors, according to the five-factor model

5 Periods of psychosexual development, according to Freud

18,000 Number of human traits catalogued by Gordon Allport

40% to 60% Heritability of the extraverted personality

Ready to study? In the book, you can:

- ❍ Review what you've read with Fill-Ins and Multiple Choice quizzes (below).
- ❍ Rip out Chapter Review card (in the back).

Or you can go online to CourseMate at www.cengagebrain.com for these resources:

- ❍ Complete Practices Quizzes to prepare for tests.
- ❍ Review Key Terms Flash Cards (online or print).
- ❍ Play games to master concepts.

Answers can be found in the back of the book, starting on page 368.

1. According to Freud, the unconscious psychic structure called the _____ is present at birth and operates according to the pleasure principle.

2. The _____ is the moral sense and develops by internalizing the standards of parents and others.

3. The stages of psychosexual development include the oral, _____, phallic, latency, and genital stages.

4. Jung believed that in addition to a personal unconscious mind, people also have a(n) _____ unconscious.

5. Adler believed that people are motivated by a(n) _____ complex.

6. Raine found brain impairments that are related to the development of a(n) _____ personality.

7. Maslow argued that people have growth-oriented needs for self-_____.

8. According to Rogers, we see the world through unique frames of _____.

9. According to sociocultural theory, _____ define themselves in terms of the groups to which they belong and give priority to group goals.

10. Projective tests present _____ stimuli and permit the respondent a broad range of answers.

1. Marisa is five months old and always chews her rattle. According to Freud, she is in the _____ stage.

   a. anal
   b. oral
   c. phallic
   d. latency

2. Which best illustrates a child undergoing the Oedipus complex?

   a. Billy acts out to get his mother's attention whenever she is alone with his father.
   b. Kelly seeks out strangers for sexual encounters.
   c. Alan always goes shopping with his father.
   d. Maria has not had conscious sexual desires for the past year.

3. Which of the following is an assumption of most trait theories?

   a. Traits are flexible and change with time.
   b. Traits are generally learned from parents.
   c. Traits are somehow inherited and embedded in the nervous system.
   d. Traits are hard to categorize.

4. The five-factor model includes which five basic personality factors?

   a. depression, obsessiveness, conscientiousness, agreeableness, openness
   b. narcissism, neuroticism, conscientiousness, agreeableness, openness
   c. extraversion, neuroticism, conscientiousness, agreeableness, openness
   d. extraversion, psychosis, conscientiousness, agreeableness, openness

5. The views of Watson and Skinner largely ignore the notion of

   a. environmental variables.
   b. personal freedom.
   c. reinforcement and punishment.
   d. shaping.

6. Social-cognitive theory differs from behaviorism in that social-cognitive theory argues that

   a. rewards shape behaviors.
   b. the ego follows the moral principle.
   c. wants and desires are the result of our environment.
   d. people influence their environments.

7. Lisa is studying musical theater. She is convinced that if she works hard enough, she will one day make it to Broadway. Her sense of conviction is an example of

   a. self-efficacy expectations.
   b. competencies.
   c. modeling.
   d. encoding strategies.

8. Carl Rogers believed that every person has his or her own unique

   a. frame of character.
   b. grey eminence.
   c. frame of reinforcement.
   d. frame of reference.

9. A test in the format of a questionnaire that has specific correct answers is an example of

   a. an acculturated test.
   b. an innate test.
   c. an objective test.
   d. a projective test.

10. The ability to give a response that accurately reflects the shape of the inkblot on the stimulus card is a sign of intact

   a. neuroticism.
   b. reality testing.
   c. acculturation.
   d. collectivism.

MULTIPLE CHOICE

Personality: Theory and Measurement 265

© Blend Images Photography/Veer

LEARNING OUTCOMES

11-1 Define stress and identify various sources of stress

11-2 Identify the psychological moderators of stress

11-3 Describe the impact of stress on the body

11-4 Explain the relationships between psychology and health

 After you read the chapter, go to the Study Tools at the end of the chapter, page 282.

Discussion of the effects of stress on the immune system paves the way for understanding the links between psychological factors and physical illness.

11-3b EFFECTS OF STRESS ON THE IMMUNE SYSTEM

Psychologists, biologists, and medical researchers have combined their efforts in a field of study called *psychoneuroimmunology* that addresses the relationships among psychological factors, the nervous system, the endocrine system, the immune system, and disease. One of its major concerns is the effect of stress on the immune system (Kemeny, 2009). Research shows that stress suppresses the immune system, as measured by the presence of various substances in the blood that make up the immune system (Calcagni & Elenkov, 2006).

The Immune System

The **immune system** combats disease in several ways (Iwasaki & Medzhitov, 2010). One way is the production of white blood cells, which engulf and kill pathogens such as bacteria, fungi, and viruses, and worn-out and cancerous body cells. The technical term for white blood cells is **leukocytes**. They engage in search-and-destroy missions in which they "recognize" and eradicate foreign agents and unhealthy cells.

Leukocytes recognize foreign substances, or antigens, by their shapes. The body reacts to **antigens** by generating specialized proteins, or **antibodies**. Antibodies attach themselves to the antigens, deactivating them and marking them for destruction. The immune system "remembers" how to battle antigens by maintaining their antibodies in the bloodstream, often for years.[1]

---

[1] A vaccination introduces a weakened form of an antigen (usually a bacteria or a virus) into the body to stimulate the production of antibodies. Antibodies can confer immunity for many years, in some cases for a lifetime.

immune system
the system of the body that recognizes and destroys foreign agents (antigens) that invade the body

leukocytes
white blood cells (derived from the Greek words *leukos*, meaning "white," and *kytos*, literally meaning "a hollow" but used to refer to cells)

antigen
a substance that stimulates the body to mount an immune system response to it (short for *anti*body *gen*erator)

antibodies
substances formed by white blood cells that recognize and destroy antigens

---

✳ Are There Gender Differences in Response to Stress?

For a century, it has been widely believed that humans are prewired to experience what biologist Walter Cannon labeled a "fight-or-flight" reaction to stress. Cannon believed we are instinctively pumped up to fight like demons or, when advisable, to beat a hasty retreat.

Or are we? According to reviews of the literature by psychologist Shelley E. Taylor and her colleagues (Taylor, 2006; Taylor et al., 2000), women under stress are more likely to care for their children and seek social contact and support from others. The "woman's response" to stress, the "tend-and-befriend" response, involves nurturing and seeking social support rather than fighting or fleeing.

This response may be prewired in female humans and in females of other mammalian species. Evolutionary psychologists might suggest that the tend-and-befriend response may have become sealed in human genes because it promotes the survival of females who are tending their young. Females who choose to fight might die or be separated from their young—no evolutionary brass ring there.

Gender differences in behavior are frequently connected with gender differences in hormones and other biological factors. This one is no different. Taylor (2006) points to the effects of the pituitary hormone oxytocin, which is connected with nurturing behaviors such as cuddling one's young (Taylor, 2006). The literature shows that when oxytocin is released during stress, it tends to have a calming effect on both rats and humans. It makes them less afraid and more social.

But men also release oxytocin when they are under stress. So why the gender difference? The answer may lie in other hormones—estrogen and testosterone. Females have more estrogen than males, and estrogen appears to enhance the effects of oxytocin. Males, on the other hand, have more testosterone than females, and testosterone may mitigate the effects of oxytocin (Taylor, 2006).

It is thus possible that males are more aggressive than females under stress because of the genetic balance of hormones in their bodies. Due to such differences, women tend to outlive men. "Men are more likely than women to respond to stressful experiences by developing certain stress-related disorders, including hypertension, aggressive behavior, or abuse of alcohol or hard drugs," Taylor added in a press release (May 2000).

Torff/plainpicture

inflammation
increased blood flow to an injured area of the body, resulting in redness, warmth, and an increased supply of white blood cells

biopsychosocial
having to do with the interactions of biological, psychological, and sociocultural factors

Inflammation is another function of the immune system. When injury occurs, blood vessels in the area first contract (to stem bleeding) and then dilate. Dilation increases the flow of blood, cells, and natural chemicals to the damaged area, causing the redness, swelling, and warmth that characterize inflammation (Leonard, 2005). The increased blood supply also floods the region with white blood cells to combat invading microscopic life-forms such as bacteria, which otherwise might use the local damage as a port of entry into the body.

Stress and the Immune System

One of the reasons that stress eventually exhausts us is that it stimulates the production of steroids. Steroids suppress the functioning of the immune system. Suppression has

TRUTH LEUKOCYTES CONTINUOUSLY CARRY ON MICROSCOPIC WARFARE, DESTROYING FOREIGN AGENTS (SUCH AS GERMS) AND OTHER HARMFUL FACTORS, SUCH AS CANCEROUS CELLS.

negligible effects when steroids are secreted occasionally. But persistent secretion of steroids decreases inflammation and interferes with the formation of antibodies. As a consequence, we become more vulnerable to infections, including the common cold (Cohen et al., 2012). By weakening the immune system, stress may also be connected with a more rapid progression of HIV infection to AIDS (Cohen et al., 2012).

Studies with college students have shown that the stress of exams depresses the immune system's response to the Epstein-Barr virus, which causes fatigue and other problems (Glaser et al., 1993). Students who were lonely showed greater suppression of the immune system than students who had more social support. The Epstein-Barr virus remains dormant in 90% of people who recover from an episode. Stress elevates blood levels of cortisol and adrenaline (epinephrine) and heightens the probability that the virus will be reactivated (Coskun et al., 2010).

11-4 Psychology and Chronic Health Problems

Why do people become ill? Why do some people develop cancer? Why do others have heart attacks? Why do still others seem to be immune to these illnesses? The **biopsychosocial** approach to health recognizes that there is no single, simple answer to these questions. The likelihood of contracting an illness—be it a case of the flu or cancer—can reflect the interaction of many factors, including biological, psychological, and sociocultural factors (Benke & Fallin, 2010; Schneiderman et al., 2005).

Biological factors such as pathogens, injuries, age, gender, and a family history of disease may strike us as the most obvious causes of illness. Genetics, in particular, tempts some people to assume that there is little they can do about their health. It is true that there are some severe health problems that are unavoidable for people with certain genes. However, in many cases, especially with cardiovascular problems and cancer, genes only create *predispositions* toward the health problem.

Genetic predispositions interact with the environment to express themselves (Benke & Fallin, 2010; Hunter, 2005). For example, genetic factors are involved in breast cancer. However, rates of breast cancer among women who have recently emigrated to the United States from rural Asia are similar to those in their countries of origin and nearly 80% lower than the rates among third-generation Asian American women, whose rates are

"THE ONLY WAY TO KEEP
YOUR HEALTH IS TO EAT
WHAT YOU DON'T WANT,
DRINK WHAT YOU DON'T
LIKE, AND DO WHAT
YOU'D RATHER NOT."
—MARK TWAIN

similar to those of European American women (Hoover, 2000; Wu et al., 2009). Thus, factors related to one's lifestyle are also intimately connected with the risk of breast cancer—and most other kinds of cancer.

As shown in Figure 11.4, biological factors (such as genetics and obesity), psychological factors (such as behaviors and personality), sociocultural factors (such as socioeconomic status), environmental factors, and stressors all play roles in health problems such as heart disease and cancer.

FIGURE 11.4 | Factors in Heart Disease and Cancer

HEART DISEASE

Biological:

Family history

Physiological conditions:
Obesity
High serum cholesterol
Hypertension

Psychological (personality and behavior):

Type A behavior

Hostility and holding in feelings of anger

Job strain

Chronic fatigue, stress, anxiety, depression, and emotional strain

Patterns of consumption:
Heavy drinking (but a drink a day may be helpful with heart disease)
Smoking
Overeating

Sudden stressors

Physical inactivity

Sociocultural:

African Americans are more prone to hypertension and heart disease than European Americans

Access to health care

Timing of diagnosis and treatment

CANCER

Biological:

Family history

Physiological conditions:
Obesity

Psychological (personality and behavior):

Patterns of consumption:
Smoking
Drinking alcohol (especially in women)

Eating animal fats?

Sunbathing (skin cancer)

Prolonged depression

Stress? Especially prolonged stress

Sociocultural:

Socioeconomic status

Access to health care

Timing of diagnosis and treatment

Higher death rates are found in nations with higher rates of fat intake

Goodshoot/Jupiterimages

Many health problems are affected by psychological factors, such as attitudes, emotions, and behavior (Frasure-Smith & Lespérance, 2008; Kiecolt-Glaser et al., 2002b). Nearly one million deaths each year in the United States are preventable (Health, United States, 2002). Stopping smoking, eating right, exercising, and controlling alcohol use would prevent nearly 80% of these. Psychological states such as anxiety and depression can impair the functioning of the immune system, rendering us more vulnerable to physical disorders ranging from viral infections to cancer (Kiecolt-Glaser et al., 2002a; Salovey et al., 2000).

Let's now discuss the chronic health problems of heart disease and cancer. Each involves biological, psychological, and sociocultural factors. Although these are medical problems, we also explore ways in which psychologists have contributed to their prevention and treatment.

11-4a CORONARY HEART DISEASE

Coronary heart disease (CHD) is the leading cause of death in the United States, most often from heart attacks (Arias et al., 2010).

Risk Factors

The risk factors for CHD are as follow (Glynn, 2010):

- *Family history:* People with a family history of CHD are more likely to develop the disease themselves.
- *Physiological conditions:* Obesity, high *serum cholesterol* levels, and *hypertension* (high blood pressure) are risk factors for CHD. About one American in five has hypertension, which can lead to CHD. *Essential hypertension*—that is, hypertension without an identifiable cause—has a genetic component. However, blood pressure is also connected with emotions like depression and anxiety. In addition, it rises when we inhibit the expression of strong feelings or are angry or on guard against threats. When we are under stress, we may believe that we can feel our blood pressure "pounding through the roof," but most people cannot sense hypertension. Therefore, it is important to check blood pressure regularly.
- *Patterns of consumption:* Patterns include heavy drinking, smoking, and overeating. On the other hand, a little alcohol seems to be good for the heart.
- *Type A behavior:* Most studies suggest that there is at least a modest relationship between Type A behavior and CHD. Hostility seems to be the component of the Type A behavior pattern that is most harmful (Chida & Steptoe, 2009). People who are highly prone to anger are about three times as likely

as other people to have heart attacks (J. E. Williams et al., 2000). The stress hormones connected with anger can constrict blood vessels to the heart, leading to a heart attack.

- *Job strain:* Overtime work, assembly line labor, and exposure to conflicting demands can all contribute to CHD. High-strain work, which makes heavy demands on workers but gives them little personal control, puts workers at the highest risk (Aboa-Éboulé et al., 2007; Ferrario et al., 2011).
- *Chronic fatigue, stress, anxiety, depression, and emotional strain.* Depression is connected with irregularities in the heart rate and may make blood platelets "sticky," which may, in turn, cause clots that lead to CHD (Kramer, 2003).
- *A physically inactive lifestyle.*

African Americans are more likely than any other ethnic group in the United States to have heart attacks and to die from them (National Center for Health Statistics, 2010). Figure 11.5 compares the death rates from heart disease of American men and women of various ethnic backgrounds. Asian Americans, Native Americans, and Latin Americans are less likely than European Americans or African Americans to die from heart disease. Early diagnosis and treatment might help decrease the racial gap.

Reducing Risk

Measures such as the following may help reduce the risk of CHD: stopping smoking; eating fewer saturated fats and more fruits, vegetables, and whole grains; reducing hypertension and lowering LDL (harmful) serum cholesterol, through medicine if necessary; modifying Type A behavior; managing feelings of anger; and exercising regularly (get a medical checkup first).

11-4b CANCER

According to the National Vital Statistics Reports, cancer is the second-leading cause of death in the United States (Jemal et al., 2009). Cancer is characterized by the development of abnormal, or mutant, cells that may take root anywhere in the body: in the blood, bones, digestive tract, lungs, and sex organs. If their spread is not controlled early, the cancerous cells may *metastasize*—that is, establish colonies elsewhere in the body. It appears that our bodies develop cancerous cells frequently. However, these are normally destroyed by the immune system. People whose immune system is damaged by physical or psychological factors may be more likely to develop tumors (Antoni & Lutgendorf, 2007; Mantovani & Sica, 2010).

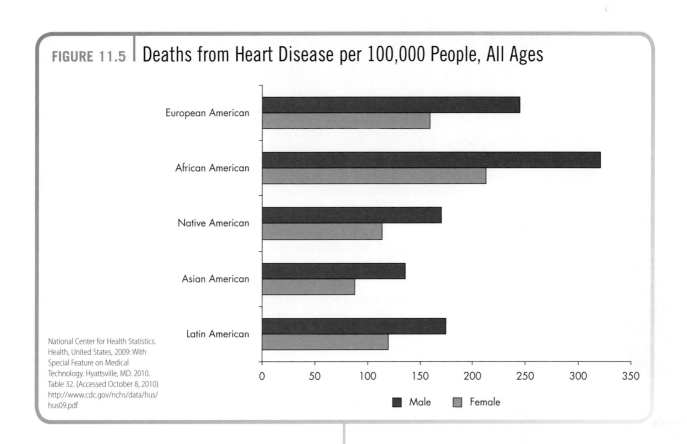

FIGURE 11.5 | Deaths from Heart Disease per 100,000 People, All Ages

National Center for Health Statistics. Health, United States, 2009: With Special Feature on Medical Technology. Hyattsville, MD. 2010. Table 32. (Accessed October 8, 2010) http://www.cdc.gov/nchs/data/hus/hus09.pdf

■ Male ■ Female

Risk Factors

As with many other disorders, people can inherit a disposition toward cancer (Santarius et al., 2010). So-called carcinogenic genes may remove the brakes from cell division, allowing cells to multiply wildly. Or they may allow mutations to accumulate unchecked. Many behavior patterns, however, markedly heighten the risk for cancer. These include smoking, more than a drink or two a day (especially for women), eating animal fats, and sunbathing (which may cause skin cancer due to exposure to ultraviolet light). Prolonged psychological conditions such as depression or stress may heighten the risk of some kinds of cancer by depressing the functioning of the immune system (Antoni & Lutgendorf, 2007; Gross et al., 2010).

African Americans are more likely than European Americans to contract most forms of cancer (National Center for Health Statistics, 2010). Once they contract cancer, African Americans are more likely than European Americans to die from it. The results for African Americans may reflect genetic factors to some degree, but are also connected with their lower socioeconomic status and relative lack of access to health care (Orsi et al., 2010).

Also consider cultural differences in health. Death rates from cancer are higher in such nations as the Netherlands, Denmark, England, Canada, and—yes—the United States, where average rates of daily fat intake are high (Bagchi & Preuss, 2007). Death rates from cancer are lower in such nations as Thailand, the Philippines, and Japan, where fat intake is lower. Thailand, the Philippines, and Japan are Asian nations, but do not assume that the difference is racial! The diets of Japanese Americans are similar in fat content to those of other Americans—and so are their rates of death from cancer.

Researchers have also suggested possible links between stress and cancer (Salovey et al., 2000). For example, Rachel Yehuda (2002) suggests that stress sometimes lowers levels of cortisol and impairs the ability of the immune system to destroy cancer cells. But here, too, the research evidence calls these theoretical links into question.

Reducing Risk

Measures such as the following may help reduce the risk of developing or dying from cancer: getting regular medical checkups to detect cancer early; stopping smoking; eating fewer saturated fats and more fruits, vegetables, and whole grains; and exercising regularly (get a medical checkup first). Cancer is most curable when it is detected early, before it metastasizes.

Ready to study? In the book, you can:

- �𝗢 Review what you've read with Fill-Ins and Multiple Choice quizzes (below).
- �𝗢 Rip out Chapter Review card (in the back).

Or you can go online to CourseMate at www.cengagebrain.com for these resources:

- �𝗢 Complete Practices Quizzes to prepare for tests.
- �𝗢 Review Key Terms Flash Cards (online or print).
- �𝗢 Play games to master concepts.

FILL-INS

Answers can be found in the back of the book, starting on page 368.

1. Daily _____ are regularly occurring conditions and experiences that threaten or harm our well-being.

2. The feeling of being pulled in two or more directions by opposing motives is called _____.

3. Albert _____ notes that our beliefs about events, as well as the events themselves, can be stressors.

4. People with (higher or lower?) self-efficacy expectations tend to cope better with stress.

5. Psychologically hardy people are high in _____, challenge, and control.

6. The GAS has three stages: _____, resistance, and exhaustion.

7. Cannon dubbed the alarm reaction the _____ or _____ reaction.

8. Women may show a tend-and-_____ response to stress rather than fight-or-flight.

9. Psychological states such as anxiety and depression impair the functioning of the _____ system, rendering us more vulnerable to health problems.

10. Risk factors for coronary heart disease include family history, obesity, hypertension, high levels of serum _____, heavy drinking, smoking, hostility, Type A behavior, and job strain.

1. Life changes that are positive can still be stressful because _____ is required.
    a. loneliness
    b. adjustment
    c. depression
    d. none of these

2. According to Ellis, a situation like failing a test, which results in stress, is called a(n)
    a. stimulus event.
    b. causal event.
    c. initiating event.
    d. activation event.

3. Edward's professor told him that his first paper could have been shorter in length. Edward starts sweating and ruminating because he jumps to the conclusion that he does not know how to write papers and will definitely fail this class. This is an example of
    a. imbibing.
    b. imbuing.
    c. catastrophizing.
    d. impetuous behavior.

4. Which quotation best represents the Type A personality?
    a. "Do unto others as you would have them do unto you."
    b. "Winning isn't everything; it's the only thing."
    c. "Don't worry, be happy."
    d. "All for one and one for all."

5. Moderators of stress include all of the following except
    a. pretending that stressors do not exist.
    b. psychological hardiness.
    c. sense of humor.
    d. predictability and control.

6. Psychological hardiness consists of three characteristics. These include
    a. expectations, humor, and control.
    b. power, control, and commitment.
    c. commitment, challenge, and control.
    d. confidence, competence, and efficacy.

7. Candace has an internal locus of control. This means that she
    a. can only control her inner emotions.
    b. can only control her outward appearance.
    c. feels she is controlled by others.
    d. feels she can control her own life.

8. The three stages of GAS (in their correct order) are
    a. alarm, snooze, rest.
    b. alarm, rest, snooze.
    c. alarm, resistance, exhaustion.
    d. resistance, alarm, exhaustion.

9. Boris has been under a great deal of stress. Which of the following is most likely true?
    a. His immune system is weakened.
    b. His immune system is strengthened.
    c. His immune system is unaffected.
    d. None of the above

10. Clarice wants to assess her risk for coronary heart disease (CHD). Which of the following is a risk factor for CHD?
    a. low serum cholesterol
    b. family history
    c. low blood pressure
    d. physically active lifestyle

LEARNING OUTCOMES

12-1 Define psychological disorders and describe their prevalence

12-2 Describe the symptoms and possible origins of anxiety disorders

12-3 Describe the symptoms and possible origins of dissociative disorders

12-4 Describe the symptoms and possible origins of somatoform disorders

12-5 Describe the symptoms and possible origins of mood disorders

12-6 Describe the symptoms and possible origins of schizophrenia

12-7 Describe the symptoms and possible origins of personality disorders

STUDY TOOLS ▶ After you read the chapter, go to the Study Tools at the end of the chapter, page 306.

CHAPTER 12

Psychological DISORDERS

During one long fall semester, the Ohio State campus lived in terror. Four college women were abducted, forced to cash checks or obtain money from automatic teller machines, and then raped. A mysterious phone call led to the arrest of a 23-year-old drifter—let's call him "William"—who had been dismissed from the Navy.

William was not the boy next door.

Psychologists and psychiatrists who interviewed William concluded that 10 personalities—8 male and 2 female—resided within him (Scott, 1994). His personality had been "fractured" by an abusive childhood. His several personalities displayed distinct facial expressions, speech patterns, and memories. They even performed differently on psychological tests.

Arthur, the most rational personality, spoke with a British accent. Danny and Christopher were quiet adolescents. Christine was a 3-year-old girl. Tommy, a 16-year-old, had enlisted in the Navy. Allen was 18 and smoked. Adelena, a 19-year-old lesbian personality, had committed the rapes. Who had made the mysterious phone call? Probably David, 9, an anxious child.

The defense claimed that William's behavior was caused by a psychological disorder termed *dissociative identity disorder* (previously referred to as *multiple personality disorder*). Several distinct identities or personalities dwelled within him. Some of them were aware of the others. Some believed that they were unique. Billy, the core identity, had learned to sleep as a child to avoid his father's abuse. A psychiatrist asserted that Billy had also been "asleep," or in a "psychological coma," during the abductions. Billy should therefore be found not guilty by reason of **insanity**.

William was found not guilty. He was committed to a psychiatric institution and released 6 years later.

In 1982, a man named John Hinckley was also found not guilty of an assassination attempt on President Reagan's life, although the shooting was witnessed on television by millions. Expert witnesses testified that he should be diagnosed with *schizophrenia*. Hinckley, too, was committed to a psychiatric institution. William and

> William was not the boy next door.

TRUTH OR FICTION

WHAT DO YOU THINK? FOLKLORE, COMMON SENSE, OR NONSENSE? CIRCLE THE T FOR "TRUTH" OR THE F FOR "FICTION," AND CHECK THE ACCURACY OF YOUR ANSWERS AS YOU READ THROUGH THE CHAPTER.

T	F	A MAN SHOT THE PRESIDENT OF THE UNITED STATES IN FRONT OF MILLIONS OF TELEVISION WITNESSES AND WAS FOUND NOT GUILTY BY A COURT OF LAW.
T	F	ANXIETY IS ABNORMAL.
T	F	FEELING ELATED IS NOT ALWAYS A GOOD THING.
T	F	PEOPLE WHO THREATEN TO COMMIT SUICIDE ARE JUST SEEKING ATTENTION.
T	F	PEOPLE WITH SCHIZOPHRENIA MAY SEE AND HEAR THINGS THAT ARE NOT REALLY THERE.
T	F	SOME PEOPLE CAN KILL OR MAIM OTHERS WITHOUT ANY FEELINGS OF GUILT.

Hinckley were diagnosed with psychological disorders, which is the topic of this chapter.

12-1 What Are Psychological Disorders?

Psychology is the study of behavior and mental processes. **Psychological disorders** are behaviors or mental processes that are connected with various kinds of

insanity

a legal term descriptive of a person judged to be incapable of recognizing right from wrong or of conforming his or her behavior to the law

psychological disorders

patterns of behavior or mental processes that are connected with emotional distress or significant impairment in functioning

hallucination

a perception in the absence of sensory stimulation that is confused with reality

ideas of persecution

erroneous beliefs that one is being victimized or persecuted

distress or significant impairment in functioning. However, they are not predictable responses to specific events.

Some psychological disorders are characterized by anxiety, but many people are anxious now and then without being considered disordered. For example, it is appropriate to be anxious before a midterm exam. When, then, are feelings like anxiety deemed to be signs of a psychological disorder? For one thing, anxiety may suggest a disorder when it is not appropriate to the situation. For example, there is (usually) no reason to be anxious when looking out a fourth-story window. The magnitude of the problem may also suggest disorder. Some anxiety can be expected before a job interview. However, feeling that your heart is pounding so intensely that it might leap out of your chest—and then avoiding the interview—are not usual.

Behaviors or mental processes are suggestive of psychological disorders when they meet some combination of the following criteria:

1. *They are unusual.* Rarity or statistical deviance may not be sufficient for behavior or mental processes to

FICTION ANXIETY CAN ACTUALLY BE PERFECTLY NORMAL, AS ON THE EVE OF A BIG TEST OR WHEN ON A FIRST DATE.

be labeled abnormal, but it helps. After all, only a few people obtain a score of 700 or more on the verbal part of the SAT, but that achievement is not considered disordered. Only a few "see things" or "hear things" as Hinckley did, and those behaviors are deemed disordered because of their bizarre quality. We must also consider the situation. Although many of us feel "panicked" when we realize that a term paper is due the next day, most of us do not have panic attacks out of the blue. Unpredictable panic attacks thus are suggestive of psychological disorder.

2. *They suggest faulty perception or interpretation of reality.* Our society considers it normal to be inspired by religious beliefs but abnormal to believe that God is literally speaking to you. "Hearing voices" and "seeing things" are considered **hallucinations**. Similarly, **ideas of persecution**, such as believing that the FBI is "out to get you," are considered signs of disorder. (Unless, of course, they *are* out to get you.) Hinckley testified that he believed he would be impressing a popular young actress, Jodie Foster, by killing the president—an idea that was delusional.

3. *They suggest severe personal distress.* Anxiety, exaggerated fears, and other psychological states cause personal distress, and severe personal distress may be considered abnormal. William and Hinckley

---

✳ The Insanity Plea

John Hinckley was found not guilty of a 1981 assassination attempt on President Ronald Reagan by reason of insanity. Hinckley was diagnosed with schizophrenia and was committed to a psychiatric institution rather than given a prison term. What does it mean to be "insane"? What is the "insanity plea"?

In pleading insanity, lawyers use the M'Naghten rule, named after Daniel M'Naghten, who tried to assassinate British Prime Minister Robert Peel in 1843. M'Naghten had delusions that Peel was persecuting him, and he killed the minister's secretary in the attempt. The court found M'Naghten not guilty by reason of insanity. That is, the defendant did not understand what he was doing at the time of the act or did not realize it was wrong. The insanity plea is still used in much the same way today (Zapf et al., 2009).

Many people would like to ban the insanity plea because they equate it with people's "getting away with murder." But there may not be all that much cause for concern. The insanity defense is raised in only about 1% of cases (Silver, 1994). Moreover, people found to be not guilty by reason of insanity are institutionalized for indefinite terms—supposedly until they are no longer insane.

AP Photo/Judy Lineberger

While on trial, John Hinckley, Jr., looks on while his father cries and claims responsibility for "John's tragedy" because he prevented his son from coming home when he desperately needed help.

acute stress disorder
a disorder, like PTSD, that is characterized by feelings of anxiety and helplessness and caused by a traumatic event; acute stress disorder occurs within a month of the event and lasts from two days to four weeks

FIGURE 12.1 | Sleep Problems Among Americans Before and After September 11, 2001

Insomnia is one of the symptoms of stress disorders. A poll by the National Sleep Foundation found that Americans had a greater frequency of sleep problems after the terrorist attacks of September 11, 2001.

half of Americans had difficulty falling asleep compared with about one-quarter of Americans before the attacks (see Figure 12.1). Women, who are more likely than men to ruminate about stressors (Nolen-Hoeksema et al., 2008), were also more likely than men to report difficulty falling asleep (50% versus 37%).

Acute stress disorder, like PTSD, is characterized by feelings of anxiety and helplessness that are caused by a traumatic event. However, PTSD can occur six months or more after the traumatic event and tends to persist. Acute stress disorder occurs within a month of the event and lasts from two days to four weeks. Women who have been raped, for example, experience acute distress that tends to peak in severity about three weeks after the assault (Bryant, 2006). Yet the same women may go on to experience PTSD (Kilpatrick et al., 2007; Koss et al., 2002).

12-2e ORIGINS OF ANXIETY DISORDERS

What is known about the origins of anxiety disorders?

Psychological Views

Some learning theorists—particularly behaviorists—consider phobias to be conditioned fears that were acquired in early childhood. Avoidance of feared stimuli is reinforced by the reduction of anxiety. Observa-

tional learning may also play a role in the acquisition of fears (Mineka & Oehlberg, 2008). If parents squirm, grimace, and shudder at the sight of mice, blood, or dirt on the kitchen floor, children might assume that these stimuli are awful and imitate their parents' behavior.

Cognitive theorists note that people's appraisals of the magnitude of threats help determine whether they are traumatic and can lead to PTSD (Koster et al., 2009). People with panic attacks tend to misinterpret bodily cues and to view them as threats. Obsessions and compulsions may serve to divert attention from more frightening issues, such as "What am I going to do with my life?" When anxieties are acquired at a young age, we may later interpret them as enduring traits and label ourselves as "someone who fears _____" (you fill it in). We then live up to the labels. We also entertain thoughts that heighten and perpetuate anxiety such as "I've got to get out of here" or "My heart is going to leap out of my chest." Such ideas intensify physical signs of anxiety, disrupt planning, make stimuli seem worse than they really are, motivate avoidance, and decrease self-efficacy expectations. The belief that we will not be able to handle a threat heightens anxiety. The belief that we are in control reduces anxiety (Bandura et al., 1985).

dissociative disorders
disorders in which there are sudden, temporary changes in consciousness or self-identity

dissociative amnesia
a dissociative disorder marked by loss of memory or self-identity; skills and general knowledge are usually retained

dissociative fugue
a dissociative disorder in which one experiences amnesia and then flees to a new location

Michael Blann/Stone/Getty Images

Biological Views

Genetic factors are implicated in most psychological disorders, including anxiety disorders (Low et al., 2008). Anxiety disorders tend to run in families. Identical (MZ) twins are much more likely to both have the disorder than fraternal (DZ) twins (Kendler et al., 2001). Adoptee studies show that the biological parent places the child at greater risk for anxiety and related traits than does the adoptive parent.

Evolutionary psychologists suggest that anxiety may reflect natural selection. Humans (and nonhuman primates) are genetically predisposed ("biologically prepared") to fear stimuli that may have posed a threat to their ancestors (Gerdes et al., 2009; Mineka & Oehlberg, 2008; Starratt & Shackelford, 2010). Evolutionary forces would have favored the survival of individuals who were predisposed toward acquiring fears of large animals, spiders, snakes, heights, entrapment, sharp objects, and strangers. Thus, people who fearlessly encounter potentially harmful stimuli may be at a disadvantage, evolutionarily speaking, rather than at an advantage.

Perhaps a predisposition toward anxiety—in the form of a highly reactive autonomic nervous system—can be inherited (Beesdo et al., 2010; Binder & Nemeroff, 2009). What might make a nervous system "highly reactive"? The autonomic nervous system may stimulate the production of excessive quantities of adrenaline (epinephrine) and noradrenaline (norepinephrine). These chemicals normally pump up the body in preparation for the fight-or-flight response—both sides of which can make up self-preserving responses to threats. But when their production is so intense that they flood the body, we can feel shaky and drenched with sweat and incapable of doing anything useful.

Biopsychosocial Views

Many cases of anxiety disorders reflect the interaction of biological, psychological, and social factors. Biological imbalances may initially trigger attacks in panic disorder. But subsequent fear of attacks—and of the bodily cues that signal their onset—may heighten discomfort

Evolutionary forces at work? Why do so many people fear spiders?

and give one the idea there is nothing one can do about them (Olatunji & Wolitzky-Taylor, 2009). Feelings of helplessness increase fear. People with panic disorder therefore can be helped by psychological methods that provide ways of reducing physical discomfort—including regular breathing—and show them that there are, after all, things they can do to cope with attacks (Olatunji & Wolitzky-Taylor, 2009).

12-3 Dissociative Disorders

William's disorder, described at the beginning of the chapter, was a dissociative disorder. In the **dissociative disorders**, mental processes such as thoughts, emotions, memory, consciousness, even knowledge of one's own identity—the processes that make a person feel whole—may seem to be split off from one another. The *DSM* lists several dissociative disorders. Among them are dissociative amnesia, dissociative fugue, and dissociative identity disorder (previously termed multiple personality disorder).

12-3a DISSOCIATIVE AMNESIA

A person with **dissociative amnesia** is suddenly unable to recall important personal information (that is, explicit episodic memories). The loss of memory cannot be attributed to organic problems such as a blow to the head or alcoholic intoxication. It is thus a psychological dissociative disorder and not an organic one. In the most common example, the person cannot recall events for a number of hours after a stressful incident, as in warfare or in the case of an uninjured survivor of an accident. In *generalized* dissociative amnesia, people forget their entire lives. Amnesia may last for hours or years.

12-3b DISSOCIATIVE FUGUE

A person with **dissociative fugue** abruptly leaves his or her home or place of work and travels to another place, having lost all memory of his or her past life. While at the new location, the person either does not think about the past or reports a past filled with invented memories. The new personality is often more outgoing and less inhibited than the "real" identity. Following recovery, the events that occurred during the fugue are not recalled.

12-3c DISSOCIATIVE IDENTITY DISORDER

Dissociative identity disorder (DID) (formerly termed **multiple personality disorder**) is the name given to William's disorder. In dissociative identity disorder, two or more identities or personalities, each with distinct traits and memories, "occupy" the same person. Each identity may or may not be aware of the others or of events experienced by the others (Huntjens et al., 2003).

The identities of an individual with dissociative identity disorder might have different eyeglass prescriptions and different allergic responses (Braun, 1988). In one person, an identity named Timmy was not sensitive to orange juice. But when other identities gained control over him and drank orange juice, he would break out with hives. Hives would also erupt if another identity emerged while the juice was being digested. If Timmy reappeared when the allergic reaction was present, the itching of the hives would cease, and the blisters would start to subside. In other cases reported by Braun, different identities within a person might show various responses to the same medicine. Or one identity might exhibit color blindness while others have normal color vision.

12-3d ORIGINS OF DISSOCIATIVE DISORDERS

The dissociative disorders are some of the odder psychological disorders. According to learning theorists and cognitive psychologists, people with dissociative disorders have learned not to think about bad memories or disturbing impulses to avoid feelings of anxiety, guilt, and shame. Both psychodynamic and learning theories suggest that dissociative disorders help people keep disturbing memories or ideas out of mind. Of what could such memories be? Research suggests that many cases involve memories of sexual or physical abuse during childhood, usually by a relative or caregiver (Foote et al., 2006; Ross, 2006; Simeon et al., 2007).

Whereas some disorders—major depressive disorder and schizophrenia among them—are found around the world, most cases of dissociative disorders have been limited to the United States and Canada (Ross, 2006). Perhaps dissociative disorders, especially DID, are culture-bound. It might also be the case, as suggested by skeptics, that many people who claim to have multiple personalities are fabricating it (Kong et al., 2008).

Dissociative identity disorder (DID) (formerly termed **multiple personality disorder**) a disorder in which a person appears to have two or more distinct identities or personalities that may alternately emerge

SHOWTIME/Landov

In the Showtime series *United States of Tara*, Toni Collette plays Tara Gregson, a homemaker with two children and several other personalities. Tara has dissociative identity disorder, and within her "reside" the flirty "T," a suburban housewife plucked from the 1950s, and a beer-guzzling Vietnam veteran named "Buck."

12-4 Somatoform Disorders

somatoform disorders
disorders in which people complain of physical (somatic) problems even though no physical abnormality can be found

conversion disorder
a disorder in which anxiety or unconscious conflicts are "converted" into physical symptoms that often have the effect of helping the person cope with anxiety or conflict

la belle indifférence
a French term descriptive of the lack of concern for their (imagined) medical problem sometimes shown by people with conversion disorders

hypochondriasis
a somatoform disorder characterized by persistent belief that one is ill despite lack of medical findings

People with **somatoform disorders** complain of physical problems such as paralysis, pain, or a persistent belief that they have a serious disease. Yet no evidence of a physical abnormality can be found. In this section, we discuss two somatoform disorders: *conversion disorder* and *hypochondriasis*.

12-4a CONVERSION DISORDER

Conversion disorder is characterized by a major change in, or loss of, physical functioning, although there are no medical findings to explain the loss of functioning. The behaviors are not intentionally produced. That is, the person is not faking. Conversion disorder is so named because it appears to "convert" a source of stress into a physical difficulty.

If you lost the ability to see at night or if your legs became paralyzed, you would understandably show concern. But some people with conversion disorder show indifference to their symptoms, a symptom termed **la belle indifférence**. The lack of concern suggests awareness, on some level, that the physical problems have their benefits.

During World War II, some bomber pilots developed night blindness. They could not carry out their nighttime missions, although no damage to the optic nerves was found. In rare cases, women with large families have been reported to become paralyzed in the legs, again with no medical findings. More recently, a Cambodian woman who had witnessed atrocities became blind as a result.

12-4b HYPOCHONDRIASIS

A more common type of somatoform disorder is **hypochondriasis** (also called *hypochondria*). People with this disorder insist that they are suffering from a serious physical illness, even though no medical evidence of illness can be found. They become preoccupied with minor physical sensations and continue to believe that they are ill despite the reassurance of physicians that they are healthy. They may run from doctor to doctor, seeking the one who will find the causes of the sensations. Fear of illness may disrupt their work or home life.

12-4c ORIGINS OF SOMATOFORM DISORDERS

The somatoform disorders offer a fascinating study in the biopsychosocial perspective. Psychologically speaking, the somatoform disorders have much to do with what one focuses on—actual social and financial problems, for example, or one's body. There is evidence that people with conversion disorder are susceptible to being hypnotized (R. J. Brown et al., 2007), and some investigators consider conversion disorder to be a form of self-hypnosis in which people focus so intently on an imaginary physical problem that they exclude conflicting information (Roelofs et al., 2002). Research evidence suggests that people who develop hypochondriasis are particularly sensitive to bodily sensations and tend to ruminate about them (Marcus et al., 2008).

Biologically speaking, tendencies toward perfectionism and rumination, which are found among many people with somatoform disorders, are thought to be at least partly heritable. Squeamishness about one's body may be too much of a good thing from the evolutionary perspective. That is, concern about bodily harm will presumably encourage one to avoid danger and provide advantages in survival and reproduction. But too much concern may lead to useless preoccupations.

"I DIDN'T KNOW MY MOTHER HAD IT.

I THINK A LOT OF WOMEN DON'T KNOW THEIR MOTHERS HAD IT; THAT'S THE SAD THING ABOUT DEPRESSION. YOU KNOW, YOU DON'T FUNCTION ANYMORE. YOU SHUT DOWN. YOU FEEL LIKE YOU ARE IN A VOID."

—MARIE OSMOND

In 2011, actress Catherine Zeta-Jones revealed that she was seeking treatment for bipolar disorder.

12-5 Mood Disorders

Mood disorders are characterized by disturbance in expressed emotions. The disruption generally involves sadness or elation. Most instances of sadness are normal, or "run-of-the-mill." If you have failed an important test, if you have lost money in a business venture, or if your closest friend becomes ill, it is understandable and fitting for you to be sad about it. It would be odd, in fact, if you were *not* affected by adversity. In this section, we discuss two mood disorders: *major depressive disorder* and *bipolar disorder*.

12-5a MAJOR DEPRESSIVE DISORDER

People with run-of-the-mill depression may feel sad, blue, or "down in the dumps." They may complain of lack of energy, loss of self-esteem, difficulty concentrating, loss of interest in activities and other people, pessimism, crying, and thoughts of suicide.

These feelings are more intense in people with **major depressive disorder**. According to a nationally representative sample of more than 9,000 adults in the United States, major depressive disorder affects 5% to 7% of us within any given year and one person in six or seven over the course of our lives (Hasin et al., 2005; Kessler et al., 2003). About half of those with major depressive disorder experience severe symptoms such as poor appetite, serious weight loss, and agitation or **psychomotor retardation**. They may be unable to concentrate and make decisions. They may say that they "don't care" anymore and in some cases attempt suicide. A minority may display faulty perception of reality— so-called psychotic behaviors. These include delusions of unworthiness, guilt for imagined wrongdoings, even the notion that one is rotting from disease. There may also be delusions, as of the devil administering deserved punishment, or hallucinations, as of strange bodily sensations.

12-5b BIPOLAR DISORDER

People with **bipolar disorder**, formerly known as *manic–depressive disorder*, have mood swings from ecstatic elation to deep depression. The cycles seem to be unrelated to external events. In the elated, or **manic** phase, the person may show excessive excitement or silliness, carrying jokes too far. The manic person may be argumentative, show poor judgment, destroy property, make huge contributions to charity, or give away expensive possessions. People often find manic individuals abrasive and avoid them. They are often oversexed and too restless to sit still or sleep restfully. They often speak rapidly (showing *pressured speech*) and jump from topic to topic (showing **rapid flight of ideas**). It can be hard to get a word in edgewise.

Depression is the other side of the coin. People with bipolar depression often sleep more than usual and are lethargic. People with major (or unipolar) depression are more likely to have insomnia and agitation. Those with bipolar depression also exhibit social withdrawal and irritability. Some people with bipolar disorder attempt suicide when the mood shifts from the elated phase toward depression (Jamison, 2000). They

mood disorders
a disturbance in expressed emotions, generally involving excessive or inappropriate sadness or elation

major depressive disorder
a serious to severe depressive disorder in which the person may show loss of appetite, psychomotor retardation, and impaired reality testing

psychomotor retardation
slowness in motor activity and (apparently) in thought

bipolar disorder
a disorder in which the mood alternates between two extreme poles (elation and depression); also referred to as *manic depression*

manic
elated, showing excessive excitement

rapid flight of ideas
rapid speech and topic changes, characteristic of manic behavior

will do almost anything to escape the depths of depression that lie ahead.

12-5c ORIGINS OF MOOD DISORDERS

What is known about the origins of the mood disorders?

Psychological Views

Many learning theorists suggest that depressed people behave as though they cannot obtain reinforcement. For example, they appear to be inactive and apathetic. Many people with depressive disorders have an external locus of control. That is, they do not believe they can control events so as to achieve reinforcements (Tong, 2001; Weinmann et al., 2001).

Research conducted by learning theorists has also found links between depression and **learned helplessness**. In classic research, psychologist Martin Seligman (1975) taught dogs that they were helpless to escape an electric shock. The dogs were prevented from leaving a cage in which they received repeated shocks.

IT IS TRUE THAT FEELING "UP" IS NOT ALWAYS A GOOD THING, AS IN THE MANICKY PHASE OF BIPOLAR DISORDER.

Later, a barrier to a safe compartment was removed, offering the animals a way out. When they were shocked again, however, the dogs made no effort to escape. They had apparently learned that they were helpless. Seligman's dogs were also, in a sense, reinforced for doing nothing. That is, the shock *eventually* stopped when the dogs were showing helpless behavior—inactivity and withdrawal. "Reinforcement" might have increased the likelihood of repeating the "successful behavior"—that is, doing nothing—in a similar situation. This helpless behavior resembles that of people who are depressed.

Cognitive factors also contribute to depression. For example, perfectionists set themselves up for depression by making irrational demands on themselves. They are likely to fall short of their (unrealistic) expectations and to feel depressed as a result (Flett et al., 2007).

Still other cognitions involve the ways people explain their failures and shortcomings to themselves. Seligman (1996) suggests that when things go wrong, we may think of the causes of failure as either *internal* or *external*, *stable* or *unstable*, *global* or *specific*. These **attributional styles** can be illustrated using the example of having a date that does not work out. An internal attribution involves self-blame (as in "I really loused it up"). An external attribution places the blame elsewhere (as in "Some couples just don't take to each other," or "She was the wrong sign for me"). A stable attribution ("It's my personality") suggests a problem that cannot be changed. An unstable attribution ("It was because I had a head cold") suggests a temporary condition. A global attribution of failure ("I have no idea what to do when I'm with other people") suggests that the problem is quite large. A specific attribution ("I have problems making small talk at the beginning of a relationship") chops the problem down to a manageable size. How does this connect to depression? Research has shown that people who are depressed are more likely to attribute the causes of their failures to internal, stable, and global factors—factors that they are relatively powerless to change (Safford et al., 2007).

Biological Views

Researchers are also searching for biological factors in mood disorders. Depression, for example, is often associated with the trait of **neuroticism**, which is heritable (Dunkley et al., 2009). Anxiety is also connected with neuroticism, and mood and anxiety disorders are

An internal attribution involves self-blame, as in "I really loused it up." An external attribution places the blame elsewhere.

Paul Sutherland/Stone/Getty Images

The Case of Women and Depression

Women are nearly twice as likely to be diagnosed with depression as men (Keyes & Goodman, 2006; Kramer et al., 2008). This gender difference begins to emerge in adolescence. In any given year, about 12% of women and 7% of men in the United States are diagnosed with depression. It was once assumed that depression was most likely to accompany menopause in women, because women could no longer carry out their "natural" function of childbearing. However, women are more likely to encounter depression during the childbearing years (Deecher et al., 2008; Keyes & Goodman, 2006).

Many people assume that biological sex differences largely explain why women are more likely to become depressed (Deecher et al., 2008). Low levels of estrogen are widely seen as the culprit. Estrogen levels plummet prior to menstruation, and the deficit may trigger psychological changes. How often do we hear degrading remarks such as "It must be that time of the month" when a woman expresses feelings of anger or irritation? Some theorists suggest that women may also have a "cognitive vulnerability" to depression, connected with greater tendencies than men to ruminate about stresses and other negative events (Hughes et al., 2008; Wisco & Nolen-Hoeksema, 2009).

Some of the gender difference may also reflect the greater stresses placed on women, which tend to be maximized when they are working a triple shift—one in the workforce and the others meeting the demands of homemaking, child rearing, and aging parents (Plaisier et al., 2008; Rathus, 2009–2010). Women are more likely to experience physical and sexual abuse, poverty, single parenthood, and sexism. Single mothers, in particular, have lower socioeconomic status than men, and depression and other psychological disorders are more common among poor people (Nicholson et al., 2008). A part of treatment for depressed women, then, is to modify the demands on women. The pain may lie in the individual, but the cause often lies in society.

roman makhmutov/Flickr/Getty Images

frequently found in the same person (Spinhoven et al., 2010). Twin and adoption studies also support a role for genetic factors in bipolar disorder (Willcutt & McQueen, 2010).

Much research into depression focuses on underutilization of the neurotransmitter serotonin in the brain (Artigas, 2008; Leach, 2008). It has been shown, for example, that learned helplessness is connected with lower serotonin levels in rats' brains (Wu et al., 1999). Moreover, people with severe depression often respond to drugs (selective serotonin reuptake inhibitors, or SSRIs) that heighten the action of serotonin (Leonard, 2008).

The Biopsychosocial Perspective

Relationships between mood disorders and biological factors are complex and under intense study. Even if people are biologically predisposed toward depression, self-efficacy expectations and attitudes—particularly attitudes about whether one can change things for the better—may play a role.

Although the mood disorders are connected with processes within the individual, many kinds of situations are also connected with depression. Depression may be a reaction to losses and stress (Cowen, 2002; Mazure et al., 2000). Sources of chronic strain such as marital discord, physical discomfort, and failure or pres-

sure at work all contribute to feelings of depression. We tend to be more depressed by things we bring on ourselves, such as academic and financial problems, unwanted pregnancy, and arguments (Greenberger et al., 2000). However, some people recover from depression less readily than others. People who remain depressed have lower self-esteem (Sherrington et al., 2001), are less likely to be able to solve social problems (Reinecke et al., 2001), and have less social support.

12-5d SUICIDE

Each year about 33,000 people in the United States take their own lives (Centers for Disease Control and Prevention, 2009). Suicide is the third leading cause of death among 15- to 24-year-olds, behind accidents and assaults (Heron & Tejada-Vera, 2009).

We discuss suicide in the section on mood disorders because most suicides are linked to feelings of depression and hopelessness (Dwivedi, 2010; Zaitsoff & Grilo, 2010). Jill Rathus and her colleagues (A. L. Miller et al., 2007) have found that suicidal adolescents experience four kinds of psychological problems: (a) confusion about the self, (b) impulsiveness, (c) emotional instability, and (d) interpersonal problems. Some suicidal teenagers, like suicidal adults, are highly achieving, rigid perfectionists who have set impossibly high expectations for themselves (A. L. Miller et al., 2007). Many people throw themselves into feelings of depression and hopelessness by comparing themselves negatively with others (Barber, 2001).

Contributors to suicidal behavior among adolescents include concerns over sexuality, sexual abuse, grades, problems at home, and substance abuse (Duke et al., 2010; A. L. Miller et al., 2007; Zayas et al., 2010). It is not always a stressful event itself that precipitates suicide but the individual's anxiety or fear of being "found out" about something, such as failing a course or getting arrested. People who consider suicide are apparently less capable of solving problems, especially social problems, than others (A. L. Miller et al., 2007). They are thus less likely to find productive ways of changing the stressful situation. They want a magical solution to problems that require work or else a quick way out (Shneidman, 2001).

There is a tendency for suicide to run in families (Goldston & Compton, 2010). Many suicide attempters have family members with serious psychological problems, and about 25% have family members who have taken their own lives (Sorensen & Rutter, 1991). The

FICTION IT IS NOT TRUE THAT PEOPLE WHO THREATEN SUICIDE ARE ONLY SEEKING ATTENTION.

causal connections are unclear, however. Do people who attempt suicide inherit disorders that can lead to suicide? Does the suicide of a family member give a person the idea of committing suicide or create the impression that he or she is "fated" to commit suicide?

Sociocultural Factors in Suicide

Suicide is connected not only with feelings of depression and stressful events but also with age, educational status, ethnicity, and gender. Suicide is more common among college students than among people of the same age who are not in college. Each year, about 10,000 college students attempt suicide. Although teenage suicides loom large in the media spotlight, older people are more likely to commit suicide (Centers for Disease Control and Prevention, 2009). The suicide rate among older people who are unmarried or divorced is double that of older people who are married.

Rates of suicide and suicide attempts also vary among different ethnic groups and according to gender. For example, about one in every six Native Americans (17%) has attempted suicide—a rate higher than that of other Americans (Centers for Disease Control and Prevention, 2009). About one in eight Latin Americans has attempted suicide and three in ten have considered it. European Americans are next, with 8% attempting and 28% contemplating suicide. African Americans are least likely to attempt suicide (6.5%) or to think about it (20%). The actual suicide rates for African Americans are about two-thirds of those for European Americans, despite the fact that African Americans are more likely to live in poverty and suffer from discrimination (Centers for Disease Control and Prevention, 2009).

About three times as many females as males attempt suicide, but about five times as many males "succeed" (Centers for Disease Control and Prevention, 2009). Males are more likely to shoot or hang themselves; females more often use drugs, such as overdoses of tranquilizers or sleeping pills, or poisons. It takes

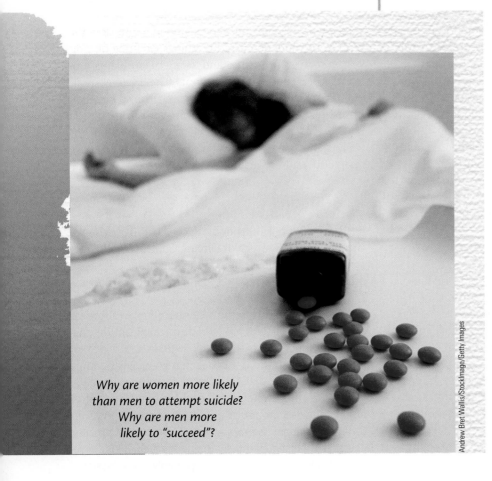

Why are women more likely than men to attempt suicide? Why are men more likely to "succeed"?

Andrew Bret Wallis/StockImage/Getty Images

FIGURE 12.4 | The Biopsychosocial Model of Schizophrenia

According to the biopsychosocial model of schizophrenia, people with a genetic vulnerability to the disorder experience increased risk for schizophrenia when they encounter problems such as viral infections, birth complications, stress, and poor parenting. People without the genetic vulnerability would not develop schizophrenia despite such problems.

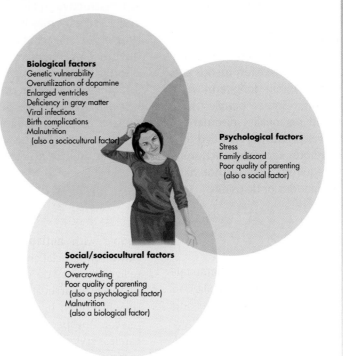

Biological factors
Genetic vulnerability
Overutilization of dopamine
Enlarged ventricles
Deficiency in gray matter
Viral infections
Birth complications
Malnutrition
    (also a sociocultural factor)

Psychological factors
Stress
Family discord
Poor quality of parenting
    (also a social factor)

Social/sociocultural factors
Poverty
Overcrowding
Poor quality of parenting
    (also a psychological factor)
Malnutrition
    (also a biological factor)

also larger numbers of dopamine receptors (Kegeles et al., 2010). It's a sort of "double hit" of neural transmission that may be connected with the confusion that characterizes schizophrenia.

Biopsychosocial View

Because biological, psychological, and sociocultural factors are implicated in schizophrenia, most investigators today favor the biopsychosocial model. According to this model, genetic factors create a predisposition toward—or vulnerability to—schizophrenia (see Figure 12.4). Genetic vulnerability to the disorder interacts with other factors, such as complications of pregnancy and birth, stress, quality of parenting, and social conditions to give rise to the disorder (Bishop, 2009; Buckley et al., 2000; Sawa & Snyder, 2002).

12-7 Personality Disorders

Personality disorders, like personality traits, are characterized by enduring patterns of behavior. Personality disorders, however, are inflexible and maladaptive. They impair personal or social functioning and are a source of distress to the individual or to other people. There are a number of personality disorders. They include the *paranoid*, *schizotypal*, *schizoid*, *borderline*, *antisocial*, and *avoidant personality disorders*.

12-7a PARANOID PERSONALITY DISORDER

The defining trait of the **paranoid personality disorder** is a tendency to interpret other people's behavior as threatening or demeaning. People with the disorder do not show the grossly disorganized thinking of paranoid schizophrenia. However, they are mistrustful of others, and their relationships suffer for it. They may be suspicious of coworkers and supervisors, but they can generally hold a job.

12-7b SCHIZOTYPAL AND SCHIZOID PERSONALITY DISORDERS

Schizotypal personality disorder is characterized by peculiarities of thought, perception, or behavior, such as excessive fantasy and suspiciousness, feelings of being unreal, or the odd use of words. There are no complex delusions, no hallucinations, and no unusual motor activities, so this disorder is schizo*typal*, not schizophrenic.

© PRNewsFoto/Gentex Corporation

schizoid personality disorder

a personality disorder characterized by social withdrawal

borderline personality disorder

a personality disorder characterized by instability in relationships, self-image, mood, and lack of impulse control

antisocial personality disorder

the diagnosis given a person who is in frequent conflict with society, yet who is undeterred by punishment and experiences little or no guilt and anxiety

avoidant personality disorder

a personality disorder in which the person is unwilling to enter into relationships without assurance of acceptance because of fears of rejection and criticism

Schizoid personality disorder is characterized by indifference to relationships and flat emotional response. People with this disorder are "loners." They do not develop warm, tender feelings for others. They have few friends and rarely maintain long-term relationships. Some people with schizoid personality disorder do very well on the job provided that continuous social interaction is not required. They do not have hallucinations or delusions.

12-7c BORDERLINE PERSONALITY DISORDER

People with **borderline personality disorder** show instability in their relationships, self-image, and mood and a lack of control over impulses (Stanley & Siever, 2010). They tend to be uncertain of their values, goals, loyalties, careers, choices of friends, and sometimes even their sexual orientations (Roepke et al., 2011). Instability in self-image or identity may leave them with feelings of emptiness and boredom. Many cannot tolerate being alone and make desperate attempts to avoid feelings of abandonment. They may be clinging and demanding in social relationships, but clinging often pushes away the people on whom they depend. They alternate between extremes of adulation in their relationships (when their needs are met) and loathing (when they feel scorned). They tend to view other people as all good or all bad, shifting abruptly from one extreme to the other. As a result, they may flit from partner to partner in brief and stormy relationships. People they had idealized are treated with contempt when they feel the other person has failed them.

Instability of moods is a central characteristic of borderline personality disorder. Moods run the gamut from anger and irritability to depression and anxiety, with each lasting from a few hours to a few days. People with the disorder have difficulty controlling anger and are prone to fights or smashing things. They often act on impulse, like eloping with someone they have just met. This impulsive and unpredictable behavior is often self-destructive and linked to a risk of suicidal attempts and gestures. It may involve spending sprees, gambling, drug abuse, engaging in unsafe sexual activity, reckless driving, binge eating, or shoplifting. People with the disorder may also engage in self-mutilation, such as scratching their wrists or burning their arms with cigarettes (Zanarini et al., 2010). Self-mutilation is sometimes a means of manipulating others, particularly in times of stress. Frequent self-mutilation is also associated with suicide attempts.

12-7d ANTISOCIAL PERSONALITY DISORDER

People with **antisocial personality disorder** often show a superficial charm and are at least average in intelligence. They do not form strong bonds with other people (Kumari et al., 2009; Romero et al., 2001). Though they are often heavily punished by their parents and rejected by peers, they continue in their impulsive, careless styles of life. Women are more likely than men to have anxiety and depressive disorders. However, antisocial personality disorder is more common among men than women (McCormick et al., 2007).

12-7e AVOIDANT PERSONALITY DISORDER

People with **avoidant personality disorder** are generally unwilling to enter a relationship without some assurance of acceptance because they fear rejection and criticism. As a result, they may have few close relationships outside their immediate families. Unlike people with schizoid personality disorder, however, they have some interest in, and feelings of warmth toward, other people.

12-7f ORIGINS OF PERSONALITY DISORDERS

Numerous biological, psychological, and sociocultural factors have been implicated in the personality disorders. Cognitive psychologists find that antisocial adolescents tend to interpret other people's behavior as threatening, even when it is not (Dodge, 2006; Ellis et al., 2009). Aggressive individuals often find it difficult to solve social problems in useful ways (Fontaine et al., 2010).

Biological Factors

Genetic factors are apparently involved in some personality disorders (Jang et al., 2007; Livesley & Jang, 2008). Personality traits are to some degree heritable,

> **TRUTH** IT IS TRUE THAT SOME PEOPLE CAN KILL OR MAIM OTHERS WITH NO FEELINGS OF GUILT AT ALL. WHEN THEY PERSISTENTLY VIOLATE THE RIGHTS OF OTHERS AND ARE IN REPEATED CONFLICT WITH THE LAW, THEY MAY BE DIAGNOSED WITH ANTISOCIAL PERSONALITY DISORDER.

and many personality disorders seem to be extreme variations of normal personality traits. An analysis of 51 twin and adoption studies estimated that genetic factors were the greatest influences on antisocial behavior (Rhee & Waldman, 2002). Referring to the five-factor model of personality, people with schizoid personalities tend to be highly introverted (Widiger & Simonsen, 2005). People with avoidant personalities tend to be both introverted and emotionally unstable (neurotic) (Widiger & Simonsen, 2005).

Perhaps the genetics of antisocial personality involve the prefrontal cortex of the brain, which is connected with emotional responses. There is some evidence that people with antisocial personality, as a group, have less gray matter (associative neurons) in the prefrontal cortex than other people do (Narayan et al., 2007; Raine et al., 2009). Adrian Raine (2008) suggests that specific genes lead to this impairment and also predispose people to antisocial behavior.

Psychological Factors

Learning theorists suggest that childhood experiences can contribute to maladaptive ways of relating to others in adulthood—that is, can lead to personality disorders. Cognitive psychologists find that antisocial adolescents encode social information in ways that bolster their misdeeds. For example, they tend to interpret other people's behavior as threatening, even when it is not (Lochman et al., 2011). Aggressive individuals often find it difficult to solve social problems in useful ways (McMurran et al., 2002). Cognitive therapists have encouraged some antisocial male children and adolescents to view social provocations as problems to be solved rather than as threats to their "manhood," with some favorable initial results (Lochman et al., 2011).

Sociocultural Factors

The label of borderline personality has been applied to people as diverse as Marilyn Monroe and Lawrence of Arabia. Some theorists believe we live in fragmented and alienating times that tend to create problems in forming a stable identity and stable relationships. "Living on the edge," or border, can be seen as a metaphor for an unstable society.

Although the causes of many psychological disorders remain in dispute, various methods of therapy have been devised to deal with them. Those methods are the focus of Chapter 13.

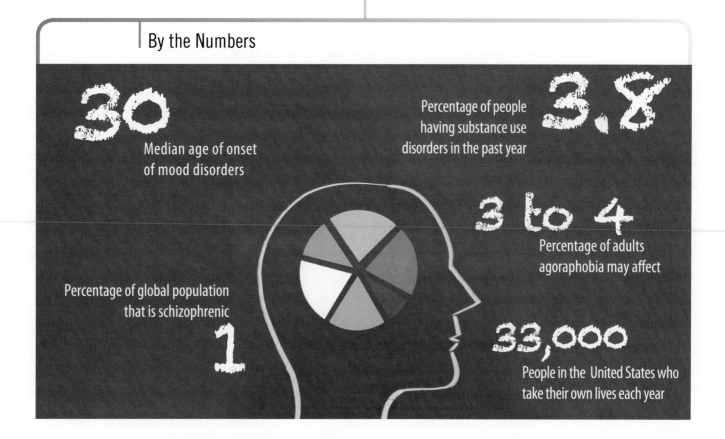

By the Numbers

30 Median age of onset of mood disorders

3.8 Percentage of people having substance use disorders in the past year

3 to 4 Percentage of adults agoraphobia may affect

Percentage of global population that is schizophrenic **1**

33,000 People in the United States who take their own lives each year

Ready to study? In the book, you can:

- ➲ Review what you've read with Fill-Ins and Multiple Choice quizzes (below).
- ➲ Rip out Chapter Review card (in the back).

Or you can go online to CourseMate at www.cengagebrain.com for these resources:

- ➲ Complete Practices Quizzes to prepare for tests.
- ➲ Review Key Terms Flash Cards (online or print).
- ➲ Play games to master concepts.

FILL-INS

Answers can be found in the back of the book, starting on page 368.

1. Behavior is labeled abnormal when it is unusual, is socially unacceptable, involves faulty _____ of reality (as with hallucinations), is dangerous, self-defeating, or distressing.

2. A(n) _____ is an irrational, excessive fear.

3. In _____–_____ disorder, people are troubled by intrusive thoughts or impulses to repeat some activity.

4. People with dissociative _____ forget their own identities but retain general knowledge and skills.

5. In dissociative _____ disorder, the person behaves as if distinct personalities occupy the body.

6. In _____ disorders, people complain of physical problems or persist in believing they have a serious disease, even though no medical problem can be found.

7. Manicky people may have grand delusional schemes and show rapid _____ of ideas.

8. Depressed people are more likely than other people to make (internal or external?) attributions for failures.

9. _____ schizophrenia is characterized by impaired motor activity and waxy flexibility.

10. _____ disorders are inflexible, maladaptive behavior patterns that impair personal or social functioning and are a source of distress to the individual or to others.

1. The news just reported that a hurricane is headed toward your home. You feel anxious and can't decide what to do first to prepare. This response is indicative of

   a. unusual behavior. c. abnormal behavior.
   b. normal behavior. d. faulty behavior.

2. A man cancels an important business trip to the mountains because he cannot control his fear of heights. He goes to a psychologist to discuss the problem. What diagnosis is the psychologist likely to consider?

   a. agoraphobia
   b. acrophobia
   c. conversion disorder
   d. avoidant personality disorder

3. A woman has difficulty concentrating on her job at work because of her preoccupation with the possibility that she has left the stove on or the iron plugged in at home. She imagines that her house will catch fire because of her mistake. She confides in her doctor. What diagnosis is the doctor most likely to use to describe her behavior?

   a. obsessive-compulsive disorder
   b. panic disorder
   c. specific phobia
   d. schizophrenia

4. Dissociative disorders involve _____ that cannot be attributed to organic problems.

   a. a loss of memory
   b. lack of feelings of guilt and shame
   c. hallucinations
   d. explosive behavior

5. For as long as Shelley can remember, grandmother has always been sick. She goes from doctor to doctor even though they keep telling her she is in excellent health. Her grandmother insists the doctors don't know what they are talking about. She is sure she has some terrible disease. Shelley checks her psychology textbook and finds that her grandmother's behavior is closest to fitting the category of

   a. dissociative amnesia.
   b. panic disorder.
   c. catatonic schizophrenia.
   d. hypochondriasis.

6. Imagery in the absence of external stimulation is the definition of _____, which are often observed in people with schizophrenia.

   a. rapid flight of ideas
   b. delusions
   c. hallucinations
   d. stress disorders

7. The difference between the emotion of sadness and an episode of major depression is that the symptoms of major depression are

   a. drastically different.
   b. more intense.
   c. only observed in females.
   d. related to stressful situations.

8. According to the text, which neurotransmitter is associated with depression?

   a. serotonin
   b. dopamine
   c. glutamate
   d. GABA

9. Your patient confides that the FBI and the CIA are "out to get me." He has stopped going to work. He keeps his blinds drawn and his doors and windows locked. The truth is that the FBI and CIA are not pursuing him or checking on him at all. Your patient can most likely be diagnosed with

   a. schizoid personality.
   b. dissociative identity disorder.
   c. paranoid personality.
   d. paranoid schizophrenia.

10. All of the following are symptoms of borderline personality disorder EXCEPT

    a. being a loner.
    b. unstable moods.
    c. fear of abandonment.
    d. self mutilation.

Zenshui/Alix Minde/Photoalto Agency RF Collections/Getty Images

LEARNING OUTCOMES

13-1 Define psychotherapy and describe the history of treatment of psychological disorders

13-2 Describe traditional psychoanalysis and short-term psychodynamic therapies

13-3 Define humanistic therapy and contrast its two main approaches

13-4 Define behavior therapy and identify various behavioral approaches to therapy

13-5 Define cognitive therapy and describe Beck's approach and REBT

13-6 Identify various types of group therapy and discuss their advantages and disadvantages

13-7 Explain whether psychotherapy works and who benefits from it

13-8 Describe methods of biological therapy—their benefits and side effects

 STUDY TOOLS ▶

After you read the chapter, go to the Study Tools at the end of the chapter, page 328.

CHAPTER 13

Methods
OF THERAPY

Joanne Cartwright (dubbed "Miss Muffet" by her therapist) had a spider phobia. "I washed my truck every night before I went to work in case there were webs," she said (cited in Robbins, 2000). "I put all my clothes in plastic bags and taped duct tape around my doors so spiders couldn't get in. I thought I was going to have a mental breakdown. I wasn't living." She checked every crack in the sidewalk for spiders—if she could push herself to go outside at all. Finally, her crippling phobia made it all but impossible for her to leave the house. After years of misery, she sought help.

Fortunately for "Miss Muffet," she wound up in the University of Washington's Human Interface Technology Laboratory, where she worked with psychologist Hunter Hoffman. Writing in *Scientific American*, Hoffman (2004) describes an elaborate virtual environment called *SpiderWorld* that helps people with spider phobias overcome their aversion by gradually approaching virtual spiders and reaching out to touch them (see Figure 13.1). A toy spider and a device that tracks the patient's hand movements provide tactile sensations akin to touching a real spider.

Twelve virtual therapy desensitization sessions changed Cartwright's life. "I'm amazed," she notes, "because I am doing all this stuff I could never do," such as camping and hiking.

Joanne Cartwright received virtual therapy to learn to cope with her phobia of spiders. If she had chosen a different kind of therapist, she might have been:

- Lying on a couch, talking about anything that popped into awareness, trying to unearth the possible symbolic meaning of spiders.

- Sitting face to face with a warm, gentle therapist who expressed faith in her ability to cope with her fears.

- Listening to a frank, straightforward therapist assert that she was catastrophizing the awfulness of spiders and compounding her problem by ruminating about it.

- Taking medication.

- Participating in some combination of these approaches.

These methods, although different, all represent methods of therapy. In this chapter, we explore methods of psychotherapy and biological therapy.

To help people deal with their problems, you must get them exposed to what they fear most.

TRUTH OR **FICTION**

WHAT DO YOU THINK? FOLKLORE, COMMON SENSE, OR NONSENSE? CIRCLE THE T FOR "TRUTH" OR THE F FOR "FICTION," AND CHECK THE ACCURACY OF YOUR ANSWERS AS YOU READ THROUGH THE CHAPTER.

T	F	RESIDENTS OF LONDON USED TO VISIT THE LOCAL INSANE ASYLUM FOR A FUN NIGHT OUT ON THE TOWN.
T	F	SOME PSYCHOTHERAPISTS LET THEIR CLIENTS TAKE THE LEAD IN PSYCHOTHERAPY.
T	F	SOME PSYCHOTHERAPISTS TELL THEIR CLIENTS EXACTLY WHAT TO DO.
T	F	LYING IN A RECLINING CHAIR AND FANTASIZING CAN BE AN EFFECTIVE WAY OF CONFRONTING FEARS.
T	F	SMOKING CIGARETTES CAN BE AN EFFECTIVE METHOD FOR HELPING PEOPLE STOP SMOKING CIGARETTES.
T	F	THERE IS NO SCIENTIFIC EVIDENCE THAT PSYCHOTHERAPY HELPS PEOPLE WITH PSYCHOLOGICAL DISORDERS.
T	F	THE ORIGINATOR OF A SURGICAL TECHNIQUE TO REDUCE VIOLENCE LEARNED THAT IT WAS NOT ALWAYS SUCCESSFUL WHEN ONE OF HIS PATIENTS SHOT HIM.

psychotherapy
a systematic interaction between a therapist and a client that brings psychological principles to bear on influencing the client's thoughts, feelings, or behavior to help the client overcome psychological disorders, adjust to problems in living, or develop as an individual

asylum
an institution for the care of the mentally ill

FIGURE 13.1 | Dr. Hunter Hoffman of the University of Washington Uses Virtual Therapy to Treat "Miss Muffet"

"Miss Muffet" is the name playfully given by Hoffman to a woman with a phobia for spiders. She is wearing virtual-reality headgear and sees the scene displayed on the monitor, which shows a large and hairy—but virtual—tarantula.

Mary Levin, UW, with permission from Hunter Hoffman, UW/www.Vrpain.com

13-1 What Is Psychotherapy?

There are many kinds of psychotherapy, but they have certain common characteristics. **Psychotherapy** is a systematic interaction between a therapist and a client that applies psychological principles to affect the client's thoughts, feelings, or behavior in an effort to help the client overcome psychological disorders, adjust to problems in living, or develop as an individual.

Quite a mouthful? True. But note the essentials:

✔ *Systematic interaction.* Psychotherapy is a systematic interaction between a client and a therapist. The therapist's theoretical point of view interacts with the client's to determine how the therapist and client relate to each other.

✔ *Psychological principles.* Psychotherapy is based on psychological theory and research in areas such as personality, learning, motivation, and emotion.

✔ *Thoughts, feelings, and behavior.* Psychotherapy influences clients' thoughts, feelings, and behavior. It can be aimed at any or all of these aspects of human psychology.

✔ *Psychological disorders, adjustment problems, and personal growth.* Psychotherapy is often used with people who have psychological disorders. Other people seek help in adjusting to problems such as shyness, weight problems, or loss of a life partner. Still other clients want to learn more about themselves and to reach their full potential as individuals, parents, or creative artists.

13-1a THE HISTORY OF THERAPIES

Historically speaking, "treatments" of psychological disorders often reflected the assumption that people who behaved in strange ways were possessed by demons. Because of this belief, treatment tended to involve cruel practices such as exorcism and execution. Some people who could not meet the demands of everyday life were tossed into prisons. Others begged in the streets, stole food, or became prostitutes. A few found their way to monasteries or other retreats that offered a kind word and some support. Generally speaking, they died early.

Asylums

Asylums originated in European monasteries. They were the first institutions meant primarily for people with psychological disorders. But their function was warehousing, not treatment. Their inmate populations mushroomed until the stresses created by noise, overcrowding, and disease aggravated the problems they were meant to ease. Inmates were frequently chained and beaten.

The word *bedlam* derives from St. Mary's of *Bethlehem*, the London asylum that opened its gates in 1547. Here unfortunate people with psychological disorders were chained, whipped, and allowed to lie in their own waste.

Humanitarian reform movements began in the 18th century. In Paris, the physician Philippe Pinel unchained the patients at La Salpêtrière. Rather than run amok, as had been feared, most patients profited from kindness and freedom. Many eventually reentered society. Later movements to reform institutions were led by William Tuke in England and Dorothea Dix in America.

Mental Hospitals

In the United States, mental hospitals gradually replaced asylums. In the mid-1950s more than a million people resided in state, county, Veterans Administration, or private facilities. The mental hospital's function is treatment, not warehousing. Still, because of high patient populations and understaffing, many patients received little attention. Even today, with somewhat improved conditions, one psychiatrist may be responsible for the welfare of several hundred residents on the weekend when other staff are absent.

The Community Mental Health Movement

Since the 1960s, efforts have been made to maintain people with serious psychological disorders in their communities. Community mental health centers at-tempt to maintain new patients as outpatients and to serve patients who have been released from mental hospitals. Today, most people with chronic psychological disorders live in the community, not in the hospital. Social critics note that many people who had resided in hospitals for decades were suddenly discharged to "home" communities that seemed foreign and forbidding to them. Many do not receive adequate follow-up care. Many join the ranks of the homeless (Drury, 2003).

psychodynamic therapy

a type of psychotherapy that is based on Freud's thinking and that assumes that psychological problems reflect early childhood experiences and internal conflicts

13-2 Psychodynamic Therapies

Psychodynamic therapies are based on the thinking of Sigmund Freud, the founder of psychodynamic theory. These therapies assume that psychological problems reflect early childhood experiences and internal conflicts. According to Freud, these conflicts involve the shifting of psychic energy among the id, ego, and superego. These shifts of psychic energy determine our behavior. When primitive urges threaten to break through from the id or

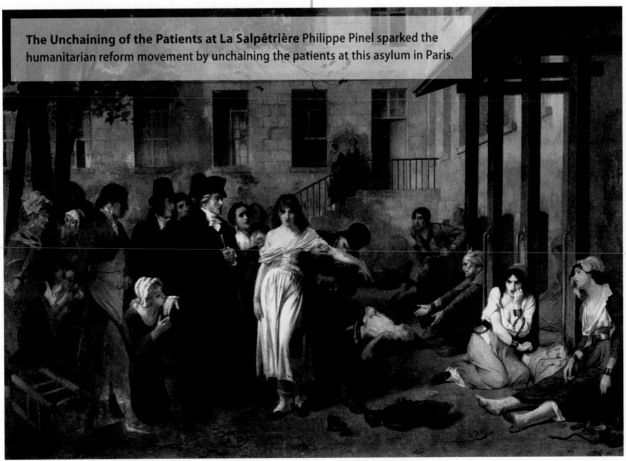

The Unchaining of the Patients at La Salpêtrière Philippe Pinel sparked the humanitarian reform movement by unchaining the patients at this asylum in Paris.

Robert-Fleury, Tony (1837-1912) (after)/Bibliotheque des Arts Decoratifs, Paris, France/Archives Charmet/TheBridgeman Art Library

psychoanalysis
Freud's method of psychotherapy

catharsis
in psychoanalysis, the expression of repressed feelings and impulses to allow the release of the psychic energy associated with them

free association
in psychoanalysis, the uncensored uttering of all thoughts that come to mind

resistance
the tendency to block the free expression of impulses and primitive ideas—a reflection of the defense mechanism of repression

In his consulting room, Freud would sit in a chair by the head of the couch while a client free-associated. The basic rule for free association is that no thought is censored. Freud did not believe that free association was really "free"; he assumed that significant feelings would rise to the surface and demand expression.

© Prisma Bildagentur AG/Alamy

when the superego floods us with excessive guilt, defenses are established and distress is created. Freud's therapy method—psychoanalysis—aims to bulwark the ego against the torrents of energy loosed by the id and the superego. With impulses and feelings of guilt and shame placed under greater control, clients are freer to develop adaptive behavior.

13-2a TRADITIONAL PSYCHOANALYSIS

Imagine your therapist asking you to lie on a couch in a slightly darkened room. She or he would sit behind you and encourage you to talk about anything that comes to mind, no matter how trivial, no matter how personal. To avoid interfering with your self-exploration, she or he might say little or nothing for session after session. That would be par for the course. A traditional psychoanalysis can extend for months, even years.

Psychoanalysis is the clinical method devised by Freud. It aims to provide *insight* into the conflicts that are presumed to lie at the roots of a person's problems. Insight means many things, including knowledge of the experiences that lead to conflicts and maladaptive behavior, recognition of unconscious feelings and conflicts, and conscious evaluation of one's thoughts, feelings, and behavior.

Psychoanalysis also aims to help the client express feelings and urges that have been repressed. By so doing, Freud believed that the client spilled forth the psychic energy that had been repressed by conflicts and guilt. He called this "spilling forth" **catharsis**. Catharsis would provide relief by alleviating some of the forces assaulting the ego. Freud also sought to replace impulsive and defensive behavior with coping behavior. In this way, for example, a man with a phobia for knives might discover

that he had been repressing the urge to harm someone who had taken advantage of him. He might also find ways to confront the person verbally.

Early in his career as a therapist, Freud found that hypnosis allowed his clients to focus on repressed conflicts and talk about them. He also found, however, that some clients denied the accuracy of this material once they were out of the trance. Others found the memories to be brought out into the open prematurely and painfully. Freud therefore turned to **free association**, a more gradual method of breaking through the walls of defense that block a client's insight into unconscious processes. In free association, the client is made comfortable—for example, by lying on a couch—and asked to talk about any topic that comes to mind. No thought is to be censored—that is the basic rule. Psychoanalysts ask their clients to wander "freely" from topic to topic, but they do not believe that the process occurring *within* the client is fully free. Repressed impulses clamor for release.

The ego persists in trying to repress unacceptable impulses and threatening conflicts. As a result, clients might show **resistance** to recalling and discussing threatening ideas. The therapist observes the dynamic struggle between the compulsion to talk about disturbing ideas and resistance. Through discreet comments and questions, the analyst hopes to encourage the client to discuss his or her problems. Talking helps the client gain insight into his or her true wishes and explore ways of fulfilling them.

Transference

Freud believed that clients not only responded to him as an individual but also in ways that reflected their attitudes and feelings toward other people in their lives.

He labeled this process **transference**. For example, a young woman client might respond to him as a father figure and displace her feelings toward her father onto Freud, perhaps seeking affection and wisdom. Analyzing and working through transference has been considered a key aspect of psychoanalysis.

Dream Analysis

Freud often asked clients to jot down their dreams upon waking so they could discuss them in therapy. Freud considered dreams the "royal road to the unconscious." He believed that the content of dreams is determined by unconscious processes as well as by the events of the day. Unconscious impulses were expressed in dreams as **wish fulfillment**.

13-2b MODERN PSYCHODYNAMIC APPROACHES

Although some psychoanalysts still adhere to Freud's techniques, modern psychodynamic therapy is briefer and less intense and makes treatment available to clients who do not have the time or money for long-term therapy. Some modern psychodynamic therapies continue to focus on revealing unconscious material and breaking through psychological defenses. Nevertheless, they differ from traditional psychoanalysis in that the client and therapist usually sit face to face (i.e., the client does not lie on a couch) (Prochaska & Norcross, 2010). Modern therapists are usually directive as well. They suggest helpful behavior instead of focusing on insight alone. Finally, there is more focus on the ego as the "executive" of personality and less emphasis on the id. For this reason, many modern psychodynamic therapists are called **ego analysts**.

13-3 Humanistic Therapies

Psychoanalytic therapies focus on internal conflicts and unconscious processes. **Humanistic therapies** focus on the quality of the client's subjective, conscious experience. Traditional psychoanalysis focuses on early childhood experiences. Humanistic therapies are more likely to focus on what clients are experiencing here and now.

13-3a CLIENT-CENTERED THERAPY

Carl Rogers (1902–1987) believed that we are free to make choices and control our destinies, despite the burdens of the past. He also believed that we have natural tendencies toward health, growth, and fulfillment. Psychological problems arise from roadblocks placed in the path of self-actualization—that is, what Rogers believed was an inborn tendency to strive to realize one's potential. If, when we are young, other people approve of us only when we are doing what they want us to do, we may learn to disown the parts of ourselves to which they object. We may learn to be seen but not heard—not even by ourselves. As a result, we may experience stress and discomfort and the feeling that we—or the world—are not real.

transference
responding to one person (such as a psychoanalyst) in a way similar to how one responded to another person (such as a parent) in childhood

wish fulfillment
in dreams, the acting out of ideas and impulses that are repressed when one is conscious

ego analyst
a psychodynamically oriented therapist who focuses on the conscious, coping behavior of the ego instead of the hypothesized, unconscious functioning of the id

humanistic therapy
a form of psychotherapy that focuses on the client's subjective, conscious experience in the "here and now"

CARL ROGERS

©Roger Ressmeyer/Corbis

Rogers believed that our psychological well-being is connected with our freedom to develop our unique frames of reference and potentials. Do you think you can separate your "real self" from your sociocultural experiences and religious training?

client-centered therapy
Carl Rogers's method of psychotherapy, which emphasizes the creation of a warm, therapeutic atmosphere that frees clients to engage in self-exploration and self-expression

David Buffington/Digital Vision/Getty Images

By showing the qualities of unconditional positive regard, empathic understanding, and genuineness, client-centered therapists create an atmosphere in which clients can explore their feelings.

Client-centered therapy aims to provide insight into the parts of us that we have disowned so that we can feel whole. It creates a warm, therapeutic atmosphere that encourages self-exploration and self-expression. The therapist's acceptance of the client is thought to foster self-acceptance and self-esteem. Self-acceptance frees the client to make choices that develop his or her unique potential.

Client-centered therapy is nondirective. An effective client-centered therapist has several qualities:

1. *Unconditional positive regard:* respect for clients as human beings with unique values and goals.

2. *Empathy:* recognition of the client's experiences and feelings. Therapists view the world through the client's *frame of reference* by setting aside their own values and listening closely.

3. *Genuineness:* Openness and honesty in responding to the client. Client-centered therapists must be able to tolerate differentness because they believe that every client is different in important ways.

The following excerpt from a therapy session shows how Carl Rogers uses empathetic understanding and paraphrases a client's (Jill's) feelings. His goal is to help her recognize feelings that she has partially disowned:

Jill: *I'm having a lot of problems dealing with my daughter. She's twenty years old; she's in college; I'm having a lot of trouble letting her go.... And I have a lot of guilt feelings about her; I have a real need to hang on to her.*

TRUTH IT IS TRUE THAT IN CLIENT-CENTERED THERAPY, THE CLIENT TAKES THE LEAD, STATING AND EXPLORING PROBLEMS.

C. R.: *A need to hang on so you can kind of make up for the things you feel guilty about. Is that part of it?*
Jill: *There's a lot of that.... Also, she's been a real friend to me, and filled my life.... And it's very hard.... a lot of empty places now that she's not with me.*
C. R.: *The old vacuum, sort of, when she's not there.*
Jill: *Yes. Yes. I also would like to be the kind of mother that could be strong and say, you know, "Go and have a good life," and this is really hard for me, to do that.*
C. R.: *It's very hard to give up something that's been so precious in your life, but also something that I guess has caused you pain when you mentioned guilt.*
Jill: *Yeah. And I'm aware that I have some anger toward her that I don't always get what I want. I have needs that are not met. And, uh, I don't feel I have a right to those needs. You know ... she's a daughter; she's not my mother. Though sometimes I feel as if I'd like her to mother me ... it's very difficult for me to ask for that and have a right to it.*
C. R.: *So, it may be unreasonable, but still, when she doesn't meet your needs, it makes you mad.*
Jill: *Yeah, I get very angry, very angry with her.*
C. R.: *(Pauses) You're also feeling a little tension at this point, I guess.*
Jill: *Yeah. Yeah. A lot of conflict.... (C. R.: M-hm.) A lot of pain.*
C. R.: *A lot of pain. Can you say anything more about what that's about? (Farber et al., 1996, pp. 74–75)*

Client-centered therapy is practiced widely in college and university counseling centers, not just to help students experiencing, say, anxieties or depression but also to help them make decisions. Many college students have not yet made career choices, or wonder whether they should become involved with particular people or in sexual activity. Client-centered therapists do not tell clients what to do. Instead, they help clients arrive at their own decisions.

13-3b GESTALT THERAPY

Gestalt therapy was originated by Fritz Perls (1893–1970). Like client-centered therapy, Gestalt therapy assumes that people disown parts of themselves that might meet with social disapproval or rejection. People also don social masks, pretending to be things that they are not. Therapy aims to help individuals integrate conflicting parts of their personality. Perls used the term *Gestalt* to signify his interest in giving the conflicting parts of the personality an integrated form or shape. (The German word *Gestalt* means "unified whole.") Perls adopted the term because he wanted to help clients integrate conflicting parts of their personalities.

TRUTH GESTALT THERAPISTS AND BEHAVIOR THERAPISTS MAY USE SPECIFIC PROCEDURES—TELLING THEIR CLIENTS WHAT TO DO.

Although Perls's ideas about conflicting personality elements owe much to psychodynamic theory, his form of therapy, unlike psychoanalysis, focuses on the here and now. Exercises heighten clients' awareness of their current feelings and behavior. Perls also believed, along with Rogers, that people are free to make choices and to direct their personal growth. But the charismatic and forceful Perls was unlike the gentle and accepting Rogers in temperament (Prochaska & Norcross, 2010). Thus, unlike client-centered therapy, Gestalt therapy is directive. The therapist leads the client through planned experiences to heighten their awareness of inner conflict and take responsibility for their behavior.

13-4 Behavior Therapy

Psychodynamic and humanistic forms of therapy tend to focus on what people think and feel. Behavior therapists tend to focus on what people *do*. **Behavior therapy**—also called *behavior modification*—applies principles of learning to directly promote desired behavioral changes. Behavior therapists rely heavily on principles of conditioning and observational learning. They help clients discontinue self-defeating behavior patterns such as overeating, smoking, and phobic avoidance of harmless stimuli. They help clients acquire adaptive behavior patterns such as the social skills required to start social relationships or say no to insistent salespeople.

Behavior therapists may help clients gain "insight" into maladaptive behaviors such as feelings of anxiety by helping the person become aware of the circumstances in which the behaviors occur. They do not help unearth the childhood origins of problems and the symbolic meanings of maladaptive behaviors as psychoanalysts do. Behavior therapists, like other therapists, may also build warm, therapeutic relationships with clients, but they see the effectiveness of behavior therapy as deriving from specific, learning-based procedures (Rachman, 2000). They insist that their methods be established by experimentation and that results be assessed in terms of measurable behavior. In this section we consider some frequently used behavior-therapy techniques.

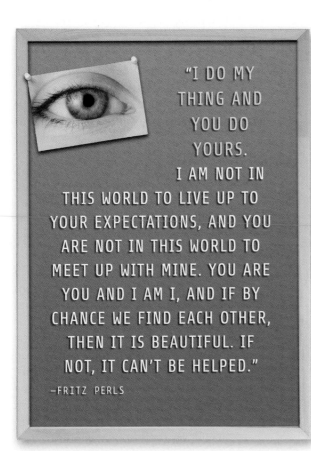

"I DO MY THING AND YOU DO YOURS. I AM NOT IN THIS WORLD TO LIVE UP TO YOUR EXPECTATIONS, AND YOU ARE NOT IN THIS WORLD TO MEET UP WITH MINE. YOU ARE YOU AND I AM I, AND IF BY CHANCE WE FIND EACH OTHER, THEN IT IS BEAUTIFUL. IF NOT, IT CAN'T BE HELPED."

—FRITZ PERLS

systematic desensitization

Wolpe's method for reducing fears by associating a hierarchy of images of fear-evoking stimuli with deep muscle relaxation

modeling

a behavior-therapy technique in which a client observes and imitates a person who approaches and copes with feared objects or situations

13-4a FEAR-REDUCTION METHODS

Many people seek therapy because of fears and phobias that interfere with their functioning. This is one of the areas in which behavior therapy has made great inroads. Behavior-therapy methods for reducing fears include *flooding* (see Chapter 5, page 118), *systematic desensitization*, *virtual therapy*, and *modeling*.

Systematic Desensitization

Adam has a phobia for receiving injections. His behavior therapist treats him as he reclines in a comfortable padded chair. In a state of deep muscle relaxation, Adam observes slides projected on a screen. A slide of a nurse holding a needle has just been shown three times, 30 seconds at a time. Each time Adam has shown no anxiety. So now a slightly more discomforting slide is shown: one of the nurse aiming the needle toward someone's bare arm. After 15 seconds, our armchair adventurer notices twinges of discomfort and raises a finger as a signal (speaking might disturb his relaxation). The projector operator turns off the light, and Adam spends 2 minutes imagining his "safe scene"—lying on a beach beneath the tropical sun. Then the slide is shown again. This time Adam views it for 30 seconds before feeling anxiety.

THE AUTHOR'S FILES

Adam is undergoing **systematic desensitization**, a method for reducing phobic responses originated by

TRUTH USING SYSTEMATIC DESENSITIZATION, A PERSON CAN IN EFFECT CONFRONT HIS OR HER FEAR WHILE LYING IN A RECLINER AND RELAXING.

psychiatrist Joseph Wolpe (1915–1997). Systematic desensitization is a gradual process in which the client learns to handle increasingly disturbing stimuli while anxiety to each one is being counterconditioned. About 10 to 20 stimuli such as slides are arranged in a sequence, or *hierarchy*, according to their capacity to trigger anxiety. In imagination or by being shown photos, the client travels gradually up through this hierarchy, counterconditioning anxiety with relaxation step by step as he or she approaches the target. In Adam's case, the target was the ability to receive an injection without undue anxiety.

Virtual Therapy

Virtual therapy may use more elaborate equipment than slides, but the principle is desensitization. New York Fire Chief Stephen King was in the north tower at the World Trade Center on September 11, 2001, which was hit first by the airplanes. The experience led him to retire from the department, avoid bridges and tunnels, and stay out of Manhattan (King, 2005). "Where I was and what I saw that day—the many people that jumped, the magnitude of it—was just overwhelming."

But virtual therapy has helped King face the past—and his future. Using the technology we find in video games, programs mimic traumatic settings and events—public speaking in an auditorium, flying in an airplane, spiders, or, in King's case, images of the World Trade Center (see Figure 13.2). "The idea behind the treatment," explains Dr. JoAnn Difede (2005), "is to systematically expose the patient to aspects of their experience in a graded fashion so they can confront their fear of the trauma."

Modeling

Modeling relies on observational learning. In this method, clients observe and then imitate people who approach and cope with the objects or situations that the clients fear. Albert Bandura and his colleagues (1969) found that modeling worked as well as systematic desensitization—and more rapidly—in reducing fear of snakes. Clients observed models handling snakes. In the same session, they were able to touch the snakes, pick them up, and let them crawl on their bodies. Modeling also

FIGURE 13.2

A Program Containing Images of the World Trade Center Intended to Help People with Posttraumatic Stress Disorder

Virtual therapy clients are exposed to virtual stimuli that represent their source of anxiety and stress to help them gradually confront their fears.

Image and Copyright by Hunter Hoffman, U.W. Virtual World Programmed by Howard Abrams.

increases self-efficacy expectations in coping with feared stimuli.

13-4b AVERSIVE CONDITIONING

Many people also seek behavior therapy because they want to break bad habits, such as smoking, excessive drinking, nail-biting, and the like. One behavior-therapy approach to helping people do so is **aversive conditioning**. Aversive conditioning is a controversial procedure that pairs painful or aversive stimuli with unwanted impulses to make the impulse less appealing. For example, to help people control alcohol intake, tastes of different alcoholic beverages can be paired with drug-induced nausea and vomiting or with electric shock.

TRUTH IN THE METHOD OF RAPID SMOKING, BEHAVIOR THERAPISTS USE SMOKING AS A WAY OF MAKING CIGARETTE SMOKE UNAPPEALING TO SMOKERS, HELPING THEM TO STOP SMOKING.

Aversive conditioning has been used with problems as diverse as cigarette smoking and sexual abuse. *Rapid smoking* is an aversive conditioning method designed to help smokers quit. In this method, the would-be quitter inhales every six seconds. In another method, the hose of a hair dryer is hooked up to a chamber containing several lit cigarettes. Smoke is blown into the quitter's face as he or she also smokes a cigarette. A third method uses branching pipes so that the smoker draws in smoke from several cigarettes at the same time. In these methods, overexposure makes once-desirable cigarette smoke aversive. The quitter becomes motivated to avoid, rather than seek, cigarettes. Interest in aversive conditioning for quitting smoking has waned, however, because of side effects such as raising blood pressure and the availability of nicotine-replacement techniques.

13-4c OPERANT CONDITIONING PROCEDURES

We tend to repeat behavior that is reinforced. Behavior that is not reinforced tends to become extinguished. Behavior therapists have used these principles of operant conditioning with psychotic patients as well as with clients with milder problems.

The staff at one mental hospital was at a loss about how to encourage withdrawn schizophrenic patients to eat regularly. Psychologists observed that staff members were making the problem worse by coaxing patients into the dining room and even feeding them. Staff attention apparently reinforced the patients' lack of cooperation. Some rules were changed (Dickerson et al., 2005). Patients who did not arrive at the dining hall within 30 minutes after serving were locked out. Staff could not interact with patients at mealtime. With uncooperative behavior no longer reinforced, patients quickly changed their eating habits. Then patients were required to pay one penny to enter the dining hall. Pennies were earned by interacting with other patients and showing other socially appropriate behaviors. These target behaviors also became more frequent.

Health professionals are concerned about whether people who are, or have been, dependent on alcohol can exercise control over their drinking. One study showed that rewards for remaining abstinent from alcohol can exert a powerful effect (Petry et al., 2000). In the study, one group of alcohol-dependent veterans was given a standard treatment while another group received the treatment *plus* the chance to win prizes for remaining alcohol-free, as measured by a Breathalyzer test. By the end of the eight-week treatment period, 84% of the veterans who could win prizes remained in the program, as compared with 22% of the standard treatment group. The prizes had an average value of $200, far less than what alcohol-related absenteeism from work and other responsibilities can cost.

In aversive conditioning, unwanted behaviors take on a noxious quality as a result of being repeatedly paired with aversive stimuli. Overexposure is making cigarette smoke aversive to this smoker.

©Lester Sloan/Woodfin Camp & Associates

aversive conditioning
a behavior therapy technique in which undesired responses are inhibited by pairing repugnant or offensive stimuli with them

AVERSIVE CONDITIONING

Glossary (margin)

token economy
a controlled environment in which people are reinforced for desired behaviors with tokens (such as poker chips) that may be exchanged for privileges

successive approximations
in operant conditioning, a series of behaviors that gradually become more similar to a target behavior

social skills training
a behavior-therapy method for helping people in their interpersonal relations that uses self-monitoring, behavior rehearsal, and feedback

biofeedback training (BFT)
the systematic feeding back to an organism of information about a bodily function so that the organism can gain control of that function

The Token Economy

Many psychiatric wards and hospitals use **token economies** in which patients need tokens such as poker chips to purchase TV viewing time, extra visits to the canteen, or a private room (Comaty et al., 2001). The tokens are dispensed as reinforcers for productive activities such as making beds, brushing teeth, and socializing. Token economies have not eliminated all symptoms of schizophrenia but have increased patients' activity and cooperation. Tokens have also been used to modify the behavior of children with conduct disorders.

Successive Approximations

The operant conditioning method of **successive approximations** is often used to help clients build good habits. For example: You want to study three hours each evening but can concentrate for only half an hour. Rather than attempting to increase your study time all at once, you could do so gradually by adding, say, five minutes each evening. After every hour or so of studying, you could reinforce yourself with five minutes of people-watching in a busy section of the library.

Social Skills Training

In **social skills training**, behavior therapists decrease social anxiety and build social skills through operant-conditioning procedures that employ *self-monitoring* (keeping a record of one's own behavior to identify problems and record successes), coaching, modeling, role-playing, *behavior rehearsal* (practicing), and *feedback* (receiving information about the effectiveness of behavior). Social skills training has been used to help formerly hospitalized mental patients maintain jobs and apartments in the community. For example, a worker can rehearse politely asking a supervisor for assistance or asking a landlord to fix the plumbing in an apartment. Social skills training is effective in groups. Group members can role-play key people—such as parents, spouses, or potential dates—in the lives of other members.

Biofeedback Training

Through **biofeedback training (BFT)**, therapists help clients become more aware of, and gain control over, various bodily functions. Therapists attach clients to devices that measure bodily functions such as heart rate. "Bleeps" or other electronic signals are used to indicate (and thereby reinforce) changes ("operants") in the desired direction—for example, a slower heart rate. (Knowledge of results is a powerful reinforcer.) One device, the electromyograph (EMG), monitors muscle tension. It has been used to increase control over muscle tension in the forehead and elsewhere, thereby al-

---

✳ Eye-Movement Desensitization and Reprocessing

Helping professionals are often inspired to develop therapy methods based on their personal experiences. As Francine Shapiro (1989) paints it, she had troubling thoughts on her mind when she entered a park. But as her eyes darted about, taking in the scene, she found her troubled thoughts disappearing. Thus, she developed a therapy method called *eye-movement desensitization and reprocessing (EMDR)* to join the arsenal of therapeutic weapons against stress disorders. With this method, the client is asked to imagine a traumatic scene while the therapist moves a finger rapidly back and forth before his or her eyes for about 20–30 seconds. The client follows the finger while keeping the troubling scene in mind. The client tells the therapist what he or she was thinking and how he or she felt during the procedure. The procedure is repeated until the client's anxiety is relieved. Treatment takes about three 90-minute sessions.

Evidence from a number of studies suggests that EMDR helps decrease the anxiety associated with traumatic events (Engelhard et al., 2010; Van der Kolk et al., 2007). One study, for example, compared the effectiveness of EMDR with two alternative treatments: exposure therapy (as in virtual therapy for spider phobia) and relaxation training (Taylor et al., 2003). Another study looked at the effectiveness of EMDR on numerous people following September 11 (Silver et al., 2005). These studies and others suggest that EMDR is effective, but it remains unclear how effective EMDR is and why it works (May, 2005; Schubert & Lee, 2009). Research also challenges the idea that eye movements are necessary (Devilly, 2002; Schubert & Lee, 2009). Perhaps clients receiving EMDR profit from their relationship with the therapist and from expectations of success. Moreover, the client is to some degree exposed to the trauma that haunts him or her under circumstances in which the client believes he or she will be able to manage the trauma.

Conclusion? Exposure helps people cope with trauma. Eye movements may not be needed.

Bananastock/Jupiterimages

---

leviating anxiety, stress, and headaches (Nestoriuc et al., 2008).

BFT also helps clients voluntarily regulate functions once thought to be beyond conscious control, such as heart rate and blood pressure. Hypertensive clients use a blood-pressure cuff and electronic signals to gain control over their blood pressure. The electroencephalograph (EEG) monitors brain waves and can be used to teach people how to produce alpha waves, which are associated with relaxation. Some people have overcome insomnia by learning to produce the kinds of brain waves associated with sleep.

13-5 Cognitive Therapies

What thoughts do you have when things go wrong at school or on the job? Do you tell yourself that you're facing a problem that needs a solution? That you've successfully solved problems before and will be able to create a solution this time? Or do you think, "Oh no! This is awful! It's going to get worse, and I'm going to flunk (or get fired)!" If you go the "This is awful" route, you are probably heightening your discomfort and impairing your coping ability. Cognitive therapy focuses directly on your thoughts and encourages ideas that will help you solve problems rather than blow them out of proportion and magnify your discomfort.

Cognitive therapy focuses on changing the beliefs, attitudes, and automatic types of thinking that create and compound people's problems (Butler et al., 2006; David et al., 2010). Cognitive therapists, like psychoanalytic and humanistic therapists, aim to foster self-insight, but they mainly aim to help make people more aware of their *current cognitions*. Cognitive therapists also aim to directly change maladaptive thoughts in an effort to reduce negative feelings and help clients solve problems.

Many behavior therapists incorporate cognitive procedures in their methods. For example, techniques such as systematic desensitization, covert sensitization, and covert reinforcement ask clients to focus on visual imagery. Behavioral methods for treating bulimia nervosa focus on clients' irrational attitudes toward their weight and body shape as well as foster good eating habits. Let's look at the approaches and methods of the cognitive therapists Aaron Beck and Albert Ellis.

"There is nothing either good or bad, but thinking makes it so."
—SHAKESPEARE, HAMLET

13-5a AARON BECK'S COGNITIVE THERAPY

cognitive therapy
a form of therapy that focuses on how clients' cognitions (e.g., expectations, attitudes, beliefs) lead to distress and may be modified to relieve distress and promote adaptive behavior

Psychiatrist Aaron Beck began his professional life as a psychoanalyst. He became impatient, however, with analysis's lengthy methods and reluctance to offer specific advice. In his own life he had successfully defeated his fear of blood by assisting in surgical operations and argued himself out of irrational fear of driving through tunnels. Similarly, his methods of cognitive therapy focus on arguing clients out of beliefs that are making them miserable and exposing them to situations they avoid because of irrational fear (Berk et al., 2004; Warman et al., 2005). Beck encourages clients to become their own personal scientists and challenge feelings and beliefs that make no sense.

Beck encourages clients to see the irrationality of their ways of thinking. For example, depressed people tend to minimize their accomplishments and to assume that the worst will happen. Minimizing accomplishments and expecting the worst are (usually) distortions of reality that lead to feelings of depression. Cognitive distortions can be fleeting and automatic, difficult to detect. Beck's methods help clients become aware of such distortions and challenge them.

Beck notes a number of "cognitive errors" that contribute to clients' miseries:

1. Clients may *selectively perceive* the world as a harmful place and ignore evidence to the contrary.

2. Clients may *overgeneralize* on the basis of a few examples. For example, they may perceive themselves as worthless because they were laid off at work or as unattractive because they were refused a date.

3. Clients may *magnify*, or blow out of proportion, the importance of negative events. They may catastrophize failing a test by assuming they will flunk out of college or catastrophize losing a job by believing that they will never find another one and that serious harm will befall their family as a result.

4. Clients may engage in *absolutist thinking*, or looking at the world in black and white rather than in shades of gray. In doing so, a rejection on a date takes on the meaning of a lifetime of loneliness; an uncomfortable illness takes on life-threatening proportions.

Becoming aware of cognitive errors and modifying catastrophizing thoughts help us cope with stress. Internal, stable, and global attributions of failure lead to depression and feelings of helplessness. Cognitive therapists also alert clients to cognitive errors or irrational thoughts so that the clients can change their attitudes and pave the way for more effective overt behavior.

13-5b ALBERT ELLIS'S RATIONAL EMOTIVE BEHAVIOR THERAPY

In **rational emotive behavior therapy (REBT)**, Albert Ellis (1913–2007) pointed out that our beliefs *about* events, not only the events themselves, shape our responses to them. Moreover, many of us harbor a number of irrational beliefs that can give rise to problems or magnify their impact. Two of the most important ones are the belief that we must have the love and approval of people who are important to us and the belief that we must prove ourselves to be thoroughly competent, adequate, and achieving.

Ellis, like Beck, began his career as a psychoanalyst. And, also like Beck, he became disturbed by the passive role of the analyst and by the slow rate of obtaining results—if they were obtained at all. Ellis's REBT methods are active and directive. He did not sit back like the traditional psychoanalyst and occasionally offer an interpretation. Instead, he urged clients to seek out their irrational beliefs, which can be unconscious, though not as deeply buried as Freud believed. Nevertheless, they can be hard to pinpoint without some di-

Aaron Beck (left) and Albert Ellis (right)

"I get people to truly accept themselves unconditionally, whether or not their therapist or anyone loves them."
—ALBERT ELLIS

rection. Ellis showed clients how those beliefs lead to misery and challenged clients to change them. When Ellis saw clients behaving according to irrational beliefs, he refuted the beliefs by asking "Where is it written that you must …?" or "What evidence do you have that …?" According to Ellis, we need less misery and less blaming in our lives, and more action.

13-5c TOWARD A COGNITIVE-BEHAVIORAL THERAPY

Many theorists consider cognitive therapy to be a collection of techniques that are a part of behavior therapy. Aaron Beck himself appears to be comfortable referring to his approach as *cognitive* in one article and *cognitive-behavioral* in another (Clark & Beck, 2011; Warman & Beck, 2003). We are apparently headed toward an integration of the two approaches that is termed **cognitive-behavioral therapy (CBT)**.

Ellis straddled behavioral and cognitive therapies. He originally dubbed his method of therapy *rational-emotive therapy*, because his focus was on the cognitive—irrational beliefs and how to change them. However,

Group therapy is more economical than individual therapy, group members can practice social skills with one another, and members can learn from the experiences of others.

Ellis also always promoted behavioral changes to cement cognitive changes. In keeping with his broad philosophy, he recently changed the name of rational-emotive therapy to rational-emotive *behavior* therapy.

13-6 Group Therapies

When a psychotherapist has several clients with similar problems—anxiety, depression, adjustment to divorce, lack of social skills—it often makes sense to treat them in a group rather than in individual sessions. The methods and characteristics of the group reflect the needs of the members and the theoretical orientation of the leader. In group psychoanalysis, clients might interpret one another's dreams. In a client-centered group, they might provide an accepting atmosphere for self-exploration. Members of behavior therapy groups might be jointly desensitized to anxiety-evoking stimuli or might practice social skills together.

Group therapy has the following advantages:

1. It is economical (Prochaska & Norcross, 2010). It allows the therapist to work with several clients at once.

2. Compared with one-to-one therapy, group therapy provides more information and life experience for clients to draw on.

3. Appropriate behavior receives group support. Clients usually appreciate an outpouring of peer approval.

4. When we run into troubles, it is easy to imagine that we are different from other people or inferior to them. Affiliating with people with similar problems is reassuring.

5. Group members who show improvement provide hope for other members.

6. Many individuals seek therapy because of problems in relating to other people. People who seek therapy for other reasons also may be socially inhibited. Members of groups have the opportunity to practice social skills in a relatively nonthreatening atmosphere. In a group consisting of men and women of different ages, group members can role-play one another's employers, employees, spouses, parents, children, and friends. Members can role-play asking one another out on dates, saying no (or yes), and so on.

But group therapy is not for everyone. Some clients fare better with individual treatment. Many prefer not to disclose their problems to a group. They may be overly shy or want individual attention. It is the responsibility of the therapist to insist that group disclosures be kept confidential, to establish a supportive atmosphere, and to ensure that group members obtain the attention they need.

Many types of therapy can be conducted either individually or in groups. Couple therapy and family therapy are conducted only with groups.

13-6a COUPLE THERAPY

Couple therapy helps couples enhance their relationship by improving their communication skills and helping them manage conflict (Prochaska & Norcross, 2010). There are often power imbalances in relationships, and couple therapy helps individuals find "full membership" in the couple. Correcting power imbalances increases happiness and can decrease the incidence of domestic violence. Ironically, in situations of domestic violence, the partner with *less* power in the relationship is usually the violent one. Violence sometimes appears to be a way of compensating for inability to share power in other ways (Rathus & Sanderson, 1999).

Today the main approach to couple therapy is cognitive-behavioral (Rathus & Sanderson, 1999). It teaches couples communications skills (such as how to listen and express feelings), ways of handling feelings like anger, and ways of solving problems.

13-6b FAMILY THERAPY

Family therapy is a form of group therapy in which one or more families constitute the group. Family therapy may be undertaken from various theoretical viewpoints. One is the *systems approach*, in which family interaction is studied and modified to enhance the growth of individual family members and of the family unit as a whole (Prochaska & Norcross, 2010).

Family members with low self-esteem often cannot tolerate different attitudes and behaviors in other family members. Faulty communication within the family also creates problems. In addition, it is not uncommon for the family to present an "identified patient"—that is, the family member who has *the* problem and is *causing* all the trouble. Yet family therapists usually assume that the identified patient is a scapegoat for other problems among family members. It is a sort of myth: Change the "bad apple," or identified patient, and the "barrel," or family, will be functional once more. The family therapist attempts to teach the family to communicate and encourage growth and autonomy in each family member.

> It is a sort of myth: Change the "bad apple," or identified patient, and the "barrel," or family, will be functional once more.

13-6c SELF-HELP AND SUPPORT GROUPS

Millions of people in the United States and elsewhere are involved in self-help and support groups that meet in person, online, or even by telephone. Some self-help and support groups enable people who have been treated for psychological disorders to reach out to others who have had similar experiences (Greidanus & Everall, 2010). These groups tend to be specific, such as groups for parents of children with autistic disorders, intellectual deficiency, or Down syndrome. Members share problems and possible solutions.

The best known of self-help and support groups is Alcoholics Anonymous (AA), whose 12-step program has been used by millions of people in the United States and around the world. Members meet regularly and call other members between meetings when they are tempted to drink. The 12 steps require admitting before the group that one's drinking is out of control, calling upon a higher power for strength, examining injurious behavior, and attempting to make amends.

Does AA work? The organization itself admits that the majority of new recruits drop out within a year. Of greater concern is a meta-analysis that concluded that AA is actually less effective than no treatment at all (Kownacki & Shadish, 1999). But most analyses suggest that AA is as effective as all forms of psychotherapy tested. When treatments, including AA, *are* effective, it seems to be because alcoholics remain in treatment for many years (Moos & Moos, 2006), alleviate feelings of depression (Kelly et al, 2010), and heighten their confidence that they can navigate challenges without drinking (Forcehimes & Tonigan, 2008).

13-7 Does Psychotherapy Work?

In 1952, the British psychologist Hans Eysenck published a review of psychotherapy research—"The Effects of Psychotherapy"—that sent shock waves through the psychotherapy community. On the basis of his review of the research, Eysenck concluded that the rate of improvement among people in psychotherapy was no greater than the rate of "spontaneous remission"—that is, the rate of improvement that would be shown by people with psychological disorders who received no treatment.

Eysenck was not addressing people with schizophrenia, who typically profit from biological forms of therapy, but he argued that whether or not people with problems such as anxiety and depression received therapy, two of three reported substantial improvement within two years.

That was over half a century ago. Research on the effectiveness of therapy conducted since then has been encouraging (Driessen et al., 2010; Shedler, 2010). In their classic early use of meta-analysis, Mary Lee Smith and Gene Glass (1977) analyzed the results of dozens of studies and concluded that people who obtained psychodynamic therapy showed greater well-being, on average, than 70% to 75% of those who did not obtain treatment. Similarly, nearly 75% of the clients who obtained client-centered therapy were better off than people who did not obtain treatment. Psychodynamic and client-centered therapies appear to be most effective with well-educated, verbal, strongly motivated clients who report problems with anxiety, depression (of light to moderate proportions), and interpersonal relationships. Neither form of therapy appears to be effective with people with psychotic disorders such as major depression, bipolar disorder, and schizophrenia.

FICTION ACTUALLY, THERE IS NOW A GREAT DEAL OF RESEARCH EVIDENCE THAT SHOWS THAT PSYCHOTHERAPY IS EFFECTIVE.

Studies of cognitive therapy have shown that modifying irrational beliefs of the type described by Albert Ellis helps people with problems such as anxiety and depression (David et al., 2010). Modifying self-defeating beliefs of the sort outlined by Aaron Beck also frequently alleviates anxiety and depression (Butler et al., 2006). Cognitive therapy may help people with severe depression, who had been thought responsive only to biological therapies (Hollon & Shelton, 2001; Simons et al., 1995). Cognitive therapy has also helped people with personality disorders (Beck et al., 2001; Trull et al., 2003).

Behavioral and cognitive therapies have provided strategies for treating anxiety disorders, social skills deficits, and problems in self-control (DeRubeis & Crits-Christoph, 1998). These therapies have helped couples and families in distress (Baucom et al., 2002). Moreover, they have modified behaviors related to health problems such as headaches (Verhagen et al., 2009), smoking, chronic pain, and bulimia (Agras et al., 2000; Butler et al., 2006). Cognitive-behavior therapists have innovated treatments for sexual dysfunctions for which there previously were no effective treatments.

13-7a EVIDENCE-BASED PRACTICES

Experimentation is the gold standard for research in psychology, and a number of methods of therapy have been shown to be effective in carefully conducted,

random controlled experiments (RCEs)—that is, experiments in which participants are assigned at random to a specific treatment or to a control treatment. The researchers in many of these studies also rely on treatment manuals that concretely outline the treatment methods. Treatment methods that survive these grueling tests are called *evidence-based practices* (Anchin & Pincus, 2010; Bruce & Sanderson, 2004). Table 13.1 shows a number of evidence-based practices and the problems for which they have been found effective. Other treatments may eventually be added as more evidence accumulates.

Many therapists argue that evidence-based practices favor cognitive-behavioral therapies because they are more readily standardized in treatment manuals and can be followed more accurately by practitioners in experiments (Kazdin, 2008; Levy & Ablon, 2009). Alternative treatments, such as psychodynamic therapy, are not so easily standardized or practiced. Therefore, they may not hold up as well in controlled trials. Second, critics assert that most studies supportive of evidence-based practices do not capture the complexity and uniqueness of real clients seen in community settings (Westen et al., 2006). And as we see in the following section on ethnicity and psychotherapy, we must also consider the sociocultural features of clients in determining how to make therapy most effective.

TABLE 13.1

Examples of Evidence-Based Practices

TREATMENT	CONDITION FOR WHICH TREATMENT IS EFFECTIVE
Cognitive therapy	Depression Headache
Behavior therapy or behavior modification	Depression Developmental disabilities Enuresis (bed-wetting)
Cognitive-behavior therapy	Panic disorder with and without agoraphobia Generalized anxiety disorder Bulimia nervosa
Exposure treatment	Agoraphobia and specific phobia
Exposure and response prevention	Obsessive–compulsive disorder
Parent training programs	Children with oppositional behavior

© Cengage Learning 2012

13-7b ETHNICITY AND PSYCHOTHERAPY

Americans from ethnic minority groups are less likely than European Americans to seek therapy (Chen & Rizzo, 2010; Sue et al., 2009). Reasons for their lower participation rate include:

- Lack of awareness that therapy would help
- Lack of information about the availability of professional services or inability to pay for them
- Distrust of professionals, particularly European American professionals and (for women) male professionals
- Language barriers
- Reluctance to open up about personal matters to strangers—especially strangers who are not members of one's own ethnic group
- Cultural inclinations toward other approaches to problem solving, such as religious approaches and psychic healers
- Negative experiences with professionals and authority figures

There are thus many reasons that clinicians need to be sensitive to the cultural heritage, language, and values of their clients. That is, they need to develop multicultural competence (Sue et al., 2009). Let's consider some of the issues involved in conducting psychotherapy with African Americans, Asian Americans, Latin Americans, and Native Americans.

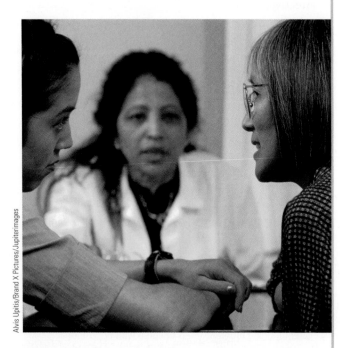

Alvis Upitis/Brand X Pictures/Jupiterimages

Psychologists need to be sensitive to the cultural heritages, languages, and values of their clients.

African Americans

African Americans often are reluctant to seek psychological help because of cultural assumptions that people should manage their own problems (González et al., 2010; Jackson & Greene, 2000). Many African Americans are also suspicious of their therapists—especially when the therapist is a European American (Mohr et al., 2010). They may withhold personal information because of society's history of racial discrimination (Dana, 2002).

Asian Americans

Asian Americans tend to stigmatize people with psychological disorders. As a result, they may deny problems and refuse to seek help for them (Spencer et al., 2010). Asian Americans, especially recent immigrants, also may not understand or believe in Western approaches to psychotherapy. For example, Western psychotherapy typically encourages people to express their feelings. This mode of behavior may conflict with the Asian tradition of public restraint. Many Asians also experience psychological problems as physical symptoms (Kim & Omizo, 2003; Sue et al., 2009). Rather than thinking of themselves as anxious, they may focus on physical features of anxiety such as a pounding heart and heavy sweating.

Latin Americans

Therapists need to be aware of potential conflicts between the traditional Latin American value of interdependence in the family and the typical European American belief in independence and self-reliance (Garza & Watts, 2010). Measures like the following may help bridge the gaps between psychotherapists and Latin American clients:

- Interacting with clients in the language requested by them or, if this is not possible, referring them to professionals who can do so.
- Using methods that are consistent with the client's values and levels of acculturation, as suggested by fluency in English and level of education.
- Developing therapy methods that incorporate clients' cultural values (Cervantes & Parham, 2005). Malgady and his colleagues (1990), for example, use *cuento therapy* with Puerto Ricans. *Cuento therapy* uses traditional folktales (*cuentos*) with characters who serve as models for adaptive behavior.

Native Americans

Many psychological disorders experienced by Native Americans involve the disruption of their traditional culture caused by European colonization (Olson, 2003; Viets et al., 2009). Loss of cultural identity and social disorganization have set the stage for problems such as alcoholism, substance abuse, and depression. Efforts to prevent psychological disorders do well to focus on strengthening Native American cultural identity, pride, and cohesion.

Psychotherapy is most effective when therapists attend to and respect people's cultural as well as individual differences. Although it is the individual who experiences psychological anguish, the fault can often be traced to cultural issues.

13-8 Biological Therapies

The kinds of therapy we have discussed are psychological in nature—forms of *psycho*therapy. Psychotherapies apply *psychological* principles to treatment, principles based on psychological knowledge of matters such as learning and motivation. However, people with psychological disorders are also often treated with biological therapies. Biological therapies apply what is known of people's *biological* structures and processes to the amelioration of psychological disorders. For example, they may work by altering events in the nervous system, as by changing the action of neurotransmitters. In this section, we discuss three biological, or medical, approaches to treating people with psychological disorders: drug therapy, electroconvulsive therapy, and psychosurgery.

13-8a DRUG THERAPY

In the 1950s, Fats Domino popularized the song "My Blue Heaven." Fats was singing about the sky and happiness. Today, "blue heavens" is one of the street names for the 10-milligram dose of the antianxiety drug Valium. Clinicians prescribe Valium and other drugs

for people with various psychological disorders.

rebound anxiety
anxiety that can occur when one discontinues use of a tranquilizer

Antianxiety Drugs

Most antianxiety drugs, such as Valium and Ativan, belong to the chemical class known as *benzodiazepines*. Antianxiety drugs are usually prescribed for outpatients who complain of generalized anxiety or panic attacks, although many people also use them as sleeping pills. Valium and other antianxiety drugs depress the activity of the central nervous system (CNS). The CNS, in turn, decreases sympathetic activity, reducing the heart rate, respiration rate, and feelings of nervousness and tension. Many people come to tolerate antianxiety drugs very quickly. When tolerance occurs, dosages must be increased for the drug to remain effective.

Sedation (feeling of being tired or drowsy) is the most common side effect of antianxiety drugs. Problems associated with withdrawal from these drugs include **rebound anxiety**. That is, some people who have been using these drugs regularly report that their anxiety becomes worse than before once they discontinue them. Antianxiety drugs can induce physical dependence, as evidenced by withdrawal symptoms such as tremors, sweating, insomnia, and rapid heartbeat.

Antipsychotic Drugs

People with schizophrenia are often given antipsychotic drugs (also called *major tranquilizers*). In most cases, these drugs reduce agitation, delusions, and hallucinations. Many antipsychotic drugs, including phenothiazines (e.g., Thorazine) and clozapine (Clozaril) are thought to act by blocking dopamine receptors in the brain (Porsolt

PhotoLink/Photodisc/JGetty Images

In electroconvulsive therapy (ECT), electrodes are placed on each side of the patient's head and a current is passed between them, inducing a seizure. ECT is used mainly in cases of major depression when antidepressant drugs and psychotherapy are not sufficient.

WILL MCINTYRE/Photo Researchers/Getty Images

et al., 2010). Research along these lines supports the theory that schizophrenia is connected with overactivity of the neurotransmitter dopamine.

Antidepressants

People with major depression often take so-called **antidepressant** drugs. These drugs are also helpful for some people with eating disorders, panic disorder, obsessive–compulsive disorder (OCD), and social phobia (Zohar & Westenberg, 2007). Problems in the regulation of noradrenaline and serotonin may be involved in eating and panic disorders as well as in depression. Antidepressants are believed to work by increasing levels of these neurotransmitters, which can affect both depression and the appetite (Dagyte et al., 2010).

There are various antidepressants. Each increases the concentration of noradrenaline or serotonin in the brain (Dagyte et al., 2010). **Selective serotonin-reuptake inhibitors (SSRIs)** such as Prozac and Zoloft block the reuptake of serotonin by presynaptic neurons. As a result, serotonin remains in the synaptic cleft longer, influencing receiving neurons. SSRIs appear to be more effective than other antidepressants.

Mood Stabilizers

The ancient Greeks and Romans were among the first to use the metal lithium as a mood stabilizer. They prescribed mineral water—which contains lithium—for people with bipolar disorder. They had no inkling as to why this treatment sometimes helped. A salt of the metal lithium (lithium carbonate), in tablet form, flattens out cycles of manic behavior and depression in most people. It is not known exactly how lithium works, although it affects the functioning of neurotransmitters. Lithium can also be used to strengthen the effects of antidepressant medication (Redrobe & Bourin, 2009).

People with bipolar disorder may have to use lithium indefinitely, as a person with type 1 diabetes must use insulin to control the illness. Many other drugs are also used to help stabilize the moods of patients with bipolar disorder. Among these are divalproex sodium (brand name: Depakote), lamotrigine (Lamictal), carbamazepine (Tegretol), and oxcarbazepine (Trileptal).

13-8b ELECTROCONVULSIVE THERAPY

Electroconvulsive therapy (ECT) is a biological form of therapy for psychological disorders that was introduced by the Italian psychiatrist Ugo Cerletti in 1939. Cerletti had noted that some slaughterhouses used electric shock to render animals unconscious. The shocks also produced convulsions. Along with other European researchers of the period, Cerletti erroneously believed that convulsions were incompatible with schizophrenia and other major psychological disorders.

ECT was originally used for a variety of psychological disorders. Because of the advent of antipsychotic drugs, however, it is now used mainly for people with major depression who do not respond to antidepressants (Piccinni et al., 2009). People typically obtain one ECT treatment three times a week for up to 10 sessions. Electrodes are attached to the temples and an electrical current strong enough to produce a convulsion is induced. The shock causes unconsciousness, so the patient does not recall it. Nevertheless, patients are given a sedative (a drug that relieves nervousness or agitation or puts one to sleep) so that they are asleep during the treatment.

ECT is controversial for many reasons, such as the fact that many professionals are distressed by the thought of passing an electric shock through a patient's head and producing convulsions. There are also side effects, including memory problems. However, research suggests that for most people, cognitive impairment tends to be temporary (Rayner et al., 2009).

13-8c PSYCHOSURGERY

Psychosurgery is more controversial than ECT. The best-known modern technique, **prefrontal lobotomy**, has been used with people with severe disorders. In this method, a picklike instrument severs the nerve pathways that link the prefrontal lobes of the brain to the thalamus. It is intended to sever thought from emotion and enable severely disturbed patients to regain control. The method was pioneered by the Portuguese neurologist Antonio Egas Moniz and was brought to the United States in the 1930s. The theoretical rationale for the operation was vague and misguided, and Moniz's reports of success were exaggerated. Nevertheless, by 1950 prefrontal lobotomies had been performed on thousands of people in an effort to reduce violence and agitation. Anecdotal evidence of the method's unreliable outcomes is found in an ironic footnote to history: one of Dr. Moniz's patients returned to shoot him.

The prefrontal lobotomy also has side effects, including hyperactivity and distractibility, impaired learning ability, overeating, apathy and withdrawal, epileptic-type seizures, reduced creativity, and, occasionally, death. Because of these side effects, and because of the advent of antipsychotic drugs, the prefrontal lobotomy has been largely discontinued in the United States.

But new methods of psychosurgery are being undertaken with caution and have had mixed success in debilitating cases of OCD and phobias. They are used only when psychotherapy and drug therapy have failed to be of help, and when patients are made fully aware of success rates and potential risks (Carey, 2009). In *gamma knife surgery*, for example, physicians beam streams of radiation deep into the skull, destroying spots of tissue believed to be overactive in severe OCD (Tyagi et al., 2010). Other psychosurgery procedures are also undergoing small-scale trials (Bear et al., 2010). But there are some side effects, and the treatments are not always effective.

13-8d DOES BIOLOGICAL THERAPY WORK?

There are thus a number of biological approaches to treat psychological disorders. But what do we know about the effectiveness of biological therapies?

There is little question that drug therapy has helped many people with psychological disorders. For example,

TRUTH ONE OF DR. MONIZ'S "FAILURES" DID INDEED SHOOT HIM, LEAVING A BULLET LODGED IN HIS SPINE AND PARALYZING HIS LEGS.

antipsychotic drugs largely account for the reduced need for the use of restraint and supervision (e.g., padded cells, straitjackets, hospitalization, and so on) with people diagnosed with schizophrenia. Antipsychotic drugs have also enabled many former mental hospital residents to lead largely normal lives in the community, hold jobs, and maintain family lives. Most of the problems related to these drugs concern their side effects.

Comparisons of the effectiveness of psychotherapy and pharmacotherapy (medicine) for depression have yielded mixed results. Cognitive therapy provides coping skills that reduce the risk of recurrence of depression once treatment ends (Hollon & Shelton, 2001). Pim Cuijpers and his colleagues (2009) undertook a meta-analysis of randomly controlled experiments to attempt to answer the question of whether there was a difference in effectiveness of the treatment of depression when an antidepressant drug was added to a psychological treatment. They found that a treatment package that included psychotherapy and pharmacotherapy was more effective than psychological treatment alone, but it was not clear that the antidepressants offered much of an advantage.

In some cases, cognitive-behavior therapy appears to have helped relieve the positive symptoms of schizophrenia (Gregory, 2010; Wykes et al., 2008). Cognitive-behavior therapy is apparently more effective, however, when it is combined with medication in the treatment of schizophrenia (Chadwick & Lowe, 1990).

Many professionals are comfortable with the short-term use of antianxiety drugs in helping clients manage periods of unusual anxiety or tension. However, many people use antianxiety drugs routinely to dull the arousal stemming from anxiety-producing lifestyles or interpersonal problems. Rather than make the often painful decisions required to confront their problems, they take a pill.

Despite the controversies surrounding ECT, it helps many people who do not respond to antidepressant drugs (Piccinni et al., 2009). ECT may be a useful "last resort" when other treatment methods are of no avail.

In sum, drug therapy and perhaps ECT seem to be effective for some disorders that do not respond to psychotherapy alone. Yet common sense and research evidence suggest that psychotherapy is preferable for problems such as anxiety and mild depression. No chemical can show a person how to change an idea or solve an interpersonal problem.

psychosurgery
surgery intended to promote psychological changes or to relieve disordered behavior

prefrontal lobotomy
the severing or destruction of a section of the frontal lobe of the brain

STUDY TOOLS ▶ 13

Ready to study? In the book, you can:

- Review what you've read with Fill-Ins and Multiple Choice quizzes (below).
- Rip out Chapter Review card (in the back).

Or you can go online to CourseMate at www.cengagebrain.com for these resources:

- Complete Practices Quizzes to prepare for tests.
- Review Key Terms Flash Cards (online or print).
- Play games to master concepts.

FILL-INS

Answers can be found in the back of the book, starting on page 368.

1. Psychotherapy is a systematic interaction between a therapist and a client that applies _____ principles to influence clients' thoughts, feelings, and/or behavior.

2. Freud's method of psychoanalysis attempts to shed light on _____ conflicts that are presumed to lie at the roots of clients' problems.

3. _____-conditioning methods reinforce desired responses and extinguish undesired responses.

4. The chief psychoanalytic method is _____ association.

5. _____ therapies focus on clients' subjective, conscious experience.

6. _____-_____ therapy is a nondirective method that provides clients with an accepting atmosphere that enables them to overcome roadblocks to self-actualization.

7. _____ therapists focus on the beliefs, attitudes, and automatic thoughts that create and compound their clients' problems.

8. Behavior-therapy methods for reducing fears include systematic _____, in which a client is gradually exposed to more fear-arousing stimuli.

9. Albert Ellis's form of therapy confronts clients with the ways in which _____ beliefs contribute to anxiety and depression.

10. (Minor or Major?) tranquilizers are usually prescribed for people who complain of anxiety or tension.

1. Your therapist is accepting and warm. You are encouraged to feel good about yourself and to make choices that develop your potential. Your therapist uses a(n) _____ approach to treatment.
   a. psychoanalytic   c. client-centered
   b. ego analytic   d. behavioral

2. Hannah's therapist believes her anxiety is the result of unconscious impulses breaking through to the conscious level. Her therapist endorses the _____ perspective.
   a. behavioral   c. cognitive
   b. psychodynamic d. humanistic

3. A client avoids talking about their relationship with their father. The psychoanalyst asks them to talk about this relationship. The client becomes restless and claims, "There is nothing to tell." This is indicative of
   a. transference.   c. catharsis.
   b. resistance.   d. free association.

4. Which of the following examples best represents using operant conditioning to change behavior?
   a. Using electroconvulsive therapy for depression.
   b. Withdrawing attention whenever a child has a temper tantrum.
   c. Fostering insight by using examples.
   d. Giving your sister money to see a therapist.

5. _____ therapists focus on beliefs and attitudes that create and compound their clients' psychological problems.
   a. Cognitive   c. Learning
   b. Psychoanalytic d. Gestalt

6. Client-centered therapy is to _____ as Gestalt therapy is to _____.
   a. directive; nondirective
   b. nondirective; directive
   c. objective; subjective
   d. present; past

7. Family therapists usually see the "identified patient" as the
   a. cause of the family's problem.
   b. scapegoat for other problems in the family.
   c. key to the family system.
   d. black sheep of the family.

8. Social skills training is facilitated in a group setting because
   a. members of the group can practice the skills with one another.
   b. members can observe and learn from each other.
   c. members can give each other feedback.
   d. all of these

9. Dr. Schwiesow wants to use the best methods when treating her patients with depression. She should search out _____ practices.
   a. evidence-based c. researched
   b. treatment   d. experimental

10. You have advised a patient to discontinue use of antianxiety drugs. After two weeks, your patient calls to complain that his anxiety symptoms are now worse than before he started to take the drug. You tell the patient that his feelings are a predictable response to discontinuing antianxiety medication. In fact, he is experiencing what is called
   a. addiction.   c. rebound anxiety.
   b. tolerance.   d. relapse.

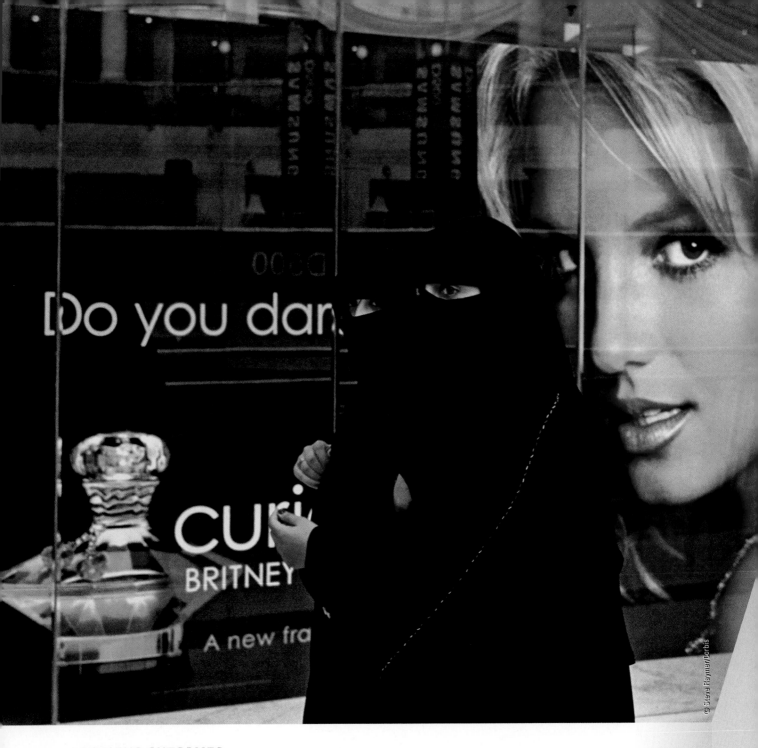

LEARNING OUTCOMES

14-1 Define *attitude* and discuss factors that shape attitudes

14-2 Discuss prejudice and discrimination

14-3 Discuss factors that contribute to interpersonal attraction and love

14-4 Define *social perception* and describe factors that influence it

14-5 Explain why people obey authority figures and conform to social norms

14-6 Discuss factors that contribute to aggression

14-7 Describe differences between the ways in which people behave as individuals and as members of a group

 STUDY TOOLS ▶ After you read the chapter, go to the Study Tools at the end of the chapter, page 351.

Social
PSYCHOLOGY

CHAPTER 14

Consider some news items from the early years of the 21st century:

- 2011: A suicide bomber drove a car laden with explosives up to a Coptic Christian church in Egypt as worshipers exited a New Year's mass, killing 21 people and wounding at least 80 more.

- 2005: Four suicide bombers blew themselves up aboard three London commuter trains and a bus, killing more than 50 people and wounding 700.

- 2001: And of course, on September 11, 2001, 19 suicide terrorists in the United States used fully fueled airplanes as bombs, flying them into the World Trade Center and the Pentagon, killing nearly 3,000 people.

Although you might think of suicide terrorism as a recent development, it dates back thousands of years (Kazim et al., 2008). The word *suicide* in the phrase "suicide bomber" leads people to turn to psychologists for understanding, with the idea that something must be psychologically wrong with these terrorists. But many social scientists assert that suicide terrorists have no telltale psychological profile (Consortium of Social Science Associations, 2003; Shi & Jia, 2011). Ariel Merari and his colleagues (2010) at the University of Tel Aviv interviewed and tested would-be suicide bombers—people who had been caught in the act and arrested. They found two groups among the would-be suicide terrorists: (1) dependent types with a tendency to follow leaders and public influences, and (2) emotionally unstable and impulsive types. Among both types, some were depressed but would not be diagnosed with major depressive disorder.

Because of the difficulty in identifying suicide terrorists, social psychologist Philip Zimbardo (2004) argues that we must look to the psychology of *social influence* to understand them. As we will see, social psychologist Stanley Milgram (1974), who conducted famous studies on obedience some 50 years ago, concluded, "Often, it is not so much the kind of person a man is, as the kind of situation in which he finds himself that determines how he will act."

> *People can be goaded by social influences into doing things that are not necessarily consistent with their personalities.*

TRUTH OR FICTION

WHAT DO YOU THINK? FOLKLORE, COMMON SENSE, OR NONSENSE? CIRCLE THE T FOR "TRUTH" OR THE F FOR "FICTION," AND CHECK THE ACCURACY OF YOUR ANSWERS AS YOU READ THROUGH THE CHAPTER.

T	F	PEOPLE VOTE THEIR CONSCIENCES.
T	F	WE APPRECIATE THINGS MORE WHEN WE HAVE TO WORK FOR THEM.
T	F	PEOPLE HAVE CONDEMNED BILLIONS OF OTHER PEOPLE WITHOUT EVER MEETING THEM OR LEARNING THEIR NAMES.
T	F	BEAUTY IS IN THE EYE OF THE BEHOLDER.
T	F	OPPOSITES ATTRACT.
T	F	WE TEND TO HOLD OTHERS RESPONSIBLE FOR THEIR MISDEEDS BUT TO SEE OURSELVES AS VICTIMS OF CIRCUMSTANCES WHEN WE MISBEHAVE.
T	F	MOST PEOPLE WILL TORTURE AN INNOCENT PERSON IF THEY ARE ORDERED TO DO SO.
T	F	SEEING IS BELIEVING.
T	F	NEARLY 40 PEOPLE STOOD BY AND DID NOTHING WHILE A WOMAN WAS BEING STABBED TO DEATH.

social psychology
the field of psychology that studies the nature and causes of people's thoughts and behavior in social situations

attitude
an enduring mental representation of a person, place, or thing that typically evokes an emotional response and related behavior

A–B problem
the issue of how well we can predict behavior on the basis of attitudes

Social psychology is the field of psychology that studies the nature and causes of behavior and mental processes in social situations. Social psychologists study the ways people can be goaded by social influences into doing things that are not necessarily consistent with their personalities. The social psychological topics we discuss in this chapter include attitudes, social perception, social influence, and group behavior. As we explore each of these, we will ask what they might offer to those of us who have difficulty imagining why people would surrender their own lives to take the lives of others. We begin with attitudes.

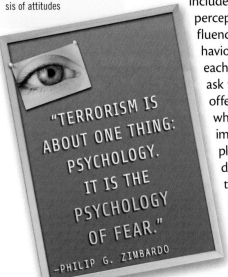

"TERRORISM IS ABOUT ONE THING: PSYCHOLOGY. IT IS THE PSYCHOLOGY OF FEAR."
—PHILIP G. ZIMBARDO

14-1 Attitudes

How do you feel about abortion, amnesty for illegal immigrants, and exhibiting the Ten Commandments in public buildings such as courthouses? These are hot-button topics because people have strong attitudes toward them. They each give rise to cognitive evaluations (such as approval or disapproval), feelings (such as liking, disliking, or something stronger), and behavioral tendencies (such as approach or avoidance). Although I asked you how you "feel," attitudes are not just feelings or emotions. Many psychologists view thinking—or judgment—as more basic. Feelings and behavior follow. **Attitudes** are enduring behavioral and cognitive tendencies that are expressed by evaluating particular people, places, or things with favor or disfavor (Bohner & Dickel, 2011).

Attitudes are largely learned. For example, if you learn that an Apple iPad is a wonderful "toy," you may feel the urge to buy one. Attitudes can foster love or hate. They can give rise to helping behavior or to mass destruction. They can lead to social conflict or to the resolution of conflicts. Attitudes can change, but not easily.

14-1a PREDICTING BEHAVIOR FROM ATTITUDES

Our definition of *attitude* implies that our behavior is consistent with our attitudes. But do people really do as they think? When we are free to do as we wish, the answer is often yes. But as indicated by the term **A–B problem**, there are exceptions. In fact, the links between attitudes (A) and behaviors (B) tend to be weak to moderate (Petty et al., 2009a, 2009b). People do not always vote "their consciences." Moreover, research reveals that people who say that drinking alcohol, smoking, and drunken driving are serious threats to their health do not necessarily curb these activities (Kiviniemi & Rothman, 2010).

Several factors affect the likelihood that we can predict behavior from attitudes:

1. *Specificity.* We can better predict specific behavior from specific attitudes than from global attitudes. For example, we can better predict church attendance by knowing people's attitudes toward church attendance than by knowing whether they are Christian.

Do people always vote their "conscience"? This A–B problem refers to the research finding that people do not always act in accord with their attitudes.

2. *Strength of attitudes.* Strong attitudes are more likely to determine behavior than weak attitudes (DeMarree et al., 2007). A person who believes that the nation's destiny depends on Democrats taking control of Congress is more likely to vote than a person who leans toward that party but does not believe that elections make much difference.

3. *Vested interest.* People are more likely to act on their attitudes when they have a vested interest in the outcome. People are more likely to vote for (or against) unionization of their workplace when they believe that their job security depends on it (Bohner & Dickel, 2011).

4. *Accessibility.* People are more likely to behave in accord with their attitudes when they are accessible—that is, when they are brought to mind (DeMarree et al., 2007). This is why politicians attempt to "get out the vote" by means of media blitzes just prior to an election. Attitudes with a strong emotional impact are more accessible, which is one reason that politicians strive to get their supporters "worked up" over issues.

FICTION ACTUALLY, PEOPLE DO NOT ALWAYS ACT IN ACCORD WITH THEIR CONSCIENCES. THE LINKS BETWEEN ATTITUDES (A) AND BEHAVIORS (B) TEND TO BE WEAK TO MODERATE.

14-1b ATTITUDE FORMATION

You were not born a Republican or a Democrat. You were not born a Christian, Jew, a Muslim, or a Hindu—although your parents may have practiced one of these religions when you came along. Political, religious, and other attitudes are learned or derived from cognitive processes. In this section, we describe some of the processes that result in acquiring attitudes.

Conditioning and Observational Learning

Conditioning may play a role in attitude formation (Walther et al., 2005). Laboratory experiments have shown that attitudes toward national groups can be influenced by associating them with positive words (such as *gift* or *happy*) or negative words (such as *ugly* or *failure*) (De Houwer et al., 2001). Parents often reward children for saying and doing things that agree with their own attitudes. Patriotism is encouraged by showing children approval when they sing the national anthem or wave the flag.

Attitudes formed through direct experience may be stronger and easier to recall, but we also acquire attitudes by observing, listening to, or reading the works of other people. The approval or disapproval of peers leads adolescents to prefer short or long hair, baggy jeans, or preppy sweaters. How do the things you read in newspapers or hear on the radio influence your attitudes?

Cognitive Appraisal

Nevertheless, attitude formation is not fully mechanical. People are also motivated to understand the environment so that they can make predictions and exercise some control over it (Bizer et al., 2004). People also sometimes form or change attitudes on the basis of new information (Petty et al., 2009a, 2009b). For example, we may believe that a car is more reliable than we had thought if a survey by *Consumer Reports* finds that it has an excellent repair record. Even so, initial attitudes act as *cognitive anchors* (Bohner & Dickel, 2011). We often judge new ideas in terms of how much they deviate from our existing attitudes. Accepting larger deviations requires more information processing—that is, more intellectual work (Petty et al., 2009a, 2009b). For this reason, perhaps, great deviations—such as changes from liberal to conservative attitudes, or vice versa—are apt to be resisted.

elaboration likelihood model the view that persuasive messages are evaluated (elaborated) on the basis of central and peripheral cues

14-1c CHANGING ATTITUDES THROUGH PERSUASION

Let advertisers spend the same amount of money improving their product that they do on advertising and they wouldn't have to advertise it.

—WILL ROGERS

Will Rogers's comment sounds on the mark, but he was probably wrong. It does little good to have a wonderful product if it remains a secret.

The **elaboration likelihood model** describes the ways in which people respond to persuasive messages (Bohner & Dickel, 2011). Consider two routes to persuading others to change attitudes. The *central route* inspires thoughtful consideration of arguments and evidence. The *peripheral route* associates objects with positive or negative cues. When politicians avow, "This bill is supported by liberals (or conservatives)," they are seeking predictable, knee-jerk reactions rather than careful consideration of a bill's merits. Other cues are rewards (such as a smile or a hug), punishments (such as parental disapproval), and such factors as the trustworthiness and attractiveness of the communicator.

Advertisements, which are a form of persuasive communication, also rely on central and peripheral routes. Some ads focus on the quality of the product (central route). Others attempt to associate the product with appealing images (peripheral route). For example, ads for Total cereal, which highlight its nutritional benefits, provide information about the quality of the product, but ads that show football players heading for Disney World or choosing a brand of beer offer no information about the product itself.

In this section we look at one central factor in persuasion—the nature of the message—and three peripheral factors: the messenger, the context of the message, and the audience.

The Persuasive Message

How do we respond when TV commercials are repeated until we have memorized the dimples on the actors' faces? Research suggests that familiarity breeds content, not contempt (Bohner & Dickel, 2011; Förster, 2009). It appears that repeated exposure to people and things as diverse as political candidates, photos of college students, and abstract art enhances their appeal (Banaji & Heiphetz, 2008; Reis et al., 2011).

When trying to persuade someone, is it helpful or self-defeating to alert them to the arguments presented by the opposition? In two-sided arguments, the communicator recounts the arguments of the opposition in an effort to refute them. In research concerning a mock trial, college undergraduates were presented with two-sided arguments—those of the prosecution and those of the defendant (McKenzie et al., 2002). When one argument was weak, the college "jurors" expressed more confidence in their decision than when they did not hear the other side at all. Theologians and politicians sometimes forewarn their followers about the arguments of the opposition and then refute each one. Forewarning creates a kind of psychological immunity to them (Eisend, 2007; Taber et al., 2009).

It would be nice to think that people are too sophisticated to be persuaded by emotional factors in attitude formation, but they usually aren't (DeSteno et al., 2004). Consider the **fear appeal**: Women who are warned of the dire risk they run if they fail to be screened for breast cancer are more

likely to obtain mammograms than women who are informed of the *benefits* of mammography (Ruiter et al., 2001). Interestingly, although sun tanning has been shown to increase the likelihood of skin cancer, warnings against sun tanning were shown to be more effective when students were warned of risks to their *appearance* (e.g., premature aging, wrinkling, and scarring of the skin) than when the warning dealt with the risk to their health. Fear appeals are most effective when the audience believes that the risks are serious—as in causing wrinkles!—and that the audience members can change their behavior to avert the risks—as in preventing cancer or wrinkling (de Hoog et al., 2007; Thompson et al., 2009).

Audiences also tend to believe arguments that appear to run counter to the vested interests of the communicator (Bohner & Dickel, 2011). If the president of Ford or General Motors said that Toyotas and Hondas were superior, you can bet that we would prick up our ears.

The Persuasive Communicator

Would you go to a doctor who admitted that he or she was behind the times? Research shows that persuasive communicators are characterized by expertise, trustworthiness, attractiveness, or similarity to their audiences (Petty et al., 2009a, 2009b). Because of the adoration of their fans, sports superstars such as Peyton Manning are the most valuable endorsers.

People find it painful when they are confronted with information that counters their own views (Garrett, 2009). Therefore, they often show **selective avoidance** and **selective exposure** (Bryant & Davies, 2006). That is, they switch channels when the news coverage runs counter to their own attitudes. They also seek communicators whose outlook coincides with their own. Whom would you prefer to listen to: Rush Limbaugh and Sean Hannity or Chris Matthews and Rachel Maddow?

We often selectively expose ourselves to opinions with which we agree—and vice versa.

Rubberball/Mike Kemp/Jupiterimages

The Context of the Message

You are too shrewd to let someone persuade you by buttering you up, but perhaps someone you know would be influenced by a sip of wine, a bite of cheese, and a sincere compliment. Aspects of the immediate environment, such as music, also increase the likelihood of persuasion. When we are in a good mood, we apparently are less likely to evaluate the situation carefully (Briñol et al., 2007).

It is also counterproductive to call your friends foolish when they differ with you—even though their ideas are bound to be "foolish" if they do not agree with yours. Agreement and praise are more effective ways to encourage others to embrace your views.

The Persuaded Audience

Why can some people say no to salespeople? Why do others enrich the lives of every door-to-door salesperson? It may be that people with high self-esteem and low social anxiety are more likely to resist social pressure (Ellickson et al., 2001).

A classic study by Schwartz and Gottman (1976) describes the cognitive nature of the social anxiety that can make it difficult to refuse requests. They found that people who comply with unreasonable requests are more apt to report thoughts such as:

- "I was worried about what the other person would think of me if I refused."
- "It is better to help others than to be self-centered."
- "The other person might be hurt or insulted if I refused."

People who refuse unreasonable requests reported thoughts like these:

- "It doesn't matter what the other person thinks of me."
- "I am perfectly free to say no."
- "This request is unreasonable."

14-1d CHANGING ATTITUDES AND BEHAVIOR BY MEANS OF COGNITIVE DISSONANCE

According to **cognitive-dissonance theory**, people are thinking creatures who seek consistency in their behaviors and their attitudes—that is, their views of the world. People must apparently mentally represent the world accurately to predict and control events. Consistency in beliefs, attitudes, and behavior helps make the

"The brain within its groove
Runs evenly and true . . ."
—EMILY DICKINSON

world seem like a predictable place. Therefore, if we find ourselves in the uncomfortable spot where two cherished ideas conflict, we are motivated to reduce the discrepancy.

In the first and still one of the best-known studies on cognitive dissonance, one group of participants received $1 (worth $5 to $10 today) for telling someone else that a boring task was interesting (Festinger & Carlsmith, 1959). Members of a second group received $20 (worth $100 to $200 today) to describe the chore positively. Both groups were paid to engage in **attitude-discrepant behavior**—that is, behavior that ran counter to what they actually thought. After presenting their fake enthusiasm for the boring task, the participants were asked to rate their own liking for it. Ironically, those who were paid *less* rated the task as actually more interesting than their better-paid colleagues reported. Similarly, being compelled by the law to recycle can lead to people's supporting recycling as opposed to throwing out all trash and garbage in a bundle.

Learning theorists might predict that the more we are reinforced for doing something (given more money, for example), the more we should like it (not find the task quite as boring, that is). But that is not what happened here. Cognitive-dissonance theorists rightly predicted that because the ideas (cognitions) of (a) "I was paid very little" and (b) "I told someone that this assignment was interesting" are dissonant, people will tend to engage in **effort justification**. The discomfort of cognitive

cognitive-dissonance theory the view that we are motivated to make our cognitions or beliefs consistent with each other and with our behavior

attitude-discrepant behavior behavior inconsistent with an attitude that may have the effect of modifying an attitude

effort justification in cognitive-dissonance theory, the tendency to seek justification (acceptable reasons) for strenuous efforts

TRUTH WE DO TEND TO APPRECIATE THINGS MORE WHEN WE HAVE TO WORK FOR THEM (STONE & FERNANDEZ, 2008). THIS IS AN EXAMPLE OF EFFORT JUSTIFICATION.

prejudice

an attitude toward a group that leads people to evaluate members of that group negatively

discrimination

hostile behavior that results is directed against groups toward whom one is prejudiced

stereotyping

erroneous assumptions that all members of a group share the same traits or characteristics

dissonance motivates people to explain their behavior to themselves in such a way that unpleasant undertakings seem worth it. Participants who were paid only $1 may have justified their lie by concluding that they may not have been lying in the first place.

14-2 Prejudice and Discrimination

Prejudice is an attitude toward a group that leads people to evaluate members of that group negatively—even though they have never met them. On a cognitive level, prejudice is linked to expectations that members of the target group will behave poorly, say, in the workplace, or engage in criminal behavior or terrorism. On an emotional level, prejudice is associated with negative feelings such as fear, dislike, or hatred. Prejudice is the most troubling kind of attitude.

In behavioral terms, prejudice is connected with avoidance, aggression, and discrimination. **Discrimination** refers to behavior that results from prejudice. Many groups in the United States have

TRUTH IT IS TRUE THAT PEOPLE HAVE CONDEMNED BILLIONS OF OTHER PEOPLE WITHOUT EVER MEETING THEM OR LEARNING THEIR NAMES. SUCH CONDEMNATION OCCURS BECAUSE OF PREJUDICE AGAINST GROUPS OF PEOPLE. IT IS CONNECTED WITH THE GENOCIDE OF MILLIONS OF PEOPLE.

experienced discrimination—women, gays and lesbians, older people, and ethnic groups such as African Americans, Asian Americans, Latin Americans, Irish Americans, Jewish Americans, and Native Americans. Discrimination takes many forms, including denial of access to jobs, the voting booth, and housing.

14-2a STEREOTYPING

Prejudice involves **stereotyping**—that is, erroneous assumptions that all members of a group share the same traits or characteristics. Have people you know characterized African Americans as superstitious and musical? What about gays and lesbians? Are they unfit for military service? Stereotypes may lead people to view members of groups in a biased fashion.

On the other hand, some stereotypes are positive, such as stereotypes about physically attractive people. By and large, we assume that "good things come in pretty packages." Attractive children and adults are judged and treated more positively than their unattractive peers (Langlois et al., 2000). We expect attractive people to be poised, sociable, popular, intelligent, mentally healthy, fulfilled, persuasive, and successful in their jobs and marriages (Principe & Langlois, 2011). Attractive people are also more likely to be judged innocent of crimes in mock jury experiments, and when they are found guilty, they are given less severe sentences (Sporer & Goodman-Delahunty, 2009).

14-2b SOURCES OF PREJUDICE

The sources of prejudice are many and varied:

1. *Dissimilarity.* We are apt to like people who share our attitudes (Cunningham, 2008). People of different religions and races often have different backgrounds, however, giving rise to dissimilar attitudes. Even when people of different races share important values, people may assume that they do not.

2. *Social conflict.* There is often social and economic conflict between people of different races and religions (Reid, 2008).

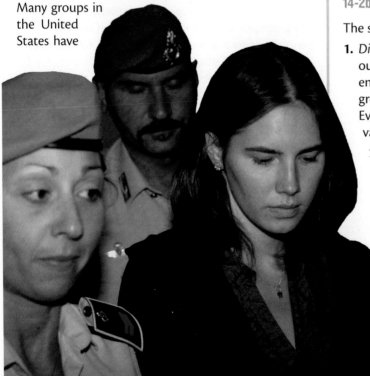

Here we see convicted murderer Amanda Knox being escorted to a hearing at which her conviction was overturned. Do stereotypes of attractive people lead us to assume that they are less likely to resort to deviant behavior to reach their goals?

OliScarff/Getty Images

3. *Social learning.* Children acquire some attitudes from other people, especially their parents. Children tend to imitate their parents, and parents reinforce their children for doing so (Durlez, 2011). In this way prejudices can be transmitted from generation to generation.

4. *Information processing.* Prejudices act as cognitive filters through which we view the social world. We tend to think of people as "familiar" or "foreign," or "good" or "bad." Our feelings and reactions toward others may be biased by these perceptions (Crisp & Nicel, 2004).

5. *Social categorization.* We also tend to divide our social world into "us" and "them." People usually view those who belong to their own groups—the "in-group"—more favorably than those who do not—the "out-group" (Park & Judd, 2005). Isolation from the out-group makes it easier to maintain our stereotypes.

FICTION 👉 ALTHOUGH THERE MAY BE INDIVIDUAL PREFERENCES, IT DOES NOT SEEM THAT STANDARDS FOR BEAUTY ARE SO FLEXIBLE THAT THEY ARE FULLY "IN THE EYE OF THE BEHOLDER."

14-3 Attraction and Love

Attitudes of liking and loving can lead to important, lasting relationships. They are the flip side of the coin of prejudice—positive attitudes that are associated with interpersonal **attraction** rather than avoidance. Among the factors contributing to attraction are physical appearance, similarity, and reciprocity.

14-3a PHYSICAL APPEARANCE

Physical appearance is a key factor in attraction and in the consideration of romantic partners (Sprecher et al., 2008). What determines physical allure? Are our standards subjective—that is, "in the eye of the beholder"? Or is there general agreement on what is appealing?

Many standards for beauty appear to be cross-cultural (Buss, 2009; Singh & Singh, 2011). For example, a study of people in England and Japan found that both British and Japanese men consider women with large eyes, high cheekbones, and narrow jaws to be most attractive (Perrett et al., 1994). In

his research, Perrett created computer composites of the faces of 60 women and, as shown in part A of Figure 14.1, of the 15 women who were rated the most attractive. He then used computer enhancement to exaggerate the differences between the composite of the 60 and the composite of the 15 most attractive women. He arrived at the image shown in part B of Figure 14.1.

Part B, which shows higher cheekbones and a narrower jaw than Part A, was rated as the most attractive image. Similar results were found for the image of a Japanese woman. Works of art suggest that the ancient Greeks and Egyptians favored similar facial features.

An examination of the Internet dating profiles of 5,810 Yahoo personal ads shows that "thin" is more "in" in the expressed preferences for partners of European Americans and males (Glasser et al., 2009). European American males are more likely than African American

attraction
in social psychology, an attitude of liking or disliking (negative attraction)

FIGURE 14.1
What Features Contribute to Facial Attractiveness?

In both England and Japan, features such as large eyes, high cheekbones, and narrow jaws contribute to perceptions of the attractiveness of women. Part A shows a composite of the faces of 15 women rated as the most attractive of a group of 60. Part B is a composite in which the features of these 15 women are exaggerated—that is, developed further in the direction that separates them from the average of the entire 60.

A.

B.

When It Comes To Sex, Red May Mean "Go"

When you go to buy a box of Valentine's Day candy, what color will the box be? Green? Blue? The answer, of course, is red. What is the most popular color of women's lipstick? Yellow? Brown? Again, the answer is red (Elliot et al., 2007). Red has been the most popular lipstick color since the hot days that saw the construction of the pyramids in ancient Egypt (Elliot & Niesta, 2008). At a traffic light, the color red means stop. But when it comes to sexual attraction, the color red is more likely to mean go.

Why is the color red associated with feelings of attraction? The link between red and physical attraction may be rooted in our biological heritage. Many female primates, including baboons, chimpanzees, gorillas, and rhesus monkeys, show reddened genital regions when they are nearing ovulation—the time of the month when they are fertile (Barelli et al., 2008). Reddening of the skin is caused by elevated estrogen levels, which increase the blood flow under the skin. Male primates are more likely to attempt sexual relations with females who display red (Waitt et al., 2006). Women's estrogen levels are also elevated near ovulation, slightly reddening the skin (Lynn et al., 2007). For men, as with other male primates, the reddening of a woman's skin at the time of ovulation may be a sexual signal.

Experiments find that men rate the same woman as more attractive when her photograph is shown against a red background as opposed to other colors (Elliot & Niesta, 2008). Women also rate photos of men as more attractive when the photos are bordered in red or the men are wearing red clothing (Eliot et al., 2010). The male sex hormone testosterone is involved in oxygenating blood and increasing its flow to the skin—giving off a reddish hue—and to the genitals, leading to sexual excitement. Red coloration can signal good health in men because high blood levels of oxygen are maintained only by organisms in good health (Elliot et al., 2010).

Why did they deck her out in red? Cultural conditioning and the human biological heritage provide two good answers.

Fancy Photography/Veer

and Latinos to want to date slender and buff women. African American and Latino men are significantly more likely to be interested in women with large or thick bodies.

14-3b GENDER DIFFERENCES IN SELECTION OF A ROMANTIC PARTNER

Physical appearance may be a major factor in the selection of a romantic partner, but cross-cultural studies on mate selection find that women tend to place greater emphasis on traits such as professional status, consideration, dependability, kindness, and fondness for children. Men tend to place relatively greater emphasis on physical allure, cooking ability, even thrift (Buss, 2011).

Susan Sprecher and her colleagues (1994) surveyed more than 13,000 Americans, attempting to represent the ethnic diversity we find in the United States. They found that women were more willing than men to marry someone who was not good-looking, but less willing to marry someone who did not hold a steady job.

Why do males tend to place relatively more emphasis than females on physical appearance in mate selection?

Why do females tend to place relatively more emphasis on personal factors such as financial status and reliability? Evolutionary psychologists believe that evolutionary forces favor the survival of women who desire status in their mates and men who emphasize physical allure because these preferences provide reproductive advantages. According to the "parental investment model," a woman's appeal is more strongly connected with her age and health, both of which are markers of reproductive capacity. The value of men as reproducers, however, is more intertwined with factors that contribute to a stable environment for child rearing—such as social standing and reliability (Schmitt, 2003).

14-3c THE ATTRACTION–SIMILARITY HYPOTHESIS

The *attraction–similarity hypothesis* holds that people tend to develop romantic relationships with people who are similar to themselves in physical attractiveness and other traits. Apparently, opposites do *not* attract. Researchers have found that our marital and sex partners tend to be similar to us in race and ethnicity, age, level of education, and religion (Montoya et al., 2008; van Straaten et al., 2009). Note that nearly 95% of marriages and 80% to 90% of cohabiting unions were be-

ACTUALLY, IT IS NOT TRUE THAT "OPPOSITES ATTRACT." PEOPLE WHO SHARE ATTITUDES ARE MORE LIKELY TO BE ATTRACTED TO ONE ANOTHER.

tween partners of the same race at the time of the 2010 U.S. census (U.S. Census Bureau, 2011). Even so, highly educated people are more likely than poorly educated people to marry people of other races (Batson et al., 2006).

Another reason people tend to have partners from the same background is *propinquity*. Marriages are made in the neighborhood and not in heaven (Sprecher & Felmlee, 2008). We tend to live among people who are similar to us in background, and we therefore come into contact with them more often.

Reciprocity is another powerful determinant of attraction (Fehr, 2008). We tend to be more open, warm, and helpful when we are interacting with people who seem to like us (Sprecher et al., 2008).

14-3d LOVE

Love is a strong positive emotion. We had a look at love between children and parents in Chapter 9. Here we will focus on that most dramatic, heated, passionate love we label *romantic love*.

There are a number of theories about romantic love. One theory is Robert Sternberg's (1988) **triangular model of love**, which can be thought of as a love triangle. This love triangle does not refer to two men wooing the same woman. It refers to Sternberg's view that love involves three components: intimacy, passion, and commitment (see Figure 14.2).

Intimacy refers to a couple's closeness, to their mutual concern and sharing of feelings and resources. **Passion** means romance and sexual feelings. **Commitment** means deciding to enhance and maintain the relation-

triangular model of love
Sternberg's view that love involves combinations of three components: intimacy, passion, and commitment

intimacy
close acquaintance and familiarity; a characteristic of a relationship in which partners share their innermost feelings

passion
strong romantic and sexual feelings

commitment
the decision to maintain a relationship

FIGURE 14.2 | The Triangular Model of Love

According to this model, love has three components: intimacy, passion, and commitment. The ideal of consummate love consists of romantic love plus commitment.

Source: From *The Psychology of Love* by R. J. Sternberg. Copyright 1988. Yale University Press. Reprinted by permission of the publisher.

Liking = Intimacy alone (true friendships without passion or long-term commitment)

Intimacy

Romantic love = Intimacy + Passion (lovers physically and emotionally attracted to each other but without commitment, as in a summer romance)

Consummate love = Intimacy + Passion + Commitment (a complete love consisting of all three components—an ideal difficult to attain)

Companionate love = Intimacy + Commitment (long-term committed friendship such as a marriage in which the passion has faded)

Passion

Commitment

Infatuation = Passion alone (passionate, obsessive love at first sight without intimacy or commitment)

Fatuous love = Passion + Commitment (commitment based on passion but without time for intimacy to develop—shallow relationship such as a whirlwind courtship)

Empty love = Commitment alone (commitment to remain together without intimacy or passion)

consummate love
the ideal form of love within Sternberg's model, which combines passion, intimacy, and commitment

romantic love
an intense, positive emotion that involves sexual attraction, feelings of caring, and the belief that one is in love

social perception
a subfield of social psychology that studies the ways in which we form and modify impressions of others

primacy effect
the tendency to evaluate others in terms of first impressions

recency effect
the tendency to evaluate others in terms of the most recent impression

attribution
a belief concerning why people behave in a certain way

dispositional attribution
an assumption that a person's behavior is determined by internal causes such as personal traits

situational attribution
an assumption that a person's behavior is determined by external circumstances such as the social pressure found in a situation

ship. Passion is most crucial in short-term relationships. Intimacy and commitment are more important in enduring relationships. The ideal form of love—**consummate love**—combines all three. Consummate love is made up of romantic love plus commitment.

Romantic love, in Sternberg's scheme, is characterized by passion and intimacy. Passion involves fascination (preoccupation with the loved one), sexual craving, and the desire for exclusiveness (Berscheid, 2009). Intimacy involves closeness and caring—championing the interests of the loved one, even if it entails sacrificing one's own. People are cognitively biased toward evaluating their partners positively (Loving & Agnew, 2001). That is, we idealize those we love.

 14-4 Social Perception

An important area of social psychology concerns the ways in which we perceive other people—for example, the importance of the first impressions they make on us. Next we explore some factors that contribute to **social perception**: the primacy and recency effects and attribution theory.

14-4a PRIMACY AND RECENCY EFFECTS

Why do you wear a suit to a job interview? Why do defense attorneys make sure that their clients dress neatly and get their hair cut before they are seen by the jury? Do first impressions really matter? Apparently they do—a great deal.

Whether we are talking about the business or social worlds, or even the relationship between a therapist and a client, first impressions are important (Bidell et al., 2002). First impressions are an example of the **primacy effect**—the tendency to evaluate others in terms of first impressions.

Participants in a classic experiment on the primacy effect read different stories about "Jim" (Luchins, 1957). The stories consisted of one or two paragraphs. The one-paragraph stories portrayed Jim as either friendly or unfriendly. These paragraphs were also used in the two-paragraph stories, but in this case the paragraphs were read in the reverse order. Of those reading only the "friendly" paragraph, 95% rated Jim as friendly. Of those who read just the "unfriendly" paragraph, 3% rated him as friendly. Seventy-eight percent of those who read two-paragraph stories in the "friendly-unfriendly" order labeled Jim as friendly. When participants read the paragraphs in the reverse order, only 18% rated Jim as friendly.

How can we encourage people to pay more attention to impressions occurring after the first encounter? Abraham Luchins accomplished this by allowing time to pass between the presentations of the two paragraphs. In this way, fading memories allowed more recent information to take precedence. The tendency to respond to the most freshly presented piece of information is known as the **recency effect.** Luchins also found a second way to counter first impressions: He simply asked participants to avoid making snap judgments and to weigh all the evidence.

14-4b ATTRIBUTION THEORY

An **attribution** is an assumption or belief about why people behave in a certain way. When you assume that one child is mistreating another child because she is "mean," you are making an attribution. This section focuses on *attribution theory*, or the processes by which people draw conclusions about the factors that influence one another's behavior. Attribution theory is important because attributions lead us to perceive others either as purposeful actors or as victims of circumstances.

Dispositional and Situational Attributions

Social psychologists describe two types of attributions. **Dispositional attributions** ascribe a person's behavior to internal factors such as personality traits and free will. If you assume that one child is mistreating another because she is "mean," you are making a dispositional attribution. **Situational attributions** attribute a person's actions to external factors such as circumstances, social influence, or socialization. If you assume that one child is mistreating the other because her parents have given her certain attitudes toward the other child, you are making a situational attribution.

STUDY TOOLS ▶ 14

Ready to study? In the book, you can:

- ◯ Review what you've read with Fill-Ins and Multiple Choice quizzes (below).
- ◯ Rip out Chapter Review card (in the back).

Or you can go online to CourseMate at www.cengagebrain.com for these resources:

- ◯ Complete Practices Quizzes to prepare for tests.
- ◯ Review Key Terms Flash Cards (online or print).
- ◯ Play games to master concepts.

FILL-INS

Answers can be found in the back of the book, starting on page 368.

1. Attitudes are acquired through conditioning, observational learning, and _____ appraisal.

2. According to cognitive-_____ theory, we are motivated to make our cognitions consistent with one another and with our behavior.

3. One factor in prejudice is social _____, or the tendency to divide the world into us and them.

4. According to the _____-_____ hypothesis, we tend to be attracted to people who are similar to ourselves.

5. According to the triangular model of love, love can include combinations of intimacy, _____, and commitment.

6. The tendency to perceive others in terms of first impressions is an example of the _____ effect.

7. The following factors contribute to obedience: socialization, lack of _____ comparison, perception of experimenters as legitimate authority figures, the foot-in-the-door technique, and inaccessibility of values.

8. Social _____ refers to the enhancement of performance that results from the presence of others.

9. Members of a group may experience _____, which is a state of reduced self-awareness and lowered concern for social evaluation.

10. Kitty Genovese's death has been attributed to the _____ effect.

1. The A–B problem focuses on
   a. activities we do and behaviors we avoid.
   b. attitudes and beliefs.
   c. the relationship between achievement and behavior.
   d. consistency between our attitudes and behavior.

2. Mary prefers living in the country away from the noise and crowds of the city, but her sister Denise prefers the excitement and pace of city life. They differ in _____.
   a. avoidance
   b. attitude
   c. polarization
   d. deindividuation

3. One major reason that groups tend to take greater risks than their members would take as individuals is
   a. diffusion of responsibility.
   b. the reciprocity norm.
   c. group intelligence.
   d. all of these.

4. The _____ route is to facts and research results as the _____ route is to status and prestige.
   a. peripheral; central
   b. central; peripheral
   c. secondary; primary
   d. primary; secondary

5. The "Save the World by Praying" association predicted the world would end on Nov. 1, 1999. When the world did not end on that day their group made a statement that supported the theory of cognitive dissonance. Which of the statements below would fit that description?
   a. "We were wrong, prayer does not help."
   b. "God did not listen to us."
   c. "Our praying must have saved the world."
   d. "We are confused about all this."

6. The first time you met your fiancée you fell down and spilled a glass of wine on her dress. You obviously didn't make a very good first impression. However, it was several months later before you saw her again. Your second meeting went much better and it was almost as if your first encounter never happened. This change in her perception of you is probably due to the
   a. primary effect.
   b. recency effect.
   c. repression.
   d. discrimination.

7. Yevhen is standing in line in school. While he isn't looking, another boy steps on his toe. Yevhen says to himself: "He must have stepped on my toe because it's so crowded in here and somebody else pushed this guy; it was probably an accident." Yevhen is making a _____ attribution.
   a. dispositional
   b. situational
   c. fundamental
   d. motivational

8. If there had been two teachers acting together rather than one in Milgram's experiment, and the teachers could discuss the situation before complying with the demands of the experimenter, this change in procedure would probably have
   a. decreased the level of obedience.
   b. had no affect on obedience.
   c. increased the level of obedience.
   d. none of these

9. The process by which the presence of others improves our performance is known as
   a. reciprocation.
   b. social facilitation.
   c. social lubrication.
   d. reciprocity.

10. The self-serving bias is the tendency to
    a. repeat ourselves when we think we're right.
    b. take care of our own needs first, and worry about others later.
    c. credit our successes to internal, dispositional factors and our failures to situational influences.
    d. describe our successes in greater detail than our failures.

4LTR Press solutions are designed for today's learners through the continuous feedback of students like you. Tell us what you think about PSYCH3 and help us improve the learning experience for future students.

YOUR FEEDBACK MATTERS.

© PhotoSpin

Pixland/Jupiterimages

LEARNING OUTCOMES

APP-1 Explain how statistics are used in psychology

APP-2 Calculate values using descriptive statistics

APP-3 Describe and apply the normal curve

APP-4 Calculate values using the correlation coefficient

APP-5 Explain the logic behind inferential statistics

App-1 Statistics

Imagine that aliens from outer space arrive outside Madison Square Garden in New York City. Their goal this dark winter evening is to learn all they can about planet Earth. They are drawn inside the Garden by lights, shouts, and warmth. The spotlighting inside rivets their attention to a wood-floored arena where the New York Big Apples are hosting the California Quakes in a briskly contested basketball game.

Our visitors use their sophisticated instruments to take measurements of the players. Some statistics are sent back to their home planet: It appears that (1) 100% of Earthlings are male and (2) the height of Earthlings ranges from 6'1" to 7'2".

These measurements are called **statistics**. Statistics is the name given to the science concerned with obtaining and organizing numerical information or measurements. Our visitors have sent home statistics about the gender and size of humans that are at once accurate and misleading. Although they accurately measured the basketball players, their small sample of Earth's population was, shall we say, distorted.

A **population** is a complete group of people, other animals, or measures from which a sample is drawn. For example, all people on Earth could be defined as the population of interest. So could all women, or all women in the United States. A **sample** is a group of measures drawn from a population. Fortunately for us Earthlings, about half of the world's population is female. And the *range* of heights observed by the aliens, of 6'1" to 7'2", is both restricted and too high—much too high. People vary in height by more than 1 foot and 1 inch. And our **average** height is not between 6'1" and 7'2"; rather, it is a number of inches below.

Psychologists, like our imagined visitors, are concerned with measuring human as well as animal characteristics and traits—not just physical characteristics as height, but also psychological traits such as intelligence, aggressiveness, and depression. By observing the *central tendencies* (averages) and variations in measurement

> To what degree do you think the people in your school represent the population of the United States? North America? The world?

TRUTH OR FICTION

WHAT DO YOU THINK? FOLKLORE, COMMON SENSE, OR NONSENSE? CIRCLE THE T FOR "TRUTH" OR THE F FOR "FICTION," AND CHECK THE ACCURACY OF YOUR ANSWERS AS YOU READ THROUGH THE CHAPTER.

T	F	PROFESSIONAL BASKETBALL PLAYERS COULD BE SAID TO BE ABNORMAL.
T	F	BEING A "10" IS NOT ALWAYS A GOOD THING.
T	F	YOU SHOULD NOT ASSUME THAT YOU CAN WALK ACROSS A RIVER WITH AN AVERAGE DEPTH OF 4 FEET.
T	F	ADDING PEOPLE'S INCOMES AND THEN DIVIDING THEM BY THE NUMBER OF PEOPLE CAN BE AN AWFUL WAY OF SHOWING THE AVERAGE INCOME.
T	F	PSYCHOLOGISTS EXPRESS YOUR IQ SCORE IN TERMS OF HOW DEVIANT YOU ARE.
T	F	AN IQ SCORE OF 130 IS MORE IMPRESSIVE THAN AN SAT SCORE OF 500.

statistics

numerical facts assembled in such a manner that they provide useful information about measures or scores (from the Latin *status*, meaning "standing" or "position")

population

a complete group from which a sample is selected

sample

part of a population

average

the central tendency of a group of measures, expressed either as the mean, median, or mode of a distribution

descriptive statistics

the branch of statistics that is concerned with providing descriptive information about a distribution of scores

TRUTH BASKETBALL PLAYERS COULD BE SAID TO BE ABNORMAL IN THE SENSE THAT THEY ARE TALLER, STRONGER, AND MORE AGILE THAN THE REST OF US.

from person to person, psychologists can say that one person is average or above average in intelligence, or that someone else is less anxious than, say, 60% of the population. But psychologists, unlike our aliens, attempt to select a sample that accurately represents the entire population. Professional basketball players do not represent the entire human species.

In this appendix, we survey some statistical methods used by psychologists to draw conclusions about the measurements they take. First we discuss *descriptive statistics* and learn what types of statements we can make about height and other human traits. Then we discuss the *normal curve* and learn why basketball players are abnormal— at least in terms of height. We explain *correlation coefficients* and provide you with some less-than-shocking news: As a group, students who study obtain higher grades than students who do not study. Finally, we have a look at *inferential statistics* and see why basketball players are in fact *statistically significantly* taller than the general population.

Does this basketball player represent all earthlings? In what ways might he do so, and in what ways might he differ?

App-2 Descriptive Statistics

Being told that someone is a "10" may sound great at first. However, it is not very descriptive unless you know something about how the scores on the scale are distributed and how frequently one finds a 10. Fortunately— for 10s, if not for the rest of us—one usually means that the person is a 10 on a scale of from 1 to 10, and that 10 is the highest score. If this is not sufficient, one will also be told that 10s are few and far between—unusual statistical events.

The idea of the scale from 1 to 10 may not be very scientific, but it does suggest something about descriptive statistics. **Descriptive statistics** is the branch of statistics that provides information about distributions of scores. We can use descriptive statistics to clarify our understanding of a distribution of scores such as heights, test grades, IQs, or even increases or decreases in measures of aggressive behavior following the drinking of alcohol. For example, descriptive statistics can help us determine measures of central tendency (averages) and to determine how much fluctuation or variability there is in the scores. Being a 10 loses much of its charm if the average score is an 11. Being a 10 is more remarkable in a distribution whose scores range from 1 to 10 than it is in a distribution whose scores range from 9 to 11.

TRUTH BEING A "10" IS NOT ALWAYS A GOOD THING BECAUSE A SCALE CAN VARY, SAY, FROM 0 TO 100, IN WHICH CASE A SCORE OF 10 WOULD PLACE ONE NEARER TO THE BOTTOM OF THE SCALE, MAKING A SCORE OF 50 THE CENTER POINT OF THE SCALE.

Let's now consider some of the concerns of descriptive statistics: the frequency distribution, measures of central tendency (types of averages), and measures of variability.

Being a 10 may not be such a good thing if the average score is 11.

TABLE A.1 | Roster of Quakes Versus Big Apples at New York

A glance at the rosters for a recent basketball game in which the New York Big Apples "entertained" the California Quakes shows that the heights of the team members, combined, ranged from 6'1" to 7'2". Do the heights of the team members represent those of the general male population? What do you think?

CALIFORNIA QUAKES			NEW YORK BIG APPLES		
2	Callahan	6'7"	3	Roosevelt	6'1"
5	Daly	6'11"	12	Chaffee	6'5"
6	Chico	6'2"	13	Baldwin	6'9"
12	Capistrano	6'3"	25	Delmar	6'6"
21	Brentwood	6'5"	27	Merrick	6'8"
25	Van Nuys	6'3"	28	Hewlett	6'6"
31	Clemente	6'9"	33	Hollis	6'9"
32	Whittier	6'8"	42	Bedford	6'5"
41	Fernando	7'2"	43	Coram	6'2"
43	Watts	6'9"	45	Hampton	6'10"
53	Huntington	6'6"	53	Ardsley	6'10"

© Cengage Learning 2012

TABLE A.2 | Frequency Distribution of Basketball Players (Quakes and Big Apples Combined), with a 1-Inch Class Interval

CLASS INTERVAL	NUMBER OF PLAYERS IN CLASS
6'1"–6'1.9"	1
6'2"–6'2.9"	2
6'3"–6'3.9"	2
6'4"–6'4.9"	0
6'5"–6'5.9"	3
6'6"–6'6.9"	3
6'7"–6'7.9"	1
6'8"–6'8.9"	2
6'9"–6'9.9"	4
6'10"–6'10.9"	2
6'11"–6'11.9"	1
7'0"–7'0.9"	0
7'1"–7'1.9"	0
7'2"–7'2.9"	1

© Cengage Learning 2012

App-2a THE FREQUENCY DISTRIBUTION

A **frequency distribution** takes scores or items of raw data, puts them into order from the lowest to the highest, and indicates how often a score appears. Table A.1 shows the rosters for a recent basketball game between the California Quakes and the New York Big Apples. The players are listed according to the numbers on their uniforms.

It would also be possible to use other class intervals, such as 3 inches, as shown in Table A.3. In determining the size of a class interval, the researcher tries to collapse the data into a small-enough number of classes to ensure that they will be meaningful at a glance. But the researcher also tries to keep a large-enough number of categories (classes) to ensure that important differences are not obscured.

Table A.3 obscures the fact that no players are 6'4" tall. If the researcher believes that this information is important, a class interval of 1 inch may be maintained.

Figure A.1 shows two methods of graphing the information in Table A.3: the **frequency histogram** and the **frequency polygon**. Students sometimes have difficulty interpreting graphs, but the purpose of graphs is to reveal key information about frequency distributions at a glance. Note that in both kinds of graph, the frequency histogram and the frequency polygon, the class intervals are usually drawn along the horizontal line. The horizontal line is also known as the *x*-axis. The numbers of cases (scores, persons, or events) in each class interval are shown along the vertical line, which is also known as the *y*-axis. In the histogram, the number of

frequency distribution
an ordered set of data that indicates the frequency (how often) with which scores appear

frequency histogram
a graphic representation of a frequency distribution that uses rectangular solids (bars) to represent the frequency with which scores appear

frequency polygon
a graphic representation of a frequency distribution that connects the points that show the frequencies with which scores appear, thereby creating a multi-sided geometric figure

TABLE A.3 | Frequency Distribution of Heights of Basketball Players, Using a 3-Inch Class Interval

CLASS INTERVAL	NUMBER OF PLAYERS IN CLASS
6'1"–6'3.9"	5
6'4"–6'6.9"	6
6'7"–6'9.9"	7
6'10"–7'0.9"	3
7'1"–7'3.9"	1

© Cengage Learning 2012

mean

a type of average that is calculated by adding all the scores and then dividing by the number of scores

median

the central score in a frequency distribution; the score beneath which 50% of the cases fall

scores in each class interval is represented by a bar—a rectangular solid—so that the graph looks like a series of steps. In the polygon, the number of scores in each class interval is plotted as a point. The points are connected to form a many-sided geometric figure (polygon). Note that empty class intervals were added at each end of the frequency polygon so that the sides of the figure could be brought down to the *x*-axis to close the geometric figure.

App-2b MEASURES OF CENTRAL TENDENCY

Never try to walk across a river just because it has an average depth of four feet.

—MARTIN FRIEDMAN

Measures of central tendency are "averages" that show the center, or balancing points, of a frequency distribution. There are three commonly used types of measures of central tendency: the *mean*, the *median*, and the *mode*. Each attempts to describe something about the scores in a frequency distribution through the use of a typical or representative number.

The **mean** is what most people think of as "the average." We obtain the mean of a distribution by adding up the scores and then dividing the sum by the number of scores. In the case of the basketball players, it would be advisable to first convert the heights into a single unit, such as inches (6'1" becomes 73", and so on). If we add all the heights in inches and then divide by the number of players (22), we obtain a mean height of 78.73". If we convert that number back into units of feet and inches, we obtain 6'6.73".

The **median** is the score of the *middle case* in a distribution. It is the score beneath which 50% of the cases fall. In a distribution with an even number of cases, such as the distribution of the heights of the 22 basketball players as shown in Table A.2, we obtain the median by finding the mean of the two middle cases. When we list the 22 cases in ascending order (moving from lowest to highest), the 11th case is 6'6" and the

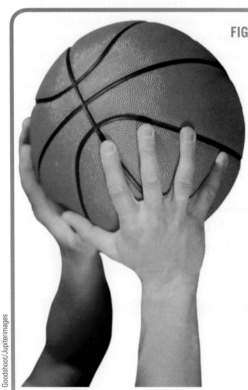

FIGURE A.1 | Two Graphical Representations of the Data in Table A.3

The graph on the left is called a frequency histogram, or bar graph. The graph on the right is called a frequency polygon.

Histogram

Height: 6'1–6'3.9, 6'4–6'6.9, 6'7–6'9.9, 6'10–7'0.9, 7'1–7'3.9

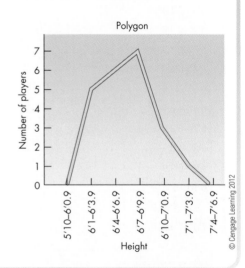

Polygon

Number of players

Height: 5'10–6'0.9, 6'1–6'3.9, 6'4–6'6.9, 6'7–6'9.9, 6'10–7'0.9, 7'1–7'3.9, 7'4–7'6.9

Goodshoot/Jupiterimages

© Cengage Learning 2012

12th case is 6'7". Therefore, the median of the distribution is (6'6" + 6'7") /2, or 6'6.5".

When we analyze the heights of the basketball players, we find that the mean and the median are similar. Either one serves as a useful indicator of the central tendency of the data. But suppose we are trying to find the average savings of 30 families living on a suburban block. Let's assume that 29 of the 30 families have savings between $8,000 and $12,000, adding up to $294,000. But the 30th family has savings of $1,400,000! The mean savings for a family on this block would thus be $56,467. The mean can be greatly distorted by one or two extreme scores. An IQ score of 145 would similarly distort the mean of the IQ scores of a class of 20 students, among whom the other 19 IQ scores ranged from 93 to 112. Then, too, if a few basketball players signed up for one of your classes, the mean of the students' heights would be distorted in an upward direction.

When there are a few extreme scores in a distribution, the median is a better indicator of central tendency. The median savings on our hypothetical block would lie between $8,000 and $12,000. Thus it would be more representative of the central tendency of savings. Studies of the incomes of families in the United States usually report median rather than mean incomes just to avoid the distortion of findings that would occur if the incomes of a handful of billionaires were treated in the same way as more common incomes. On the other hand, one could argue that choosing the median as the average obscures or hides the extreme scores, which are just as "real" as the other scores. Perhaps it is best to use the median and a footnote—a rather big footnote.

TRUTH ADDING PEOPLE'S INCOMES AND THEN DIVIDING THEM BY THE NUMBER OF PEOPLE CAN BE AN AWFUL WAY OF SHOWING THE AVERAGE INCOME. A FEW EXTREMELY HIGH INCOMES, OR IQ SCORES, OR HEIGHTS CAN DISTORT THE AVERAGE OF A GROUP IN AN UPWARD DIRECTION.

The **mode** is simply the most frequently occurring score or measure in a distribution. The mode of the data in Table A.1 is 6'9" because this height occurs most often among the players on the two teams. The median class interval for the data shown in Table A.3 is 6'6.5" to 6'9.5". With this particular distribution, the mode is somewhat higher than the mean or the median.

In some cases the mode is a more appropriate description of the central tendency of a distribution than the mean or the median. Figure A.2 shows a **bimodal** distribution—that is, a distribution with two modes. This is a hypothetical distribution of test scores obtained by a class. The mode at the left indicates the most common class interval (45 to 49) for students who did not study, and the mode to the right shows the most common class interval (65 to 69) for students who did study. (Don't be alarmed. I'm sure that the professor, who is extremely fair, will be delighted to curve the grades so that the interval of 75 to 79 is an A+ and the interval of 65 to 69 is at least a B.) The mean and median test scores would probably lie within the 55 to 59 class interval, yet use of that interval as the measure of central tendency could obscure rather than reveal the important aspects of this distri-

FIGURE A.2 | A Bimodal Distribution

This hypothetical distribution represents students' scores on a test. The mode at the left represents the central tendency of the test scores of students who did not study. The mode at the right represents the mode of the test scores of students who did study.

range
a measure of variability defined as the high score in a distribution minus the low score

standard deviation
a measure of the variability of a distribution, obtained by the formula

$$S.D. = \sqrt{\frac{\text{Sum of } d^2}{N}}$$

FIGURE A.3 | Hypothetical Distributions of Student Test Scores

Each distribution has the same number of scores, the same mean, even the same range, but the standard deviation (a measure of variability) is greater for the distribution on the left because the scores tend to be farther from the mean.

© Cengage Learning 2012

bution of test scores. It might suggest that the test was too hard, not that a number of students chose not to study. Similarly, one of the distribution's modes might be a bit larger than the other, so one could follow the exact rule for finding the mode and report just one of them. But this approach would also hide the meaning of this particular distribution of scores. All in all, it is clearly best to visualize this distribution of scores as bimodal.

App-2c MEASURES OF VARIABILITY

Our hypothetical class obtained test scores ranging from class intervals of 35 to 39 to class intervals of 75 to 79. That is, the scores *varied* from the lower class interval to the higher class interval. Now, if all the students had obtained scores from 55 to 59 or from to 65 to 69, the scores would not have varied as much; that is, they would have clustered closer to one another and would have had lower variability.

The measures of the variability of a distribution inform us about the spread of scores—that is, about the typical distances of scores from the average score. Two commonly used measures of variability are the *range* of scores and the *standard deviation* of scores.

The **range** of scores in a distribution is defined as the difference between the highest score and the lowest score. The range is obtained by subtracting the lowest score from the highest score. The range of

TRUTH PSYCHOLOGISTS MAY EXPRESS YOUR IQ SCORE IN TERMS OF HOW DEVIANT YOU ARE FROM THE AVERAGE OR MEAN SCORE.

heights in Table A.2 is obtained by subtracting 6'1" from 7'2", or 1'1". It is useful to know the range of temperatures when we move to an area with a different climate so that we may anticipate the weather and dress for it appropriately. A teacher must have some understanding of the range of abilities or skills in a class to teach effectively. An understanding of the range of human heights can be used to design doorways, beds, and headroom in automobiles. Even so, the typical doorway is 6'8" high; and, as we saw with the California Quakes and New York Big Apples, some people will have to duck to get through.

The range is an imperfect measure of variability because of the manner in which it is influenced by extreme scores. The range of savings of the 30 families on our suburban block is $1,400,000 minus $8,000, or $1,392,000. This is a large number, and it is certainly true. However, it tells us little about the *typical* variation of savings accounts, which lie within a more restricted range of $8,000 to $12,000.

The **standard deviation** is a statistic that does a better job of showing how the scores in a distribution are distributed (spread) about the mean. It is usually better than the range because it considers every score in the distribution, not just the extreme (highest and lowest) scores. Consider Figure A.3. Each distribution in the figure has the same number of scores, the same mean, and the same range of scores. However, the scores in the distribution on the right side cluster more closely about the mean. Therefore, the standard deviation of the distribution on the right is smaller. That is, the typical score deviates less from the mean score.

The standard deviation is usually abbreviated as S.D. It is calculated by the formula

$$\text{S.D.} = \sqrt{\frac{\text{Sum of } d^2}{N}}$$

where d equals the deviation of each score from the mean of the distribution and N equals the number of scores in the distribution.

Let's find the mean and standard deviation of the IQ scores listed in column 1 of Table A.4. To obtain the mean we add all the scores, attain 1,500, and then divide by the number of scores (15) to obtain a mean of 100. We obtain the deviation score (d) for each IQ score by subtracting the score from 100. The d for an IQ score of 85 equals 100 minus 85, or 15, and so on. Then we

square each d and add the squares. The S.D. equals the square root of the sum of squares (1,426) divided by the number of scores (15), or 9.75.

As an additional exercise, we can show that the S.D. of the test scores on the left (in Figure A.3) is greater than that for the scores on the right. First, we assign the grades a number according to a 4.0 system. Let A = 4, B = 3, C = 2, D = 1, and F = 0. The S.D. for each distribution is computed in Table A.5. The larger S.D. for the distribution on the left indicates that the scores in that distribution are more variable, or tend to be farther from the mean.

TABLE A.4 | Hypothetical Scores Obtained from an IQ Testing

IQ SCORE	d (DEVIATION SCORE)	d² (DEVIATION SCORE SQUARED)
85	15	225
87	13	169
89	11	121
90	10	100
93	7	49
97	3	9
97	3	9
100	0	0
101	−1	1
104	−4	16
105	−5	25
110	−10	100
112	−12	144
113	−13	169
117	−17	289

Sum of IQ scores = 1,500   Sum of d^2 scores = 1,426

$$\text{Mean} = \frac{\text{Sum of scores}}{\text{Number of scores}} = \frac{1,500}{15} = 100$$

$$\text{Standard Deviation (S.D.)} = \sqrt{\frac{\text{Sum of } d^2}{N}} = \sqrt{\frac{1,426}{15}} = \sqrt{95.07} = 9.75$$

© Cengage Learning 2012

TABLE A.5 | Computation of Standard Deviations for Test-Score Distributions in Figure A.3

DISTRIBUTION AT LEFT			DISTRIBUTION TO THE RIGHT		
GRADE	d	d²	GRADE	d	d²
A (4)	2	4	A (4)	2	4
A (4)	2	4	B (3)	1	1
A (4)	2	4	B (3)	1	1
B (3)	1	1	B (3)	1	1
B (3)	1	1	B (3)	1	1
B (3)	1	1	C (2)	0	0
B (3)	1	1	C (2)	0	0
C (2)	0	0	C (2)	0	0
C (2)	0	0	C (2)	0	0
C (2)	0	0	C (2)	0	0
C (2)	0	0	C (2)	0	0
D (1)	−1	1	C (2)	0	0
D (1)	−1	1	C (2)	0	0
D (1)	−1	1	D (1)	−1	1
D (1)	−1	1	D (1)	−1	1
F (0)	−2	4	D (1)	−1	1
F (0)	−2	4	D (1)	−1	1
F (0)	−2	4	F (0)	−2	4

Sum of grades = 36
Mean grade = 36/18 = 2
Sum of d^2 = 32
Sum of grades = 36
Mean grade = 36/18 = 2
Sum of d^2 = 32
S.D. = $\sqrt{32/18}$ = 1.33

Sum of grades = 36
Mean grade = 36/18 = 2
Sum of d^2 = 16
Sum of grades = 36
Mean grade = 36/18 = 2
Sum of d^2 = 16
S.D. = $\sqrt{16/18}$ = 0.94

© Cengage Learning 2012

normal distribution
a symmetrical distribution that is assumed to reflect chance fluctuations; approximately 68% of cases lie within a standard deviation of the mean

normal curve
graphic presentation of a normal distribution, which shows a characteristic bell shape

App-3 The Normal Curve

Many human traits and characteristics, including height and intelligence, seem to be distributed in a pattern known as a normal distribution. In a **normal distribution**, the mean, the median, and the mode all fall at the same data point or score. Scores cluster most heavily about the mean, fall off rapidly in either direction at first (as shown in Figure A.4), and then taper off more gradually.

The curve in Figure A.4 is bell-shaped. This type of distribution is also called a **normal curve** or bell-shaped curve. This curve is hypothesized as the distribution of variables in which different scores are determined by chance variation. Height is thought to be largely determined by chance combinations of genetic material. A distribution of the heights of a random sample of the population approximates normal distributions for men and women, with the mean of the distribution for men a few inches higher than the mean for women.

Test developers traditionally assumed that intelligence was also randomly or normally distributed among the population. For that reason, they constructed intelligence tests so that scores would be distributed as close to "normal" as possible. In actuality, IQ scores are also influenced by environmental factors and chromosomal abnormalities, so that the resultant curves are not perfectly normal. The means of most IQ tests are defined as scores of 100 points. The Wechsler scales are constructed to have standard deviations of 15 points, as shown in Figure A.4. A standard deviation of 15 points causes 50% of the Wechsler scores to fall between 90 and 110, which is called the "broad average" range. About 68% of scores (two out of three) fall between 85 and 115 (within a standard deviation of the mean), and more than 95% fall between 70 and 130—that is, within two standard deviations of the mean. The more extreme high (and low) IQ scores deviate more from the mean score.

The Scholastic Assessment Tests (SATs) were constructed so that the mean scores would be 500 points and the S.D. would be 100 points. Thus a score of 600 would equal or excel that of some 84% to 85% of the test takers. Because of the complex interaction of variables that determine SAT scores, their distribution is not exactly normal either. Moreover, the actual mean scores and standard deviations tend to vary from year to year, and, in the case of the SAT IIs, from test to test. The normal curve is an idealized curve.

The IQ score of 130 is two standard deviations above the mean and exceeds that of more than 97% of the population. An SAT score of 500 is the mean SAT score and thus equals or excels that of about 50% of the population.

FIGURE A.4 | A Bell-Shaped or Normal Curve

In a normal curve, approximately two out of three cases (68%) lie within a standard deviation (S.D.) from the mean. The mean, median, and mode all lie at the same score. IQ tests and the Scholastic Assessment Tests (SATs) are constructed so that their distributions approximate the normal curve.

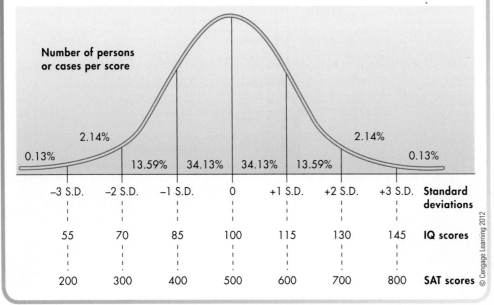

	–3 S.D.	–2 S.D.	–1 S.D.	0	+1 S.D.	+2 S.D.	+3 S.D.	Standard deviations
IQ scores	55	70	85	100	115	130	145	
SAT scores	200	300	400	500	600	700	800	

Number of persons or cases per score

0.13%   2.14%   13.59%   34.13%   34.13%   13.59%   2.14%   0.13%

App-4 The Correlation Coefficient

What is the relationship between intelligence and educational achievement? Between cigarette smoking and lung cancer among humans? Between the personality trait of introversion and numbers of dates among college students? We cannot run experiments to determine whether the relationships between these variables are causal, because we cannot manipulate the independent variable. That is, we cannot assign high or low intelligence at random. Nor can we (ethically) assign some people to smoke cigarettes and others not to smoke. People must be allowed to make their own decisions, so it is possible that the same factors that lead some people to smoke—or to continue to smoke after they have experimented with cigarettes—also lead to lung cancer. (Even if we were to assign a group of people to a nonsmoking condition, could we monitor them continuously to make sure that they weren't sneaking puffs?) Nor can we designate who will be introverted and who will be extraverted. True, we could encourage people to act as if they are introverted or extraverted, but behavior is not the same thing as a personality trait. We cannot run true experiments to answer any of these questions, but the *correlation coefficient* can be used to reveal whether there is a relationship between intelligence and achievement, a relationship between smoking and cancer, or a relationship between personality and dating. Correlational research shows that smoking and cancer are related but does not reveal cause and effect. However, experimental research with animals does strongly suggest that smoking will cause cancer in humans.

TRUTH AN IQ SCORE OF 130 IS MORE IMPRESSIVE THAN AN SAT SCORE OF 500. THE IQ SCORE IS TWO STANDARD DEVIATIONS ABOVE THE MEAN, AND THE SAT SCORE IS THE MEAN FOR THAT TEST.

The **correlation coefficient** is a statistic that describes the relationship between two variables. A correlation coefficient can vary from +1.00 to −1.00. A correlation coefficient of +1.00 is called a perfect positive correlation, and it describes the relationship between temperatures as measured by the Fahrenheit and Centigrade scales. A correlation coefficient of −1.00 is a perfect negative correlation, and a correlation of 0 (zero) reveals no relationship between variables.

As suggested by Figures A.5 and A.6, most correlation coefficients in psychological research are less than perfect. The left graph in Figure A.5 reveals a positive relationship between time spent studying and grade point averages. Because there is a positive correlation between the variables but the relationship is not perfect, the correlation coefficient will lie between 0.00 and +1.00. Perhaps it is about +0.60 or +0.70. However, we cannot absolutely predict what a person's GPA will be if we know the hours per week that he or she

correlation coefficient a number between −1.00 and +1.00 that indicates the direction (negative or positive) and extent (from none to perfect) of the relationship between two variables

---

FIGURE A.5 | **Positive and Negative Correlations**

When there is a positive correlation between variables, as there is between intelligence and achievement, one increases as the other increases. By and large, the more time students spend studying, the better their grades are likely to be, as suggested in the diagram to the left. (Each dot represents the amount of time a student spends studying each week and his or her grade point average.) But there is a negative correlation between grades and juvenile delinquency. As the number of delinquent acts per year increases, one's grade point average tends to decline. Correlational research may suggest but does not demonstrate cause and effect.

Positive correlation, as found between intelligence and academic achievement

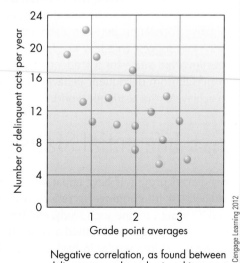

Negative correlation, as found between delinquency and academic achievement

© Cengage Learning 2012

FIGURE A.6 | Correlational Relationships, Cause and Effect

Correlational relationships may suggest but do not demonstrate cause and effect. In part A, there is a correlation between variables X and Y. Does this mean that either variable X causes variable Y or that variable Y causes variable X? Not necessarily. Other factors could affect both variables X and Y. Consider the examples of academic grades (variable X) and time spent studying (variable Y) in part B. There is a positive correlation between the two. Does this mean that studying contributes to good grades? Perhaps. Does it mean that good grades encourage studying? Again, perhaps. But there could also be other variables—such as cultural belief in the value of education, enjoyment of learning, even parental pressure to do well—that contribute both to time spent studying and good grades.

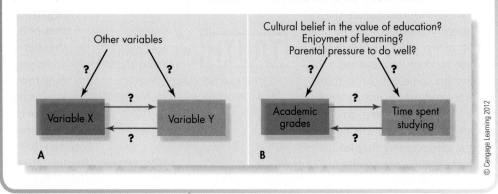

© Cengage Learning 2012

spends studying (nor can we predict exactly how much time the person spends studying on the basis of his or her GPA). Nevertheless, it would seem advisable to place oneself among those who spend a good deal of time studying if one wishes to achieve a good GPA.

The right drawing in Figure A.5 reveals a negative relationship between number of delinquent acts committed per year and GPA. The causal connection is less than perfectly clear. Does delinquency interfere with studying and academic achievement? Does poor achievement weaken a student's commitment to trying to get ahead through work? Do feelings of distance from "the system" contribute both to delinquent behavior and a low GPA? The answers are not to be found in Figure A.5, but the negative correlation between delinquent behavior and GPA does suggest that it is worthwhile to study the issues involved and—for a student—to distance himself or herself from delinquent behavior if he or she wishes to achieve in the academic world.

App-5 Inferential Statistics

Head Start programs have apparently raised children's intellectual functioning, as reflected in their grades and IQ scores. In one such study, children enrolled in a Head Start program obtained a mean IQ score of 99, whereas children similar in background who were not enrolled in Head Start obtained a mean IQ score of 93.

Is this difference of six points in IQ *significant*, or does it represent a chance fluctuation in scores? Inferential statistics help us determine whether we can conclude that the differences between such samples reflect real differences that are found in the populations that they represent.

Descriptive statistics enables us to provide descriptive information about samples of scores. **Inferential statistics** assist us in determining whether we can generalize differences among samples to the populations that they represent.

Figure A.7 shows the distribution of heights of 1,000 men and 1,000 women who were selected at random from the general U.S. population. The mean height for men is greater than the mean height for women. Can we conclude, or *infer*, that this difference in height is not just a chance fluctuation but represents an actual difference between the general populations of men and women? Or must we avoid such an inference and summarize our results by stating only that the mean height of the sample of men in the study was greater than the mean height of the sample of women in the study?

If we could not draw inferences about populations from studies of samples, our research findings would be limited indeed. We could speak only about the specific individuals studied. There would be no point to learning about any study in which you did not participate because it would not apply to you! Fortunately, that is not the case. Inferential statistics permits us to

FIGURE A.7 | Distribution of Heights for Random Samples of Men and Women

Note that the mean height of the men is greater than that of the women. Is the group mean difference in height statistically significant? Researchers use a tool called inferential statistics to determine the answer.

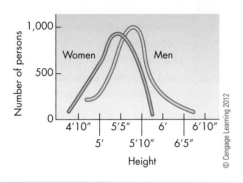

© Cengage Learning 2012

extend findings with samples to the populations from which they were drawn.

App-5a STATISTICALLY SIGNIFICANT DIFFERENCES

We asked whether the differences in height between our samples of men and women were simply a chance fluctuation or whether they represented actual differences between the heights of men and women. Researchers tend not to talk about "real differences" or "actual differences" between groups, however. Instead, they speak of statistically significant differences. Similarly, researchers asked whether differences in IQ scores

between children in Head Start programs and other children from similar backgrounds were chance fluctuations or statistically significant differences.

Statistically significant differences are differences that are unlikely to be due to chance fluctuation. Psychologists usually do not accept a difference as being statistically significant unless the probability (p) that it is due to chance fluctuation is less than 1 in 20 (i.e., $p < .05$). They are more comfortable labeling a difference as statistically significant when the probability (p) that it is due to chance fluctuation is less than 1 in 100 (i.e., $p < .01$).

Psychologists use formulas involving the means (e.g., mean IQ scores of 93 versus 99) and the standard deviations of sample groups to determine whether differences in means are statistically significant. As you can see in Figure A.8, the farther apart group means are, the more likely it is that they are statistically significant. In other words, if the men are on average 5 inches taller than the women, it is more likely that the difference is statistically significant than if the men are only one-quarter of an inch taller on average. *Principle 1: Everything else being equal, the greater the difference between means, the greater the probability that the difference is statistically significant.* This makes sense. After all, if you were told that your neighbor's car had gotten one-tenth of a mile more per gallon of gas than your car in the past year, you would probably attribute the difference to chance fluctuation. But if the difference were greater, say 14 miles per gallon, you would probably assume that the difference reflected an actual difference in driving habits or the efficiency of the automobile.

As you can see in Figure A.9, the smaller the standard deviations (a measure of variability) of the groups, the more likely it is that the difference between means is statistically significant. Consider the extreme example in which there is *no* variability within each group.

FIGURE A.8 | Decreasing and Increasing the Mean Group Difference in Heights

Everything else being equal, the greater the difference in group means, the greater the probability that the difference is statistically significant. The distribution on the right shows a greater difference in group means; therefore, there is a greater probability that the difference is statistically significant.

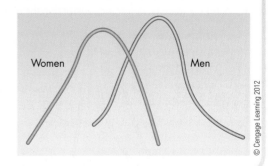

© Cengage Learning 2012

That is, imagine that every woman in the randomly selected sample of 1,000 women is exactly 5'5" tall. Similarly, imagine that every man in the randomly selected sample of 1,000 men is exactly 5'10" tall. In such a case the heights of the men and women would not overlap at all, and it would appear that the differences were statistically significant. Consider the other extreme—one with unnaturally large variability. Imagine that the heights of the women vary from 2' to 14' and that the heights of the men vary from 2'1" to 14'3". In such a case we might be more likely to assume that the difference in group means of 5" was a chance fluctuation. *Principle 2: Everything else being equal, the smaller the variability of the distributions of scores, the greater the probability that the difference in group means is statistically significant.*

Therefore, we cannot conclude that men are taller than women unless we know the average heights of men and women and how much the heights within each group vary. We must know both the central tendencies (means) and variability of the two distributions of heights to infer that the mean heights are statistically significantly different.

We have been "eyeballing" the data and making assumptions. We have been relying on what one professor of mine called the "Wow!" effect. As noted, psychologists and other researchers actually use mathematical techniques that take group means and standard deviations into account to determine whether group differences are statistically significant. It is often the case that eyeballing real data does not yield clear results or even good guesses.

"SMOKING IS ONE OF THE LEADING CAUSES OF ALL STATISTICS."
—LIZA MINNELLI

App-5b SAMPLES AND POPULATIONS

Inferential statistics are mathematical tools that psychologists apply to samples of scores to determine whether they can generalize or extend their findings to populations of scores. They must, therefore, be quite certain that the samples involved actually represent the populations from which they were drawn. Sampling techniques are crucial. Random sampling is the best method, and sampling is random only if every member of the target population has an equal chance of being selected.

It matters little how sophisticated our statistical methods are if the samples studied do not represent the target populations. We could use a variety of sophisticated statistical techniques to analyze the heights

"Statistics show that of those who contract the habit of eating, very few survive."
—GEORGE BERNARD SHAW

of the New York Big Apples and the California Quakes, but none of these methods would tell us much about the height of the general population. Or about the height of women. (Or about the height of people who can't pass the ball, shoot, or play defense.)

FIGURE A.9 | Decreasing and Increasing the Variability of the Distributions of Scores

Everything else being equal, the smaller the variability in group scores, the greater the probability that the difference in group means is statistically significant. The distribution on the right shows a greater difference in the variability of the groups; therefore, there is a *lower* probability that the difference in group means is statistically significant.

© Cengage Learning 2012

WHY CHOOSE?

Every 4LTR Press solution comes complete with a visually engaging textbook in addition to an interactive eBook. Go to CourseMate for PSYCH3 to begin using the eBook. Access at **www.cengagebrain.com**

Complete the Speak Up survey in CourseMate at **www.cengagebrain.com**

 Follow us at **www.facebook.com/4ltrpress**

ANSWERS TO STUDY TOOLS QUESTIONS

Chapter 1

FILL-INS
1. behavior
2. Clinical
3. Wilhelm Wundt
4. Gestalt
5. Evolutionary
6. Clark
7. population
8. survey
9. control
10. ethical

MULTIPLE CHOICE
1. A
2. B
3. C
4. A
5. D
6. D
7. A
8. A
9. C
10. C

Chapter 2

FILL-INS
1. neurotransmitters
2. axon
3. myelin
4. schizophrenia
5. autonomic
6. cerebellum
7. existence
8. instincts
9. Down
10. monozygotic (identical)

MULTIPLE CHOICE
1. C
2. B
3. A
4. B
5. A
6. D
7. D
8. A
9. A
10. D

Chapter 3

FILL-INS
1. Perception
2. absolute
3. rods; cones
4. optic
5. retina
6. olfactory
7. taste
8. position
9. semicircular
10. file-drawer

MULTIPLE CHOICE
1. C
2. B
3. A
4. D
5. C
6. C
7. A
8. D
9. A
10. B

Chapter 4

FILL-INS
1. awareness
2. paradoxical
3. five
4. activation
5. trance
6. mantra
7. abuse
8. abstinence
9. Cocaine
10. Hallucinogenic

MULTIPLE CHOICE
1. D
2. C
3. B
4. A
5. C
6. B
7. D
8. A
9. B
10. A

Chapter 5

FILL-INS
1. unconditioned
2. conditioned
3. extinguish
4. spontaneous
5. Albert
6. flooding
7. Negative
8. fixed-interval
9. Programmed
10. contingency

MULTIPLE CHOICE
1. B
2. D
3. C
4. C
5. A
6. C
7. D
8. D
9. C
10. A

Chapter 6

FILL-INS
1. episodic
2. Semantic
3. maintenance
4. elaborative
5. sensory; short-term; long-term
6. eidetic
7. flashbulb
8. retroactive
9. proactive
10. synapses

MULTIPLE CHOICE
1. B
2. C
3. D
4. A
5. A
6. D
7. C
8. D
9. B
10. C

Chapter 7

FILL-INS
1. Concepts
2. algorithm
3. Heuristic
4. mental
5. linguistic
6. overregularization
7. *g*
8. multiple
9. practical
10. intelligence quotient

MULTIPLE CHOICE
1. D
2. D
3. B
4. B
5. C
6. D
7. C
8. D
9. B
10. C

Chapter 8

FILL-INS
1. Motives
2. incentive
3. homeostasis
4. self-actualization
5. Anorexia
6. excitement
7. organizing
8. Apperception
9. performance
10. action

MULTIPLE CHOICE
1. C
2. A
3. A
4. B
5. C
6. D
7. C
8. D
9. D
10. A

Chapter 9

FILL-INS
1. reflexes
2. concrete
3. zone
4. initial-preattachment
5. secondary
6. formal
7. imaginary
8. diffusion
9. fluid
10. do not

MULTIPLE CHOICE
1. B
2. A
3. C
4. D
5. B
6. C
7. D
8. B
9. C
10. B

Chapter 10

FILL-INS
1. id
2. superego
3. anal
4. collective
5. inferiority
6. antisocial
7. actualization
8. reference
9. collectivists
10. ambiguous

MULTIPLE CHOICE
1. B
2. A
3. C
4. C
5. B
6. D
7. A
8. D
9. C
10. B

Chapter 11

FILL-INS
1. hassles
2. conflict
3. Ellis
4. higher
5. commitment
6. alarm
7. fight; flight
8. befriend
9. immune
10. cholesterol

MULTIPLE CHOICE
1. B
2. D
3. C
4. B
5. A
6. C
7. D
8. C
9. A
10. B

Chapter 12

FILL-INS
1. perception
2. phobia
3. obsessive-compulsive
4. amnesia
5. identity
6. somatoform
7. flight
8. internal
9. Catatonic
10. Personality

MULTIPLE CHOICE
1. B
2. B
3. A
4. A
5. D
6. C
7. B
8. A
9. D
10. A

Chapter 13

FILL-INS
1. psychological
2. unconscious
3. Operant
4. free
5. Humanistic
6. Client-centered
7. Cognitive
8. desensitization
9. irrational
10. Minor

MULTIPLE CHOICE
1. C
2. B
3. B
4. B
5. A
6. B
7. B
8. D
9. A
10. C

Chapter 14

FILL-INS
1. cognitive
2. dissonance
3. categorization
4. attraction-similarity
5. passion
6. primacy
7. social
8. facilitation
9. deindividualization
10. bystander

MULTIPLE CHOICE
1. D
2. B
3. A
4. B
5. C
6. B
7. B
8. A
9. B
10. C

REFERENCES

A

Abele, S., & Diehl, M. (2008). Finding teammates who are not prone to sucker and free-rider effects: The Protestant work ethic as a moderator of motivation losses in group performance. *Group Processes and Intergroup Relations, 11*(1), 39–54.

Aboa-Éboulé, C., Brisson, C., Maunsell, E., Mâsse, B., Bourbonnais, R., Vézina, M., ... Dagenais, G. R. (2007). Job strain and risk of acute recurrent coronary heart disease events. *Journal of the American Medical Association, 298,* 1652–1660.

Ackard, D. M., Fulkerson, J. A., & Neumark-Sztainer, D. (2007). Prevalence and utility of *DSM-IV* eating disorder diagnostic criteria among youth. *International Journal of Eating Disorders, 40*(5), 409–417.

Adams, A. L., Doucette, T. A., James, R., & Ryan, C. L. (2009). Persistent changes in learning and memory in rats following neonatal treatment with domoic acid. *Physiology and Behavior, 96*(4–5), 505–512.

Agras, W. S., Walsh, T., Fairburn, C. G., Wilson, G. T., & Kraemer, H. C. (2000). A multicenter comparison of cognitive-behavioral therapy and interpersonal psychotherapy for bulimia nervosa. *Archives of General Psychiatry, 57*(5), 459–466.

Agrawal, A., Silberg, J. L., Lynskey, M. T., Maes, H. H., & Eaves, L. J. (2010). Mechanisms underlying the lifetime co-occurrence of tobacco and cannabis use in adolescent and young adult twins. *Drug and Alcohol Dependence, 108* (1–2), 49–55.

Ahs, F., Pissiota, A., Michelgård, A., Frans, O., Furmark, T., Appel, L., & Fredrikson, M. (2009). Disentangling the web of fear: Amygdala reactivity and functional connectivity in spider and snake phobia. *Psychiatry Research, 172*(2), 103–108.

Ainsworth, M. D. S., Blehar, M. C., Waters, E., & Wall, S. (1978). *Patterns of attachment: A psychological study of the strange situation.* Hillsdale, NJ: Erlbaum.

Ainsworth, M. D. S., & Bowlby, J. (1991). An ethological approach to personality development. *American Psychologist, 46,* 333–341.

Alarcón, R. D., Becker, A. E., Lewis-Fernández, R., Like, R. C., Desai, P., Foulks, E., ... Primm, A. (2009). Issues for *DSM-V*: The role of culture in psychiatric diagnosis. *Journal of Nervous and Mental Disease, 197*(8), 559–660.

Alberts, A., Elkind, D., & Ginsberg, S. (2007). The personal fable and risk-taking in early adolescence. *Journal of Youth and Adolescence, 36*(1), 71–76.

Alexander, G. M., Wilcox, T., & Woods, R. (2009). Sex differences in infants' visual interest in toys. *Archives of Sexual Behavior, 38*(3), 427–433.

Allen, J. P., & Antonishak, J. (2008). Adolescent peer influences: Beyond the dark side. In M. J. Prinstein & K. A. Dodge (Eds.), *Understanding peer influence in children and adolescents* (pp. 141–160). New York: Guilford.

Allport, G. W., & Odbert, H. S. (1936). Traitnames: A psycho-lexical study. *Psychological Monographs, 47,* 211.

Amanatullah, E. T., & Morris, M. W. (2010). Negotiating gender roles: Gender differences in assertive negotiating are mediated by women's fear of backlash and attenuated when negotiating on behalf of others. *Journal of Personality and Social Psychology, 98*(2), 256–267.

Ambrosius, U., Lietzenmaier, S., Wehrle, R., Wichniak, A., Kalus, S., Winkelman, J., ... E. Friess. (2008). Heritability of sleep electroencephalogram. *Biological Psychiatry, 64*(4), 344–348.

American Cancer Society. (2010). Retrieved from http://www.cancer.org/

American Lung Association. (2010). Smoking. Retrieved from http://www.lungusa.org/stop-smoking/about-smoking/health-effects/smoking.html

American Psychiatric Association. (2000). *Diagnostic and statistical manual of mental disorders, DSM–IV–TR* (4th ed., text revision). Washington, DC: Author.

American Psychological Association. (2002). Ethical principles of psychologists and code of conduct. *American Psychologist, 57*(12), 1060–1073.

American Psychological Association. (2008). Award for distinguished scientific contributions: Michael S. Gazzaniga. *American Psychologist, 63*(8), 636–638.

American Psychological Association, Center for Workforce Studies. (2009). *Doctoral psychology workforce fast facts. Health service provider subfields.* Retrieved from http://research.apa.org/fastfacts-09.pdf

American Psychological Assoiacation. (2012). Stress in America 2009: Executive summary. Retrieved from www.apa.org/news/press/releases/stress/2011/final-2011.pdf

The anatomy of anxiety. (2002). *Time, 159,* 50.

Anchin, J. C., & Pincus, A. L. (2010). Evidence-based interpersonal psychotherapy with personality disorders: Theory, components, and strategies. In J. J. Magnavita (Ed.), *Evidence-based treatment of personality dysfunction: Principles, methods, and processes* (pp. 113–166). Washington, DC: American Psychological Association.

Andersen, A. E., & Ryan, G. L. (2009). Eating disorders in the obstetric and gynecologic patient population. *Obstetrics and Gynecology, 114*(6), 1353–1367.

Anderson, C. A., Sakamoto, A., Gentile, D. A., Ihori, N., & Shibuya, A. (2008). Longitudinal effects of violent video games on aggression in Japan and the United States. *Pediatrics, 122*(5), e1067–e1072.

Anderson, C. A., Shibuya, A., Ihori, N., Swing, E. L., Bushman, B. J., Sakamoto, A., ... Bartlett, C. P. (2010). Violent video game effects on aggression, empathy, and prosocial behavior in Eastern and Western countries: A meta-analytic review. *Psychological Bulletin, 136*(2), 151–173.

Anderson, O. (1995). The buzz on exercise. *Men's Health, 10,* 88–89.

Andreano, J. M., & Cahill, L. (2009). Sex influences on the neurobiology of learning and memory. *Learning and Memory, 16,* 248–266.

Ansburg, P.I. (2000). Individual differences in problem solving via insight. *Current Psychology, 19,* 143.

Antoni, M. H., & Lutgendorf, S. (2007). Psychosocial factors and disease progression in cancer. *Current Directions in Psychological Science, 16*(1), 42–46.

Apovian, C. M. (2010). The causes, prevalence, and treatment of obesity revisited in 2009: What have we learned so far? *American Journal of Clinical Nutrition, 91*(1), 277S–279S.

Archer, J. (2009). The nature of human aggression. *International Journal of Law and Psychiatry, 32*(4), 202–208.

Archer, R. P., Buffington-Vollum, J. K., Stredny, R. V., & Handel, R. W. (2006). A survey of psychological test use patterns among forensic psychologists. *Journal of Personality Assessment, 87*(1), 84–94.

Arden, G. (2003, February 21). Test for color vision;-and save sight. *Optician,* p. 2.

Arendt, J. (2009). Managing jet lag: Some of the problems and possible new solutions. *Sleep Medicine Reviews, 13*(4), 249–256.

Arias, E., Rostron, B. L., & Tejada-Vera, B. (2010). United States life tables, 2005. *National Vital Statistics Report, 58*(10). National Center for Health Statistics. Retrieved from http://198.246.98.21/nchs/data/nvsr/nvsr58/nvsr58_10.pdf

Arnett, J. J. (1999). Adolescent storm and stress, reconsidered. *American Psychologist, 54*(5), 317–326.

Arnett, J. J. (2000). Emerging adulthood. *American Psychologist, 55*(5), 469–480.

Arnett, J. J. (2012). New horizons in research on emerging and young adulthood. *National Symposium on Family Issues, 2*(5), 231–244.

Arthritis Foundation. (2000, April 6). Pain in America: Highlights from a Gallup survey. Retrieved from http://www.arthritis.org/answers/sop_factsheet.asp

Artigas, F. (2008). Serotonin receptors: Role in depression. *Actas Españolas de Psiquiatría, 36*(Suppl. 1), 28–30.

Asch, S. E. (1952). *Social psychology.* Englewood Cliffs, NJ: Prentice Hall.

Ashtari, M., Cervellione, K., Cottone, J. Ardekani, B. A., Serge Sevy, S., & Kumra, S. (2009). Diffusion abnormalities in adolescents and young adults with a history of heavy cannabis use. *Journal of Psychiatric Research, 43*(3), 189–204.

Atkins, M. S., McKay, M. M., Frazier, S. L., Jakobsons, L. J., Arvanitis, P., Cunningham, T., … Lambrecht, L. (2002). Suspensions and detention in an urban, low-income school: Punishment or reward? *Journal of Abnormal Child Psychology, 30*(4), 361–371.

Atkinson, R. C., & Shiffrin, R. M. (1968). Human memory: A proposed system and its control processes. In K. Spence (Ed.), *The psychology of learning and motivation* (Vol. 2). New York: Academic Press.

Auyeung, B., Baron-Cohen, S., Ashwin, E., Knickmeyer, R., Taylor, K., Hackett, G., & Hines, M. (2009). Fetal testosterone predicts sexually differentiated behavior in girls and in boys. *Psychological Science, 20*(2), 144–148.

B

Back, S. E., Brady, K. T., Waldrop, A. E., Yeatts, S. D., McRae, A. L., & Spratt, E. (2008). Early life trauma and sensitivity to current life stressors in individuals with and without cocaine dependence. *American Journal of Drug and Alcohol Abuse, 34*(4), 389–396.

Baddeley, A. (1982). *Your memory: A user's guide.* New York: Macmillan.

Bae, S., Holloway, S. D., Li, J., & Bempechat, J. (2008). Mexican-American students' perceptions of teachers' expectations: Do perceptions differ depending on student achievement levels? *Urban Review, 40*(2), 210–225.

Bagchi, D., & Preuss, H. G. (2007). *Obesity: Epidemiology, pathophysiology, and prevention.* Boca Raton, FL: CRC Press.

Bahrick, H. P., Bahrick, P. O., & Wittlinger, R. P. (1975). Fifty years of memory for names and faces. *Journal of Experimental Psychology: General, 104*, 54–75.

Bahrick, H. P., Hall, L. K., & Da Costa, L. A. (2008). Fifty years of memory of college grades: Accuracy and distortions. *Emotion, 8*(1), 13–22.

Baker, L. A., DeFries, J. C., & Fulker, D. W. (1983). Longitudinal stability of cognitive ability in the Colorado adoption project. *Child Development, 54*, 290–297.

Bakst, S., Rabinowitz, J., & Bromet, E. (2009). Is premorbid functioning a risk factor for suicide attempts in first-admission psychosis? *Schizophrenia Research, 116*(2), 210–216.

Baltes, P. B., & Staudinger, U. M. (2000). Wisdom: A metaheuristic (pragmatic) to orchestrate mind and virtue toward excellence. *American Psychologist, 55*, 122–136.

Banaji, M. R., & Heiphetz, L. (2008). Attitudes. In S. T. Fiske, D. T. Gilbert, & G. Lindzey (Eds.), *Handbook of social psychology* (5th ed., Vol. 1., pp. 353–393). Hoboken, NJ: Wiley.

Bandelow, B., Wedekind, D., Pauls, J., Broocks, A., Hajak, G., & Ruther, E. (2000). Salivary cortisol in panic attacks. *American Journal of Psychiatry, 157*, 454–456.

Bandura, A. (1986). *Social foundations of thought and action: Associal-cognitive theory.* Englewood Cliffs, NJ: Prentice Hall.

Bandura, A. (1999). Social cognitive theory: An agentic perspective. *Asian Journal of Social Psychology, 2*(1), 21–41.

Bandura, A. (2008). An agentic perspective on positive psychology. In S. J. Lopez (Ed.), *Positive psychology: Discovering human strengths* (pp. 167–214). Santa Barbara, CA: ABC-CLIO.

Bandura, A., Blanchard, E. B., & Ritter, B. (1969). The relative efficacy of desensitization and modeling approaches for inducing behavioral, affective, and cognitive changes. *Journal of Personality and Social Psychology, 13*, 173–199.

Bandura, A., & Locke, E. A. (2003). Negative self-efficacy and goal effects revisited. *Journal of Applied Psychology, 88*(1), 87–99.

Bandura, A., Ross, S. A., & Ross, D. (1963). Imitation of film-mediated aggressive models. *Journal of Abnormal and Social Psychology, 66*, 3–11.

Bandura, A., Taylor, C. B., Williams, S. L., Medford, I. N., & Barchas, J. D. (1985). Catecholamine secretion as a function of perceived coping self-efficacy. *Journal of Consulting and Clinical Psychology, 53*, 406–414.

Barber, J. G. (2001). Relative misery and youth suicide. *Australian and New Zealand Journal of Psychiatry, 35*(1), 49–57.

Barbey, A. K., & Barsalou, L. W. (2009). Reasoning and problem solving: Models. *Encyclopedia of Neuroscience, 8*, 35–43.

Barbor, C. (2001). The science of meditation. *Psychology Today, 34*, 54.

Bard, P. (1934). The neurohumoral basis of emotional reactions. In C. A. Murchison (Ed.), *Handbook of general experimental psychology.* Worcester, MA: Clark University Press.

Barelli, C., Heistermann, M., Boesch, C., & Reichard, U. H. (2008). Mating patterns and sexual swellings in pair-living and multiple groups of wild white-handed gibbons, *Hylobates lar. Animal Behaviour, 75*(3), 991–1001.

Baron, R. A., Branscombe, N. R., & Byrne, D. R. (2009). *Social psychology* (12th ed.). Boston: Allyn & Bacon.

Bartone, P. T., Roland, R. R., Picano, J. J., & Williams, T. J. (2008). Psychological hardiness predicts success in U.S. Army special forces candidates. *International Journal of Selection and Assessment, 16*(1), 78–81.

Bartoshuk, L. M. (2000). Psychophysical advances aid the study of genetic variation in taste. *Appetite, 34*(1), 105.

Basic Behavioral Science Task Force of the National Advisory Mental Health Council. (1996c). Basic behavioral science research for mental health: Sociocultural and environmental practices. *American Psychologist, 51*, 722–731.

Bassok, M., & Novick, L. R. (2012). Problem solving. In K. J. Holyoak & R. G. Morrison (Eds.), *The Oxford handbook of thinking and reasoning* (pp. 413–432). New York: Oxford University Press.

Bates, E. (2001) Plasticity, localization and language development. In S. T. Parker, J. Langer, & C. Milbrath (Eds.), *Biology and knowledge revisited* (pp. 205–254). London: Routledge.

Batson, C. D., Qian, Z., & Lichter, D. T. (2006). Interracial and intraracial patterns of mate selection among America's diverse Black populations. *Journal of Marriage and the Family, 68*, 658–672.

Baucom, D. H., Epstein, N. B., LaTaillade, J. J., & Kirby, J. S. (2002). Cognitive-behavioral couple therapy. In A. S. Gurman (Ed.), *Handbook of couple therapy* (pp. 31–72). New York: Guilford Press.

Baumeister, R. F. (1996). *Evil: Inside human cruelty and violence.* New York: W. H. Freeman /Times Books/ Henry Holt & Co.

Baumrind, D. (1989). Rearing competent children. In W. Damon (Ed.), *Child development today and tomorrow.* San Francisco: Jossey-Bass.

Baumrind, D. (2005). Taking a stand in a morally pluralistic society: Constructive obedience and responsible dissent in moral/character education. In L. Nucci (Ed.), *Conflict, contradiction, and contrarian elements in moral development and education* (pp. 21–50). Mahwah, NJ: Erlbaum.

Bear, R. E., Fitzgerald, P., Rosenfeld, J. V., & Bittar, R. G. (2010). Neurosurgery for obsessive–compulsive disorder: Contemporary approaches. *Journal of Clinical Neuroscience, 17*(1), 1–5.

Beck, A. T., Butler, A. C., Brown, G. K., Dahlsgaard, K. K., Newman, C. F., & Beck, J. S. (2001). Dysfunctional beliefs discriminate personality disorders. *Behaviour Research and Therapy, 39*(10), 1213–1225.

Beesdo, K., Pine, D. S., Lieb, R., & Wittchen, H.-U. (2010). Incidence and risk patterns of anxiety and depressive disorders and categorization of generalized anxiety disorder. *Archives of General Psychiatry, 67*(1), 47–57.

Behar, E., Dobrow DiMarco, I., Hekler, E. B., Mohlman, J., & Staples, A. M. (2009). Current theoretical models of generalized anxiety disorder (GAD): Conceptual review and treatment implications. *Journal of Anxiety Disorders, 23*(8), 1011–1023.

Belsky, J. (2006). Determinants and consequences of infant–parent attachment. In L. Baker & C. S. Tamis-LeMonda (Eds.), *Child psychology: A handbook of contemporary issues* (2nd ed.) (pp. 53–57). New York: Psychology Press.

Belsky, J., & Pluess, M. (2009). Beyond diathesis stress: Differential susceptibility to environmental influences. *Psychological Bulletin, 135*(6), 885–908.

Belsky, J., Weinraub, M., Owen, M., & Kelly, J. (2001, April). Quantity of child care and problem behavior. In J. Belsky (Chair), *Early childcare and children's development prior to school entry.* Symposium conducted at the 2001 biennial meetings of the Society for Research in Child Development, Minneapolis, MN.

Bem, D. J. (2011). Feeling the future: Experimental evidence for anomalous retroactive influences on cognition and affect. *Journal of Personality and Social Psychology, 100*(3), 407–425.

Bender, H. L., Allen, J. P., Boykin McElhaney, K. J., Antonishak, C. M., Moore, H., O'Beirne K., & Davis, S. M. (2007). Use of harsh physical discipline and developmental outcomes in adolescence. *Development and Psychopathology, 19*(1) 227–242.

Benke, K., & Fallin, M. (2010). Methods: Genetic epidemiology. *Psychiatric Clinics of North America, 33*(1), 15–34.

Benson, H. (1975). *The relaxation response.* New York: Morrow.

Ben-Zur, H. (2002). Associations of Type A behavior with the emotional traits of anger and curiosity. *Anxiety, Stress and Coping: An International Journal, 15*(1), 95–104.

Berk, M. S., Henriques, G. R., Warman, D. M., Brown, G. K., & Beck, A. T. (2004). A cognitive therapy intervention for suicide attempters: An overview. *Cognitive and Behavioral Practice. 11*(3), 265–277.

Berkowitz, L. (2004). Two views of evil: Evil is not only banal. *PsycCRITIQUES.*

Bermudez, P., Lerch, J. P., Evans, A. C., & Zatorre, R. J. (2009). Neuroanatomical correlates of musicianship as revealed by cortical thickness and voxel-based morphometry. *Cerebral Cortex, 19*(7), 1583–1596.

Bernardin, H. J., Cooke, D. K., & Villanova, P. (2000). Conscientiousness and agreeableness as predictors of rating leniency. *Journal of Applied Psychology, 85*(2) 232–236.

Bernstein, D. M., & Loftus, E. F. (2009). How to tell if a particular memory is true or false. *Perspectives on Psychological Science, 4*(4), 370–374.

Berscheid, E. (2009). Love in the fourth dimension. *Annual Review of Psychology, 61*, 1–25.

Berten, H., & Rossem, R. V. (2009). Doing worse but knowing better: An exploration of the relationship between HIV/AIDS knowledge and sexual behavior among adolescents in Flemish secondary schools. *Journal of Adolescence, 32*(5), 1303–1319.

Bexton, W. H., Heron, W., & Scott, T. H. (1954). Effects of decreased variation in the sensory environment. *Canadian Journal of Psychology, 8*, 70–76.

Bidell, M. P., Turner, J. A., & Casas, J. M. (2002). First impressions count: Ethnic/racial and lesbian/gay/bisexual content of professional psychology application materials. *Professional Psychology: Research and Practice, 33*(1), 97–103.

Bienvenu, O. J., et al. (2005). Anxiety and depressive disorders and the five-factor model of personality: A higher- and lower-order personality trait investigation in a community sample. *Depression & Anxiety, 20*(2), 92–97.

Bierman, K. L., Domitrovich, C. E., Nix, R. L., Gest, S. D., & Welsh, J. A. (2008). flynn Promoting academic and social-emotional school readiness: The Head Start REDI program. *Child Development, 79*(6), 1802–1817.

Binder, E. B., & Nemeroff, C. B. (2009). The CRF system, stress, depression, and anxiety—Insights from human genetic studies. *Molecular Psychiatry, 15*(6), 574–588.

Bishop, D. V. M. (2009). Genes, cognition, and communication. *Annals of the New York Academy of Sciences, 1156*, 1–18.

Bizer, G. Y., et al. (2004). The impact of personality on cognitive, behavioral, and affective political processes: The effects of need to evaluate. *Journal of Personality, 72*(5), 995–1027.

Bjorklund, D. F. (2000). *Children's thinking* (3rd ed.). Pacific Grove, CA: Brooks/Cole.

Blake, P., Fry, R., & Pesjack, M. (1984). *Self-assessment and behavior change manual.* New York: Random House.

Blass, T. (2009). From New Haven to Santa Clara: A historical perspective on the Milgram obedience experiments. *American Psychologist, 64*(1), 37–45.

Blechert, J., Wilhelm, F. H., Meuret, A. E., Wilhelm, E. M., & Roth, W. T. (2010). Respiratory, autonomic, and experiential responses to repeated inhalations of 20% CO_2 enriched air in panic disorder, social phobia, and healthy controls. *Biological Psychology, 84*(1), 104–111.

Block, N. (2009). The mind as the software of the brain. In S. Schneider (Ed.), *Science fiction and philosophy: From time travel to superintelligence* (pp. 170–185). Hoboken, NJ: Wiley.

Blum, K., Chen, A. L. C., Chen, T. J. H., Bowirrat, A., Downs, B. W., Waite, R. L., ... Comings, D. E. (2009). Genes and happiness. *Gene Therapy and Molecular Biology, 13*, 91–129.

Bogen, J. E. (1969). The other side of the brain II: An appositional mind. *Bulletin of the Los Angeles Neurological Society, 34*, 135–162.

Bogen, J. E. (2000). Split-brain basics: Relevance for the concept of one's other mind. *Journal of the American Academy of Psychoanalysis, 28*(2), 341–369.

Bohner, G., & Dickel, N. (2011). Attitudes and attitude change. *Annual Review of Psychology, 62*, 391–417.

Bolinskey, K. P., & Gottesman, I. I. (2010). Premorbid personality indicators of schizophrenia-related psychosis in a hypothetically psychosis-prone college sample. *Scandinavian Journal of Psychology, 51*(1), 68–74.

Bonds-Raacke, J.M., Fryer, L.S., Nicks, S.D., and Durr, R.T. (2001). Hindsight bias demonstrated in the prediction of a sporting event. *The Journal of Social Psychology, 141*, 349.

Bonn-Miller, M. O., Zvolensky, M. J., & Bernstein, A. (2007). Marijuana use motives: Concurrent relations to frequency of past 30-day use and anxiety sensitivity among young adult marijuana smokers. *Addictive Behaviors, 32*(1), 49–62.

Boom, J., Wouters, H., & Keller, M. (2007). A cross cultural validation of stage development. A Rasch re-analysis of longitudinal socio-moral reasoning data. *Cognitive Development, 22*(2), 213–229.

Bouchard, C. (2010). Defining the genetic architecture of the predisposition to obesity: A challenging but not insurmountable task. *American Journal of Clinical Nutrition, 91*(1), 5–6.

Bouton, M. E. (2010). The multiple forms of "context" in associative learning theory. In B. Mesquita, L. F. Barrett, & E. R. Smith (Eds.), *The mind in context* (pp. 233–258). New York: Guilford Press.

Bower, B. (1997). Forbidden flavors: Scientists consider how disgusting tastes can linger surreptitiously in memory. *Science News, 151*, 198–199.

Bower, B. (1991). Oedipus Wrecked: Freud's Theory of Frustrated Incest Goes on the Defensive. *Science News, 140*, 248–250.

Bowlby, J. (1988). *A secure base.* New York: Basic Books.

Boyatzis, R. E. (1974). The effect of alcohol consumption on the aggressive behavior of men. *Quarterly Journal for the Study of Alcohol, 35*, 959–972.

Braarud, H. C., & Stormark, K. M. (2008). EJ814142—Prosodic modification and vocal adjustments in mothers' speech during face-to-face interaction with their two- to four-month-old infants: A double video study. *Social Development, 17*(4), 1074–1084.

Brackett, M. A., Rivers, S. E., & Salovey, P. (2011). Emotional intelligence: Implication for personal, social, academic, and workplace success. *Social and Personality Psychology, 5*(1), 88–103.

Bradley, R. H., et al. (1989). Home environment and cognitive development in the first 3 years of life. *Developmental Psychology, 25*, 217–235.

Bradley, R. H. (2006). The home environment. In N. F. Watt, C. Ayoub, R. H.

- Updated research on the value of social support
- Revised the box, "Are There Gender Differences in Response to Stress?"
- Added the box, "Stress Tip Sheet"
- Pared back the section on cancer

Chapter 12 Changes

- Reordered the discussion of disorders in the chapter
- Revised the Truth or Fiction questions
- Added a new chapter-opening vignette (previously an example in the dissociative disorders section)
- Revised the discussion on perspectives on psychological disorders to fall under its own head

Chapter 13 Changes

- Made small edits throughout to make areas more concise
- Added a new chapter-opening vignette (previously an example in the virtual therapy section)
- Changed psychoanalytic perspective to psychodynamic perspective
- Condensed the virtual therapy section
- Added a brief section on self-help and support groups
- Revised the "Does Psychotherapy Work?" section
- Created a new head, "Does Biological Therapy Work?," which pulls together parts of various sections

Chapter 14 Changes

- Revised the learning objectives
- Updated the chapter-opening vignette
- Added the box, "When It Comes to Sex, Red May Mean 'Go'"
- Deleted the section on body language
- Added a section on aggression
- Revised the section on groupthink

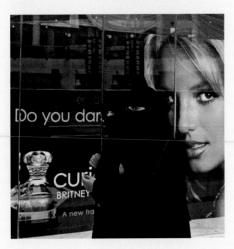

CHAPTER OUTLINE

> **Chapter at a Glance**
> The outline with page references gives you a quick snapshot of the content covered in the chapter.

WHAT'S INSIDE

Topics discussed in this chapter incl...
ogy; the history of psychology; the ...
gists; research methods for human ...
scientific model; ethical considerati...
thinking.

> **What's a Prep Card?**
> To help you prepare, we've developed a Prep Card for each chapter. Each card starts with a short list of key topics covered in the chapter.

LEARNING OUTCOMES

1-1 Define psychology

1-2 Describe the various fields of psycholog...

1-3 Describe the origins of psychology and i... ...le significant contributions to the field

1-4 Identify theoretical perspectives from w... psychologists view behavior and mental ...

1-5 Explain how psychologists study behavior and mental processes, focusing on critical thinking, research methods, and ethical considerations

> **Learning Outcomes**
> The quick list of outcomes reiterates what students should take away from the chapter.

TEACHING SUGGESTIONS

MULTIMEDIA HIGHLIGHTS
Facial Analysis 5:16

Available on *Research in Action Videos, Vol II.* Thi...
as researchers explore whether computers coul...
students: What might be some real-world appli...
analysis be a more objective measure of emoti...
of computers so important in research?

> **Videos**
> Long and short videos feature the laboratories of established and up-and-coming psychology researchers and cover current studies and research in psychology.

LECTURE TOPICS
1. **Student Expectations** Before going over the definition of psychology, break the students into groups and allow them to discuss...

   What is psychology?

   What would you like to learn...

   After giving them time to come u... ...each group report to the class what the group came... ...nd discuss each concept. This helps students preview the course content and find out what they will learn versus what they wish they could learn.

> **Lecture Topics**
> A variety of lecture topics helps you engage your students from the first minute of class.

2. **Preparing for a Future Class** End the first lecture by playing a tape of some unique music and invite students to sample a distinct aroma or taste as they file out. Provide numerous small samples of fresh basil leaves on top of summer tomatoes. Present this as simply something that is enjoyable and that you want the students to experience. Do not mention the purpose until the beginning of the unit on Memory, when you again play the music at the start of a class. If this works you will have several students spontaneously mention their association with the basil–tomato taste, and then you are off and running, having established associations as the basis for conditioning. (Note that this demonstration should work with any combination of novel and/or strong sensory stimuli.)

1 What Is Psychology?

KEY TERMS

Key Terms

This list gives you a quick view of the terminology you can expect your students to know.

TEACHING SUGGESTIONS *continued*

LECTURE TOPICS *continued*

3. **Forensic Psychology** For this lecture topic, discuss with your students the topic of forensic psychology. This topic is typically not covered in an introductory text but is an area of interest to students. Forensic psychologists apply the modern approaches to psychology in the area of law. Psychologists in this field may focus on such things as the design of correctional facilities, interrogation methods, and examination of eyewitness testimony. To help your students understand this interesting, modern approach to psychology, access the American Board of Forensic Psychology website at: www.abfp.com.

STUDENT PROJECTS

1. **American Psychological Association (APA)** One of the best resources on the web is the American Psychological Association's website, which can be found at www.apa.org. This extensive website has a plethora of information on psychology . Your textbook discusses many areas of study within the field of psychology. What career opportunities are there in psychology? The APA website can help answer this question and explain each in your own words.

   Access the website at the above address. O[...] Brochure link. Then you will be able to click [...] careers site by going to: http://www.apa.or[...]

2. **Samples of Populations** As you learn more [...] find that much of the research is conducted [...] election years when polling data is reported. Do samples used in research reflect human diversity (the whole population)? Why? For this project, bring in articles from newspapers or magazines, etc., that report research using samples. Be prepared to discuss the basic methods used in the research.

Projects

Extend course concepts beyond the class by assigning students projects. This section provides a range of ideas and guidelines for using them.

CLASSROOM DEMONSTRATIONS

1. **Current Perspectives in Psychology** This classroom activity works better after you have presented on the current perspectives in psychology. Between classes, create paper signs that you can hang on the walls in the classroom. On class day, hang the signs on the walls around the room. Have students stand in the center of the room and then ask them, "If you had to pick one perspective to study and explain behavior, which [...] priate sign on the wall. After all the students h[...] why. This can lead to some interesting group d[...]

2. **"Star Trek" Preparation:** You will need copies of [...] episodes that have captains as the main chara[...]

   One way to teach students the various aspects [...] methodology suggested by Herreinger (2000) [...] *Psychology* journal and focus on the television [...] Generation." Herreinger has students watch episodes of each and analyze the personalities of Captain Kirk and Captain Picard. Students are instructed to use information that is reliable and objective, which typically involves operationally defining variables. This activity can help students apply the concepts of research methods.

Classroom Demonstrations

Each Prep Card contains multiple classroom demonstrations that can help you bring the study of psychology alive for your students. Detailed suggestions for conducting each demonstration are given.

PSYCH was designed for instructors just like you—busy people who want choices, flexibility, and multiple teaching options.

PSYCH delivers concise, focused, thoroughly researched information in a fresh and contemporary way. In addition to your tear-out prep cards, PSYCH offers a variety of teaching materials designed with you in mind.

PowerLecture DVD with ExamView®

This one-stop lecture and class preparation tool contains ready-to-use Microsoft® PowerPoint® slides and other great tools—enabling you to assemble, edit, and present custom lectures for your course. With **PowerLecture**, you can bring together text-specific lecture outlines and art from PSYCH, along with videos or your own materials—culminating in a powerful, media-enhanced presentation. In your chapter prep cards, see Multimedia Highlights for video suggestions.

PowerLecture also includes a full *Instructor's Resource Manual* and *Test Bank* in **ExamView** format.

- **Instructor's Resource Manual**

  This easy-to-use, comprehensive manual—organized by content area—includes an array of features, activities, and review material to help you streamline your course while maximizing the effectiveness of your course preparation. The manual contains lecture topics, classroom demonstrations, student projects, learning objectives, an annotated list of suggested readings, as well as ready-made handouts to help you efficiently prepare a well-rounded lecture.

- **ExamView**

  You'll create, deliver, and customize tests (both print and online) in minutes with this easy-to-use assessment and tutorial system. **ExamView** includes over 3,000 PSYCH-specific test questions in electronic format and offers both a Quick Test Wizard and an Online Test Wizard that guide you step-by-step through the process of creating tests.

THE LIST OF GREAT TOOLS CONTINUES ON THE BACK.

instructorresources

WebTutor™

Jumpstart your course with customizable, rich text-specific content within your Course Management System. Whether you want to Web-enable your class or put an entire course online, WebTutor™ delivers. WebTutor™ offers a wide array of resources including access to the eBook, glossaries, flashcards, quizzes, videos, and more.

Video Resources

- **Wadsworth Psychology: Research in Action Videos, Vol. I & II**
  These videos take students right into the laboratories of established and up-and-coming psychology researchers! Students learn not only who is conducting this cutting-edge research but also how it's done and where the results are being applied outside the laboratory. Topics include "Trust and the Brain," "Stress and Health," "Internet Relationships," and "Issues in Multiracial Development." Creator Roger D. Klein (Ph.D., Educational Psychology) is an award-winning psychology teacher and video producer. The Multimedia Highlights on the chapter prep cards provide suggestions for **Research in Action Videos** to use in your class.
- **ABC® Videos: Introductory Psychology**
  These short, high-interest clips cover current studies and research in psychology. Perfect for engaging discussion or enriching lectures, topics include mental illness and suicide, prescription drug abuse in teenagers, stem cell research, gay teens, rules of attraction, and foster care.

PSYCH CourseMate

www.cengagebrain.com

This invaluable book companion includes resources for both instructors and students. Instructors will find the full instructor's resource manual, PowerPoint lecture slides, and more. Here are some of the study tools specifically designed for your students:

- *Learning Outcomes* Downloadable learning outcomes from PSYCH.
- *Interactive Flashcards* Key terms are also available as interactive flash cards that allow you to shuffle the deck, remove a card, view the term first, or view the definition first.
- *Printable Flashcards* Our extensive research shows that almost all students use flash cards to reinforce their understanding of core psychology concepts. To help you prepare flash cards that fit your specific study needs, the website provides three varieties of downloadable flash cards: 1) term only, 2) definition only, or 3) term and definition. Each set of cards is formatted to fit the standard Avery business card template.
- *Glossary* Select a chapter to view glossary terms and definitions.
- *Quizzes* You can practice before chapter tests, midterms, and finals by taking these interactive quizzes.
- *Study Games* Games provide fun study practice.
- *Interactive Practice* Learning Modules and Drag-and-Drops help you learn more about concepts covered in PSYCH.
- *Videos* News and research video clips bring chapter concepts to life.

YOU TOLD US HOW YOU TEACH YOUR CLASS, AND

WE LISTENED.

1

CHAPTER OUTLINE

WHAT'S INSIDE

Topics discussed in this chapter include: theories and the fields of psychology; the history of psychology; the contributions of modern-day psychologists; research methods for human behavior and mental processes; the scientific model; ethical considerations in research and practice; critical thinking.

LEARNING OUTCOMES

1-1 Define psychology

1-2 Describe the various fields of psychology

1-3 Describe the origins of psychology and identify people who made significant contributions to the field

1-4 Identify theoretical perspectives from which today's psychologists view behavior and mental processes

1-5 Explain how psychologists study behavior and mental processes, focusing on critical thinking, research methods, and ethical considerations

TEACHING SUGGESTIONS

MULTIMEDIA HIGHLIGHTS
Facial Analysis 5:16

Available on *Research in Action Videos, Vol II*. This video shows the scientific method in action as researchers explore whether computers could help us analyze facial expressions. Ask your students: What might be some real-world applications of facial analysis? Why might facial analysis be a more objective measure of emotions than our own perceptions? Why is the use of computers so important in research?

LECTURE TOPICS

1. **Student Expectations** Before going over the definition of psychology, break the students into groups and allow them to discuss the following questions:

   What is psychology?

   What would you like to learn in psychology?

   After giving them time to come up with their answers, have a member from each group report to the class what the group came up with. Write all their ideas on the board and discuss each concept. This helps students preview the course content and find out what they will learn versus what they wish they could learn.

2. **Preparing for a Future Class** End the first lecture by playing a tape of some unique music and invite students to sample a distinct aroma or taste as they file out. Provide numerous small samples of fresh basil leaves on top of summer tomatoes. Present this as simply something that is enjoyable and that you want the students to experience. Do not mention the purpose until the beginning of the unit on Memory, when you again play the music at the start of a class. If this works you will have several students spontaneously mention their association with the basil–tomato taste, and then you are off and running, having established associations as the basis for conditioning. (Note that this demonstration should work with any combination of novel and/or strong sensory stimuli.)

1 What Is Psychology?

TEACHING SUGGESTIONS *continued*

LECTURE TOPICS *continued*

3. **Forensic Psychology** For this lecture topic, discuss with your students the topic of forensic psychology. This topic is typically not covered in an introductory text but is an area of interest to students. Forensic psychologists apply the modern approaches to psychology in the area of law. Psychologists in this field may focus on such things as the design of correctional facilities, interrogation methods, and examination of eyewitness testimony. To help your students understand this interesting, modern approach to psychology, access the American Board of Forensic Psychology website at: www.abfp.com.

STUDENT PROJECTS

1. **American Psychological Association (APA)** One of the best resources on the web is the American Psychological Association's website, which can be found at www.apa.org. This extensive website has a plethora of information on psychology. Your textbook discusses many areas of study within the field of psychology. What career opportunities are there in psychology? The APA website can help answer this question. Use the site to explore five careers in psychology and explain each in your own words.

   Access the website at the above address. Once there, click on the Students link and then the Brochure link. Then you will be able to click on the Subfields link. You could go directly to the careers site by going to: http://www.apa.org/students/brochure/subfields.html.

2. **Samples of Populations** As you learn more about research methods used in psychology, you will find that much of the research is conducted using samples of people. This is commonly seen in election years when polling data is reported. Do samples used in research reflect human diversity (the whole population)? Why? For this project, bring in articles from newspapers or magazines, etc., that report research using samples. Be prepared to discuss the basic methods used in the research.

CLASSROOM DEMONSTRATIONS

1. **Current Perspectives in Psychology** This classroom activity works better after you have presented on the current perspectives in psychology. Between classes, create paper signs that you can hang on the walls in the classroom. On class day, hang the signs on the walls around the room. Have students stand in the center of the room and then ask them, "If you had to pick one perspective to study and explain behavior, which would it be?" Have students move to the appropriate sign on the wall. After all the students have made their decision, have each group explain why. This can lead to some interesting group discussions.

2. **"Star Trek"** *Preparation:* You will need copies of "Star Trek" and "Star Trek: the Next Generation" episodes that have captains as the main character. Students may have their own copies.

   One way to teach students the various aspects of research methods is to use an interesting methodology suggested by Herreinger (2000). His suggestions are found in the *Teaching of Psychology* journal and focus on the television series "Star Trek" and "Star Trek: the Next Generation." Herreinger has students watch episodes of each and analyze the personalities of Captain Kirk and Captain Picard. Students are instructed to use information that is reliable and objective, which typically involves operationally defining variables. This activity can help students apply the concepts of research methods.

CHAPTER OUTLINE

KEY TERMS

(Continued)

WHAT'S INSIDE

Topics discussed in this chapter include: nervous systems, neurotransmitters, endocrine system, split-brain patients, brain structures and functions, Charles Darwin, theory of evolution, evolutionary psychology, twin and adoptee studies, heredity, steroid controversy, and hormone imbalances.

LEARNING OUTCOMES

2-1 Describe the nervous system, including neurons, neural impulses, and neurotransmitters

2-2 List the structures of the brain and their functions

2-3 Explain the role of the endocrine system and list the endocrine glands

2-4 Describe evolutionary psychology and the connections between heredity, behavior, and mental processes

TEACHING SUGGESTIONS

MULTIMEDIA HIGHLIGHTS
Action Potential 1:26

Available on the *PowerLecture* DVD. This short clip describes the action potential. Ask your students: Can you define the action potential? Explain how an action potential travels along the axon of a neuron. Explain the relationship between the action potential and the resting potential.

Brain Organization, Structure and Function 5:52

Available on *Research in Action Videos, Vol. I*. This video shows students how psychologists are learning to map the brain in a variety of organisms. They see how researchers use different procedures to identify which brain areas are connected and how they function, and how psychologists can trace a neural message in monkeys that travels from the finger to the brain.

LECTURE TOPICS

1. **The Neuron** After you have discussed how neurons work and how the synapse offers a wide range of variability in the nervous system, have students brainstorm ideas about how the neurons could be explained using real-life analogies. (For example: The students receive information from their instructor. Which part of the neuron would the instructor be?)

2. **Phineas Gage** No lecture on the brain can be complete without a discussion of Phineas Gage and the experience he had with a tamping iron. This historical experience is found in most introductory psychology textbooks as well as many neurology textbooks. In 1994, researchers were granted access to Gage's skull to determine exactly what happened when the tamping rod passed through his skull. To learn more about what they found, access an article found in most libraries titled "What Happened to Phineas?" written by Shreeve (1995). This brief article will aid you as you explain the fascination and the lessons learned from an experience that happened over century ago.

2 Biology and Psychology

TEACHING SUGGESTIONS *continued*

STUDENT PROJECTS

1. **Endorphins** Many students can easily relate to the concept of the "runner's high." The "runner's high," which is caused by the release of endorphins, helps the body compensate for pain. Research the following questions on the Internet. (You may wish to read the article, "The Buzz on Exercise," written by Anderson (1995). Then answer the following questions: (1) What types of exercise tend to facilitate the release of endorphins? (2) How long does a person typically have to exercise before experiencing the release of endorphins? (3) Have you ever experienced a runner's high? If so, be prepared to discuss your experience in class.

2. **Biological Evidence for Evolution** To aid in your understanding of what evolution is and the evidence that exists to support this theoretical approach, read "Biological Evidence For Evolution," by Smith (2001). Then answer the following questions: (1) What is the simple definition of evolution as presented in the article? (2) What is the crux of evolution? What does the term "heritable" mean? (3) What is natural selection? (4) What are the four things about evolution that the author says "need to be clear"?

CLASSROOM DEMONSTRATIONS

1. **Timing the Neural Impulse** In order to demonstrate the time it takes for neural impulses to be processed, perform a variation of the "dollar drop." Take a dollar and ask a student to drop it from the thumb and index finger of one hand (holding onto the short side of the dollar) and catch it with the thumb and index finger of the other hand. The student should have no trouble with this part of the exercise. Then have the student try to catch it while a partner drops the bill. Ask the students to explain the difference in results.

2. **Behavioral Effects of the Split-Brain Operation** Ask for three volunteers from the class, one of whom has shoes with laces (volunteer 1). The other two volunteers should be right-handed (volunteers 2 and 3). (Make sure the rest of the class can see what will happen.) Have volunteer 1 stand on a table in the front of the classroom and untie one shoe. Have volunteer 2 retie that shoe while you explain that a "normal" functioning person has little problem tying a shoe. Explain that what will happen next is a demonstration of how it might be for someone who has experienced a split-brain operation (perhaps to help with a severe case of epilepsy). Have volunteer 1 untie the shoe. Have volunteers 2 and 3 sit on a chair in front of the table. Volunteer 2 and 3 should place their outside arms behind their backs (left hand for the left volunteer and right hand for the right volunteer). Volunteers 2 and 3 should place their inner arms on the table, one crossing over the other (to illustrate the crossing-over nature of the brain-body connection). The volunteer representing the left hand should not speak from this point on (to demonstrate the localization of brain functioning, specifically the speech areas). Now have volunteers 2 and 3 attempt to retie the shoe. *Adapted from: Morris, E.J. (1991). Classroom demonstration of behavioral effects of the split-brain operation. Teaching of Psychology, 18 (4), 226–228.*

   For the next two classroom demonstrations, you will need a computer, Internet access, and a projector.

3. **Hypothalamus and Pituitary** To help your students understand the endocrine system, show them the images at: http://arbl.cvmbs.colostate.edu/hbooks/pathphys/endocrine/hypopit/anatomy.html. The images of the hypothalamus and pituitary are from a real human cadaver, part of the Visible Human Project.

4. **Genetic Diseases** To discuss genetic diseases with your students go to: http://www.genome.gov/10001204

CHAPTER OUTLINE

KEY TERMS

(Continued)

WHAT'S INSIDE

Topics discussed in this chapter include: definition of sensation and perception; the five traditional senses; the properties of light; the parts of the eye; the parts of the ear; the chemical senses including smell and taste; the skin senses and theoretical explanations for pain; the kinesthetic and vestibular senses; and the impact of virtual reality and visual illusions.

LEARNING OUTCOMES

3-1 Define and differentiate between sensation and perception

3-2 Identify the parts of the eye; describe the properties of light and the theories of color vision

3-3 Describe the organization of visual perceptions

3-4 Identify the parts of the ear; explain the sense of hearing

3-5 Describe the chemical senses

3-6 Identify the skin senses and theoretical explanations for pain

3-7 Describe the kinesthetic and vestibular senses

3-8 Explain why psychologists are skeptical about extrasensory perception

TEACHING SUGGESTIONS

MULTIMEDIA HIGHLIGHTS
Overview of the Functioning of the Eye and Retina 0:28
Available on the *PowerLecture* DVD. This short clip provides a visual display of the eye's role in sight processes.

LECTURE TOPICS
1. **Synesthesia** Have your students imagine that they are eating something and instead of tasting the food, they see colors flashing in front of them; instead of hearing a song, they feel a soft brush on the back of their ankle. This interesting condition is known as synesthesia. To help your students understand this interesting condition, have them read "Everyday Fantasia: The World of Synesthesia," by Carpenter. This article, which was written for the *APA Monitor on Psychology*, discusses this interesting condition and provides examples of people with the condition and attempts to understand it.

2. **Somesthesis** To introduce your students to the area of the skin senses, ask them to read "Somesthesis," by Craig and Rollman (1999). This in-depth article explores the skin senses and focuses on touch, texture, touch in communication, thermal sensitivity, kinesthesis, and pain. This article will provide students with a complete understanding of the skin sense.

STUDENT PROJECTS
1. **Senses and the Brain** To better understand how our senses work, how they define our world, and how they interact with our brain, access an article found in most libraries titled "The Senses: They Delight, Heal, Define the Boundaries of our World. And They are Helping Unlock the Brain's Secrets" written by Brownlee (1997). This article explores each of the senses and suggests that most of our world is interpreted through a combination of senses working together. For this project, read the article and then write a one-page paper summarizing something interesting you learned about each of the five senses. You may also want to determine if you are a super-taster, which you can find at the end of the article.

(Continued)

STUDENT PROJECTS *continued*

2. **The Color Vision Test** For this project you will be exploring information regarding color vision and those who are colorblind. Effects have been made to imporve the ability to assess color vision to detect possible vision problems. Access an article found in most libraries titled "Test for Colour Vision; -and save sight" written by Arden (2003). After reading this article, write a one-page response paper about color blindness and the attempts being made to assess this condition. You may also want to visit the following website at: http://colorvisiontesting. com. This website has information about color vision testing.

CLASSROOM DEMONSTRATIONS

1. **Discussions of S & P** Divide the class into groups of four or five students. Ask them the following questions about sensation and perception:

   - What is the difference between sensation and perception?

   - Put out your arm and point your finger at an object across the room while you have one eye closed. Open that eye and close the other. Why isn't the finger still on the object?

   - Why is it easier to locate the source of a sound when it comes from the side than when it comes from behind?

   - Why doesn't food taste as good when you have a cold?

2. **Test for Color Blindness** *Preparation:* You will need a computer, Internet access, and a projector.

   In this demonstration, you will show your students a test to determine color blindness. You can find the test at: http://colorvisiontesting.com/ This website has a color-blindness test as well as some explanations of color blindness.

3. **The Food–Taste Bud Connection** *Preparation:* You will need three bottles of bottled water (different brands) with cups to illustrate taste preference, an artichoke and an apple to illustrate modifying proteins, an apple with salt to intensify the fruit's flavor, and soy sauce and chocolate syrup to illustrate muted tastes.

   In this demonstration, you will help students understand the complex sensation of flavor, which is an interaction of smell and taste. Taste and smell interact to help differentiate flavors. For example, bottled waters should have no taste, but do we have preferences for a certain brand? Have your students discuss this while volunteers sample different bottles of water and rank their preferences.

   Taste Modifiers: Foods can also taste different because of what you have recently eaten. For example, after you eat an artichoke, everything else you eat will taste sweet. Have a volunteer eat a piece of apple and rate its sweetness. Then have them eat some artichoke and then a piece of apple to see if the apple tastes sweeter. Putting salt on an apple should *also* intensify its taste.

   Taste Mute: Have a volunteer taste some soy sauce and then taste some chocolate syrup. The soy sauce should mute the sweet taste of the chocolate. *This information comes from* "How Food Communicates With Your Taste Buds: The Chemistry of Perception," *by Hunter (2002).* This demonstration takes some preparation time, but it can be very effective in illustrating taste and smell.

WHAT'S INSIDE

Topics discussed in this chapter include: definition of consciousness, the nature of sleep, sleep disorders, hypnosis, meditation, biofeedback techniques, substance abuse, and the various categories of drugs.

LEARNING OUTCOMES

4-1 Define consciousness

4-2 Explain the nature of sleep and various sleep disorders

4-3 Explain various nature and uses of hypnosis, meditation, and biofeedback in altering consciousness

4-4 Define substance abuse and dependence, identify categories of psychoactive drugs, and explain their allures and dangers

TEACHING SUGGESTIONS

MULTIMEDIA HIGHLIGHTS
Weight Loss Hypnosis 4:50

Available on the *PowerLecture* DVD. Hypnosis helps one woman find the motivation to eat healthier and exercise. A look at the scientific side of hypnosis, how it can help, and its limitations.

LECTURE TOPICS

1. **When Perception Becomes Consciousness** To help your students better understand the construct of consciousness, access an article found in most libraries titled "When Perception Becomes Conscious" written by Velmans (1999). This article presents a model to represent the psychological transition between perceiving the world and how that analysis becomes consciousness. The author suggests that some of the difficulty in studying consciousness comes in defining the construct. Is something conscious when a person is conscious of the process, or is it consciousness when a third person can distinguish it? The article goes on to suggest ways to determine if something is conscious or not.

2. **Power Naps** Students often hear about cultures that take siestas or naps in the afternoon. In the fast-paced lifestyle of a college student, it would seem that the day isn't long enough to do that. But could taking a nap actually help? To help your students understand how this could benefit them, ask them to read "Siesta Time: Power Napping," written for *The Economist (2002)*. This article contains a summary of research conducted in which subjects took afternoon naps and describe the influence the naps had on their visual perception. The research suggests that an afternoon nap of 60 minutes can be beneficial, news that your students will love to hear.

3. **The Science of Meditation** Research is being conducted to determine the benefits of meditation. This ancient practice has been shrouded in mystery for many years. To help your students understand the scientific approach to meditation, have them read "The Science of Meditation," written by Barbor (2001). This article discusses how groups of people have integrated meditation into every aspect of their lives. The article also discusses research conducted at Harvard Medical School using MRI technology to investigate what happens to the brain during meditation. The article suggests that the autonomic nervous system seems to be affected.

4 Consciousness

TEACHING SUGGESTIONS *continued*

STUDENT PROJECTS

1. **Friend Survey** For this project, ask three female and three male friends if they have recently had any aggressive fantasies. Perhaps they were mad at someone and had a fantasy about getting even. With their permission and maintaining confidentiality, briefly summarize the fantasies and then evaluate the summaries to see if there is any difference in the type of aggressive fantasies that males and females have. Be prepared to share your findings in class.

2. **Teaching Children about Sleep** Sleep is a fact of life. It has been estimated that people spend about a third of their life sleeping. Because this experience is so common, people (including children) don't think a lot about it. Yet some of the common sleep disturbances happen during childhood. If you were to prepare a lesson plan to teach children about sleep, a great resource is an article titled "Sleep and Dreams," written for *Science Weekly (2002)*. This article provides information about sleep in a simplistic manner, though you may find some things that will be new to you. Your task for this assignment is to develop a lesson plan to educate children about sleep and dreams. You may want to include information such as different types of sleep, what nightmares are, dreams, circadian rhythms, sleepwalking, and the amount of sleep that is necessary for children.

3. **Awareness of Advertising** For this project, you will be exploring the world of advertising. Advertisers use various methods to sell their products. Are there techniques that may facilitate us in paying attention to their ads? The textbook suggests that sudden changes, novel stimuli, intense stimuli, and repetitive stimuli can all contribute to capturing our attention. For this project watch television and keep a log of the advertisements that you see. Indicate which advertisements you enjoyed and why you enjoyed them. Did the advertisers use some of the techniques suggested in the text? Be prepared to discuss your findings in class.

CLASSROOM DEMONSTRATIONS

1. **Biofeedback Computer Games** *Preparation:* You will need a computer, Internet access, and a projector. You may need to download the games from the site first, depending on your Internet provider.

   For this demonstration go to: www.bfbgames.com. This is the homepage for Biofeedback Computer Games, actual computer games that can be downloaded and played to help a person relax. For complete biofeedback, the website would like a person to purchase the "pulse detector," which can monitor the heart rate while a person plays the games. The pulse detector connects to the computer. For the demonstration, you can play the games without the detector.

2. **Prescribe a Good Night Sleep** *Preparation:* Be familiar with the suggested techniques from the article.

   In this demonstration, you will have a discussion with your students to elicit possible suggestions to help someone get a good night's sleep. Have the students suggest techniques that they use to help them sleep and list them on the board. You can suggest ideas that have been shown to be effective through research. These techniques can be found in an article titled "Getting a Good Night's Sleep with the Help of Psychology," on the American Psychological Association website at www.apa.org/research/action/sleep.aspx. The techniques these authors suggest are having good sleep hygiene, relaxation techniques, keeping a sleep diary, sleep restriction therapy, and psychotherapy. Then compare the student's suggestions to the suggestions from the article.

3. **Hypnotist** If you know a hypnotist or hypnotherapist, ask them to come to class and talk about what they do. Have them discuss clinical and stage hypnosis and then illustrate stage hypnosis. As the students are enjoying the stage hypnosis show, they are also learning various hypnotic concepts. When they finish the show, discuss clinical hypnosis and answer questions. It is a great way to teach the various aspects of hypnosis.

WHAT'S INSIDE

Topics discussed in this chapter include: the definition of learning; behavioral and cognitive perspectives; Ivan Pavlov; classical conditioning; taste aversions and phobias; Edward Thorndike; B. F. Skinner; operant conditioning; reinforcers; schedules of reinforcement; punishment; shaping; Tolman; Bandura; and violence in the media.

LEARNING OUTCOMES

5-1 Define learning

5-2 Describe principles and methods of classical conditioning

5-3 Describe principles and methods of operant conditioning

5-4 Describe cognitive factors in learning

TEACHING SUGGESTIONS

MULTIMEDIA HIGHLIGHTS
Little Albert 0:38

Available on the *PowerLecture* DVD. Watch this classic video clip of Little Albert and the conditioning he was exposed to as a baby. Ask your students to explain the learning theory of fear that underlies this experiment by John B. Watson and Rosalie Rayner. How would you go about reversing Little Albert's conditioning?

Fear Conditioning 6:04

Available on *Research in Action Videos, Vol. I*. Many people suffer from phobias and anxiety disorders. Students learn how simple Pavlovian conditioning experiments with rats help to uncover the neurobiology of fear. Students see how surgical lesions in rats can help to determine which brain areas are critical for emotional content, and which are crucial for contextual learning.

LECTURE TOPICS
1. **Taste Aversion and Alcohol** Taste aversion research has focused on many areas of animal behavior. Comparative studies have been conducted with animals to investigate the possible influence that taste aversions could have with humans. One area of interest is alcohol consumption. Recent attempts to create taste aversion to alcohol in humans have been pursued as possible treatment options. Because of the various factors that contribute to alcohol consumption in humans, the research is ongoing. Reference the article "Conditioned Taste Aversion and Alcohol Drinking: Strain and Gender," by Cailhol and Mormede (2002). The authors investigate conditioned taste aversions in laboratory rats. One of the goals of the research was to determine the etiological basis of individual vulnerability to alcohol. This subject can be discussed with the class as ongoing research, trying to identify vulnerabilities as well as using classical conditioning procedures as possible treatment for alcohol abuse.

STUDENT PROJECTS
1. **Reinforcement or Reinforcer?** An integral part of operant conditioning is the concept of reinforcement. These "rewards" that increase the probability of responding can be powerful influences in a person's life. Students often get confused between positive and negative reinforcers. To aid in your understanding of these concepts, access an article in most libraries titled "Reward and Punishment: In the regular feature examiners and teachers will explore baffling or taken for granted concepts and topics to give you clarity and insight into their meaning and their significance" by Curtis (2001). After reading the article, define in your own words what a reinforcer and

(Continued)

5 Learning

TEACHING SUGGESTIONS *continued*

STUDENT PROJECTS *continued*

what a reinforcement is. Also, diagram the contingency table that explains positive and negative reinforcement, and punishment.

2. **Principles of Behavior Modification** This project will provide you with an opportunity to create a hypothetical plan to help a person overcome a problem behavior. Your first task will be to identify a problem behavior (in a person or animal) that needs to be changed. Then go to www.edpsychinteractive.org/topics/behavior/behmod.html. This website has proposed principles that can be used to help students in their task. Take the suggested principles and develop your plan to change the target behavior, then be prepared to discuss your plan in class.

3. **Forbidden Flavors** Researchers have surmised that how we taste may have evolved over time, and that placement of our taste buds may serve an evolutionary process, that being to warn us against poisons. Though we aren't often faced with having to detect poisons through our taste buds, we do develop taste aversions. To learn more about these aversions and the connection that flavors have with memory, access an article found in most libraries titled "Forbidden Flavors: Scientists Consider How Disgusting Tastes Can Linger Surreptitiously in Memory" by Bower (1997). After reading this article, write a one-page summary of what you learned. Connect the information presented in the article to the theory of evolution. Is it important that we remember?

CLASSROOM DEMONSTRATIONS

1. **Balloon** *Instructor Preparation:* You will need some balloons (full of air) and a pin to pop the balloons.

   Classical conditioning is difficult to demonstrate because the response that individuals have is reflexive or automatic. One demonstration that works is popping balloons. A popping balloon will typically elicit a startle response from students in the classroom. Take a few balloons and pop them with your pin. Point out the startle response in the students. Make sure you exaggerate the pin meeting the balloon. Now attempt to pop a balloon by sticking the pin in at the nipple of the balloon. The balloon will not pop. Typically students will still show the startle response. The response is in reaction to seeing the pin meet the balloon. If you do this a few times the students may develop an extinguished startle response. Toward the end of the lecture, try to pop the balloon again by going through the nipple, and see if there is a spontaneous recovery of the startle response.

2. **Invisible Fence** An interesting example of operant (and classical) conditioning principles is the invisible fence that many dog owners use. Draw a schematic of a house and yard. Ask for suggestions for how the owner might try to keep the dog in the yard. (They could tie the dog up, install a fence, or purchase a dog run.)

   The invisible fence solves this problem with a radio transmitter plugged into an electrical outlet in the home. This transmitter sends a signal to a wire embedded a few inches under the ground around the perimeter of the yard. The pet wears a radio receiver collar that emits "an audible warning tone" when the animal gets closer to the wire. If the animal ignores this signal, the collar delivers a "restraining correction" from the collar. This electrical shock is a punishment for the behavior of walking too close to the buried wire.

3. **Insight** This demonstration illustrates cognitive learning, latent learning, and insight. Challenge the students to specify the "rule" to a game wherein you state that you like X but don't like Y, X and Y being nouns. (Rule: The rule is that all Xs have double letters in their spelling whereas Ys do not.) Start with the following sentence:

   "I like cabbage, but I don't like spinach."

   If students want to suggest a solution, ask them to raise their hand and not blurt out the answer. The second sentence is:

   "I like school, but I don't like vacation."

   Presenting the words orally is tougher than presenting them in writing. You may want to create an overhead with the two sentences. It is not uncommon when conducting this demonstration to have a student blurt out the answer even though you have repeated the directions several times. Once they arrive at the solution, have the students think about how they got there. Some students will find it difficult to describe the process, i.e., it just came to them. This demonstration allows the students to experience the suddenness of insight while you explain that this type of learning could not have been conditioned.

6

WHAT'S INSIDE

Topics discussed in this chapter include: the definition of memory; explicit and implicit memories; retrospective and prospective memories; memory processes such as encoding, storage, and retrieval; stages of memory; contributors of forgetting; recognition and recall tasks; the biological aspects of memory; and memory enhancers.

LEARNING OUTCOMES

6-1 Define memory and differentiate between types of memories

6-2 Explain the processes of memory

6-3 Explain the stages of memory

6-4 Identify contributors of forgetting

6-5 Describe the biological aspects of memory

TEACHING LESSONS

MULTIMEDIA HIGHLIGHTS
The Brain and Memory 5:19

Available on *Research in Action Videos, Vol. I.* In this video, students learn how habit memory—a second robust, but unconscious memory system—plays a role in helping people with amnesia to learn a declarative task.

Reconstructive Memory 5:49

Available on the *PowerLecture* DVD. Going beyond the book, this video discusses how an understanding of memory has implications for the police, the justice system, and eyewitness testimony. Ask your students: What kinds of factors influence a person's memory? How could these factors affect eyewitness testimony? What is a "leading" question? Why does it "lead"?

LECTURE TOPICS

1. **Working Memory and Sleep** College students are on the short side of sleep and relate to sleep deficits. To help them understand the connection between sleep and memory, ask the students to read "Working Memory and Sleep in 6- to 13-year-old School Children," by Steenari et al. (2003). This article presents a research study that demonstrates that lower sleep efficiency and not getting enough sleep can adversely affect memory performance. Although the study used children, many of your students will be able to relate to the findings.

2. **Eyewitness Testimony of the *Titanic*** For an interesting topic to discuss with your students, you can present a research study, which used subjects as eyewitnesses (their testimony) to the *Titanic* accident. This study is in "An Archival Study of Eyewitness Memory of the *Titanic's* Final Plunge," by Riniolo, Koledin, Drakulic, and Payne (2003). The authors suggest that the eyewitness testimony of this tragic event was mostly accurate, lending support to eyewitness testimony in traumatic events.

3. **Gene Involved in Memory** Researchers at MIT have attempted to locate the gene involved in memory retrieval. Their hypothesis is that older people have not lost their memories but are having difficulty in retrieving them. In their laboratories, researchers are working with mice, altering their hippocampus to see what happens. Researchers use electrodes to actually "see" memories as they are formed within the brains of the mice. To help your students understand this connection, have them read "MIT Researchers ID Gene Involved in Memory Retrieval," from *Genomics & Genetics Weekly* (2002). Discussing the comparative research conducted with mice can help your students see the relationship between brain structures and memory.

6 Memory: Remembrance of Things Past—and Future

KEY TERMS

TEACHING LESSONS *continued*

STUDENT PROJECTS

1. **Learning and Memory** Although we use the words "learning" and "memory" in everyday speech, it can be instructive to start this unit by differentiating between the two. Both seem to involve the encoding, storage, and retrieval of information from our experiences. But how are they different? For this project, define the two terms in your own words, making sure to indicate the similarities and differences. Be prepared to discuss your answers in class.

2. **Memory and Misidentification** This student project will help you to better understand how memory can be affected by stereotypes. An article titled "Stereotypes Can Affect Memory When Identifying Criminal Suspects" that was written for *Ascribe Higher Education News Service*, describes a research study investigating this relationship. Read the article and then write a one-page summary of the research methods used and what the findings were.

CLASSROOM DEMONSTRATIONS

1. **Digits Forward** This class demonstration is very good at reinforcing the limitations of short-term memory. Ask your students to take out a sheet of paper. You will read a series of numbers to them. They are to write the numbers on the paper, but not until you have given them the "Go" signal. Prepare them for each set by saying "Ready."

DO NOT READ	READ	READ	READ
3 bits	Ready	9,6,3.	Go
4 bits	Ready	5,9,3,1.	Go
5 bits	Ready	8,2,7,4,5.	Go
6 bits	Ready	3,9,2,1,4,8.	Go
7 bits	Ready	4,1,8,7,9,3,6.	Go
8 bits	Ready	2,5,9,3,1,9,5,6.	Go
9 bits	Ready	9,6,3,2,5,1,7,4,8.	Go
10 bits	Ready	6,3,5,8,9,4,3,2,8,7.	Go
11 bits	Ready	3,1,8,5,1,6,4,2,7,5,1.	Go
12 bits	Ready	9,6,4,3,5,8,3,1,2,6,8,5.	Go

2. **Identifying Memory Types** *Preparation:* You will need to create a handout for each student or an overhead of the 10 memories listed below.

   After lecturing on the different types of memory, distribute the Episodic, Semantic, and Procedural Memory handout. Have students label the type of memory, and then write their own examples of each type of memory.

   Episodic, Semantic, and Procedural Memory Handout:

   1. Riding a bike
   2. Describing your trip to Texas last year
   3. Naming the 16th president of the United States
   4. Stating the details of your first kiss
   5. Executing a cartwheel
   6. Describing what you had for breakfast the day before yesterday
   7. Stating the definition of psychology
   8. Recalling the events of your 10th birthday
   9. Tying your shoelaces
   10. Knowing how to spell the word ENCYCLOPEDIA

Thinking, Language, and Intelligence
PREP CARD
7

WHAT'S INSIDE

Topics discussed in this chapter include: the definition of thinking; thinking prototypes and problem solving; algorithms, heuristics, framing, mental sets, and overgeneralization; components of language; the role of genetics and environment in developing language; the determinants of intelligence—where intelligence comes from; theoretical perspectives of intelligence from Spearman, Thurstone, Gardner, and Sternberg; emotional intelligence; and techniques used to measure intelligence.

LEARNING OUTCOMES

7-1 Define thinking and the various concepts involved in thinking

7-2 Describe how language develops

7-3 Identify the concept of intelligence and the techniques used to measure intelligence

7-4 Describe the controversy surrounding intelligence testing

TEACHING SUGGESTIONS

LECTURE TOPICS
1. **Child Care and Language Development** This lecture topic will provide you an opportunity to discuss various environmental factors that contribute to language and cognitive development. A study was conducted with children from 10 sites in the United States to determine the factors that contribute to language and cognitive development. The main independent variable explored in the study was day care and family environments. Access the article "The Relation of Child Care to Cognitive and Language Development," written for *Child Development* (2000). This article discusses quality of care, type of care, amount of care, and how these variables relate to development. One result from the article is that children in center care performed better than children in other types of care when compared at age 3.
2. **Race and Intelligence** Interesting topics to share with your students are race and intelligence. These areas more than any other in the field of psychology, are controversial. An article titled "Race and Intelligence: Separating Science from Myth," written by Reeve (2002), is a book review that focuses on this issue. Topics covered in the book (which would also make excellent topics for discussion in class) include race only as a socially defined category, racial categories used to justify and perpetuate social inequalities, the merits of intelligence testing, the misuse of statistical concepts, and alternative interpretations of the bell curve. Each of these areas can lead to lively discussions with your students.

STUDENT PROJECTS
1. **Individual Differences in Problem Solving** Insight is the solution to a problem that seems to be nonobvious and functional. For this project, you will be exploring the phenomenon of insight. Read "Individual Differences in Problem Solving via Insight," by Ansburg (2000). After reading this article, write a one-page response paper defining insight.
2. **Family Size and Intelligence** This project will give you an opportunity to explore the influence that family size can have on a person's intelligence. Before students read the assigned article, have them write down their hypothesis and answer the question, "What do you think is the influence of family size on intelligence?" The assigned article is "Family Size Tied to SAT, IQ Scores," by Greenberg (1985). After reading this article, write a one-page summary of what you learned and whether your initial hypothesis was supported by this article.

7 Thinking, Language, and Intelligence

TEACHING SUGGESTIONS *continued*

CLASSROOM DEMONSTRATIONS

1. **Sporting Events and Hindsight Bias** *Preparation:* You will need to be familiar with this demonstration and use it at the time of a major sporting event (Super Bowl, NCAA basketball final, etc.). You will also need to create both a pre-event survey and a post-event survey similar to those discussed in the article.

   For an interesting example of the hindsight bias, read "Hindsight Bias Demonstrated in the Predictions of a Sporting Event," by Bonds-Raacke, Fryer, Nicks, and Durr (2001). This article discusses a research study that used college students and a popular sporting event to demonstrate the hindsight bias. To demonstrate how powerful the hindsight bias is, have students complete the pre-event survey. The survey will have students indicate how much they watch the actual sport being discussed in the survey, demographic information (gender and age), and the predicted outcome of the event. After the event is over and you meet again as a class, have the students complete the post-event survey, which asks the students who they predicted to win and whether they were surprised by the outcome. This collected data can help you demonstrate the hindsight bias.

2. **Framing Effect** *Preparation:* Be familiar with the framing example from the article. You may want to create an overhead of the framing example.

   To help your students understand the power of framing, have them read "Influence of Elaboration on the Framing of Decision," by Takemura (1994). This article describes a framing example that can be used in class to describe an unusual disease that is expected to kill 600 people. Two alternatives are presented for students to choose between. One option is positively framed, and one option is negatively framed. After presenting the scenario to your students, have them write down which option they would choose.

3. **Intelligence Meter** *Preparation:* You will need to be familiar with the scenario presented below and with the normal bell curve. In class, explain that a fictional intelligence meter has been developed that will measure an infant's intellectual potential. This meter is so modern that testing is no longer necessary; instead, the child is passed through what appears to be an airport metal detector, and a measurement is taken.

   In this fictional scenario, two children have been measured: "Child A" and "Child B." On the day of birth, both children are measured for intelligence, and both are shown to have a potential IQ score of exactly 100, which is at the 50th percentile in the normal bell curve and considered to be average. Child A and Child B are from different families and different environments. The parents of Child A want the best for all of their children but neither parent is well educated. They lack parenting skills, and both have to work extremely long hours in order to make ends meet.

   The parents of Child B are just the opposite. Child B is able to visit museums and zoos, and has a strong vocabulary because of the parents' involvement with books and reading. Each child, due to circumstances, experiences the world differently.

   Years later both children sit next to each other in a classroom and take an intelligence test. Ask your class if it seems reasonable that the enriched environment that has been provided for Child B would be worth 15 more points on an IQ test. Next ask them if it also seems reasonable that there could be a 15-point loss in Child A's score due to the less nurturing environment. After the response from your students, illustrate for them the normal bell curve; place Child B at the first standard deviation (84th percentile) and Child A at a standard deviation below the mean (16th percentile). Child A is headed for remedial education, and Child B is close to being gifted. Solicit students' reactions to this scenario.

CHAPTER OUTLINE

WHAT'S INSIDE

Topics discussed in this chapter include: motivation (including needs, drives, and incentives), theories of motivation, hunger, sexual motivation, eating disorders, motivation of aggression, achievement motivation, emotions and their three theoretical explanations (James–Lange, Cannon–Bard, and the Schachter–Singer), positive psychology, and lie detector tests.

LEARNING OUTCOMES

8-1 Define motivation including needs, drives, and incentives

8-2 Identify the theories of motivation

8-3 Describe the biological and psychological contributions to hunger

8-4 Explain the role of sex hormones and the sexual response cycle in human sexuality

8-5 Describe achievement motivation

8-6 Identify the theoretical explanations of emotions

TEACHING SUGGESTIONS

MULTIMEDIA HIGHLIGHTS
Weight Control 5:56

Available on the *Research in Action Videos, Vol. I.* In this clip, students learn how researchers are helping people respond to the obesity epidemic. They observe how researchers determine the relative importance of intensity and duration of exercise. They are also introduced to behavioral interventions that help people overcome "obstacles" to exercise, as well as interventions that help people learn to eat less and exercise more.

Culture and Emotion 4:55

Available on *Research in Action Videos, Vol. I.* How does culture influence emotion, and how are emotional responses similar across cultures? Are there physiological differences, behavioral differences, or differences in emotional experience—depending upon the culture in which someone was raised? What implications might cultural differences have for clinical psychology? This video helps students explore these and other related questions.

LECTURE TOPICS
1. **Exercise and Well-Being** One topic that many of your students can relate to is motivation for exercise. To help your students understand the efforts made to study exercise motivation, ask them to read "The Relationship Between Exercise Motives and Psychological Well-Being," by Maltby and Day (2001). The article discusses extrinsic and intrinsic motives that people have when they exercise. The authors suggest that extrinsic motives for exercise may be what people begin exercise with, but for those who exercise for longer periods (six months or more) the motivation may change to intrinsic motivations. After discussing the article, ask your students to describe why they exercise.

(Continued)

KEY TERMS

TEACHING SUGGESTIONS *continued*

LECTURE TOPICS *continued*

2. **Eating Disorders** For an excellent review of eating disorders including: classification/diagnostic information, clinical features, and development and subsequent course of anorexia and bulimia nervosa, read "Eating Disorders," by Fairburn and Harrison (2003). This article also considers possible risk factors and management of the disorders.

3. **The Kinsey Report** Perhaps the most classic study conducted in the area of sex research was that of Alfred Kinsey. To help your students understand the research that Kinsey conducted and the lasting contributions from his research, have them read "Alfred Kinsey and the Kinsey Report: Historical Overview and Lasting Contributions," by Bullough (1998). This article summarizes sex research that took place prior to Kinsey, and then describes the research that Kinsey conducted with over 8,000 individuals that he interviewed. The summary presented in this article can help your students understand the impact that this research had.

4. **The College Transition** For the incoming freshman at college, the transition may prove difficult. Research has shown that nearly a third of college freshman do not enroll the following year. Why does this happen? In an article, "The Transition From Extrinsic to Intrinsic Motivation in the College Classroom: A First-Year Experience," by Thompson and Thorton (2002), this topic is discussed. The authors suggest that high school students are extrinsically motivated by grades, attendance, detentions, and suspensions. The college student, on the other hand, is not. The authors suggest that learning is intrinsically motivating, and the transition between the two experiences can be difficult. As an additional component to this lecture topic, you can have your students describe the difficulties they encountered when entering college.

STUDENT PROJECTS

1. **Prison Simulation** A classic study conducted in the field of psychology was initiated by Zimbardo at Stanford University and has come to be known as the Prison Simulation. This study had college students play the roles of prisoner and guard and was scheduled to last two weeks. After only six days, the experiment had to be abandoned due to unanticipated reactions. To find out more, read "The Prison Simulation Experiment," by Gross (2002), which summarizes the prison simulation study. After reading the article, write a one-page response paper focusing on your thoughts about this study and how it relates to aggressive behavior. What would you have done as a guard? As a prisoner?

2. **Emotional Intelligence** For this project, visit www.eqi.org/index.htm This website contains information about emotional intelligence and contains links to information about the construct. After you explore the website, write a one-page paper summarizing what you learned.

CLASSROOM DEMONSTRATIONS

1. **Motivation List** This classroom demonstration involves an assignment that the class will probably enjoy. Ask the students to rank-order a list of a dozen behaviors that reflect their preferences and, hence, their motivations. One way to do this is to create the list yourself ahead of time and distribute it to all the students. Typical items are studying, dancing, having sex, watching TV, shopping, buying fashionable clothes, exercising, meditating, being with friends, reading a book, and so on. You may want to let the class decide the contents of the list to ensure that you haven't left out something that is important to them.

   The fun comes when you assign them to rank-order the behaviors in two ways: first to represent their own preferences, and second to represent the preferences of a typical member of the other sex. Clarify the process, collect the data, and calculate the mean rank order to be distributed or shown on an overhead projector at the next class meeting. You can probably count on some surprises, as students eagerly debate the reasons for their accuracy or inaccuracy about the preferences of the other sex. (Typically, females state that "having sex" is the top male priority, while all those sensitive males deny such base instinctual drives.) This makes for a good review of perception, and a preview of social perception.

2. **TAT** *Preparation:* You will need to have a Thematic Apperception Test.

   It is always interesting to display some of the actual pictures from the Thematic Apperception Test (TAT). Show the pictures and allow the students to observe it for a minute. Then ask individuals what is happening in the picture. This also works well in demonstrating a projective test.

The Voyage Through the Life Span
PREP CARD
9

CHAPTER OUTLINE

KEY TERMS

zygote **218**
germinal stage **218**
amniotic sac **218**
placenta **218**
umbilical cord **218**
reflex **219**
rooting **219**
fixation time **220**
assimilation **221**
schema **221**
accommodation **222**
object permanence **222**
sensorimotor stage **222**
preoperational stage **222**
egocentrism **222**
conservation **223**
objective responsibility **223**
concrete operational stage **224**
decentration **224**
subjective moral judgment **224**
zone of proximal development (ZPD) **225**
scaffolding **225**
preconventional level **226**
conventional level **226**
attachment **227**
contact comfort **229**
ethologist **229**
critical period **229**

(Continued)

WHAT'S INSIDE

Topics discussed in this chapter include: prenatal development, including the role of sex hormones in prenatal development; the physical, cognitive, moral, social, and emotional development of children; the physical, cognitive, moral, social, and emotional development of adolescents; adolescent sexuality; and the physical, cognitive, moral, social, and emotional development of adults.

LEARNING OUTCOMES

9-1 Explain prenatal development and the role that sex hormones play

9-2 Explain the physical, cognitive, moral, social, and emotional development of children

9-3 Explain the physical, cognitive, moral, social, and emotional development of adolescents

9-4 Explain the features of emerging adulthood

9-5 Explain the physical, cognitive, moral, social, and emotional development of adults

TEACHING SUGGESTIONS

MULTIMEDIA HIGHLIGHTS
Newborns: Sensation and Perception 2:30

Available on the *PowerLecture* DVD. Watch an infant and his early sensory experiences, and listen to the explanations of infant sight and hearing. Ask your students: What does research tell us about the sensory capabilities of newborns?

Adolescence: Moral Development 2:00

Available on the *PowerLecture* DVD. Watch interviews with adolescents who are explaining their moral reasoning to understand moral development in this age group. Ask your students to describe the responses of the adolescents when presented with Kohlberg's Heinz dilemma. Are their responses typical for adolescents?

LECTURE TOPICS
1. **Scaffolding** The textbook refers to a cognitive technique known as scaffolding that helps children learn new material. Cognitive scaffolding refers to the temporary support given by a parent or teacher to a child who is learning a new task. To help students better understand scaffolding, have them read "Children's Genre Knowledge: An Examination of K–5 Students' Performance on Multiple Tasks Providing Differing Levels of Scaffolding," by Donovan and Smolkin (2002). This article discusses how scaffolding is used in children's writing. The authors suggest that it can help but can also hinder a child. Discuss scaffolding with students and ask them how they feel it both helps and hinders children.

TEACHING SUGGESTIONS *continued*

LECTURE TOPICS *continued*

2. **Attachment Theory** Attachment theory is discussed in the textbook, and Ainsworth's three stages of attachment are presented: 1) initial pre-attachment phase; 2) attachment, in-the-making phase; and 3) clear-cut attachment phase. Although this theory has gained acceptance in the United States, does it generalize to other societies? To help your students better understand this, have them read "Family Systems Theory, Attachment Theory, and Culture," by Rothbaum, Rosen, Ujiie, and Uchida (2002). This article discusses the similarities and differences in family systems theory and attachment theory. The authors also discuss how these theories apply in non-Western societies.

3. **Alzheimer's Disease** College students may appear to be indifferent to this Alzheimer's disease, but many may be able to relate to the experience because of grandparents who are in the age category. To understand the disease, have the students read "Tangled Memories: Alzheimer's Diseases: The Story So Far," by Liebman and Schardt (2002). This article discusses the disease from various theoretical perspectives. These include plaques, the dead zones between the nerve cells that are filled with protein fragments called beta-amyloid and tangles, which are neurofibrillary tangles that come from deposits of tau.

STUDENT PROJECTS

1. **Visible Embryo** This project will allow you to explore the world of a developing fetus. Access the Visible Embryo website at www.visembryo.com/baby/. Explore the site and then write a one-page response paper discussing what you learned.

2. **U.S. Teenagers and Television** For this project, you will be exploring a website about U.S. adolescents' television watching and smoking. You can find this website at: http://www.nichd.nih.gov/new/releases/tv.cfm. This website is part of the National Institute of Child Health and Human Development site. After you read through the site, write a one-page response paper about what you learned. You may actually be surprised.

3. **Male Menopause?** Female menopause is an accepted phenomenon that females experience, formally thought of as the end of menses, the end of estrogen production, and the end of reproductive capability. Hormonal imbalances, mood disturbances, vaginal dryness, and hot flashes are often associated with menopause. In a 1992 book written by Sheehy, the concept of male menopause was promoted. Is it possible that males go through a similar experience? Read "Male Menopause: Is It Myth, or a Reality of Aging?" by Curry (1993).

CLASSROOM DEMONSTRATIONS

1. **Mini Experiment for Three- to Four-Year-Olds** *Preparation:* You will need to arrange with a parent of a three- to four-year-old child to come to your class. You will need a clear glass that is tall and thin, and a second glass that is wide and a pitcher of water. You will be conducting a version of the Piaget Conservation task. This experiment is described in the textbook.

    Once your "subject" has come to class, pour water from the pitcher into the tall, thin glass. Then, with the child watching, pour water into the wide glass. Then ask the child whether the low, wide glass has more, less, or the same amount of water that was in the tall, thin glass. If the child says they are the same, the child is correct. If the child errs, then ask your students "Why?" This can lead to a discussion of Piaget's theory of conservation.

2. **The Imaginary Audience** *Preparation:* You will need to have a student confederate who can drop something that will make a loud noise during the lecture.

    Because of the novelty of the noise, a number of students will turn toward the noise. After they do this, stop your lecture and discuss with the class what happened. First, ask the student who dropped the item to describe what it felt like to have everyone look at him or her. Then have the class members describe what they were thinking when they looked. For the most part, those who looked probably didn't think anything of what happened.

3. **What Is an Adult?** For this demonstration, have your students generate a list of characteristics that they think describe adults. Write their suggestions on the board. After the students have generated a list, ask them to decide if they "qualify." Many students in introductory courses are in the early adult stage. This will help them see how they are doing.

CHAPTER OUTLINE

WHAT'S INSIDE

Topics discussed in this chapter include: personality; the psychoanalytic perspective; Freudian theory; non-Freudian contributions; trait perspective and the Big Five personality traits; learning theory; humanistic-existential perspective; sociocultural perspective; personality assessment; and gender-typing.

LEARNING OUTCOMES

10-1 Understand the psychoanalytical perspective and how it contributed to the study of personality

10-2 Explain the trait perspective and the "Big Five" trait model

10-3 Identify the contributions of learning theory to understanding personality

10-4 Describe the humanistic-existential perspective on personality

10-5 Describe the sociocultural perspective on personality

10-6 Describe the different kinds of tests psychologists use to measure personality

TEACHING SUGGESTIONS

MULTIMEDIA HIGHLIGHTS
Personality Traits 5:34

Available on the *Research in Action Videos, Vol. I.* How should we measure personality? Some researchers focus on broad traits, but others are looking at how we behave in different situations. In this clip students learn about the person-in-the-situation model of personality, how it differs from trait approaches, and how it might be used to help people learn to regulate their emotions. Ask your students to define the "person-in-the situation" phenomenon. Can you think of a time you were in a social situation and behaved in such a way that you surprised yourself? Can you explain your behavior in terms of the requirements of the situation?

LECTURE TOPICS

1. **The Psychodynamic Perspective** For a succinct, organized approach to the psychodynamic perspective, read "The Psychodynamic Perspective," written for *Psychology Review (1999)*. This article describes the major components of the psychodynamic perspective in a manner that is easily understood and organized. The article begins with the levels of consciousness and then proceeds through the psychosexual stages of development and defense mechanisms. This is a nice review of this perspective.

2. **Karen Horney** In the history of psychology, women played major roles but often didn't get the recognition they deserved. Karen Horney was one of those women. To learn more about her life and contributions to the field of psychology, visit http://webspace.ship.edu/cgboer/horney.html. This website discusses her life and can provide you with information for your students.

3. **Leadership and Self-Efficacy** Often thought of as synonyms, self-efficacy and self-confidence are similar but not exactly the same. Both would seem to have an influence in the area of leadership ability. To help your students understand the relationship between these three concepts (self-

(Continued)

10 Personality: Theory and Measurement

TEACHING SUGGESTIONS *continued*

LECTURE TOPICS *continued*

efficacy, self-confidence, and leadership) access an article titled "Self-efficacy and Leadership Effectiveness: Applying Social Cognitive Theory to Leadership," by McCormick (2001). This article describes a model for leadership that includes self-efficacy and self-confidence as it relates to social cognitive theory. This article can help your students see an applied aspect to personality traits learned through social cognitive theory.

4. **Sociocultural Influences and Self-Esteem**   There is an interest in determining the factors that contribute to the self-esteem of those with eating disorders. People with eating disorders tend to have low self-esteem related to their poor body image. To help your students understand the complex interaction of self-esteem and sociocultural factors, read "Self-Esteem and Negative Affect as Moderators of Sociocultural Influences on Body Dissatisfaction, Strategies to Decrease Weight, and Strategies to Increase Muscles Among Adolescent Boys and Girls," by Ricciardelli and McCabe (2001). This article explores how media, family, and peers play an important role in transmitting sociocultural messages regarding the ideal body weight. The connection is then made to eating disorders.

STUDENT PROJECTS

1. **Oedipus Wrecked?**   One aspect of Freud's theory, which was controversial from the beginning, was that of the Oedipus complex. The idea that each child has incestuous desires toward their opposite-sex parent has left many cringing at the thought. To learn more about the difficulties that this theory has encountered, access an article found in most libraries titled "Oedipus Wrecked: Freud's Theory of Frustrated Incest Goes on the Defensive" by Bower (1991). This article discusses this controversial concept and explores the supposed evidence . . . or lack thereof.

2. **Defense Mechanisms**   Watch a favorite television show and record the various defense mechanisms that the characters use. Come to class prepared to summarize the episode, characters, and the defense mechanisms.

3. **Keirsey Sorter**   Complete the Keirsey Temperament Sorter, which you can access online at www.keirsey.com, and summarize the results. Do you think the results truly reflect yourself? Do you think the test is reliable and valid?

CLASSROOM DEMONSTRATIONS

1. **Sigmund Freud**   *Preparation:* Create note cards with the terms from the article. To help your students learn the terms from Freudian theory, play a version of the board game Taboo. An article titled "Psychoanalyst: Sigmund Freud," by Gay (1999), reviews a number of the terms found in Freudian theory. Take the terms and write them on the note cards. Have a student come up to the front of the room and randomly pick one of the cards. The student's task is to get the class to say what is written on the card without using the word(s) on the card. They also have to describe the word based on its psychological meaning. Continue playing the game, choosing other students from the class to pick a card.

2. **Traits of the Famous**   Before starting your presentation of the trait perspective of personality to the class, ask students to describe the personality of someone they know very well or a television or movie character. Students usually use an average of five traits to describe their person (you may need to screen out repetitive traits such as nice and kind, and things not considered personality traits such as intelligence or weight). Write down some of the descriptions on the board. Discuss the trait perspective and how one of the major theories describes personality along five dimensions (five-factor model).

Stress, Health, and Coping
PREP CARD
11

WHAT'S INSIDE

Topics discussed in this chapter include: health psychology; stress—its sources, moderators, and effects on the body; the relationship between psychology and health; prevention measures for stress-related health problems.

LEARNING OUTCOMES

11-1 Define stress and identify various sources of stress

11-2 Identify the psychological moderators of stress

11-3 Describe the impact of stress on the body

11-4 Explain the relationship between psychology and health

TEACHING SUGGESTIONS

MULTIMEDIA HIGHLIGHTS
Health and Stress 5:09

Available on the *PowerLecture* DVD. In this clip your students will learn how researchers are determining the mechanisms by which stress affects the immune system, and how emotional states like happiness and loneliness may influence the ability to fight off infection. Ask your students to explain what happens to the immune system when a person becomes stressed. What is the role of cytokine? How can you differentiate between "good stress" and "bad stress"?

LECTURE TOPICS
1. **Road Rage** A phenomenon that is seen more and more is road rage. Road rage is a reaction to stress and frustration in which a person becomes aggressive in their driving, leading to unsafe situations for all. To begin the discussion you could share with them the article "Road Rage: Understandings and Experiences," by Lupton (2002). This article reports a qualitative study in which 77 people were interviewed about road rage. The results indicate that many people find driving to be a source of autonomy and self-expression. Driving can become frustrating when the roads become crowded and when the individuals experience frustrations at work. Drivers do characterize road rage as negative yet understandable, considering the stress people face.

2. **Nutrition and Health** For this topic you can help your students understand the connection between stress and nutrition. Have your students read "Break the Chain-Control Stress with Optimal Nutrition," by Langer (1997). This article discusses hardy personalities and less obvious signs of stress, and then suggests proper nutrition to alleviate and prevent stress. Suggestions include vitamin B-complex, vitamin C, vitamin E, and amino acids.

3. **The Mind and the Immune System, Part I and Part II** For this lecture topic you can help your students understand the connection between the mind and the immune system by accessing two articles written for the *Harvard Mental Health Letter (2002)*—"The Mind and the Immune System-Part I" and "The Immune System and the Mind-Part II." The first article introduces the immune system and suggests that the immune system can actually learn through association. The first article also discusses hormonal effects on stress, and how stress is related to physical illness. In part two the discussion expands to include HIV infection and cancer.

11 Stress, Health, and Coping

KEY TERMS

TEACHING SUGGESTIONS *continued*

STUDENT PROJECTS

1. **An Antidote for Stress** Find and read the article titled "Humor: An Antidote for Stress," by Wooten (1996). Although this article is written for nurses, who have a high-stress occupation, the suggestions are for all. Answer these questions in a one-page paper. (1) How does humor tie to the Middle Ages and what are the four humors mentioned in the article? (2) How does laughter stimulate the immune system? (3) What are the three hardiness factors discussed in the article? (4) How does humor influence locus of control? (5) How is humor processed in the brain?

2. **Stress Warning Signs** Experiencing stress is a natural reaction to situations in which our body needs to be in a state of readiness. But long-term exposure to stress can be negative. How much is too much? Find and read "Stressed: Warning Signs That You Could Be Hitting the Danger Zone," by MacNeill (2003) and write a one-page response paper focusing on the reactions our bodies have to stress.

CLASSROOM DEMONSTRATIONS

1. **Locus of Control** *Preparation:* You will need a computer, projector, and an internet connection.

   To illustrate how stress can come from within a person, have your students take the self-assessment found in Chapter 10 titled "Self-Assessment: Locus of Control Scale" at the book companion website. After they take the assessment, they can bring their scores to class and a class discussion can take place about locus of control and how a person's perceived control over situations can alleviate or lead to stress. While the discussion is taking place, you can revisit the questionnaire and discuss individual items found on the instrument.

2. **Stop a Headache in Five Minutes** *Preparation:* This demonstration will require you to prepare a guided imagery for relaxation.

   Many headaches that individuals suffer are tension headaches. People can find relief from these tension headaches by relaxing. If possible, the person should attempt to relax within the first five minutes of feeling the headache. To help your students learn how to relax, present your guided imagery. Examples of visualizations can be found in an article in *Prevention*, "Stop a Headache in 5 Minutes," by Stocker (1994). These visualizations include "imagine your pain is a dial and turn down the ache" and "imagine pain is a fiery color and see it turning a cool blue like calm water."

3. **Sources of Stress Among College Students** *Preparation:* You will need to create a handout of the list of stressful life events experienced by college students, as reported in the article, for each student. You may want to create an overhead to present the results for the class.

   There are many stress scales designed to assess stress in everyday life. In this demonstration you can show the results of a study designed specifically for college students. The list of stressful events can be found in "Sources of Stress Among College Students," by Ross, Niebling, and Heckert (1999). The student stress events are categorized under four areas: (1) Interpersonal, (2) Intrapersonal, (3) Academic, and (4) Environmental. For the demonstration you can have students check which events they have experienced and then tally the results, which can be presented in the next class period.

Psychological Disorders
PREP CARD 12

WHAT'S INSIDE

Topics discussed in this chapter include: definition, classification, and prevalence of psychological disorders; schizophrenia; mood disorders and suicide; anxiety disorders; somatoform disorders; dissociative disorders; and personality disorders.

LEARNING OUTCOMES

12-1 Define psychological disorders and describe their prevalence

12-2 Describe the symptoms and possible origins of anxiety disorders

12-3 Describe the symptoms and possible origins of dissociative disorders

12-4 Describe the symptoms and possible origins of somatoform disorders

12-5 Describe the symptoms and possible origins of mood disorders

12-6 Describe the symptoms and possible origins of schizophrenia

12-7 Describe the symptoms and possible origins of personality disorders

TEACHING SUGGESTIONS

MULTIMEDIA HIGHLIGHTS
Home Videos and Schizophrenia 5:44

Available on *Research in Action Videos, Vol. I.* Can we learn to predict who will develop schizophrenia? In this video, students see how psychologists are using low-tech procedures like home videos, and high-tech procedures like hormonal measures and brain scans, to better understand who might develop this very serious mental health disorder.

Bipolar Disorder: Expression of Moods 1:38

Available on the *PowerLecture* DVD. In this clip, Mary talks about her experience with bipolar disorder and expressions of mood.

Obsessive-Compulsive Disorder 1:22

Available on the *PowerLecture* DVD. In this clip, Chuck explains his struggles with obsessive-compulsive disorder.

Antisocial Personality Disorder 0:57

Available on the *PowerLecture* DVD. In this clip, George describes the symptoms of his antisocial personality disorder.

LECTURE TOPICS
1. **Exorcism** From a historical perspective, disorders were once thought to be the work of demons possessing a person's body. One method of "therapy" was to perform exorcisms to drive the demon from the person's body. In an article titled "Exorcism! Driving Out the Nonsense," by Nickell (2001), this topic is discussed. The article discusses the possible reasons that people thought that disorders might be due to demon possession. The author continues into more modern days and focuses on people's opinions about the movie "The Exorcist." This article can help you present to your students the interesting history of psychological disorders and how some thoughts have endured through time.

(Continued)

12 Psychological Disorders

TEACHING SUGGESTIONS *continued*

LECTURE TOPICS *continued*

2. **Medical Student Syndrome** Many students will be interested in the "medical student syndrome," also known as "intern's syndrome." First-year medical students read so much about symptoms of diseases that they convince themselves they are suffering from one or more of them. A little knowledge can be a dangerous thing, even for the highly intelligent. The chapter on abnormal behavior is usually introduced at a time in the semester when the workload has piled up for the students, and they may be feeling particularly vulnerable. Students will often approach you to discuss the symptoms of one of the disorders listed in the textbook. Warning students about medical student syndrome is not to deny that some students may be experiencing real problems, but it could provide an "inoculation" against seeing these troubles in their own behaviors.

3. **Experts Are Split** To help your students understand the controversy surrounding multiple personality disorder, read "Multiple Personalities: The Experts Are Split," by Sileo. This article describes one aspect of the controversy, the increased numbers of MPD patients seen. Are the larger numbers due to greater awareness or due to therapeutic misbehavior? The article presents information from both sides.

STUDENT PROJECTS

1. **Diagnosing** Research a famous person whom you believe has had a mental disorder. (Possible examples include Jeffrey Dahmer, Ted Kaczynski, Charles Manson, David Koresh, John Hinckley, Roseanne Barr, Sybil Lively, Karen Carpenter, Margot Kidder, Ted Bundy, Howard Hughes, Howie Mandel, Catherine Zeta Jones.) Write a one- to two-page paper on the evidence (or lack thereof) in support of a particular diagnosis of a mental disorder, using the *DSM*.

2. **Men and Depression** To learn more differences between men and women with depression, access a page from the National Institute of Mental Health website at http://menanddepression.nimh.nih.gov/. After exploring the site, write a one-page response paper summarizing what you have learned.

CLASSROOM DEMONSTRATIONS

1. **Accuracy in the Media** *Preparation*: You will need to identify a specific media source that provides information about psychological disorders. An interesting source for your students is music lyrics, including songs by Pink Floyd, Jimi Hendrix, Metallica, etc. Share your source in class (you may want to create an overhead of the lyrics so that your students can see them while the song is playing) and then assign the students to find one of their own to bring to the next class for discussion.

2. **The 23-Year-Old Schizophrenic** *Preparation*: Be familiar with the article and provide either overheads or handouts of relevant sections of the article.

   To help your students understand the difficulties that a patient with schizophrenia encounters, share with them the story of Mr. X, a 23-year-old schizophrenic. His story can be found in most libraries in an article titled "A 23-Year-Old Man With Schizophrenia" written by Goff (2002). This article details the life of Mr. X. This article can help bring to life this devastating disorder.

3. **The Anatomy of Anxiety** *Preparation:* You will need overheads (presentation slides) of the brain (from your lectures in biopsychology).

   For this demonstration, you can show your students how anxiety impacts various structures in the brain. For this demonstration, access an article found in most libraries titled "The Anatomy of Anxiety" written for Time (2002). This article describes how the body responds to anxiety, targeting specific brain structures. This information can help your students understand the connection between biopsychology and anxiety.

PREP CARD

13

WHAT'S INSIDE

Topics discussed in this chapter include: the history of treatment of people with psychological disorders; psychoanalytic therapy, client-centered therapy, and Gestalt therapy; behavior therapy, cognitive therapy, and rational emotive behavior therapy; group therapy; an evaluation of the effectiveness of psychotherapy; and biological methods of therapy.

LEARNING OUTCOMES

13-1 Define psychotherapy and describe the history of treatment of psychological disorders

13-2 Describe traditional psychoanalysis and short-term psychodynamic therapies

13-3 Define humanistic therapy and contrast its two main approaches

13-4 Define behavior therapy and identify various behavioral approaches to therapy

13-5 Define cognitive therapy and describe Beck's approach and REBT

13-6 Identify various types of group therapy and discuss their advantages and disadvantages

13-7 Explain whether psychotherapy works and who benefits from it

13-8 Describe methods of biological therapy and their benefits and side effects

TEACHING SUGGESTIONS

MULTIMEDIA HIGHLIGHTS
Virtual Reality Therapy 4:59

Available on *Research in Action Videos, Vol. I*. In this clip students learn how high-tech procedures—usually associated with the entertainment industry—are helping people overcome fear as virtual reality moves into the clinician's office. They also learn how virtual reality can speed up treatment, make treatment more convenient, and bridge the gap to real-life exposure.

LECTURE TOPICS

1. **Bethlem** Perhaps the most famous mental hospital is St. Mary of Bethlehem hospital in London. Possibly the oldest psychiatric facility in Europe, the hospital came to be known as Bethlem and subsequently Bedlam (a metaphor for madness). An excellent history of this hospital can be found in an article titled "Bethlem/Bedlam: Methods of Madness?" by Porter (1997). The article presents a history and descriptions of the facility and patients. Discussion of this early attempt to "house" individuals with psychiatric disorders is interesting to students.

2. **The Baby and the Bathwater** Some psychologists today suggest that Freudian concepts are outdated and should receive mention for historical perspective only. In essence, Freud did a fairly good job considering that he was one of the first to propose such a complete theory, but the theory has little relevance today. There are some who suggest that to throw it all away would be inappropriate. To see a postmodernist view of Freud's theory, read "The Baby and the Bathwater: Some Thoughts on Freud as a Postmodernist," written by Freud—that is, Sophie

(Continued)

KEY TERMS

TEACHING SUGGESTIONS *continued*

LECTURE TOPICS *continued*

Freud (1998). Freud suggests that aspects of Sigmund's theory have relevance today: meaning making, the unconscious, defense mechanisms, and psychoanalytic treatment. Ask students to form their own opinions and be ready to discuss them in class.

3. **Solution-Focused Therapy** At the beginning of your lecture on therapy, ask students to describe what happens in therapy. You will probably get responses that suggest that a client goes to see a therapist to talk about their problems. The therapist then helps them work through their problems. This type of response implies that a majority of therapy may be spent talking about what is not working, i.e., the problems. In an interesting article titled "What is Solution-Focused Therapy?" by Kingsbury (1997) this topic is discussed. The author suggests that problem behaviors are present only intermittently. Solutions-based therapy attempts to help the client notice those times when symptoms are diminished or absent. It is actually that time that needs to be expanded. Kingsbury suggests that this type of approach works well with anxiety disorders, depression, dependence, and family conflicts. This short article can aid you as you present to your students that not all of therapy need focus on the negative.

STUDENT PROJECTS

1. **Asylums** Mental institutions, mental hospitals, asylums, etc., continue to be somewhat controversial aspects of therapy. With a checkered past, asylums have survived and continue to be used. What is the fate of the severely mentally ill? Should they be hospitalized, or not? For this project, read two articles. The first article is "Asylum: The Complex and Controversial Story of Mental Institutions in the U.S.A.," written by McGovern (1993). In this article, McGovern reviews a film that explores the history of asylums and the controversy surrounding them. The second article, "Second Thoughts," written for *The Economist* (1989), focuses on this issue in Britain. After reading these articles, write a response paper stating and supporting your view: Is there a need for mental institutions or not? Use evidence from these articles to support your view.

2. **What to Do?** Whether you or someone you know struggles with depression, there are resources available to help. To research the options that exist, explore the website at: http://depression.about.com. This site contains information for those who may be struggling with depression or for those who may have a friend or family member experiencing depression. For this assignment, explore the website and write a response containing information you learned while on the site.

CLASSROOM DEMONSTRATIONS

1. **Systematic Desensitization: The Eraser Phobia** *Preparation:* You will need a chalkboard eraser (white board eraser), a cage that the eraser can fit in, and a picture of an eraser. You will also need a student confederate, preferably one who sits away from the chalkboard.

   As you begin class, present to the students the three steps typically used in systematic desensitization: (1) relaxation techniques, (2) creating an anxiety hierarchy, and (3) progressive associations with each hierarchy item and relaxation. Explain to the class that you are going to demonstrate how systematic desensitization works. Take the photograph of the eraser and begin to approach the confederate student. Explain to the class that you have already worked with this student to overcome this hierarchical item. The student takes the photograph. Explain that you are going to work on the next item in the hierarchy. Remove the caged eraser from your case. Begin walking toward the student. The student should act somewhat nervous as you explain to the "client" to take deep breaths and to relax. As the demonstration continues, you can remove the eraser from the cage while the client continues to practice the relaxation techniques. Near the end of the demonstration the student should be able to actually hold the eraser. At this point, explain to the class that the student really has no eraser phobia and that actual systematic desensitization would take more than just one session. This humorous demonstration is adapted from an article written by Lawson and Reardon (1997) found in the *Teaching of Psychology* journal, a great teaching tool.

2. **Counselor Visit** Your campus's health or wellness center is an excellent resource for your students. Often these centers have a mental health component with therapists who work for the institution. Arrange for one of the counselors who conducts group therapy to come to your class and discuss the techniques they use in conducting group therapy.

CHAPTER OUTLINE

WHAT'S INSIDE

Topics discussed in this chapter include: definition of social psychology; attitudes, including the A–B problem, persuasion, prejudice, and interpersonal attraction; social perception, including the primacy and recency effects, attribution theory, and body language; social influence, focusing on obedience to authority figures and conformity to social norms; aggression; and group behavior, including the effects of deindividuation.

LEARNING OUTCOMES

14-1 Define *attitude* and discuss factors that shape attitudes

14-2 Discuss prejudice and discrimination

14-3 Discuss factors that contribute to interpersonal attraction and love

14-4 Define *social perception* and describe the factors that influence it

14-5 Explain why people obey authority figures and conform to social norms

14-6 Discuss factors that contribute to aggression

14-7 Describe differences between the ways in which people behave as individuals and as members of a group

TEACHING SUGGESTIONS

MULTIMEDIA HIGHLIGHTS
Stereotype Threat 5:22

Available on *Research in Action Videos, Vol. I.* Each of us belongs to groups that have stereotypes associated with them. Can belonging to a stereotyped group affect academic performance? In this clip, students learn about what's called stereotype threat—how it affects people and what might be done about it. Ask your students: What is the theory of stereotype threat, and what is its effect on people? Have you ever wondered whether people from your ethnic background or gender can do something as well as people from another ethnic background or gender? How did your uncertainty make you feel?

LECTURE TOPICS

1. **The Psychology of Prejudice** For this lecture, discuss with your students the underlying possibilities of prejudice. In an article titled "The Psychology of Prejudice: Ingroup Love or Outgroup Hate?" by Brewer (1999), two different possibilities are explored. The authors suggest that many prejudices are a result of attempts to maintain positive relationships within the group rather than any negative ideas of the outgroup. This information can lead to a classroom discussion about prejudice.

2. **Attribution Change** The fundamental attribution error suggests that individuals tend to overestimate the importance of personal variables and underestimate the importance of the situation when making judgments about other people's behavior. But do those attributions exist over time? To expand your student's knowledge of this area, read "Do Attributions Change Over Time When the Actor's Behavior Is Hedonically Relevant to the Perceiver?" by Truchot, Maure, and Patte (2003). This article explores whether the attributions made continue to exist over time with the added component that the behavior is negative to the observer. The results indicate that they do not.

(Continued)

14 Social Psychology

KEY TERMS *continued*

attitude **332**
A–B problem **332**
elaboration likelihood model **333**
fear appeal **334**
selective avoidance **334**
selective exposure **334**
cognitive-dissonance theory **335**
attitude-discrepant behavior **335**
effort justification **335**
prejudice **336**
discrimination **336**
stereotyping **336**
attraction **337**
triangular model of love **339**
intimacy **339**
passion **339**
commitment **339**
consummate love **340**
romantic love **340**
social perception **340**
primacy effect **340**
recency effect **340**
attribution **340**
dispositional attribution **340**
situational attribution **340**
fundamental attribution error **341**
actor–observer effect **341**
self-serving bias **341**
social influence **342**
foot-in-the-door technique **344**
social facilitation **347**
evaluation apprehension **347**
diffusion of responsibility **348**
social decision schemes **348**
groupthink **349**
deindividuation **350**
altruism **350**
bystander effect **350**

TEACHING SUGGESTIONS *continued*

LECTURE TOPICS *continued*

3. **Gender Differences in Attributions** Use this lecture topic to help your students better understand the interaction of gender differences, attributions, and helping behavior. These three topics are discussed in an article titled "Gender Differences in Attributions and Emotions in Helping Contexts," by MacGeorge (2003). This article presents research findings suggesting that there are gender differences in attribution that are consistent with the application of moral orientation.

4. **Variations of Milgram** Milgram's classic study on obedience to authority spawned much research. These variations on his original work continue. To illustrate for your students the additional knowledge gained through similar research, read "Self and Other Obedience Estimates: Biases and Moderators," by Geher, Bauman, Hubbard, and Legare (2002). This article describes a project to determine how knowledge of Milgram's experiment would impact perceptions of self and another person in hypothetical replications of Milgram's original experiment. How far would they actually go? This information can help your students see the creative nature of research and how Milgram continues to influence the field.

STUDENT PROJECTS

1. **Family Observation** Make observations the next time you witness friends or family members having an argument. Ask afterward why the argument occurred—who had done something wrong and why. If an individual admits to having done something wrong himself or herself, does he or she make a dispositional or a situational attribution? If he or she blames the other person, does he or she make a dispositional or a situational attribution? Keep track of the responses and be prepared to share your results in class.

2. **Helping Behavior** The author presents information suggesting that women are more likely than men to help people in need. Yet in the South, it is traditional for men to help women. Gather some change and then "stage" a situation in which you drop the change on the ground while both men and women are present and note who helps and who doesn't. Bring your results to class for discussion.

3. **Discussing Prejudice with Your Child** Prejudice needs to be discussed, especially during periods of wartime or national crisis. For this project you will explore some suggestions on how to discuss prejudice with children. Read the article "Discussing Prejudice with Your Child," by Reeve (2002). This article presents five suggestions. For this project, list and briefly summarize each of the five suggestions and think of at least one additional factor to include in the discussion.

CLASSROOM DEMONSTRATIONS

1. **Persuasion** For this demonstration, assign your students to watch television (you probably won't get too much resistance to this assignment). Specifically, ask them to watch commercials. As they watch the commercials, have them note what type of persuasion method the commercial uses. Does the commercial utilize the foot-in-the-door technique, setting the context and mood, familiarity, pointing out weakness as well as strengths, or persuasive communicators? See if they can find an example of each and possibly even other attempts at persuasion. Have them write down the examples and be prepared to share what they found in class.

2. **Truth or Lie?** Before discussing with your class the idea that information can be transmitted through the eyes, have the students in the class pair up. Then have each student think of three things about themselves, two of which are truthful and one that is a lie. Then have them tell their partner the three things while the partner attempts to determine the lie. After they finish this activity, discuss with your students that when someone looks them squarely in the eye, they typically are being more honest and open. If they avoid eye contact, this may mean deception. Ask the students if they used these cues to help them determine the lie.

3. **Social Psychology Topics** For this demonstration, have your students take the following ten social psychology terms and try to provide current examples from the media that would support the psychological principles. Encourage them to use both their books and notes and to be prepared to support their examples. During the next class period have them share what they found.

1. Gender polarization
2. Fundamental attribution error
3. Prejudice
4. Obedience to authority
5. Conformity
6. Social Facilitation
7. Group decision making
8. Groupthink
9. Mob behavior
10. Bystander effect